BUSINESS
SCHOOLS
and their contribution to
SOCIETY

SAGE has been part of the global academic community since 1965, supporting high quality research and learning that transforms society and our understanding of individuals, groups, and cultures. SAGE is the independent, innovative, natural home for authors, editors and societies who share our commitment and passion for the social sciences.

Find out more at: **www.sagepublications.com**

edited by
METTE MORSING AND ALFONS SAUQUET ROVIRA

BUSINESS
SCHOOLS
and their contribution to
SOCIETY

Los Angeles | London | New Delhi
Singapore | Washington DC

Editorial arrangement and prologue © Mette Morsing and Alfons Sauquet Rovira 2011
Epilogue © Mette Morsing, Alfons Sauquet Rovira and Marc Vilanova 2011

Chapter 1 © Rakesh Khurana and
Daniel Penrice 2011
Chapter 2 © Maria Tereza Leme Fleury
and Thomaz Wood Jr. 2011
Chapter 3 © Bernard Yeung and
Kulwant Singh 2011
Chapter 4 © Valery S. Katkalo 2011
Chapter 5 © Barış Tan 2011
Chapter 6 © Lluis Pugès 2011
Chapter 7 © Juliet Roper 2011
Chapter 8 © Alan Irwin, Dorte Salskov-
Iversen and Mette Morsing 2011
Chapter 9 © Michael Barzelay and Saul
Estrin 2011
Chapter 10 © Thomas M. Begley and
Patrick T. Gibbons 2011
Chapter 11 © Thomas Bieger 2011

Chapter 12 © Muel Kaptain and George
S. Yip 2011
Chapter 13 © Christoph Badelt and
Barbara Sporn 2011
Chapter 14 © Guido Tabellini 2011
Chapter 15 © Adam Budnikowsyi 2011
Chapter 16 © Judith Samuelson 2011
Chapter 17 © Carlos Losada, Josep M.
Lozano and Janette Martell 2011
Chapter 18 © Valérie Swaen, Philippe de
Woot and Didier de Callataÿ 2011
Chapter 19 © Eero Kasanen and Robert
Grosse 2011
Chapter 20 © Manuel Escudero 2011
Chapter 21 © Robert Strand 2011
Chapter 22 © Nigel Roome, David
Bevan and Gilbert Lenssen 2011

First published 2011

SAGE Publications Ltd
1 Oliver's Yard
55 City Road
London EC1Y 1SP

SAGE Publications Inc.
2455 Teller Road
Thousand Oaks, California 91320

SAGE Publications India Pvt Ltd
B 1/I 1 Mohan Cooperative Industrial Area
Mathura Road
New Delhi 110 044

SAGE Publications Asia-Pacific Pte Ltd
33 Pekin Street #02-01
Far East Square
Singapore 048763

Library of Congress Control Number: 2011925162

British Library Cataloguing in Publication data

A catalogue record for this book is available from the British Library

ISBN 978-0-85702-386-5
ISBN 978-0-85702-387-2 (pbk)

Typeset by C&M Digitals (P) Ltd, Chennai, India
Printed by MPG Books Group, Bodmin, Cornwall
Printed on paper from sustainable resources

MIX
Paper from
responsible sources
FSC
www.fsc.org FSC® C018575

CONTENTS

NOTES ON CONTRIBUTORS

Christoph Badelt has been Rector at WU (Vienna University of Economics and Business) since 2002. Since 1989, he has been Professor for economic and social policy at WU. From 1998 to 2002, he was Vice-Rector for infrastructure and has been Rector since 2002. He was President of Universities Austria from 2005 to 2009 and has been Vice-President, WIFO (Austrian Institute of Economic Research) since 2008.

Michael Barzelay is Professor of Public Management based in the London School of Economics's Department of Management. A political scientist by background, he is author of a number of books, including *Breaking through Bureaucracy* (University of California Press, 1992), *The New Public Management: Improving Research and Policy Dialogue* (University of California Press, 2001), and *Preparing for the Future: Strategic Planning in the US Air Force* (Brookings Institution Press, 2003). He has served as Co-Editor of *Governance: An International Journal of Policy, Institutions, and Administration* and is Executive Director of the Center for Transformation and Strategic Initiatives in Washington, DC. He received an honorary doctorate from the University of St Gallen in 2010.

Thomas M. Begley is a Professor, and currently Dean of University College Dublin (UCD) Business School in Ireland, which includes the Michael Smurfit Graduate School and the Quinn School. He formerly held the Governor Hugh L. Carey Chair in Organizational Behavior at UCD. He has a Bachelor's degree from Seton Hall University and Master's and PhD degrees from Cornell University, New York.

David Bevan completed his PhD in Accounting at King's College London. He is currently Academic Director of the Academy of Business in Society; Professor of Management and Applied Ethics at Grenoble Graduate Business School. David is a Senior Wicklander Fellow at the Institute for Professional and Business Ethics (DePaul).

Thomas Bieger is President of the University of Gallen and is a full Professor of Business Administration with specialization in Tourism since 1999 and Director of the Institute for Systemic Management and Public Governance since December 2010. He was Secretary General of the AIEST (International Association of scientific Experts in Tourism) and he is the Chairman of CEMS (Global Alliance in Management Education). From 2003 to 2005, he served as Dean of the Faculty of Management at the University of St Gallen. From 2005 to 2010, he was Vice President of the University of St Gallen.

Adam Budnikowski has been the Rector of the Warsaw School of Economics since 2005, currently serving his second term. He was born in 1948 and is a graduate of the Poznan University of Economics (MA) and the Warsaw School of Economics (PhD). Fulbright scholar at the Massachusetts Institute of Technology in 1985–1987 and Visiting Professor at the Goethe University in Frankfurt am Main in 1989–1990, his area of expertise is international economics.

Didier de Callataÿ is President of the Louvain School of Management and a Senior Lecturer at the Université Catholique de Louvain. He graduated as a civil engineer and followed this with a postgraduate in Management Studies awarded by the 'Université Catholique de Louvain'. He is one of the founding partners of 'Callataÿ and Wouter', a leading provider of innovative IT solutions for banks where he is now Chairman of the Board. Callataÿ and Wouters employs more than 500 consultants, with an international reach spanning more than 15 countries. Didier de Callataÿ is also.

Manuel Escudero is General Director of Deusto Business School. He was Executive Director of the Research Centre for the UN Global Compact of the New York State University. Since 2003, he has worked for the United Nations as a Special Advisor to UN Global Compact and Director of the Secretariat of the UN Principles for Responsible Management Education.

Saul Estrin is Professor of Management and Head of the Department of Management at the London School of Economics. He is best known for his work on privatization, foreign direct investment and entrepreneurship. He was formerly Adecco Professor of Business and Society at London Business School where he was also Deputy Dean (Faculty and Research) and Acting Dean. His publications include the widely cited *Privatisation in Central and Eastern Europe* (1996); *Foreign Direct Investment into Transition Economies* (2004); and *Investment Strategies in Emerging Markets (2004).* He is on the Editorial Advisory Boards of several scholarly journals including the *Journal of Business Venturing* and *Emerging Markets and Finance*. He also writes for policy journals such as *Business Strategy Review*, of which he was Editor.

Maria Tereza Leme Fleury is Dean of the Fundação Getulio Vargas, EAESP. She is Research Fellow at the IFM Cambridge University and Director of ANPAD, the Brazilian Academy of Management. Professor Fleury has authored or edited 20 books and published over 65 academic papers in the field of strategy and competence management and international management.

Patrick T. Gibbons is the Jefferson Smurfit Professor of Strategic Management at University College Dublin (UCD), Ireland. He is currently Associate Dean at the School and is a member of the Governing Authority of UCD. He graduated with a PhD in Strategy from the University of Pittsburgh. Previous academic appointments have included Peking University; HKUST; Penn State; the University of Pittsburgh, and Nanyang Business School in Singapore.

Robert Grosse is a Professor, and Dean of the EGADE Business School at Monterrey Tec in Mexico. Previously, he was the head of Leadership Development and Learning at Standard Bank of South Africa. He holds a BA from Princeton University and a PhD from the

University of North Carolina, both in international economics. He has taught at Thunderbird, the University of Miami, the University of Michigan, Instituto de Empresa (Madrid, Spain), and in many universities in Latin America.

Alan Irwin has been Dean of Research at Copenhagen Business School since 2007. He is currently also Acting President. His PhD is from the University of Manchester. He has previously been a Dean at the University of Liverpool and at Brunel University. His academic work is on science and technology policy.

Muel Kaptein PhD is Professor of Business Ethics and Integrity Management at the Department of Business-Society Management at RSM Erasmus University. His research interests include the management of ethics, the measurement of ethics, and the ethics of management. Muel is also partner of KPMG. More information can be found at muelkaptein.com.

Eero Kasanen is Professor of Finance at Aalto University School of Economics, Finland, a former Rector of Helsinki School of Economics and Dean of Aalto University School of Economics. He has doctorates from Harvard Business School and Turku School of Economics and has served on the CEMS Strategy and Executive Board, the EFMD Board and the EQUIS Awarding Body. Research interests cover financial reporting, real options, research methodology, and business ethics. He has served on the boards of several listed companies and research foundations.

Valery S. Katkalo is Vice-Rector of St. Petersburg State University and Dean of the Graduate School of Management. He received undergraduate and Doctoral degrees in Economics from SPbSU, and completed a postdoctoral program at Haas Business School, UC Berkeley. He was taught at business schools in France, Finland, and Denmark. His research focuses on strategic management and network organizations. He is co-founder and chief editor of the Russian Management Journal and serves on the EFMD Board of Trustees, EPAS Accreditation Committee, and several Boards for international and Russian business schools and companies.

Rakesh Khurana is the Marvin Bower Professor of Leadership Development at the Harvard Business School. He is also the Master of Cabot House at Harvard College. He teaches a doctoral seminar on Management and Markets and The Board of Directors and Corporate Governance in the MBA program. Professor Khurana's research uses a sociological perspective to focus on the processes by which elites and leaders are selected and developed.

Gilbert Lenssen is President of the European Academy of Business in Society. He was Professor of Management at Leiden University, Professor of International Management at the College of Europe (Bruges/Warsaw) and Visiting Fellow at Templeton College, University of Oxford. He is a member of the Board of the European Foundation for Management Development (EFMD) and a member of the Editiorial Board of Corporate Governance, *The International Journal of Business in Society*, *The Journal for Strategy and Management* and *The Journal for Management Development*. He is Visiting Professor at Cranfield University, Henley Management College, and ENPC Paris and has been a Life Fellow of the Royal Society of Arts (London) since 1995.

Carlos Losada has a PhD in Management Sciences from Ramon Llull University, an undergraduate degree and a Master's in Business Administration from ESADE, a degree in Law from the University of Barcelona, and a diploma from the JFK School of Government (Harvard University). In 1986, he began his academic career in the Department of Business Policy at ESADE Business School. He lectured in Executive Functions, Strategy and Organization, which he combined with strategic consulting. In 1997, he joined the Inter-American Development Bank in Washington, DC. In 2000, he returned to ESADE as Director General, a position he held until 2010. During this period, he served as a member of various boards of directors and government bodies. He currently combines his academic activities with involvement in various government bodies, among which are the boards of Gas Natural Fenosa, SFL (France) and the European company InnoEnergy.

Josep M. Lozano is currently Full Professor in the Department of Social Sciences at ESADE and Senior Researcher in CSR at the Institute for Social Innovation (ESADE). His academic and professional activity encompasses the fields of Applied Ethics, Corporate Social Responsibility, and Values, Leadership and Spirituality. Josep M. Lozano's books to date include *The Relational Company* (Peter Lang), *Governments and Corporate Social Responsibility* (Palgrave; also translated into Chinese), and *Ethics and Organizations: Understanding Business Ethics as a Learning Process* (Kluwer). His personal website is www.josepmlozano.cat.

Janette Martell (MBA, MSOD, PhD candidate at ESADE). Her research interests focus on organizational change centered on social responsibility in universities and business schools. Her work has been published in the *Journal of the World Universities Forum* and in the book *Toward Assessing Business Ethics Education*, Swanson and Fisher (Ed.). She has worked at Monterrey Tec in Mexico for 16 years, last post as General Director of a campus of the Tec System. She has been a Lecturer in Leadership and Human Development and Social Commitment at the Monterrey Tec.

Mette Morsing PhD is a Professor at Copenhagen Business School (CBS) and Director of CBS Centre for Corporate Social Responsibility (cbsCSR) and was recently appointed as co-chair of CBS Sustainability Initiative. She has authored or edited more than twenty books and published extensively in international journals on management, communication, organizational identity and corporate social responsibility. She has also researched at New York University, Stanford University and Ilisimatusarfik Greenland University and is a member of the LEGO Foundation Board, the National Ministerial Council for Corporate Responsibility and Board member of the European Academy of Business in Society.

Daniel Penrice is a Research Associate at Harvard Business Schools. He has more than 10 years of experience as a writer and editor for consulting firms including Accenture, Arthur D. Little, the Boston Consulting Group, and PRTM as well as the Winthrop Group. He has published articles in the Harvard Business Review and several Harvard Business School publications. Recently he collaborated with Professor Rakesh Khurana on *From Higher Aims to Hired Hands* (Princeton University Press, 2007), a sociological history of the American business school.

Lluis Pugès graduated in Philosophy from the University of Barcelona and in Economics from the University of Leuven (Belgium) and received his doctorate in Social and Moral Sciences from the University of Rome. He served as Dean at ESADE, where he was also Director General and the advocate of numerous academic and economic initiatives.

Bernard Ramanantsoa was Chairman of the CEMS Alliance from 2007 until 2010 and has been the Dean of HEC Paris from 1995 till 2010. He is a specialist on strategy and corporate culture in the business place and himself advocate of an open-minded approach and a multi-cultural scope in the corporate world. He joined the HEC faculty in 1979 as Professor of Business Strategy.

Nigel Roome is Professor of Governance, Corporate Responsibility and Sustainable Development at Vlerick Leuven Gent Management School and Academic Director of the International MBA program. Nigel has worked on curriculum development and reform for over 20 years. He has held professorships in Canada, Netherlands and Belgium and is currently Academic Chair of EABIS.

Juliet Roper is Professor of Management Communication and Associate Dean, sustainability, at the University of Waikato Management School, New Zealand. She is also President of the Asia Pacific Academy of Business in Society (APABIS).

Salskov-Iversen, PhD, is Vice-President for International Relations at Copenhagen Business School, where she is also an Associate Professor and Head of the Department of Intercultural Communication and Management. Her research is located at the interface between (public) management, organizational studies and international political economy.

Judith Samuelson is Executive Director of the Aspen Institute of Business and Society Program, which is dedicated to developing leaders for a sustainable global society. Among its signature programs are Beyond Grey Pinstripes – a global survey of MBA education – and the Corporate Values Strategy Group – a forum to curb capital market short-termism.

Alfons Sauquet Rovira is Dean of the ESADE Business School, where previously he was Vice-Dean of Research and Director of the Undergraduate Programs. He is the principal investigator of the research group on learning and knowledge in organizations (GRACO). His field of expertise is organizational learning and organizational development.

Kulwant Singh PhD is Deputy Dean and Professor of Strategy and Policy at the NUS Business School, Singapore. His research and teaching address firm strategy and competition in rapidly changing environments, with a particular focus on Asia. his research has been published in leading strategy journals, and he has co-authored three books on strategy in Asia.

Barbara Sporn is Vice-Rector for Research, International Affairs and External Relations and Professor of University Management at WU (Vienna University of Economics and Business). Among others, she has also served as Acting Assistant Professor at Stanford University. She is a known expert in the field of globalization of higher education.

Robert Strand is a PhD Fellow at the Copenhagen Business School Centre for Corporate Social Responsibility in affiliation with PwC Denmark. Robert received his MBA from the University of Minnesota and was the inaugural Net Impact Fellow to Europe in 2009–10. His research focuses on leadership and corporate social responsibility.

Valérie Swaen is Professor at the Louvain School of Management (Université catholique de Louvain) and at the IESEG School of Management. She is an active member of the Center of Excellence on Consumers and Marketing Strategy and the head of the Louvain CSR Network at the Louvain School of Management. Her research interests include consumer behavior, CSR implementation and CSR communication.

Guido Tabellini is Professor of Economics at Università Bocconi and Rector, since November 2008. He taught at Stanford University and UCLA. He has been President of the European Economic Association. The main focus of his research is on how political and policymaking institutions influence policy formation and economic performance.

Barış Tan is the Dean of College of Administrative Sciences and Professor of Operations Management at Koç University, Istanbul, Turkey. His research interests are on design, control and improvement of production systems and supply chain management. Professor Tan serves on the EFMD Board of Trustees, CEMS Strategic Board, and Academic Advisory Board of Business Council for Sustainable Development Turkey.

Marc Vilanova is a Lecturer and Researcher at the Institute for Social Innovation at ESADE Business School. He specializes in the exploration of the relationship between competitiveness and sustainability, with published research on responsible competitiveness, sustainable innovation, organizational sustainability and learning for sustainable development. He has a background in economics and more than 10 years' experience as a Consultant.

Thomaz Wood Jr is Professor at FGV-EAESP, Brazil, where he teaches operations strategy and organizational theory. He also serves a mandate as Associate Dean for Research. Professor Wood has authored or edited 25 books and published over 40 academic papers in the field of organization studies.

Philippe de Woot is Professor at Louvain Catholic University (196–1995) and a member of the Royal Academy of Belgium. His fields of research and teaching are corporate strategy; change processes in a turbulent environment; and business ethics, corporate raison d'être and societal responsibilities. Considered as a whole, the works of Philippe de Woot have aimed to give back economic activity its ethical and its political dimensions.

Bernard Yeung PhD is Dean and Stephen Riady Distinguished Professor in Finance and Strategic Management at the NUS Business School, Singapore. Bernard's research covers international corporate finance, corporate strategy, foreign direct investment, and the relationship between institutions, development and firm behavior. He has published more than 100 research articles in top journals across multiple fields.

George S. Yip wrote this chapter while he was Dean of the Rotterdam School of Management, Erasmus University. He is now Professor of Management at the China Europe International Business School in Shanghai. He conducts research on innovation, strategic transformation and international business. His books include *Total Global Strategy* (2nd edn, Prentice Hall, 2002) and *Managing Global Customers* (Oxford University Press, 1992).

ABOUT CEMS

Founded in 1988, CEMS is a strategic global alliance of leading business schools and universities from 26 countries and 4 continents, working in close collaboration with over 70 multinational companies and NGOs. Together they deliver the CEMS Master's in International Management (CEMS MIM), offering a unique blend of top-level education and business experience.

Consistently ranked by the *Financial Times* as one of the top pre-experience Master's in Management programs in the world, the CEMS MIM is the most international and culturally diverse MSc on the marketplace. It is awarded to multilingual, multicultural postgraduate students seeking a career in international management.

With a current cohort of 900 students of over 60 different nationalities and a global network of over 6000 alumni working in 70 different countries, CEMS has grown from European roots to become a truly global alliance of schools and companies integrally involved in the definition and teaching of the curriculum, as well as the implementation of a series of joint research projects.

The aim of the CEMS alliance is to equip students and graduates of the program with the skills and knowledge required to become responsible business leaders and global citizens.

CEMS MEMBER SCHOOLS AND COUNTRIES

Australia	University of Sydney Business School
Austria	WU, Vienna University of Economics & Business
Belgium	Louvain School of Management
Brazil	Escola de Administração de Empresas de São Paulo-FGV
Canada	Richard Ivey School of Business, University of Western Ontario
China (Beijing)	School of Economics & Management, Tsinghua University
Czech Republic	University of Economics, Prague
Denmark	Copenhagen Business School
Finland	Aalto University School of Economics
France	HEC Paris
Germany	University of Cologne
Hungary	Corvinus University of Budapest
Ireland	UCD, Michael Smurfit Graduate Business School
Italy	Università Bocconi
Japan	Keio University, Tokyo
Norway	NHH, Norwegian School of Economics & Business Administration
Poland	Warsaw School of Economics
Portugal	Nova School of Business & Economics
Russia	Graduate School of Management, St. Petersburg State University
Singapore	National University of Singapore Business School
Spain	ESADE Business School
Sweden	Stockholm School of Economics
Switzerland	University of St. Gallen
The Netherlands	Rotterdam School of Management, Erasmus University
Turkey	Koç University Graduate School of Business
United Kingdom	LSE, London School of Economics & Political Science

FOREWORD

Bernard Ramanantsoa
CEMS and HEC, France

Thinking about education is always particularly challenging because it is so interconnected with who we are and who we want to be as human beings. In the end our memories from our days as students are contradictory: on the one hand, the world was waiting for us, it belonged to us; but on the other hand, we were constrained by rules which, at the time, seemed unshakable. That is precisely why we wanted to present this collection of reflections on the past, present and future of business schools: to discuss different voices on how business schools can and should contribute to a better and more sustainable society.

Business schools have been challenged with reports of all kinds of wrongdoings: of conducting research without links to the 'real world', of being obsessed with rankings, of being incapable of developing cross-disciplinary learning, or preferring analytical competencies to the detriment of managerial aptitude … Not all these criticisms are accurate, but certainly there is something to be said about the need for business schools to address more fundamental questions, such as the sustainability of the economic model and the roles and responsibilities that businesses should have.

As we see in this book, there are many business schools, as well as other relevant business actors, who have been reflecting on their responsibilities, vision and mission – not only in terms of the global crisis, but also as a more in-depth reflection of what type of society is needed for a sustainable world and the role business schools could play in achieving that goal. Some of these schools insist, for example, on teaching students that a long-term perspective is not merely a succession of short-term decisions. This means giving students the capacity to face new challenges that have not yet been identified, which forces schools to rethink the dialectical link that binds them to the economic world. In this regard, every day more business schools generate alternative ideas and models, rather than adhering to a single model. Thus, as the authors of this book point out, business schools aim to contribute to the emergence of a pluralistic vision, embracing contradictions and paradoxes as fundamental tools for creativity and innovation, and understanding that businesses are not only not the centre of the universe, but are also only a small and interdependent part of it.

A little over two years ago, the Community of European Management Schools (CEMS) received the proposal to write a book on the challenges facing business schools, particularly after the economic crisis that has shaken the world and has led us to question some of the central ideas, institutions and systems that confirm who we are as a society. This idea was quickly and enthusiastically accepted within CEMS, and a number of our member schools quickly proposed to contribute a chapter, as it fits very well with our culture and our mission. However, as we wanted the book to be representative of different voices, we decided to open up the process to other scholars, schools and organizations.

CEMS is an association of management schools, originally European but currently international, that aims to reflect precisely on the central aspects of business school education: future challenges, the teaching curricula, or the pedagogy of management education. In this regard at CEMS, we approach these issues as teachers as well as researchers, with an ultimate goal: to constantly question what we teach and how this contributes to creating the sort of future business executives society needs. Thus, the mission is not reduced to reproducing knowledge, but is largely focused on creating new knowledge. This is especially vital in the field of business education which is characterized by the constant, rapid evolution of knowledge. With this book, we want to commit to paper this permanent reflection process around the challenges for business education.

Thus, this book is above all the result of a collective work that through the collection of different voices allows us to construct our own voice around the challenges facing business education. We present different points of view rather than a doctrine which would have been, by definition, monolithic. In this regard, not only we do not want to shy away from debate and contradiction, we also want to embrace them as central tools for advancement. The editors of this book, Mette Morsing and Alfons Sauquet Rovira, have worked very hard not only to keep the discussion alive, and give ear to the different voices, but also to find and render the links between the different ideas, thus allowing them to propose some common themes, challenges and visions for the future. I would like to thank them for their devotion to the project and for their hard work.

Personally, I hope that after reading this book, you will be left with at least two central ideas: first, that there are a number of very interesting voices exploring and questioning business education from within business schools, with no issue too controversial to discuss; second, that there are clear and concrete proposals for the future of business education and business schools, alive with creativity and innovation, enthusiastic motivation and a sincere wish to contribute to a better and more sustainable world.

Bernard Ramanantsoa
CEMS *Chairman, 2007–2010*
HEC *Director General, 1995–2010*

PROLOGUE

BUSINESS SCHOOLS AS USUAL?

Mette Morsing and Alfons Sauquet Rovira

CBS and ESADE

Business schools are one of the most influential institutions in contemporary society, and have a particular role to play in setting high ethical standards for trust and fairness. They influence the way in which most socio-economic activities are conducted, inasmuch as they contribute to shaping and transforming business decisions, and how businesses develop their identities to face the challenges presented by globalization. Business school norms and values can help to provide a standard and professional grounding for thousands and thousands of young people educated to lead and form businesses tomorrow. How business schools in practice integrate values into research, education and outreach programs influences the way in which socio-economic activity is conducted over generations. Like other education institutions, business schools have a responsibility. However, recently, their handling of this responsibility has been questioned and challenged.

Strong critique has been raised from outside and inside business schools. It has been suggested that business schools might do more harm than good (Ghoshal 2005; Antunes and Thomas 2007), and that they neglect the human dimension of business and their responsibility to society (Navarro 2008). Business schools have been accused of causing increasing distrust in business because they develop a narrow shareholder thinking as the underlying value permeating education, while they neglect other aspects of importance to business such as collaborative skills, intercultural abilities, trust and social responsibility (Mintzberg 2004; Blasco 2009). Businesses themselves have even complained about narcissistic, interculturally and socially inept business school graduates (Feldman 2005; Blasco 2009) as they have indicated how business schools have forgotten to help students develop their 'moral muscles' (Salbu 2002, cited in Starkey and Tempest 2004: 1625). While many business schools have developed courses on ethics and corporate social responsibility and some have introduced voluntary oaths of honor (e.g. Thunderbird and Harvard Business School) and the annual Responsibility Day for all first semester undergraduate students (e.g. CBS) as a reply to the critique after Enron, Andersen and the subsequent financial crisis, such efforts have been critiqued for being decoupled and not integrated into the mainstream 'business school as usual' and for simply enforcing a 'slavish commitment to narrow business values' (Starkey and Tempest 2006: 1522). The Harvard Business School MBA students' 'MBA oath' promises to pay equal attention to 'shareholders, co-workers, customers and the society in which we operate', with a final goal of 'sustainable prosperity'. This action has been criticized for being 'simply an effort by students to shield themselves from the populist rage at the role of MBAs played in the current financial crisis and that the ethics push will fade once the economy stabilizes' (*Business Week*, 11 June 2009). Nevertheless, the MBA oath may possibly be one more of much larger changes that are about to surface in transforming business school identities and values. For instance, it seems to have inspired other grassroots and student-led initiatives that have developed in different places around the world with one common purpose: all of them pressure business schools to rethink and integrate issues of ethics, corporate social responsibility (hereinafter CSR) and sustainability into the curriculum by way of placing these issues at the center of business school policy and strategy.

A group of business school deans and rectors decided to make a strong and collective voice to address the questioning and challenging of business school legitimacy. They wanted to emphasize that management education is inherently a normative endeavor in which assumptions about right and wrong ways of managing people, profits and businesses underpin the curriculum. They wanted to draw attention to the fact that good management virtues are also developed in informal ways – in what has been referred to as *the hidden curriculum* (Blasco 2010) – in business school settings influencing student beliefs and behavior. They wanted to emphasize in the public debate that management decisions have to do with interactions of people and social institutions with a respect and understanding for context. And that such understandings and skills build on taking 'the human factor' seriously among business schools.

This group of business school deans has taken the challenge very seriously. Important ideas and activities stemming from their work and thinking are presented to you in this book. Here, they express their thinking about business school contributions to society, and share some of their experiences and experiments, while also revealing the problems and challenges with systematically promoting and embedding social virtues of trust, fairness and responsibility into their business school identities. At that meeting in Cologna in December 2009, the deans decided to make their voices heard collectively in the public debate on business school legitimacy with the aim of stimulating debate on the approaches and challenges of that legitimacy. The general acknowledgment of the legitimacy crisis of business schools and the public interest in debating the issue has so far been led by US scholars and practitioners. While the latter may have very good reasons to engage, the non-US business school deans decided to contribute to the debate in a collective and comprehensive way. They agreed that business schools are globally faced with a legitimacy crisis, but they also agreed that it is a crisis that has different characteristics, challenges and solutions at local and regional level. For example, the Asian, Latin American and European geo-political and socio-economic contexts provide other points of departure for business schools than their Anglo-Saxon counterparts – the fact that the MBA program has been less central to the development of business schools operating within Asian universities, the fact that some business schools in Europe receive considerable support from state and public institutions, or less institutionalized frameworks of business education in some other regions like Latin America, offer the possibility of adding to the discussion a different perspective that at first sight stems from a more classical university ethos.

However, this book does not intend to serve as a comparison between Anglo-Saxon and non Anglo-Saxon models, or any other business school models. Rather, it serves to provide a global voice and insight to the experiences, approaches and perspectives of business schools' legitimacy as expressed by the deans and rectors' own voices. We also want to emphasize that none of the contributions in this book claim to represent 'best case' practices. Rather, authors agree that such 'best case' practice can only be unfolded and assessed in its local context. There is no one recipe for how to achieve business school legitimacy. We think this book provides a collection of thought-pieces in which how to stimulate business school self-reflection, learning and engagement with society is a permeating theme.

BUSINESS SCHOOLS: WHAT VIRTUES?

Economic thinking has assumed that generating shareholder value is the main goal of economic activity, and this has dominated business school values in recent years and thus heavily influenced business school education. The theories and methods taught in business schools are often seen as almost hands-on instruments to enhance business growth and reputation, and in substantive ways shareholder thinking has served as the value furnishing business schools with arguments stimulating knowledge production. Often, those values underpinning theories and methods are not surfaced and debated. But they inform the moral and political choices graduates make, as they become leaders of corporations.

The debate around the role and values of business schools has taken many turns. It has existed as long as these organizations have been perceived as powerful and influential social actors, and it has been raised when business schools have been deemed as not complying with the challenges to provide sound education. In that regard, the current economic crisis has not generated the debate, but accentuated a concern and stimulated a renewed global discussion on the issue. The criticism has been that business schools have pushed mainstream business thinking rather than foster critical and diverse thinking, narrowing the focus of management theory and fuelling practices overly concerned with short-term results. In a seminal paper, Professor Sumantra Ghoshal provocatively argued that 'bad management theories are destroying good management practices' (2005: 75). With reference to John Maynard Keynes, Ghoshal emphasized the importance of ideologies for business and society and points at their often implicit nature:

> ... the ideas of economists and political philosophers, both when they are right and when they are wrong, are more powerful than is commonly understood. Indeed the world is run by little else. Practical men, who believe themselves to be quite exempt from any intellectual influence are usually the slaves of some defunct economist ... It is ideas, not vested interests, which are dangerous for good or evil. (Keynes 1953: 306, cited in Ghoshal 2005: 75)

Ultimately, Ghoshal's arguments form an idealism that certainly opens up the possibility for an in-depth discussion, and the fact that there are many references to Ghoshal's paper throughout this book is a good indicator of its influence for stimulating debate. Ghoshal argues that prevalent theories in business schools may be uncritically disseminated. He states that business schools systematically teach students that managers cannot be trusted to do what shareholders expect of them, and therefore managers' incentives and interests must be controlled to be aligned with those of shareholders. According to Ghoshal, this distrust has led to a transaction cost economics that promotes the need for tight monitoring and the control of people to prevent 'opportunistic behavior'. One of the main explanations for managerial behavior is business school education, where 'thousands – indeed, hundreds of thousands – of executives who attend business courses have learned the same lessons, although the actual theories were not presented to them quite so directly' (Ghoshal 2005: 75). In particular, Ghoshal finds a lack of social virtues, that seem to have been decoupled from business school logics which he critiques for having reduced managerial work to 'a kind of physics' where economic, social and psychological laws inevitably shape people's actions' (2005: 77).

Business schools have, in various ways, replied to the criticism of narrow shareholder thinking, tecnification or neglect of the human factor and a lack of relevant knowledge generation. This is a serious critique for the business school as an institution that acknowledges its role for contributing to social virtues such as trust, fairness, responsibility and accountability. The critique does not indicate that business schools intentionally teach their students to be socially irresponsible. The question is rather that whatever is done at business schools has a relevant impact on the professional behavior of graduates.

BUSINESS SCHOOLS AS REFLECTIVE LEARNING ENVIRONMENTS

It has been suggested that students should be exposed to ethically challenging situations in school, otherwise they will be unprepared for and likely to fail in providing leadership for decision-making in corporations (Evans and Marcal 2005). Perhaps we should suggest the same training to scholars who teach and research at business schools? Perhaps scholars should meet 'real' business challenges and make 'real' business decisions with ethical implications before we allow them to teach students? Recently, we have seen more journals dedicating special issues to the question of business schools' contribution to society, for example *Academy of Management Learning and Education* (2009, issue 8) and *Journal of Corporate Citizenship* on 'Designing Management Education' (2011, issue 39). These special issues focus on bringing not only academic reflection and discussion but also examples from the classroom.

Regardless of the actual role business schools play – or think they play – in causing the economic crisis, they are perceived by the general public as the embodiment of managerial thinking and economic development in contemporary society, and thus directly involved in any transformations these undergo. With that in mind, business schools need to respond to the lack of trust and growing scepticism. On a positive note, this provides a perfect opportunity to carry out a self-reflective exercise among business schools.

Many have already begun a reflective process, as can be seen by the increase in the number of initiatives, codes of conduct and declarations that have been developed to show that they are listening to the critiques, and that they take seriously their responsibilities towards producing a better society. To this end, deans, rectors and professors seem to acknowledge the need for a reflective and systematic evaluation of business schools' curricula, but more specifically for a more profound debate on the values on which theories and thinking behind business school activities are constructed. In this respect, the internationalization process via accreditation systems is a clear step in that direction.

In this volume, we will not bring examples from the classroom in any detail. Rather, we take the rare opportunity of exploring the views of the deans of some of the most important business schools from around the world and around three dimensions: (1) the legitimacy of business schools from a historical perspective; (2) the future of business schools in terms of different visions; and (3) the role of business schools in shaping and transforming ethical conduct.

THE STRUCTURE OF THE BOOK

In this volume, we explore how business schools contribute to sustaining the distinctiveness of themselves as legitimate business schools in global society and how they work to infuse a 'corporate logic' that significantly addresses concerns about current economic models and theories. While the individual contributions will overlap and blend the themes of the three parts, we uphold them as thematic directions, as each contribution will take an overall point of departure in one of the three themes. Each part of the volume consists of several contributions. The authors of these contributions are deans, rectors and distinguished scholars at business schools, and in some instances to provide additional views of key stakeholders of business schools, we also invited a number of relevant expert institutions with a special interest in and knowledge about business school development to assist the role of business in society. Contributing deans, rectors, professors and business school experts have contributed because their business schools in various ways have addressed, explicitly or implicitly, the new challenges for business schools in the wake of the financial crisis. In doing so, they are already beginning to shape the contours of how to address this new problematic in practice. The invitation to contribute to this volume prompted these authors to express their views of business schools' responsibilities to society in an explicit, systematic and empirically grounded manner. Each contribution, therefore, illustrates a particular perspective on business schools' responsibilities to society, taking its point of departure in a particular business school context and framing this in a broader global approach, reflecting critical future challenges for business schools' theorizing, economic models and contributions to society.

To provide insightful reflection as well as an overall coherence, each contributor was asked to discuss a specific and different issue and simultaneously analyze two common issues: (1) the current legitimacy crisis of business schools; and (2) the future vision and challenge of the future of business schools. Furthermore, to provide some additional and different perspectives of organizations or individuals directly involved with business schools, we have also asked for a contribution from a student perspective, some business leaders, and prominent scholars within the business school debate. This way, the book aims to address gaps in knowledge by scanning the landscape of business schools from several regional and organizational perspectives, to debate how deans and rectors push and steer the frontiers of business school identity in new directions in collaboration with key stakeholders in different contextual settings. The contributing business schools are all currently engaged in developing new strategies and policies towards developing 'globally responsible citizens' and, as such, the book will explore cutting-edge developments within the business school world.

Part 1 takes its point of departure from the historical raison d'être of the business school as an institution that has developed into a powerful global institution influencing economic, institutional and cultural development. The philosophical underpinnings of business schools are outlined and contextualized. This first part of the book provides a general overview of the development globally while it also contributes more focused chapters from different regions: Europe, the USA, Latin America, Russia and Asia. Contributions discuss how the phenomenon of business schools has developed regionally, and how it has contributed to setting a new global agenda for business, and how business schools – in a variety of ways – have produced those economic theories which they themselves teach as the mainstream business school philosophy, based on shareholder thinking and criteria of success measured by what we may here refer to as 'old business school' thinking.

Part 2 – Towards a new legitimacy for business schools in global society – addresses how business schools are one of the most influential industry sectors today in educating managers and setting the agenda for global business logic and the development of international markets. Yet, in this process, business schools increasingly depend on market economic dynamics turning them into businesses driven by market logics rather than universities characterized by independent thinking and research. This part discusses how the 'marketization' of both privately and publicly funded business schools influences the legitimacy of business schools, and how business schools respond as a new economic reality has created mistrust in them, and they experience a need to demonstrate themselves as responsible institutions. One important element is how business schools approach, select and interact with stakeholders in society, i.e. policies and strategies of business schools' stakeholder management to achieve trust and confidence from the general public.

Part 3 – Business schools' role in shaping and transforming ethical business conduct – addresses the impact of business schools on corporations in terms of the current economic logics, norms and values driving theorizing and educational programs and their influence on organizations and their managers. Whereas Part 1 focuses on the trust of business schools, Part 2 focuses on how business schools may serve to create trust in business. Contributions in this part focus explicitly on how business schools directly influence leadership in corporations and how concrete approaches to program and curriculum development, as well as the selection of topics, courses, and pedagogies, set the norms and directions for future managerial decisions, rhetoric and actions. Contributions in this part discuss and exemplify how business schools may develop alternative ways of educating tomorrow's leaders as they entrust students with critical and complex ways of approaching ethical dilemmas for business in a globalized world, taking inspiration from, for example, the social and human sciences.

For us, it has been a pleasure to serve as editors of this book. We hope that readers will appreciate and learn as much as we have from reading and discussing this unique collection of important voices on business schools' contribution to society.

ACKNOWLEDGMENTS

By definition, an edited book is the fruit of the contributors. We sincerely thank those deans, rectors and professors who were dedicated enough to find the time to contribute with a book chapter. They contributed in good faith, most times going beyond their academic comfort zone and accepting the challenge to go public on their reflections. We also sincerely want to thank all of our author experts who have generously spent their time providing thoughtful reflections on the challenges of business schools in contemporary society, ensuring that the book has also delivered a glimpse from the world outside business schools.

No edited volume is simply the result of the editors' and contributors' work. This volume is not an exception. A number of people have been extremely helpful at different stages of the process. We want to thank CEMS Chairman and HEC Director General, Bernard Ramanantsoa, for providing strong support, CBS Vice-President Dorte Salskov-Iversen for taking up the challenge, and CEMS Director General François Collin for his involvement and help in all sorts of matters.

Finally, we want to give special recognition to Marc Vilanova. Marc has served as our steady, networking, hard-working and reliable editorial assistant throughout the development of this book. His social skills, academic skills, ever-presence and ability to connect and collect material and people to ensure consistency cannot be over-stated. If there is ever a role of being editor to the editors, you fulfilled it beyond expectations – our most sincere gratitude to you.

REFERENCES

Academy of Management Learning and Education (2009) 8 (1).

Antunes, D. and Thomas. H. (2007) The competitive (dis)advantage of European business schools. *Long Range Planning*, 40: 382–404.

Blasco, M. (2009) Cultural pragmatists? Student perspectives on learning culture at a business school. *Academy of Management Learning and Education*, 8 (2): 174–87.

Blasco, M. (2010) Business Schools as Usual? Towards Socially Responsible Management Education. Working paper, Copenhagen Business School.

Business Week (2009) Harvard's MBA Oath Goes Viral. http://www.businessweek.com/bschools/content/jun2009/bs20090611_522427.htmAccessed 11 June 2010.

Evans, F.E. and Marcal, J.E. (2005). Educating for ethics: business deans' perspectives. *Business in Society Review*, 110 (3): 233–48.

Feldman, D. (2005) The food's no good and they don't give us enough: reflections on Mintzberg's critique of MBA education. *Academy of Management Learning and Education*, 4 (2): 217–20.

Ghoshal, S. (2005) Bad management theories are destroying good management practices. *Academy of Management Learning and Education*, 4 (1): 75–91.

Journal of Corporate Citizenship (2011) 'Designing Management Education' [Special Issue], issue 39.

Mintzberg, H. (2004) *Managers Not MBAs: A Hard Look at the Soft Practice of Managing and Management Development.* San Francisco, CA: Berrett-Koehler.

Navarro, C. (2008) The MBA core curricula of top-ranked US business schools: a study in failure? *Academy of Management Learning and Education*, 7 (1): 108–23.

Starkey, K., Hatchuel, A. and Tempest, S. (2004) Rethinking the business school. *Journal of Management Studies*, 41 (8): 1521–31.

Starkey, K. and Tempest, S. (2006) The business school in ruins? In P. Gagliardi and B. Czarniawska (eds) *Management Education and Humanities*. Cheltenham: Edward Elgar.

Part 1

HISTORICAL AND GEOGRAPHICAL PERSPECTIVES ON BUSINESS SCHOOL LEGITIMACY

1 BUSINESS EDUCATION: THE AMERICAN TRAJECTORY

Rakesh Khurana and Daniel Penrice

Harvard Business School, USA

As business education in an academic setting becomes an increasingly global phenomenon, the university-based business school in America remains a unique institution. This holds true despite the fact that the American business school, as it evolved in the post-World War II era, has become the dominant model for business schools in Europe and elsewhere in the world.

Most observers looking at these institutions as they exist today, without an awareness of their differing historical origins and development, would likely conclude that business schools inside and outside of the USA exhibit more similarities than differences. Yet the uniqueness of the American business school lies not so much in the widely imitated strategies and practices it has developed over the last 60 years as in the way that, for more than a century, it has articulated and shaped for the larger society a set of ideas, aspirations and norms concerning business and management. Moreover, the visions and values animating the university-based business school in America – which arguably account more than any other factor for the great influence it has enjoyed in American society – have changed significantly from the era when the earliest schools were founded up until the present day. Thus, the institution that came to be the major influence on business education worldwide in the postwar era is significantly different from the one that preceded it in the first half of the twentieth century, when American and European business schools developed along largely separate lines.

Indeed, as we will argue, the loss of legitimacy with which the American business school is now threatened[1] has resulted from an evolution in which the fundamental ideas and purposes behind its original establishment in the late-nineteenth and early-twentieth centuries have been largely abandoned, both by business schools themselves and by other institutional actors with which they have become linked. If these original purposes – which committed American business schools to producing a public good in the form of a socially conscious business leadership for the nation – still survive at all, it is now mostly, to paraphrase Max Weber, as the ghosts of dead beliefs. As a consequence, in our view, the institution that became the model for business schools in Europe and elsewhere in the postwar years was a significantly diminished version of what had preceded it, while the American business school of today has little to offer by way of answers to the fundamental questions being raised about our global economic institutions in the wake of recent crises. At the same time, we maintain, even though the visions and values that originally animated American business schools have been in retreat for several decades, they offer a path out of the present crisis of legitimacy and towards a renewal of purpose that can ultimately benefit both business education and business itself as global institutions.

Prior to World War II, business education in academic institutions followed one of two models, one German in origin and the other American. The German system arose as the Prussian civil service, responding to the rapid industrialization of the newly united German nation, began a rapid expansion of engineering schools (*technische Hochschulen*) in the late nineteenth century and then of schools of commerce (*Handelshochschulen*) at the beginning of the twentieth century.[2] (Faculties of business and commercial economics were introduced in the universities of Cologne and Frankfurt-am-Main in the early twentieth century, but these institutions were focused primarily on research rather than teaching.) By the early decades of the twentieth century, the German system was thoroughly institutionalized, increasingly imitated in Switzerland, Holland and Sweden, and the dominant model for business schools in all the non-English speaking European nations (Engwal 2009). The American system, by contrast, was the creation not of the state, as in Germany, but of private institutions and individuals including universities, foundations and industrialists.[3]

The key difference between these two systems of academic business education, inherent in their historical origins, was that the German system assumed a role for the state in the administration of business and of society that, in the American conception, was to be fulfilled by creating an enlightened class of private business leaders. It is critical to note that the university-based business school in America arose in the context of what one historian has called the 'search for order' in American society in the last quarter of the nineteenth century and the first two decades of the twentieth century (Wiebe 1967). The disruption of the social order occasioned by the rise of the large corporation in America and its attendant economic and social phenomena was profoundly troubling to the nation's existing social and economic elites. The appearance, at this time, of a new class of aspiring elites known as managers occurred in a context in which industrialization, urbanization, increased mobility and the absorption of local economies into what was increasingly a single national economy dominated by large corporations had facilitated the deinstitutionalization of traditional authority structures.

In this destabilized context, three institutions – science, professions and the university – offered alternative structures and rationales on which to erect a new social order and create a new class of elites that, their proponents argued, were more suited to changed social conditions. Amid the sometimes violent clashes of interests attending the rise of the new industrial order, science, the professions and the university presented themselves as disinterested communities possessing both expertise and a commitment to the common good. The novel institution of the university-based business school – which made its first appearance with the founding of the Wharton School at the University of Pennsylvania in 1881 – drew upon the prestige of science,[4] the professions and the university itself in arguing that management could be conceived as a science and transformed into a profession on the model of the 'high' professions of medicine, law and divinity, which had all been part of the Western university from its medieval origins. The traditional professions, and particularly medicine and law as they were being reconstructed in late-nineteenth-century America, provided a rhetoric of social duty that framed business education as possessing a higher purpose than mere 'moneymaking', thus rendering it more palatable to academics who opposed its inclusion within the university.

Among the most eloquent spokesmen for the novel idea of business as a profession were several figures associated with the founding and early decades of the Harvard Business School (or the Graduate School of Business Administration, as it was known at its founding in 1908). Harvard president Charles W. Eliot, who approved the creation of the business school, explained his decision by noting that 'business in its upper walks has become a highly intellectual calling, requiring knowledge of languages, economics, industrial organization, and commercial law, and wide reading concerning the resources and habits of the different nations' (Eliot 1908; also quoted in Cruikshank 1987: 44). The school's first dean, the economist Edwin F. Gay, stated that placing the study of business on a firm intellectual footing by grounding it within the university would help develop 'a habit of intellectual respect for business as a profession, with the social implications and heightened sense of responsibility which goes with that' (Edwin F. Gay, quoted in Cruikshank 1987: 44). In an address delivered at Stanford University's business school in 1926 that was later published in *Harvard Business Review*, Gay's successor, Wallace B. Donham, showed equal concern with producing business leaders who could be called professionals, individuals who appreciated the dignity and worth of their occupation as well as the social responsibilities that accompanied it:

> *The development, strengthening, and multiplication of socially minded business men is the central problem of business ... Moreover, it is one of the great problems of civilization. Discontent with the existing condition of things is perhaps more widespread than ever before in history. The nation is full of idealists, yet our civilization is essentially materialistic. On all sides, complicated social, political, and international questions press for solution, while the leaders who are competent to solve these problems are strangely missing. These conditions are transforming the world simultaneously for better and for worse. They compel a complete reappraisal of the significance of business in the scheme of things ... The business group largely controls [the mechanisms placed in society's hands by the development of science and technology] and is therefore in a strategic position to solve [the resulting] problems. Our objective therefore, should be the multiplication of men who will handle their current business problems in socially constructive ways. (Donham 1927: 24)[5]*

From these ambitious beginnings, business schools multiplied rapidly in American universities from the beginning of the twentieth century until the Great Depression,[6] an event that only compounded the widespread sense that the nation suffered from socially irresponsible business leadership. The professionalization project in American business education faltered during the 1930s, however, and was deflected significantly from its original course after the end of World War II. Although the postwar years saw an explosion in enrollment in American colleges and universities, and in business programs in particular, American business schools in this era took a decisive turn in the direction that the Wharton School's sixth dean, Joseph Willits, had foreseen in the 1930s when he asked: 'Have we not put too much emphasis on turning out business technicians alone, and paid too little attention to the development of business men with a sense of statesmanship ...?' (American Association of Collegiate Schools of Business 1934).

The new intellectual orientation of the post-World War II business school in America arose from three momentous developments: the emergence of the new organizational society that came out of the war; the concept of the rational manager that accompanied the latter development; and the rise of a reform movement in American business education spurred by the intervention of two large private foundations, the Carnegie Corporation and – even more significantly – the Ford Foundation.[7] The successful Allied war effort was widely viewed in the USA as a triumph of American organization, planning and management rather than just a feat of arms. In the postwar era, what the sociologist Richard Scott has called 'organizational society' – a societal order characterized by large government agencies and the birth of a new and soon dominant form of business corporation, the conglomerate – had the effect of increasing the importance of management as a social function and of producing a more rational, technically rooted conception of professional management than had existed prior to World War II. The emergence of the Soviet threat and the onset of the Cold War, moreover, made the development of large cadres of highly skilled managers a national priority, considered to be as important to the struggle against communism as the nation's managers and planners had been in the defeat of fascism.

It was a widespread belief that American business schools lacked the necessary intellectual rigor that, along with Cold War fervor, motivated the Ford Foundation to spend what would eventually come to over $35 million to remake business education in the USA in the 1950s and 1960s. This concerted effort to transform American business schools was driven by a two-part premise about how best to increase the intellectual quality of business education and to make the field truly 'professional'. First, the reasoning went, business schools must increase the proportion of faculty with doctorates in existing academic disciplines, primarily the social sciences and various quantitative fields. Second, business school faculty and MBA students must be extensively trained in quantitative analysis and the behavioral sciences. The new emphasis on hiring business school faculty from the quantitative disciplines dovetailed perfectly with the new conception of the rational manager that came out of the American war effort and became established in the corporate world by the rise of the conglomerate form of organization. The appearance of the postwar industrial conglomerate, with its multiplicity of managers increasingly removed from hands-on operations, increased the seeming applicability to corporate management of sophisticated quantitative tools developed during the war. As a result of their profit-maximizing orientation and because, in the conglomerate form of organization, a single executive was often responsible for 10 or 12 different businesses, corporate management in these companies devalued concrete, industry- or firm-specific knowledge and skills in favor of the newer, more abstract and analytical tools and techniques that could be applied without regard to industry distinctions. Conversely, the human relations model of management from the 1930s, with its emphasis on interpersonal skills and motivation, felt less and less suited to the conglomerate environment.

In the Ford Foundation's program for the remaking of the postwar American business school, the first major testing ground for this new approach – which organizational scholars have called 'systems rationalism' or the 'Carnegie perspective', but which can also be described as managerialism – was the Graduate School of Industrial Administration at the

Carnegie Institute of Technology in Pittsburgh, Pennsylvania.[8] For the purpose of tracing the evolution of the visions and values that have historically underlain the university-based business school in America, the key point is that the Carnegie perspective emphasized one side of the older ideal of professionalism in business education, technical expertise, at the expense of the other, which was about producing what Wallace Donham had called 'socially minded business men'. In the last three decades of the twentieth century, however, American business schools would largely abandon both professionalism and managerialism as defining conceptions in favor of a new ideology that amounted to the antithesis of such ideas. By the 1970s, as the postwar economic boom in the USA began to come to a halt amid a series of economic shocks, the system of managerial capitalism that had prevailed in the 1950s and 1960s gave way to a new investor capitalism that both influenced and was influenced by intellectual developments within American business schools.

In the 1970s, while many talked about the American corporation being squeezed by high oil prices, new foreign competition, or excessive regulation, other Americans were becoming more sceptical about attributing all of the problems affecting the nation's corporations to such exogenous factors and began to blame corporate managers themselves – and, specifically, many of the management techniques put in place as a consequence of the business education reforms of the 1950s and 1960s – for the lackluster performance of their companies and of the economy as a whole.[9] Yet not all of the critics of the American corporation in the American business school of the 1970s and early 1980s put the blame for poor corporate performance on the new management techniques. A second camp within American business schools implicated managers in the context of a sweeping critique of what University of Chicago economists Raghuram Rajan and Luigi Zingales have called 'relationship capitalism', a system of managed competition enforced through a mixture of government policy and informal cartelization that obtained in the USA in the postwar era (Rajan and Zingales 2004: 238–43).

This group of critics – consisting mostly of economists and policy makers, many trained in the free-market tradition of the University of Chicago – was doubtful that the problems facing American corporations could be solved either through voluntary restructuring or by adopting the industrial planning and industrial welfare policies of Japan or Germany. They also argued that managers would not voluntarily reform. The solution to the problems of American competitiveness, in the view of the Chicago School critics, entailed not only minimizing the government's role in the national economy but also – in an argument that stood Alfred Chandler's famous thesis about the 'managerial revolution' in American business on its head – preventing managers themselves from standing in the way of the efficient operation of competitive markets.

In particular, business school economists such as Michael Jensen and William Meckling, propounding what they called agency theory, argued that the lack of an active market for corporate control had contributed to a lack of corporate discipline and managerial accountability. Ultimately, the agency theorists argued, the answer to poor corporate performance was to monitor managerial behavior and rely more on markets, both for the regulation of the overall economy and for corporate governance. Since all human beings, as Jensen and Meckling (1994) once opined, are (at least potentially) analogous to prostitutes, the way to motivate managers was to tie their compensation closely to their companies' stock price and let them know that, should share prices fall too far, they and their firms would be subject to hostile takeovers. Agency theory, which became enormously influential in American business schools in the mid-1980s, thus defined managers not as the socially conscious professionals envisioned by the founders of the American business school or the rational, enlightened technocrats of the era of managerialism but, rather, as all-too-human impediments to the smooth functioning of the free market's economic and corporate machinery. Managers, in this view, essentially had to be bribed to carry out what another influential Chicago School idea – the efficient market hypothesis – had proclaimed as the ultimate purpose of the corporation: maximizing shareholder value.[10]

The presence on business school faculties in the 1970s and 80s, meanwhile, of large numbers of economists who were quietly making their discipline the dominant one in American business schools was an important, if not quite foreseen, consequence of the Ford Foundation reforms. During the 1960s and 1970s, as the effects of the Ford program began to make themselves felt in schools across the country, large numbers of business school academics who had specialized training in economics came to be employed in business schools and to engage in business research. The impact on business education of scholars trained in, and primarily oriented towards, the discipline of economics went beyond the particular effects of the perspective they brought to the business school curriculum and business school research; it also signified the growing acceptance of the legitimacy of economics as the foundational discipline of business education.[11] In the environs of almost all the elite business schools, the ideas of economists came to dominate not only finance but also accounting, international business, production, negotiations and strategy. Surveying three decades of management research, Jeffrey Pfeffer concludes: 'There is little doubt that economics has won the battle for theoretical hegemony in academia and society as a whole, and that such dominance becomes stronger every year' (1997: 44).

From our perspective, the rise of economics to its current position of dominance in American business schools and the influence of concepts such as agency theory and the efficient markets hypothesis are significant because they represent a total repudiation of the older idea of professionalism in management that had given rise to the university-based business school in the first place. This transformation has had profound consequences not only for the business school curriculum (and the wider world into which ideas such as deregulation, share price as the ultimate measure of corporate success and tying the fortunes of managers to share prices, all migrated with sometimes disastrous consequences) but also for the culture of business schools themselves. As the market logic promulgated by finance professors penetrated not just the curriculum but also the very ways in which American business schools thought of themselves and their educational enterprise, there was, and is, less and less to distinguish the traditional, university-based institutions from the for-profit business schools that have sprung up and claim to offer a comparable 'value proposition'. University business education has become, even in the discourse of faculty, an 'industry' serving students who are now described as 'customers' and who often base their choice of school on media rankings, measuring factors such as the starting salaries of graduates and the quality of the services provided to corporate recruiters.[12] Having proclaimed that markets offer the ultimate measure of the value of managerial work, university-based business schools in America have, in effect, made the same argument about academic work, essentially admitting that there is nothing they do that cannot be done equally well by commercial institutions that may lack only such luxury appurtenances as PhDs, faculty publications in recondite journals and tenured and endowed professorships.

In short, by aiming to legitimate themselves, in the second half of the twentieth century, in terms of the era's successively dominant discourses – first of science and rationality, and then of the superiority of markets to all other forms of social organization, including management itself – university-based business schools in America have contributed to their own delegitimation. In so doing, they have not only undermined their competitive position vis-a-vis other providers of management education but also virtually abandoned any idea of social purpose, once part of the price of admission to the revered institution of the American university.

The idea of professionalism in management, which was ultimately what gave business schools access to the resources and prestige of the university, defined the profession of management as an institution through which self-regulation by enlightened practitioners would steer American society between the social chaos bred by unfettered markets, on the one hand, and the stifling effects of ham-handed government regulation, on the other. Such a role requires of managers far more than the technical expertise that the Ford Foundation and the business school leaders who carried out its reforms placed at the center of their programs. Yet at least for the Ford reformers, as we have seen, management education was part of a larger enterprise aimed at strengthening the foundations of a democratic capitalist order. When the new economic ideology that arose in the 1970s, however, denied even the possibility of self-regulation by managers, the university-based business school in America effectively lost its reason for existing. For in the absence of a conceptual model embedding business in a social context where private wealth creation is only one among many desired and desirable goals, what exactly do academic business schools have to offer that cannot now be purchased (and at a lower price) in many other venues?

By the beginning of the 1990s, American business schools – particularly those elite schools that had staked their reputations on their academic superiority – faced a full-blown crisis of identity and purpose. It was no longer possible for business schools to tout a mission of educating managers according to the canons of postwar managerialism (particularly at the elite schools, where increasing numbers of students now shunned traditional management careers altogether in favor of fields such as consulting and investment banking). Many faculty and business school administrators recognized that in this new era the university business education needed to re-orient itself, though there was much uncertainty as to what the new model should be.

It was in this pervasive atmosphere of drift and uncertainty that business schools turned to the notion of leadership as a way to redefine their identity and mission. Academic concern with the subject of leadership began in 1945 with a research program at Ohio State University known as the Ohio State Leadership Studies. Certain key ideas of the Ohio State researchers would be echoed and recast, in the mid-1970s, by a seminal article in *Harvard Business Review* by Harvard Business School professor Abraham Zaleznik, entitled 'Managers and Leaders: Are They Different?': '[M]anagers and leaders are very different kinds of people', Zaleznik wrote, giving rise to a conceptual distinction that has proven both popular and enduring. Characterizing a 'managerial culture' as one that 'emphasizes rationality and control', Zaleznik (1977) described the manager as essentially a 'problem solver'. 'To get people to accept solutions to problems', he stated, 'managers continually need to coordinate and balance opposing views … Managers aim to shift balances of power toward solutions acceptable as compromises among conflicting values'. However, according to Zaleznik, 'Leaders work in the opposite direction. Where managers act to limit choices, leaders develop fresh approaches to long-standing problems and open issues to new options' (1977: 72).

Zaleznik's resuscitation of Max Weber's notion of charismatic leadership – an idea that was taken up not only by other business school academics but also by management consultants, motivational speakers, and corporate trainers – found a receptive audience in the economic environment of the late 1970s, with managerialism on the wane and the rise of the new investor capitalism paving the way for the appearance of a new type of corporate leader, the charismatic CEO (Khurana 2004). Corporate America, many of its critics now contended, had become 'overmanaged' and 'underled'. By the early 1990s, as faculty members including Michael Jensen preached to their students about the venality and corruptibility of managers, Harvard Business School (2006) formally shifted its focus from its traditional concern with general management, issuing a new mission statement that described its purpose as 'to educate leaders who make a difference in the world'. Dartmouth's Tuck School of Business (2006) came to describe its primary educational goal as preparing 'students for leadership positions in the world's foremost organizations'. Stanford's Graduate School of Business (2010) now aims to 'develop innovative, principled, and insightful leaders who change the world' and MIT's Sloan School of Management (2010) hopes 'to develop principled, innovative leaders who improve the world'. Non-elite schools like Michigan State's Broad College of Business, whose mission is 'to excel in the education and development of business leaders and in the creation and dissemination of knowledge, leading to national and international prominence for our core businesses [sic]' (2010)[13] describe themselves in terms that mimic the elite institutions.

The decision by American business schools to replace the managerial paradigm – which already represented a certain dilution of the professional paradigm with which the university-based business school began – with the 'leadership' one, raises significant questions. Although it is still too early to render definitive judgment, the history of leadership scholarship and pedagogy to date suggests that, at the very least, business schools will find the task of creating a professional knowledge base around leadership no easier than they have thus far found the task of creating firm intellectual foundations for the study and teaching of management to be. Sixty-five years after the launching of the Ohio State Leadership Studies, leadership as a subject of scholarly inquiry remains without either a widely accepted theoretical framework or a cumulative empirical understanding leading to a useable body of knowledge. Moreover, none of the dominant approaches to teaching leadership in American business schools lend substance to the claim that leadership instruction constitutes, in whole or in part, a substantive contribution to business education.[14]

For all of its shortcomings as an academic field, however, 'leadership' as a subject of attention in the mission statements and curricula of university-based business schools does have the considerable virtue of calling attention to the many – and ultimately most important – aspects of management that are not merely technical or reducible to the quasi-scientific formulations of agency theory. For one thing, to talk about managers as leaders is implicitly to acknowledge the social nature of the firm, something that agency theory denies in defining the firm as a 'legal fiction' serving as 'a nexus for contracting relationships' (Jensen and Meckling 1994: 311). The concept of leadership can also be made to encompass the fact that business organizations exist in relation to an external environment in which non-economic forces influence and can be influenced by the actions of the firm. Although such phenomena lie well outside the purview of neoclassical or neoliberal economics, they have in the past merited the attention of economists as well as sociologists, social psychologists, political scientists, and others, and are gaining the attention of increasing numbers of social scientists today.

Neoliberal economics has become so dominant and taken for granted, particularly over the last 40 years, that even many economists have forgotten that it once had to compete for hegemony within the field. Institutional economics, rooted in history, sociology and politics, and supported by empirical data and comparative case studies, is the name for the school of economic thought that lost out to its neoclassical antagonist in a contest (known in Austria, where it had its original intellectual centre, as the *Methodenstreit*, or 'battle of the methods') that arose in Europe around 1880 and spilled over into the USA at the beginning of the twentieth century. In contrast to neoclassical economists, who analyzed economic behavior using a small set of selective principles, theory development through deduction and a focus on rational and self-interested individual actors, institutional economics incorporated history, political science and sociology into the analysis of economic behavior. Institutional economics was a dominant discipline in the German business school of the pre-World War II era, and many of the founding fathers of the American business school – including Edwin Gay at Harvard, Edmund James and Simon Patten at the Wharton School, and Roswell McCrea at the Columbia School of Business – were institutional economists. Their insistence that economics, particularly in its neoclassical form, could not serve as an adequate foundation for the academic study of management grew from their understanding that, as Harvard's Wallace Donham (a lawyer, not an economist, by training) put it, 'while two and two in mathematics may always be four, two and two plus the X of human relations and other "imponderables" involved in any situation is never four' (Donham 1952).

Unlike what is now mainstream economic theory, the institutional perspective starts from the nature of the social, economic and political system, not with the values and preferences of individuals. As consumer marketing professionals know, markets do not consist of atomized individuals making isolated decisions. Individuals act as members of social groups and bring their social identities to markets – just as they do to the workplace. As the organizational scholars Walter Powell and Paul DiMaggio have written, 'The new institutional economics adds a healthy dose of realism to the standard assumptions of microeconomic theory' (Powell and DiMaggio 1991; see also Moss Kanter and Khurana 2010).

In terms of management practice and business education, an institutional perspective takes the broad strategic outlook that is necessary for business leadership by looking at the wider system in which an organization operates. An institutional perspective recognizes that organizational behaviors are responses not only to market forces but also to institutional pressures that emerge from an organization's social context – a context that the organization can and does seek to influence. According to this perspective, the behavior of people and groups can be motivated by a social logic as well as a market logic. From the standpoint of management education, any analysis of organizations that fails to account for both logics would seem to be of little value for practice. If this was true in Wallace Donham's day, it has become much more true in view of profound changes over the last 60 years in the fundamental nature and structure of organizations, markets and the relationship between business and society.

As an institutional perspective changes the way in which we look at organizations and their environments, that is to say, it also provides a new look at the manager's role and the how best to prepare students to assume it. In a world in which a considerable part of a CEO's job, for example, is to act as the corporation's interface with shareholders, governments, strategic partners and other actors external to the firm itself, successful business leaders must be much more akin to the broadly educated, socially aware and responsible managers that the founders of the American business school envisioned than to the narrowly trained technocrats that the mid-twentieth-century reforms engineered by the Ford Foundation. They also need – if only to ensure the survival of an economic and political order that is hospitable to business – to commit their firms to contributing to the solution of major social problems (environmental sustainability, pandemics and severe economic inequality, to name a few) that are global in nature and cut across many disciplines and institutions. And from a perspective that recognizes that human beings are not necessarily willing prostitutes but are driven by social and cognitive motivations (such as the desire to be seen as a decent member of the group, or the need for meaning) as well as economic ones, it becomes possible to influence how future business leaders become aware of and make use of these motivations in themselves and others for the good of their organizations and the broader society.

To talk about business leaders and their roles in this way is also to hearken back to the founding vision for the university-based business school in America, which saw business schools as part of matrix of institutions enabling social order and dedicated to enhancing society's welfare, and sought to produce business leaders who – as academic business schools in America now say – will contribute to society. To live up to this self-proclaimed mission, business schools today must reverse the relentless narrowing of intellectual perspective they have countenanced over the past 60 years and once again embrace a more complex and integrative view of the relationship between business and society. To remember their forgotten history may actually be the first step that the American business school – and business schools around the world that still look to it as a leader in the field – can take towards a renewal of purpose and a better future.

NOTES

1. In the past year, questions about the legitimacy of American business schools have arisen in many corners.
2. See Locke (1984/2006). Japan, another late-industrializing country, also began expanding business education rapidly in the late-nineteenth century. Following the Sino-Japanese War of 1894–95, a long article appeared in the *Times of London* (27 August 1897) entitled 'Commercial Education in Japan'. It concluded that 'Japan's whole system of commercial education is one [that], in its completeness, even Anglo Saxon countries have not yet attained'. Rudolf Beigel of Germany wrote in 1898 that the Tokyo Higher Commercial School was 'most nearly allied to what the German people tried to establish as a Handelshochschule [college of commerce]' (as cited in 'Business Education in Japan', (Nishizawa, 2008), *Business History Review*, Volume 82: Issue 2).
3. Although the business schools at some public universities in America are among the oldest in the country, they were established on a model developed within their private counterparts.
4. It should be noted that the notion of a 'science' of management did not originate with university-based business schools. Organizational theory, of which scientific management

represented the first example, arose within the profession of engineering, and scientific management was adopted by business schools only after Frederick W. Taylor had developed the theory from his own studies of the factory production process and, in his consultant's role, introduced it to industry.

5. The 'business problems' Donham spoke of included 'the momentous labor problem', the business cycle with its 'devastating periods of alternate speculation and depression, with their corollary contribution to unemployment' and 'problems of corporate control' that pointed to a need to strengthen the 'spirit of trusteeship on the part of corporate managers' (1927: 25, 27).

6. The first school of business in the USA was established in 1881. No other university-based business schools were founded until 1900. By 1929, more than 80 university-based schools had been created.

7. That these private foundations, particularly Ford, would prove able to refashion the postwar American business school according to their own prescriptions was the result not only of their great wealth but also of an institutional vacuum within the business education establishment, itself created by the decline of the American Association of Collegiate Schools of Business (AACSB) as an instrument of self-regulation for American business schools. See Khurana 2007, Chapter 5, pp. 223–31.

8. On the central role of Carnegie's Graduate School of Administration in the transformation of the concept of management in the postwar era, see Khurana 2007, Chapter 6.

9. For example, in an influential 1980 Harvard Business Review article entitled 'Managing Our Way to Economic Decline', Harvard Business School professors Robert Hayes and William Abernathy laid the blame for America's economic woes squarely on the shoulders of American managers and on the new management techniques. 'American managers', Hayes and Abernathy wrote, 'have increasingly relied on principles which prize analytical detachment and methodological elegance over insight, based on experience, into the subtleties, and complexities of strategic decisions. As a result, maximum short-term financial returns have become the overriding criteria for many companies' [Hayes, R. H.; Abernathy, W. J.: Managing Our Way to Economic Decline. *Harvard Business Review,* Vol 58, July-August, 1980, p. 67–77.]

10. The core idea here is that stock market prices accurately reflect the intrinsic value of a firm based on all known information about factors that impact the expected value of the firm's future cash flow. Consequently, the best way to align a manager's interest to those of shareholders is to align managerial compensation to stock price, preferably through high leverage tools such as stock options.

    It is worth noting that economic theories that would prove so influential were developed in business schools rather than in the economics departments of arts and science faculties in American universities and represented a remarkable turnaround. Well into the 1970s, business school appointments were much less prestigious than departmental ones for academic economists. Indeed, the entrenchment of certain fields (finance), and certain approaches (monetarism, rational expectations, agency theory) in business schools as opposed to economics departments, denoted their (initially) somewhat marginal status relative to the mainstream of the discipline. Yet so successful were the business school economists in arguing for the technical and 'scientific' superiority of their methods to those of more mainstream economists that the evolution of American business schools toward increasingly abstract and technical knowledge rooted in the social scientific disciplines would end up transforming the economics discipline itself, extending the influence of the neoclassical school far beyond its original redoubt at the University of Chicago. See Fourcade and Khurana (2011).

11. For discussions of the role of economic theory in changing the paradigm of management education and management research, see Ferraro et al. (2005); Ghoshal and Moran (1996); and Pfeffer (1997).

12. Like the active intervention of the Ford Foundation in the 1950s, the emergence of an external authority in the form of media rankings highlighted the inability or unwillingness of business schools to engage in self-regulation – a critical element in any process of professionalization. See Khurana 2007, Chapters 5–8.
13. Michigan State University Broad College of Business (2010). The Broad mission statement defines the school's undergraduate, MBA, MS, PhD, research and executive development programs as its 'core businesses'.
14. See the introduction to Nohria and Khurana (2010), for a discussion of why the development of a body of knowledge around leadership is difficult. In particular, the editors note, definitions of leadership are highly variable both across and within the social sciences. Moreover, a corresponding pedagogy for educating leaders may not be consistent with contemporary views about the purpose of higher education. On the latter point, see Nohria et al. (forthcoming).

REFERENCES

American Association of Collegiate Schools of Business (1934) *Proceedings of the 16th Annual Meeting*, p. 37.

'Business Education in Japan' (2008) *Tamotsu Nishizawa Business History Review*, summer, p. 355.

Cruikshank, J.L. (1987) *A Delicate Experiment: The Harvard Business School, 1908–1945* (Boston: Harvard Business School Press).

Donham, W.B. (1927) 'The Social Significance of Business', *Dedication Addresses*, HBS Archives, AC 1927, 17.1, pp. 24–7.

Donham, W.B. (1952) *Administration and Blind Spots: The Biography of an Adventurous Idea*, George H. Weatherbee Lectures, pp. 13–14 (Boston: Harvard University, Graduate School of Business Administration).

Eliot, C.W. (1908) Address to the Harvard Club of Connecticut, February, Harvard Business School, Baker Library, Historical Collections Department, Notes: 1900–1909, ADE Box 1 of 2.

Engwal, L. (2009) *Mercury Meets Minerva: History of Swedish Business Education* (London: Pergamon Press).

Ferraro, F., Pfeffer, J. and Sutton, R.I. (2005) 'Economics Language and Assumptions: How Theories Can Become Self-Fulfilling', *Academy of Management Review* 30(1).

Fourcade, M. and Khurana, R. (2011) 'From Social Control to Financial Economics: The Linked Ecologies of Economics and Business in Twentieth-Century America', *Harvard Business School Working Paper*, 11–071.

Ghoshal, S. and Moran, P. (1996) 'Bad for Practice: A Critique of the Transaction Cost Theory', *Academy of Management Review* 21(1).

Harvard Business School (2006) 'Who We Are'. Available at: www.hbs.edu/about/index.html [accessed 9 October 2006].

Jensen, M.C. and Meckling, W.H. (1994) 'The Nature of Man', *Journal of Applied Finance*, 7(2): 10 (revised July 1997).

Khurana, R. (2004) 'The Rise of the Charismatic CEO', in *Searching for a Corporate Savior: The Irrational Quest for Charismatic CEOs*. Princeton, NJ: Princeton University Press.

Khurana, R. (2007) *From Higher Aims to Hired Hands: The Social Transformation of American Business Schools and the Unfulfilled Promise of Management as a Profession.* Princeton, NJ: Princeton University Press.

Locke, R. (1984/2006) *The End of the Practical Man: Entrepreneurship and Higher Education in Germany, France, and Great Britain, 1880–1940* (Greenwich, CT: JAI Press).

Michigan State University Broad College of Business (2010) 'Mission Statement'. Available at: http://broad.msu.edu/information/about/mission [accessed 11 November 2010].

MIT Sloan School of Management (2010) 'About Mit Sloan – Background: Mission'. Available at: http://mitsloan.mit.edu/about/mission.php [accessed 11 November 2010].

Moss Kanter, R. and Khurana, R. (2010) 'Advanced Leadership Note: An Institutional Perspective and Framework for Managing and Leading', *Harvard Business School Teaching Note* N9-410-076, 20 January.

Nohria, N. and Khurana, R. (eds) (2010) *The Handbook of Leadership Theory and Practice*, pp. 3–26 (Boston: Harvard Business School Press).

Nohria, N., Khurana, R. and Snook, S. (eds) (forthcoming) *The Handbook of Leadership Pedagogy and Teaching* (New York: Sage).

Pfeffer, J. (1997) *New Directions for Organization Theory: Problems and Prospects* (New York: Oxford University Press).

Powell, W.W. and DiMaggio, P.J. (eds) (1991) *The New Institutionalism in Organizational Analysis* (Chicago: University of Chicago Press).

Rajan, R. and Zingales, L. (2004) *Saving Capitalism from the Capitalists: Unleashing the Power of Financial Markets to Create Wealth and Spread Opportunity*, pp. 238–43 (Princeton, NJ: Princeton University Press).

Stanford Graduate School of Business (2010) 'Our Mission: About the GSB'. Available at: www.gsb.stanford.edu/about/mission.html [accessed 11 November 2010].

Tuck School of Business at Dartmouth (2006) 'Our Strategy'. Available at: www.tuck.dartmouth.edu/about/strategy.html [accessed 9 October 2006].

Wiebe, R.H. (1967) *The Search for Order 1877–1920.* (New York: Hill and Wang).

Zaleznik, A. (1977) 'Managers and Leaders: Are They Different?', *Harvard Business Review* 55(3): 67–78.

2 CREATING A BUSINESS SCHOOL MODEL ADAPTED TO LOCAL REALITY: A LATIN AMERICAN PERSPECTIVE

Maria Tereza Leme Fleury and Thomaz Wood Jr

Fundação Getúlio Vargas-EASEP, Brazil

The economic crisis that took place in 2008 and 2009 set off a (new) wave of criticisms of business schools in the Anglo-Saxon media. Some of the articles suggested that questionable values and methods, learned in MBA programs, were behind the risky behavior of some executives. The epicenter of the crisis and the criticisms was the USA. However, its reverberations were felt the world over, stimulating critical reflection among scholars.

In this chapter, we put forth our outlook on the crisis from the Latin American point of view, specifically from the Brazilian perspective. We seek to show how contextual differences from the Anglo-Saxon countries and Latin-America demand a re-interpretation of the crisis and go against a direct transposition of any recipes for solutions. Using an analysis of the Brazilian context, we aim to show how business schools can better serve their interest groups, strengthen their image and reputation, and foster their legitimacy as agents for social change.

Beyond seeking excellence in teaching and research, we argue that business schools should look for a more affirmative action in promoting topics related to the local context, i.e. to encourage the development and dissemination of knowledge related to, for instance, social responsibility, sustainability, entrepreneurship, and the needs of the emerging 'bottom of the pyramid'.

Along with the offer of an interdisciplinary-based curriculum, we argue that it is necessary to educate socially conscious change agents: professionals capable of understanding the complexity of the organizations in which they work, of identifying opportunities for improvement, and of developing and implementing solutions, with a humanistic and critical approach. In the following sections of this chapter, we go further into the arguments presented in this introduction.

CRITICISM OF BUSINESS SCHOOLS AND MANAGEMENT PROGRAMS: THE ANGLO-SAXON PERSPECTIVE

Business schools were created in the USA a century ago. The American model became globally accepted after the end of World War II and underwent remarkable growth in the 1980s and 1990s. With this growth, business schools began to advertise a self-congratulatory and braggartly discourse in promotional ads published in the business media. This discourse was on several occasions in contrast with texts being published in the very same business media, which carried stories of cowardly, aggressive, or even criminal conduct by executives who had sat in the classrooms of renowned business schools. This distinct contrast was seen in the 1980s with the Wall Street scandals, in the late 1990s and early 2000s with the corporate scandals and the bursting of the internet bubble, and in the late 2000s with the global financial crisis.

In fact, the debate surrounding business schools and MBA programs is nothing new. In the 1980s, critics accused MBA programs of prioritizing finance and marketing, to the detriment of operations management and technology. Critics also argued that MBA programs were encouraging a dreadful short-term vision of management. Starting in the 1990s, Henry Mintzberg began to argue that managers should not continue to be trained with fragmented case studies and disjointed theories, while companies increasingly demand broader, integrative capabilities (see Mintzberg, 2004).

In the following decade, renewed scholars added new critiques. Bennis and O'Toole (2005) argued that schools place excessive value on scientific research and put teaching and publication in non-scientific periodicals on the backburner. By intending to raise the status of research institutions, many business schools favor the ascension of research professors, who lack experience when it comes to managerial practice.

Ghoshal (2005), in turn, centered his focus on the idea that business schools have become large businesses that try to make people believe that management is a hard science. The result has been bad management theories, which are seemingly at the root of the problems related to financial scandals, since they induce their students to adopt short-term approaches in order to maximize profits.

In one study that had extensive repercussions, Pfeffer and Fong (2002) concluded that business schools have been ineffective in terms of generating positive impacts on the career of their graduates. They also suggested that scientific research carried on by business schools has dismal influence on management practice.

An even more unflattering assessment of management programs and business schools can be found among the authors associated with Critical Management Studies (CMS) and Critical Management Education (CME). These authors (e.g. Grey et al., 1996; Reynolds, 1997; Robert, 1996) point to the following problems: first, the conceptions and traditional approaches to management teaching are less and less acceptable, since they usually ignore the complexity of the object – organizations; second, the tendency towards knowledge instrumentality, through the application of ready-to-use recipes, which leads students to learn how to reproduce techniques instead of carrying out more robust diagnoses; third, students are being thought of as mere spectators to the teaching process, and there is almost no incentive for autonomy and self-learning; and fourth, management education is undergoing a significant massification process.

Together, these criticisms point to a need for a substantial reformulation of the MBA programs. In fact, several authors discuss how a renewal of management education could be carried out, covering issues such as: a review of education content and methods, the connection between theory and practice and, especially, the development of a critical outlook and analytical reasoning among students.

From the Latin American perspective, these critical appraisals should all be welcome. However, as contexts in the region may differ from those of the Anglo-Saxon world, one must be careful not to adopt nice, alien solutions for inexistent problems. For instance, Mintzberg's argument against case studies is fine, but not many business schools in Brazil apply the method, and almost all their students are working managers, studying on a part-time schedule. Bennis and O'Toole's critique of research-oriented business schools is also sound, but research in management is relatively new in Brazil and the business schools give enormous importance to teaching. Pfeffer and Fong's critique of the dismal influence of management research in management practice echoes Brazilian studies on the same theme, but their poor assessment of the impact of management education on careers may sound dubious in Latin America. On the other hand, the critiques from CMS and CME scholars look appropriate and comprehensive.

A LATIN AMERICAN VOICE, CENTERED IN THE BRAZILIAN CONTEXT

Latin America is home to 570 million people, spread over 20 countries, with huge ethnic, cultural, social and economic variations. Therefore, the region cannot be treated in a monolithic manner. However, some characteristics and trends are applicable to a considerable part of the region: almost all of the countries can be classified as developing countries, run under democratic regimes and facing problems related to poverty and inequality. In the 1980s and 1990s, many countries in the region adopted policies from the so-called Washington Consensus, which led to processes of economic liberalization, privatization and the encouragement of free initiative. In the 2000s, the election of several leftist leaders in the region, including in Brazil, softened, yet did not reverse, this trend.

Starting in the 1990s, the educational system experienced several changes and underwent a striking expansion. Latin America today has 24 top-level business schools. They are mostly institutions with international connections, established with renowned institutions from developed countries. Among the top 20 management schools classified in a recent ranking (Díaz, 2008), 18 had at least one international accreditation (AACSB, AMBA, EQUIS or SACS), and several of them had two or three accreditations. For these schools, accreditation is both an opportunity to improve their processes, a signal of international legitimization and a tool for marketing differentiation in the local market. Besides, all of them have joint degree programs with European and American business schools and several of them have a noteworthy number of papers published in top scholarly journals.

We could not find documents that provided a wide-ranging historical view of Latin American business schools. However, this gap can be somewhat filled via a portrait of the main associations related to research and the teaching of Business Administration in the region: CLADEA (the Latin American Council of Management Schools), BALAS (the Business Association of Latin American Studies) and ANPAD (the National Association of Graduate Studies and Research in Administration). Together, these and other institutions have helped to outline and foster the area of business education and research in Latin America, particularly in Brazil. Their creation, starting in the 1970s, followed an upshot in interest in management, which was reflected in the increased number of existing programs in the region.

CLADEA was created 40 years ago. The organization has over 140 affiliate institutions, including 92 business schools in Latin America and representatives from Europe, North America and Oceania. Its annual meetings constitute a forum for business school deans and professors to exchange experiences and present scientific work. BALAS aims at promoting the study of economics, management, leadership and industrial activities in Latin America and the Caribbean. In 2009, it held its 25th annual conference, gathering researchers from all over the world who are interested in the region. ANPAD was created in 1976, as an organization made up of Brazilian Master's and doctorate programs. As time passed, it became a promoter of the biggest and most important scientific management events in the country. The organization currently has 80 affiliated graduate programs. Its chief annual meeting is organized in 11 academic divisions and receives more than 3000 scientific papers per year.

BUSINESS SCHOOLS IN BRAZIL

In Brazil, as in other emerging countries, the development of management as a professional and research field can be related to the industrialization process. A milestone of this process took place in the 1940s, when the industrial and services sectors of the economy began to grow. The development of administration studies in Brazil was articulated around the creation of the School of Economics, Business and Accounting, at the University of São Paulo, and of the Schools of Business and Public Administration, at the Fundação Getúlio Vargas, in the second half of the 1950s.

The first course specifically aimed at business administration was created in 1954, at the School of Business Administration of São Paulo, at FGV (FGV-EAESP), with the support of professors from the Michigan State University. Over the following decades, business administration studies grew in the country, with the creation of undergraduate, Master's, doctorate and specialization programs.

As with the other countries in Latin America, the industrialization process in Brazil was distinguished by a policy of substituting imports, with significant participation from subsidiaries of multinational, and especially North American companies. These companies were key agents for the dissemination of management models and practices from abroad. Because these companies operated in a closed and protected local market, the demand for trained managers and for creating local knowledge was limited. Brazil's family-owned companies also had little demand for professional administrators. Indeed, a background in engineering was more valued by Brazil's private and government companies than a background in management. Thus, these few business schools were enough to meet local demand.

Liberal reforms that took place in the 1990s led Brazilian companies to improve their business and management models in order to compete with multinationals in the domestic markets and to successfully internationalize their operations. This scenario created a strong demand for better educated executives and for new knowledge in management. Therefore, hundreds of new undergraduate programs, dozens of Master's and doctorate programs, and a noteworthy number of specialization programs were created.

Data from the Ministry of Education allow for an assessment of the growth of business education in Brazil. In 1998, the undergraduate administration course ranked second in number of enrollments, with almost 260,000 students enrolled, second only to the law course, which had 300,000 students enrolled. In 2008, this number had jumped to over 860,000, surpassing Law by more than 200,000. This growth was followed by an explosive increase in the number of programs: in 2000, there were 989 administration courses in Brazil. In 2008, this figure had jumped to 1809.

On the other hand, the growth of the Brazilian business schools consolidated a situation that is different from the Anglo-Saxon situation in several respects.

First, Brazil does not have North American-style MBA programs. Hundreds of programs use the MBA acronym but are really specialization programs with the most varied purposes, focuses and formats. In Brazil, the massification of the use of the MBA acronym has reached such a proportion that some top schools, with the backing of the Ministry of Education, have created a different acronym, MPA (Professional Master in Administration), which is used to name their graduate courses aimed at executives.

Second, in Brazil, as compared to the Anglo-Saxon countries, the undergraduate course is more highly valued than the graduate courses. Undergraduate courses were the first to be created and it was in these programs that many of Brazil's top managers and some of its most famous entrepreneurs were educated. They are fêted by the business community and the business schools grant them their best attention.

Third, research-oriented business schools constitute a fresh phenomenon in Brazil. ANPAD plays an important role in promoting and disseminating scientific knowledge in the area. It was created in the 1970s and brings together over 1000 participants at its annual meetings. Brazil has over a dozen academic journals and there is growing pressure on scholars to publish their works in top-level peer-reviewed journals. Although there is also pressure to adhere to the Anglo-Saxon model, few local institutions are in fact geared towards research. As a consequence, even in those institutions that place an emphasis on research, teaching activities are also highly valued.

Fourth, the case study method, which is harshly criticized by Mintzberg, albeit disseminated in Brazil, is used to a much lesser degree than in the USA and some European countries. In Brazil, there are, to our knowledge, no programs or disciplines that are totally based on case studies. In general, case studies are used in conjunction with other teaching methods.

Fifth, the institutional context is also different: in Brazil, the presence of the State in economy is still relevant, there are a large number of family-run businesses, financial institutions operate under a rigid regulamentary regime, and the stock market is less developed than in some rich countries. Despite advancement over recent decades of liberal economic ideas, related management ideology and the cult of entrepreneurship, the country is still far from the values and attitudes fostered on Wall Street or in Silicon Valley. Significantly, Brazilian managers in general are less prone to push their companies for short-term results.

Furthermore, Brazil has an important tradition of critical thinkers. Sociology, Anthropology and even Psychoanalysis, which developed in Brazil under French influence, have established roots in the business schools. At the School of Business Administration of São Paulo, at FGV (FGV-EAESP), for instance, scholars such as Fernando Prestes Motta infused several generations of PhD students, and future professors, with critical thinking. As their colleagues from the Anglo-Saxon world, Brazilian folk build their knowledge on the shoulders of Horkheimer, Adorno, Marcuse, Benjamin and Habermas, but also studied Freud, Foucault and Brazilian classic and contemporary thinkers, such as Gilberto Freyre, Sergio Buarque de Holanda, Raymundo Faoro and Roberto da Matta.

Finally, we should consider that Brazil, like other Latin American countries, felt the economic crisis of 2008 and 2009 as a crisis that arose abroad, suffering less dramatic effects than those faced by the developed countries (with the exception of Mexico and small countries in Central America that are highly dependent on the North American economy). Generally speaking, the crisis was perceived as an external 'fabrication', without any direct relation to local problems. Among executives, the crisis was perceived as a not so dramatic turbulence, that affected business temporally and in certain industries, i.e. a small turmoil compared to the past crises that had affected the country in the 1980s and 1990s. Economic growth resumed fast and employment was barely affected. Consequently, businesspeople, and the population in general, were not affected by the dark mood that spread throughout North America and Europe.

As for corporate scandals and financial fraud, since the 1980s Brazil has also seen its share of these. Yet, these scandals and frauds were unrelated to the risky or criminal behavior of former management students, as in the Anglo-Saxon world. On the contrary, many of these scandals were associated with the conduct of businesspeople who did not have a formal education in management. Most of them were ruthless mavericks, who built their empires without giving any attention to professional management practices.

Business schools, on the other hand, have built a solid, yet low-profile reputation over the years. During the 1990s and 2000s, the business media helped build professional managers' legitimacy and credibility. In several texts, these professionals were portrayed as the right solution for poorly managed family businesses and decrypted state-owned companies.

It is worth mentioning that this analysis is based on the situation in Brazil. However, we can hypothesize that several of these traits are common to other countries in the region.

Considering all of these points, it is difficult to transpose the Anglo-Saxon crisis concerning the legitimacy of MBAs to Brazil and other Latin American countries. The issue placed before Brazil, and probably before other Latin American countries, is not how to regain legitimacy, but rather how to increase legitimacy. In the following section, we will examine this proposal further.

FACING CHALLENGES: THE CASE OF FGV-EAESP

Located in downtown São Paulo, FGV-EAESP is intimately connected to the business and public administration establishment. It co-evolves with the environment, permanently acknowledging demands and responding to challenges. Its mission, since its inception, has been to develop and disseminate knowledge in order to promote the development of Brazil.

FGV-EAESP has always had a faculty that was characterized by professional and ideological diversity. This creates a positive tension, which prevents purely instrumental attitudes and behaviors from being accepted without question. Our MBA programs have been designed to educate change agents: professionals who are capable of understanding the complexity of the environments in which they work, of identifying opportunities for improvement, and of developing and implementing solutions.

On the other hand, several challenges still persist. For instance, facing pressure to publish in top academic journals, in order to gain international prestige and legitimacy, some business schools in Brazil are nurturing elite research groups. These groups are formed with highly specialized, well-paid researchers. They are pushing research quality and rigor and helping business schools achieve their global aspirations. However, their research agenda is influenced, if not defined, by other countries, and it seldom meets local needs. To fill the void parallel research groups are created that are more concerned with management practices and the local reality. Their research often lacks rigor, but is bold in terms of relevance. Consequently, the challenge for FGV-EAESP, as for other Latin American business schools, is to make these groups get together and cooperate so that rigor and relevance can march together.

Internationalization is also a big challenge. Brazilian business schools are, for the most part, insular organizations. The (huge) size of the local market, with a language (Portuguese) that is spoken in few other nations (none else in Latin America) and an inward-looking mentality, makes internationalization an unlikely process. In this regard, FGV-EAESP has been a pioneer. It has partner business schools all over the world and numerous international double-degree programs, and receives several visiting scholars and dozens of foreign students every year. However, for the most part, classes are taught in Portuguese and so the school rarely attracts regular students from abroad.

CONCLUSION: THE CHALLENGES FOR BRAZIL AND FOR BUSINESS SCHOOLS

In a recent issue, the British magazine *The Economist* (*2009*: 12–18 November) published a photo-montage in which the vast statue of Christ the Redeemer, an iconic image of Brazil, took off like a rocket from its base on the top of the Corcovado hill, in Rio de Janeiro. The issue contained a special survey on the country. Overall, the content was optimistic, showing that Brazil seemed to finally be prepared to reach the highest levels of development.

Although there is optimism, one should not forget the huge challenges still facing the country (and which are common to many other Latin American nations): poverty and disparities in income and opportunities, corruption, environmental degradation, and, particularly, poor management. It is a scenario that surely brings opportunities, yet it also holds many challenges for teachers and researchers in the region's business schools.

As seen in this chapter, the crisis concerning the legitimacy of business schools cannot be directly transposed to the Latin American context. This does not mean that it should be ignored. In fact, many issues that have emerged with the crisis are relevant to any region in the world.

We would argue that, in Brazil and in other Latin American countries, the discussion should not focus on how to repair a damaged reputation but on how to increase the legitimacy of business schools and their social role. Such an endeavor should be undertaken through the adoption of initiatives that will consider local reality and respond to local challenges, that will promote a humanities-based and critical approach in management education, that will educate socially responsible change agents, that will generate and disseminate action-able, local knowledge with global relevance.

Pundits will frequently point out that Brazilian organizations – government agencies, state-owned enterprises, private and public companies, family businesses or social organizations – are poorly managed: strategy is erratic, planning and controlling are frail, and human resources management is dismal. The business programs in Brazil should therefore do a better job at preparing future managers for taking responsible, sustainable action. In addition, the elite schools and their research groups should help Brazilian organizations and Brazilian managers to know themselves, their strengths and weaknesses, and to improve their performance.

Brazil's reality is complex and diverse. Institutions are still evolving, regulation is maturing and markets are changing fast. Foreign managerial expertise may help, but only up to a point. Many ideas and theoretical models, no matter how shiny they look in northern countries, may be lost in translation in the tropics. Besides, top business schools in Brazil and in other Latin American countries should function as gateways: acting as a reference for those scholars and business people who are interested in knowing more about the region. These are, of course, enormous challenges, enough to fill deans', researchers' and teachers' agendas for many years to come.

REFERENCES

Bennis, W.E. and O'Toole, J. (2005) How Business Schools Lost Their Way. *Harvard Business Review*, 83(4): 96–104.

Díaz, R. (2008) As Mais Empreendedoras. *Americaeconomia*, 25 (August): 18–27.

Ghoshal, S. (2005) Bad Management Theories are Destroying Good Management Practices. *Academy of Management Learning and Education*, 4(1): 75–91.

Grey, C., Knights, D. and Willmott, H. (1996) Is a Critical Pedagogy of Management Possible? In R.E. French and C. Grey (eds), *Rethinking Management Education*, pp. 94–110. London: Sage.

Mintzberg, H. (2004) *Developing Managers, Not Mbas*. London: Prentice Hall.

Pfeffer, J. and Fong, C. (2002) The End of Business Schools? Less Success than Meets the Eye. *Academy of Management, Learning and Education* 1: 78–95.

Reynolds, M. (1997) Towards a Critical Management Pedagogy. In J. Burgoyne and M. Reynolds (eds), *Management Learning: Integrating Perspectives in Theory and Practice*, pp. 312–38. London: Sage.

Robert, J. (1996) Management Education and the Limits of Technical Rationality: The Conditions and Consequences of Management. In R.E. French and C. Grey (eds), *Rethinking Management Education*, pp. 54–75. London: Sage.

3 THE CHANGING ROLE OF BUSINESS SCHOOLS AS KEY SOCIAL AGENTS IN ASIA

Bernard Yeung and Kulwant Singh

NUS Business School, Singapore

Business schools have been influential in developing and promoting important concepts relating to the profession of management, the practice of business, the organization of industries, and the provision of goods and services. Business schools are associated with ideas that have had major impact for good in recent decades, such as the globalization of business; the management of large, complex organizations within and across geographies; the development of modern financial and accounting concepts and tools; the productive utilization of scarce resources; the efficient management of operations and logistics; and the focus on entrepreneurship and value creation.

In addition, as business schools have had to be practically and empirically relevant in research and teaching, they have facilitated the development of fields like economics, psychology and sociology, influencing their research questions, theory development, methods and contexts. Business schools have educated many leaders and managers of industry. Relying on the inputs of about 100 professors and not much else, most schools have developed hundreds of business and society leaders each year, with a substantial and largely positive impact on society. Finally, business schools have typically been the most dynamic and forward-looking units within universities, driving improvements in their internal management and external interactions.

Business schools in Asia have played similar roles and aspire to the same positive impact. Business schools in Asia are important social agents for economic and societal progress through their knowledge creation and dissemination roles. Though these roles are common to most business schools globally, these contributions are under-recognized in Asia, in part because business schools there are still developing towards achieving their potential. Using the National University of Singapore (NUS) Business School as a case, we propose how business schools in Asia can become effective academic institutions, which will enhance their contributions as social change-agents.

BUSINESS SCHOOLS IN ASIA

The recent, rapid and broad development of Asia is mirrored in the development of business schools in Asia. The establishment of a large number of business schools throughout Asia since the late 1990s greatly increased the relatively small number of schools in existence. By 2010, China, the Philippines and India each had more than 1200 institutions awarding business degrees, the largest number of any country after the USA (AACSB, 2010). This growth was driven by governments viewing business education as supporting economic growth, students perceiving business degrees as financially rewarding, and entrepreneurs identifying business schools as business opportunities.

However, most business schools in Asia are under-resourced and lack the academic processes and standards associated with established business schools. This is illustrated by China having only four AACSB accredited schools in 2010, the Philippines one and India none (AACSB, 2010). At the same time, the small and relatively advanced countries of Hong Kong, Singapore, South Korea and Taiwan had 21 AACSB accredited business schools, while 16 schools in Asia had achieved EQUIS accreditation (for details, please see the EFMD site). This suggests the parallel existence in Asia of a set of relatively advanced and well-resourced schools. As we discuss below, the co-existence of these two clusters offers challenges, opportunities and optimism for the development of business schools in Asia.

Business schools there face the challenge of operating in emerging economies undergoing an economic, social and institutional transition, in most cases under tight resource and governance constraints. Nevertheless, they have made important contributions to national and regional development, possibly even more significantly and in broader roles than established business schools in developed nations.

However, Asian business schools' contributions and impact are under-recognized; paradoxically, these schools have also under-achieved. With respect to the knowledge creation role, business schools there face the charge that most of their research is theoretical, has not created adequate value and is irrelevant for the students, managers and organizations they serve. External observers and governments often perceive research to be costly and to detract from teaching. The pressure to conduct 'practical research' and to deliver real outcomes reflects the values, pragmatic orientations and resource limitations of most governments in Asia.

The growing needs of developing economies and the rising aspiration of students have increased pressures on business schools to increase their teaching in order to develop leaders. A major issue is the need to teach appropriate content, which students can apply locally and immediately. A contradictory pressure comes from employers who desire a universal content, as they want staff to work within global contexts and across borders.

Three factors explain the under-recognition and under-delivery of business schools in Asia:

1. A post-colonial complex, which leads major stakeholders to under-value what Asian schools can do and should aspire to, and to over-rate North American and European schools.
2. Leading academics and key institutions are located in North America and Europe, creating strong isomorphic pressures and the pursuit of largely US and European benchmarks.
3. The world economy has been driven by and oriented towards North America and Europe in the past.

Despite evidence that rapid and broad development is moving the center of gravity for the world economy towards Asia, such inertia will take time to overcome. It is also likely that time in the emergence of leading business schools and broader development of business education will improve the quality and recognition of business schools within Asia. We elaborate on this below.

This broad context is characteristic of the environment in which the National University of Singapore (NUS) Business School and many business schools in Asia operate. As we discuss next, through its multiple roles, the NUS Business School has made broad contributions to Singapore's development. However, these contributions are under-recognized, and in some respects, less than could have been achieved. The NUS case supports the argument that business schools in Asia have had a similar impact and have been key social change-agents. It also clarifies the actions required to make increased contributions and achieve global standards.

THE NUS BUSINESS SCHOOL

The NUS Business School was established in 1965 from units within the Economics Department, in the same year that Singapore became an independent state. Formed as a school within the comprehensive state-supported National University, its primary task was to offer business and accounting undergraduate education. An underlying responsibility was to support a government-directed economy that was growing rapidly with the entry of MNCs, particularly in manufacturing and financial services. A tiny island focused on international trade from its modern foundation as a British colony, Singapore was among the most global of economies by the 1960s, with a significant foreign presence in its economy and society. The language of business, government and education was English, as were the foundations of most of its institutions. These characteristics had an important impact on the NUS Business School, imprinting it with the qualities that continue to characterize it today.

The shortage of local faculty and the use of English as the language of instruction allowed for the recruitment of foreign faculty, the implementation of British and North American academic practices, and the adoption of Western teaching content. As a result, the NUS Business School was born as a global business school, among the most global of all business schools at that time and since.

By the 1990s, Singapore had grown almost to the extent of becoming a developed economy. Its emergence as an attractive investment location for MNCs, an economic hub for the region, and a global trading and manufacturing center was an important driver of this growth.

Mirroring the economy, the School took on an academic leadership role in the region. Contributions included facilitating the establishment of regional organizations, conferences and academic journals, and supporting faculty development and schools in the region. Locally, it also diverted substantial resources to support the development of competitive business schools, and demonstrated substantial forbearance in allowing their development.

The government invested heavily in expanding the national university and in creating two other universities. The expectations of universities changed, from a strong focus on teaching to including knowledge creation to support innovation and entrepreneurship in the maturing economy (Ministry of Education, 2003, 2005). As a result, the NUS and the School shifted their orientations to emphasize research as a means for creating knowledge. A formal commitment was made in the late 1990s to evolve from a teaching-oriented school to an institution that would recognize and balance its twin responsibilities of research and education. A key priority was a goal of achieving the research and teaching standards expected of a global business school, but with a focus on Singapore and Asia. This focus was captured in the School's tagline: 'Asia's Global Business School'.

The revised research–teaching balance required substantial resources, major changes in administrative, resource allocation and incentive systems, and a new faculty profile. Hiring new faculty to build research competencies proved to be a particularly challenging and costly process. The difficulty in this was compounded by the spinning off of the School's accounting department and program to create Singapore's second business school. Senior faculty from the School also played key roles in subsequently creating Singapore's third business school.

The School managed the transition, albeit with considerable difficulty. It now has broad strengths in research and teaching, and is perceived to be one of the leading business schools in Asia. Key factors that supported this transition were: (1) the NUS's strong drive for high academic standards, particularly in research; (2) significant improvements in the university's corporate and academic governance systems and rewards structures; and (3) strong resource support from the government (Ministry of Education, 2003, 2005).

ROLES AND IMPACT

This overview demonstrates that the NUS Business School played four key roles, which collectively indicate its impact in supporting social change:

1. *Educating business and public leaders.* The NUS Business School played a key role in educating business and public sector leaders through its status as the only or leading business school in Singapore for most of its existence. The immaturity of business education and substantial demand for managers in a rapidly growing emerging economy in a new state made this role more significant than in larger and more mature economies. This role was particularly important, as a formal business education was rare among business and public sector managers.
2. *Supporting economic and national development.* Singapore's rapid development compressed major economic and social change into little more than three decades. The NUS Business School adapted rapidly to these changes, pioneering graduate, executive and research programs to meet the growing needs and aspirations of its stakeholders and to support the growing sophistication of the economy. Research and teaching content also evolved rapidly as the economy moved through the stages of simple assembly, sophisticated manufacturing and a services orientation. Just as Singapore was highly embedded in the political economy of the region, the NUS Business School extended its programs into parts of Asia, while also recruiting students and faculty from these locales. In general, the School developed and changed more quickly than schools in developed economies.

3. *Creating localized knowledge.* Recognizing its knowledge creation responsibilities, the School adopted a policy of undertaking theoretical research in the Asian context where appropriate, and of contextualizing teaching and teaching content to Asia. Specific research efforts evaluated aspects associated with the government's economic strategy and the growth and development of Asia.
4. *Building academic institutions.* As one of the oldest business schools in Asia, the NUS Business School played an important leadership role in establishing business education in Asia.

Many business schools, including the leading business schools in Asia, play some or all of the above roles to some degree. However, these roles were more central and more constraining for the NUS Business School. As the primary source of business education and research for the majority of Singapore's independent existence, the NUS Business School played an important role in the economic and social development of the nation. In doing so, the School acted as a key social agent in Singapore.

The challenges of these roles have increased in recent years, as Singapore seeks a new basis for its mature, high-cost economy within the context of increased competition from lower-cost neighbours and the large, high-growth economies of China and India. In recent years, the development of Singapore's business schools and of the local operations of leading foreign business schools, all with support from the government, has created a very high competitive intensity in business education. As not all of these institutions have been required to or have attempted to play the same roles, the pressures on the NUS Business School have increased significantly.

The School's societal impact is more significant when viewed against the general perception among Singapore's public and business leaders that business schools are primarily teaching institutions with little or no role in creating knowledge. This is a significant challenge.

In some respects, business schools in Singapore and in Asia lack the legitimacy of their counterparts in developed economies, as they are not viewed as useful contributors to policy debates, and until recently, were rarely called on to do so. The value of business school research is also questioned for not offering the practical benefits of, for example, engineering or medical research. This challenge is compounded by the large role of foreign multinationals in Asia. These firms generally rely on hiring and research from their home countries, and generally do not show a strong interest in local talent and locally generated ideas. Many also challenge the rigor of a business education for not offering a professional or discipline-based grounding.

In part, these issues are due to the NUS Business School's early failure to establish its credentials beyond core academic constituencies, which followed the tradition of universities in Singapore, maintaining a narrow academic focus. One unintended consequence was that the legitimacy of the School was not challenged in the aftermath of major crises – the presumption of limited influence beyond the teaching sphere undermined charges that business schools were influential enough to significantly impact the external economy. However, this highlights the need for business schools in emerging environments to establish their reputation among key stakeholders to achieve broader legitimacy.

At the same time, there are indications that as the achievement of the NUS Business School and those of other leading business schools in Asia are recognized, that their roles and potential impact are expanding. Following concerted efforts to share its knowledge outside of narrow academic confines, the NUS Business School is increasingly being sought out by senior public officials and local and foreign executives for its expertise. Expectations are growing that through relevant research and thought leadership, the NUS Business School can have a broader societal impact. Claims of having emerged as a world-class business school have created expectations that the School will provide world-class teaching and research to advance an economic and social transformation. The experience is not unique to that of the NUS Business School, as other leading business schools in Asia face similar pressures to expand their roles and impact. This challenge requires leading business schools there to develop rapidly, and faster than the very rapid development and transformation of Asia itself. A detailed discussion of the implications of this follows.

THE GROWTH AND GLOBALIZATION OF ASIA[1]

Asia has had four decades of strong and broad economic growth, built on the key foundations of economic globalization. In the past, globalization in Asia centered on assembling capabilities to produce goods and services for customers in North America and Europe. Asia has now progressed to the stage where consumption is rising rapidly, driving firms to focus on serving Asian customers.

Asia is now moving to the next stage of development, where it is increasingly a source of the innovation and investments that will drive growth within the region and beyond. This increases the need for higher-quality inputs, particularly of leadership and management. Asia's needs are especially great because of the size of the region, and because of a long-term under-investment in education, particularly in business education.

Another requirement for Asia to maintain its pace of development is to base its growth on improvements in productivity and not just on capital accumulation or increased labor participation in the economy. This requires process and management improvements, and increasing innovation that commercializes streams of products. More fundamentally, it also requires streams of ideas that will facilitate efficient exchanges and markets.

These requirements support the view that Asia needs high-quality business schools to support continued development. More broadly, Asia's continued economic growth will have a significant impact on the world economy, particularly as the economies of the USA and Europe deal with the long-term consequences of the crisis of 2008.

Hence, Asia requires business schools that will serve national needs and which will help to create the conditions to support broader growth and integration. In a sense, Asia's greatest need in business education is for the emergence of global business schools to serve as supporters and change-agents for growth and development. Business schools in Asia must produce effective leaders who have the aspiration and ability to transform their organizations into globally competitive firms. This places significant demands on business schools, while also offering them the considerable opportunity to contribute towards business education globally.

THE FUTURE AND LEGITIMACY OF BUSINESS SCHOOLS IN ASIA

A global business school accepts both knowledge creation and knowledge dissemination missions, and aspires to fulfil these to global standards of academic excellence while providing education and research that serve a broad set of stakeholders. This definition argues that business schools are social agents and that key aspects of this role revolve around their traditional core missions of research and teaching. Recognizing and accepting the challenges of being social agents and agents for social change will drive business schools to achieve greater impact in these core missions.

This context and our earlier discussion of the case of the NUS Business School offer two key implications for business schools in Asia. The first is well established – the creation of a leading business school takes time and resources, with recruiting and developing faculty representing particularly significant challenges. This is an important lesson for several schools that have been established or restructured in recent years with significant government or private organization support, which are under tremendous pressure to achieve global reputations rapidly. The vast majority of schools in Asia face severe resource constraints but have overly ambitious agendas, and can gain from paying close attention to the implications of this lesson.

A second implication is that irrespective of their resource constraints, business schools can play vital roles as social agents in Asia. The key challenge is to identify and address the needs of the specific communities they seek to serve, while striving to meet the roles and global standards of business schools. This will require balancing the knowledge creation and knowledge dissemination missions, and the particular focus of each of these missions. Emerging and resource-constrained schools should address the local community needs and contexts in their teaching and research while building on the standards and content developed by the global business school community. Established and resource-rich schools should do the same, while contributing to and influencing the standards and agenda of the global business school community. Not all business schools in Asia can or should aim to be global business schools. But all schools can and must aim to be social agents for good in their communities.

These two implications are particularly important for business schools in Asia and provide a guiding framework on how they can build on key advantages and overcome constraints to develop into effective social agents. We discuss these ideas at four levels: individual academics, individual business schools, collaboration among schools, and governments.

INDIVIDUAL ACADEMICS

Business research and economic research are often context dependent. Academics observe, develop systematic questions, derive answers and build theories. They then test these theories, refine and improve them, and draw implications. This process is enhanced by variations in the phenomena being observed and is constrained by limited variations in data and context.

The USA and Western Europe are at advanced stages of societal, institutional and economic development, and have relatively limited variations on these dimensions. Their business and economic problems differ from those of economies at earlier stages of development. Hence, business research and economic research in these advanced societies do not address some of the issues that are relevant to emerging economies or do not do so in appropriate contexts. This research, though important, may not adequately address the broader needs of Asian nations.

This raises important implications and priorities for business academics in Asia:

- They should avoid directly transplanting research. This means not replicating existing research merely for publication in international journals, which may not appreciate contextual differences. However, this does not mean abandoning scientific standards or assuming that fundamental theory and research questions are dissimilar.
- Business academics and schools in Asia must learn from the best global experiences while establishing their own development paths. Importantly, this does not mean that research and researchers should not learn or build from the economic and developmental histories of other regions.
- They should aim for the highest global standards in knowledge creation and dissemination. However, like all academics, they need to balance the sometimes-orthogonal demands posed by these tasks. They should address teaching and research opportunities in Asia, while focusing on global requirements and standards.
- They should exercise their location advantage to focus on issues that are proximate to them and distant from those of American and European schools. This approach will allow them to create the most value in both research and teaching. The priority and ambition must be to raise the standards of fundamental knowledge and knowledge that is relevant to Asia. A key advantage is that most academics in Asia are trained in the paradigms and contexts of the developed world, while also being embedded in Asia. The multiple dimensions of contrast between the developed world and Asia create fertile intellectual tensions that can propel high-level knowledge creation.
- Academics should focus their intellectual curiosity and research on addressing the following tensions:

  o Asia's growth is now of global importance. Tackling questions in vastly differing economies and societies at different stages of development is a challenge, but one that provides the advantage of variations on multiple dimensions. There are immense research opportunities.
  o Identify and contrast cross-economy and cross-time differences on basic questions, to identify a theoretical and empirical divergence. Again, Asia offers multiple opportunities to investigate these issues.
  o Focus on students' and other stakeholders' specific needs. In a region as complex and rapidly evolving as Asia, these vary significantly. This highlights the need to balance research and teaching across global, regional and local dimensions.

- Anticipate the future in research and teaching scholarship, as well as in programs. Asia's rapid development will require a more rapid change in content, context and programs than is common in most other regions.

INDIVIDUAL BUSINESS SCHOOLS

Business schools in Asia need to develop clear and realistic intents, and to strive in a coherent and systematic manner to achieve them. Pitfalls to avoid and challenges to overcome include:

- Becoming blind followers or imitators of 'advanced schools'. Differing contexts, resources and societies' needs will almost certainly cause this approach to fail.
- Focusing on 'the numbers game' or targeting appearance rather than substance. Examples include the practice of rewarding faculty financially for each published paper and for launching programs primarily to achieve higher rankings. Though these approaches may offer benefits at particular stages of development, long-term progress must be based on intellectually rigorous research and teaching.
- Becoming local hosts, to ride on the reputation of foreign partners. Business schools have learnt from their own teaching that alliances offer many advantages. However, the advantages of speed, increased visibility and market access may create dependencies that hinder Asian schools from developing independent capabilities in the long-term if the cooperation is not based on sharing between partners.

A more appropriate approach is for business schools in Asia to focus on the following key approaches:

- *Building broad research, teaching and organizational capabilities.* Business schools must learn to accommodate faculty with varying capabilities, so that individual faculty might excel in specific areas while the School succeeds on collective strengths. Though not controversial in mature organizations, this approach is not necessarily accepted in many schools in Asia.
- *Nurturing rather than dictating career development.* The organizational tradition in many parts of Asia has often been one of concentrating power and top-down management. This fundamentally restricts academic freedom and constrains the search for individual excellence.
- *Professionalizing the management of schools.* Schools need to introduce global best practices that have been adapted to their local environment. A particular priority is establishing effective organizations and administrative systems to support research and teaching. As most Asian schools are government-funded they face constraints in admissions, compensation, fees and fundraising, for example. These constraints are uncommon in many schools elsewhere. Overcoming these will be a major challenge and a major step forward.
- *Building capabilities for faculty development within the region,* particularly through PhD programs. This will help address a key constraint, the shortage of quality faculty. Equally importantly, this will ameliorate the global shortage of faculty, and help business schools outside Asia recruit faculty with a better understanding of the region.
- *Leveraging resources* within schools and universities, and in other universities and business schools, both locally and across Asia. This will address resource shortages and enhance sharing.
- *Building links with industry.* These links will provide contextual information, develop the understanding of key challenges facing businesses and their leaders, identify variations in business models and practices from those in developed environments, and allow testing of the rigor and relevance of theory. This will enhance the value of teaching and research that business schools can provide, leading to the important benefit of increased legitimacy. If developed appropriately, these links can promote intellectual curiosity and rigor, and increase the quality and relevance of teaching and research.
- *Developing global approaches.* Most business schools in Asia are characterized by local faculty and student bodies, with content, programs and aspirations grounded in domestic contexts. Schools in Asia must develop the same global mindsets and approaches that leading business schools aspire to achieve.

COLLABORATION AMONG SCHOOLS

Regional cooperation is a key initiative that will facilitate overcoming knowledge creation and dissemination challenges. Most schools in Asia have weak links within the region and thus miss the benefits of collaboration, including sharing resources, improving capabilities, growing markets and serving customers more effectively.

The following are key issues for business schools:

- Many Asian schools have good links with the West but not with other schools in Asia. A key constraint is that there are few credible regional organizations or forums that provide the opportunity to meet, share resources, accumulate knowledge and build links. At the same time, there are too many ad hoc, overlapping and competitive agreements that do not serve as adequate platforms.
- The primary challenge in developing regional organizations or forums is the willingness of business school leaders to collaborate and to recognize that this can happen within a broader context of competition. The ability to overcome territorial or competitive tendencies will support the formation of regional networks.
- Though there is a tendency for elite schools to seek exclusive networks, these can co-exist with broader and inclusive networks. All members will gain from the establishment of ties, even weak ones, with schools that they might not otherwise partner. An added advantage is the opportunity for leading schools to assist emerging schools.
- Collaborative efforts should not replicate, at least initially, existing accreditation and publications efforts. These efforts would divert resources to activities and organizations that exist elsewhere, and which schools in Asia can draw on.

GOVERNMENTS

Governance mechanisms in the context of Asia more closely resemble those of Europe than those of the USA. The involvement of Asian governments in business education is significant though varied, both in terms of providing resources and in guiding the activities of schools. In essence, most governments in Asia view education as too important and politically sensitive to leave to educators or the private sector.

Their provision of significant resources to business schools earns governments the right of influence. However, governments and society will be best served by the following approach:

- Privatizing and liberalizing business education within broad quality assurance and academic governance frameworks. Educators are best placed to drive schools towards excellence, and to attract and motivate academics. Government officials suffer substantial information disadvantages and are poorly placed to play active management and governance roles.
- Encouraging market forces. Many Asian countries have a paradoxical combination of tight control on government-supported business schools and loose or ineffective control of non-government business schools. This disadvantages government-supported schools, while often undermining the general quality of business education. A more market-driven approach, supported by mechanisms to ensure quality and provide relevant information, will generate the advantages of competition while addressing issues of market failure in education. At the same time, the negative consequences of competition, such as lowered standards,

'window dressing', an over-investment in infrastructure and excessive marketing, must be guarded against.
- Encouraging an effective concentration of resources so that governments can support and build on agglomeration principles. This could see the emergence of regional centers of business education within and across countries in Asia.

These ideas collectively provide a set of actions that can help business schools in Asia move towards fulfilling their potential contributions. To be effective social agents, however, they will have to overcome significant challenges.

CHALLENGES

Business schools in Asia are latecomers and face significant challenges in becoming global business schools. Many also face the constraints of strong government oversight, insufficient funding, a shortage of faculty and an inadequate infrastructure. However, they do enjoy the advantages of operating in munificent environments, being able to learn from the experiences of top schools, having the potential resource of large numbers of ethnic-Asian faculty in leading business schools, and strong demand.

A key challenge is the governance framework within which business schools operate. Change in the role of governments in education is likely to be slow and to lag overall social and economic liberalization. Business schools will have to work with universities and governments to liberalize educational institutions and institutional structures at a pace that is acceptable to their governments, and manageable for universities and their stakeholders. Helping to manage this process and the shift in systems for resourcing universities represents a key challenge and opportunity for business schools.

Asia's continued development will increase the pressures on business schools to undertake research and teaching that are both rigorous and relevant, and contribute to changing economies and requirements. The demands of creating knowledge to support growth, while enhancing relevant teaching, will also continue to increase. In some countries, business schools may face pressure to contribute to national and institutional building outside of their educational role, to repay governments' contribution scarce public resources. For these schools, a key challenge is to establish the argument that knowledge creation and dissemination are the primary and most effective contributions they can make as social agents. For the majority of schools in Asia, the challenge is to create a balance between their particular combination of research and teaching to serve their stakeholders, demonstrating the value of this focus for their societies, and working within their constraints towards becoming global business schools.

To a significant degree what we propose is normative and, with minor adaptions, applicable to business schools globally. This leads to the powerful position that the challenges facing business schools in Asia, and the solutions to these challenges, may be different from those elsewhere but not unique.

A small number of high-quality business schools in Asia offer role models. However, a major constraint in Asia is the absence of well-established collective efforts. Recent successful collaborative networks, such as the Association of Asia Pacific Business Schools (AAPBS) offer considerable potential. CEMS, the European-led Global Alliance for Management

Education, offers a model for guiding and coordinating regional efforts in Asia. The key challenges for these efforts are to focus on developing schools, establishing internally driven norms for research and teaching excellence, developing platforms for sharing, facilitating the development of markets for faculty, and encouraging mobility at all levels.

A related challenge is to develop a CEMS equivalent in Asia, or to undertake a 'Bologna-like' rationalization of programs in the absence of an organization similar to the European Union. Even more fundamentally, a major challenge is to overcome the almost total absence of desire for any form of integration in Asia. De facto integration through trade and economic exchange is much more likely. As business schools directly address and facilitate such integration they are a partial solution to this problem, again highlighting their role as social change-agents.

A complementary form of collaboration is with schools from the West. Schools in Asia have much to learn through such partnerships, which should focus on competency development. Their partners will gain from greater awareness of Asia, from operating globally, and from gaining new contexts for research and teaching. The challenge for Asian schools is to focus such collaboration on developmental purposes. The successful examples of business schools and programs in Asia that have emerged from such collaborative efforts are partly offset by cases of collaboration that have failed to achieve lasting impact.

A major challenge is countering an approach to governance, leadership and management that is common in Asia, one of central coordination and top-down direction. This approach may work for a small number of lead institutions, which receive disproportionate priority and resources, but it is unlikely to be broadly effective. Instead, the best approach may be to create the right starting conditions and to provide the necessary resources to nurture the growth of faculty, schools, institutions and infrastructures that are attuned to the needs of local and regional communities, while aspiring to global academic standards. A key focus must be on igniting faculty initiatives and the drive for excellence as pre-requisites for the development of good business schools. This approach is more likely to see the creation of a broad base of good business schools, from which a number of truly high-quality global business schools will emerge.

An ambitious objective would be for the emergence of 10 top-quality global business schools in Asia within 10 years. A more realistic aim would be for these schools to emerge within 20 years. Achieving these targets will require shared ambition, collective action, closer interaction, stronger competition, enhanced mobility, increased flexibility and substantial resources. Most of these requirements are within the control of business schools. Governments recognizing the key roles of business schools – as has happened in some economies – will enhance support and facilitate their emergence.

NOTE

1. We will refer to Asia without offering a definition of this complex construct. We limit our reference to the regions popularly described as East Asia, Southeast Asia and South Asia, while excluding Central Asia and the Middle East. This offers a more manageable region, but which is still too diverse, vast and complex to permit more than broad generalizations. See Singh (2004) for a discussion of the concept of Asia in the context of strategy research.

REFERENCES

AACSB International (2010) *Business School Data Trends and 2010 List of Accredited Schools.* Tampa, FL: AACSB.

EFMD (2010) www.efmd.org/index.php/accreditation-/equis/accredited-schools (accessed 1 August 2010).

Ministry of Education (2003) *Restructuring the University Sector: More Opportunities, Better Quality.* Singapore: Ministry of Education.

Ministry of Education (2005) *Autonomous Universities: Towards Peaks of Excellence.* Singapore: Ministry of Education.

Singh, K. (2004) Towards the Development of Strategy Theory: Contributions from Asia Research. In S. White and K. Leung (eds) *Handbook of Asian Management.* Dordrecht: Kluwer.

4 INSTITUTIONAL EVOLUTION AND NEW TRENDS IN RUSSIAN MANAGEMENT EDUCATION

Valery S. Katkalo

St. Petersburg University, Russia

The two decades since the beginning of the Russian transition from socialism to market economy have been a period of birth and dynamic growth in management education industry in the country. Several leading Russian business schools have received international recognition through program accreditations and alliances with some of the top European and US schools. Meanwhile, even these leaders are not yet featured in global rankings of top business schools, and most of the other local providers of management education operate on outdated business models that barely meet international professional standards. This has resulted in major gaps in ambitious goals for global competitiveness of the national economy in the twenty-first century, set up by the Russian political and business elite. However, this recent strategic request for a world-class management education, together with the high economic potential of Russia (as one of the BRIC countries), and ongoing reform of the national university system have all created unique opportunities for a further maturation of Russian business schools which must demonstrate their ability to change.

In this chapter, the analysis of institutional evolution and new trends in Russian management education is organized into three sections. A short retrospective analysis of the main phases in its evolution is provided in the first section. The second deals with a comparison of the business models on which Russian schools currently operate. In the third section, future trends in Russian management education are examined.

EMERGING RUSSIAN MANAGEMENT EDUCATION: A BRIEF SUMMARY OF THE FIRST 20 YEARS

For most of the twentieth century (70 years of socialism), the tradition of business education as it developed in the Western economies and the phenomena of the business school itself had no systemic reason for emerging in Russia. To be precise, in 1900–1910 schools of commerce were opened in several key cities, in parallel with the birth of business education in other European countries. However, in the Russian case, this trend was cut short by the socialist coup d'etat in 1917. Only in the late 1980s, when joint ventures 'with enterprises from capitalist countries' and cooperatives (private entrepreneurial firms) were legitimized under Perestroika, did the demand for business education become a Russian reality again.

The institutional rebirth of Russian business education was to start almost from scratch. In the Soviet period, higher education in business subjects was directed towards the needs of the planned economy, both in the economic departments of universities and in specialized institutes in economy, finance, engineering and trade (with scarcely no studies in corporate finance, marketing or operational management). Along with the dominance of ideological dogmas and the weak connections of academics to business, there were limited (if any) international and interdisciplinary academic interactions. Only a few elite places, such as the Moscow and St. Petersburg (then Leningrad) State Universities, and the Moscow State Institute of International Relations (MGIMO), had the privilege of organizing faculty groups to study the 'economy of contemporary capitalism', and of international academic exchanges (not surprisingly, these institutions later gave way to some of the top Russian business schools). Another major platform for the development of managers for Soviet enterprises and government – the Academy of National Economy (ANE) – was established in 1977 in Moscow. But even with this most advanced prototype of a professional business school, initial programs' design and delivery methods, as documented in Puffer (1981), differed much from the standards set by US business schools. Organized research in management was also very limited and done mostly at the Institute for USA Studies, and the Institute of World Economy and International Relations (IMEMO), both at the Academy of Sciences. By the mid-1980s, there were still no articles by Russian scholars in top international management research journals, and for faculty at the universities research was not even a predominant evaluation criterion. This is one of the critical factors which can explain the neglect of a research culture at most Russian business schools today.

During the 1990s and into the 2000s, the management education landscape in Russia changed dramatically, especially in terms of market growth and institutional evolution. This period could be structured in the following three phases.

Phase 1 – Birth of the industry (late 1980s to 1990s). The demand for business education as it boomed in Russia from the late 1980s centered mainly on the basics in accounting, entrepreneurship, international business, economics and law. This served a mass entrepreneurial movement, and the need to introduce the directors of state enterprises to managing a market-type firm. After the launch in 1992 of price liberalization, mass privatization and other radical reforms, the quest for a 'Russian management revolution' drove the explosive growth of the business education industry. However, it emerged in and reflected on Russia's decade of initial capital accumulation and of managing privatized enterprises through 'adaptation without restructuring' (low unemployment despite a major downfall in the national economy). It was from this period of transition, adaptation and survival that many Russian business schools inherited a dominance of commercial interests and short-term goals on their agenda, as well as a priority of practical focus in education, often at the expense of theory.

Newborn business schools (in major cities across the country) soon became self-organized: in 1990, the Russian Association of Business Education (RABE) was co-founded with the Graduate School of International Business at ANE, the Higher Commercial School at the Ministry of Economy, and the International Business School at MGIMO. While these all focused on executive education, the population of Russian business schools (and RABE membership) quickly increased due to opening these in-house and otherwise at classical and technical universities (usually in or as spin-offs from economics departments), at traditional providers of business training (i.e. institutes of economics and finance, and industry-level training centers), and as a result of the creation of private schools. By the mid-1990s, about 500 Russian institutions were offering programs in management.

Major changes in the state regulation of higher education created huge opportunities for these developments. In 1992, the new Federal Law on Education liberalized the formation of private institutions of higher education, and permitted tuition-based education at state universities, thus enforcing competition in higher education between entities with varying ownership. In 1994, State regulations for the management field in undergraduate university education were adopted, thus introducing 4-year Bachelor programs in management and the traditional 5-year specialist format with programs in management, marketing, public administration, etc. In 1996, the first federal regulations were adopted for pre-experience Master's programs in the management field.

Though some Russian business schools also delivered programs in the 1990s that were named MBA, this degree was not recognized officially, and graduates usually received two documents – the state diploma of 'Retraining' degree (with a required minimum of 500 contact hours) and an MBA certificate authorized by the school itself. Many business schools, though, successfully ran Retraining degree programs with no MBA label.

Quality improvements and faculty development programs were done in this period mostly with foreign assistance – via institutional development grants from US and EU agencies as well as from Eurasia and other foundations. From those, several major successes emerged, i.e. the Moscow University Graduate School of Business Administration (GSBA) (with Northeastern University), the St. Petersburg University School of Management (SOM) (projects with the Haas Business School, UC Berkeley; Stockholm University, and consortia of top Nordic business schools), and the Baikal Management Institute at Irkutsk University (with the University of Maryland).

In this period, international business schools also used various modes of entry into the attractive Russian market: creating a branch (i.e. the Stockholm School of Economics [SSE] in St. Petersburg), a new school as a joint venture with a Russian partner (i.e. the Belgian LETI-Lovanium, and the International Management Institute of St. Petersburg [IMISP], born as a joint venture of St. Petersburg University with Bocconi, and now a private school), and delivering programs at a Russian institution (i.e. California State at Hayward and Kingston University – both at ANE). Though they achieved varying results – extreme cases are 15 years of SSE success and LETI-Lovanium dissolution in the early 2000s – still none has its own academic organization in Russia.

The growth of business education was supported by: the identification of managers as a new social strata; the call for continuous professionalization of management by *Expert* magazine in 1996 (which resulted in the bestseller *Seven Notes of Management* with eight editions); the launch of RABE's *Business Education* magazine in 1996, and publication of the first Russian-authored textbooks in management and strategic management. In early

1998, the Presidential Initiative program was started with the target of retraining 5000 managers per year. Evidently, by August 1998 (when the major economic crisis began), Russian management education was walking rather than crawling .

Phase 2 – Dynamic expansion of the market (2000 until the 2008–9 economic crisis). The new millenium was a remarkably different stage in the evolution of Russian business and business education in the context of departing from 'wild capitalism', high rates of economic growth (8 per cent average), and political stabilization. In 1999, the first two Russian companies (Gazprom and Lukoil) appeared in *Fortune 500,* and within the decade Russian business in general replaced survival-type adaptation with growth strategies. Hot topics in the business community became competitive and corporate strategies, branding, IPO, organization design, and learning from international experience. Strategy consulting was booming. In 2001 the Association of Russian Managers, and in 2004 the Russian edition of *Harvard Business Review,* were launched. For business education, the turning point was the adoption by the Ministry of Education (RABE's lobbying success) of the state requirements for the MBA Degree in late 1999.

Throughout most of the 2000s, prior to the economic crisis of 2008–9, the Russian market for management education demonstrated great dynamic growth. According to an estimation by Roland Berger Strategy Consultants, the total tuition revenues of Russian business schools more than doubled during 2002–7: from $2.27 billion up to $4.89 billion (Milov, 2008). This study covered two dominating segments of the Russian business education market – undergraduate programs in economics and management (89 per cent of the total market in 2002 and 82 per cent in 2007), and MBA and EMBA programs (11 per cent and 18 per cent, accordingly). As of 2008, pre-experience Master in Management programs formed a small segment, and non-degree executive education was not included in this study.

The new decade also came with a strong request for business schools to progress according to the growing needs of the Russian economy. Despite the expansion of business schools, a continuous dramatic shortage of modern managers and (in general) the insufficient quality of business education at Russian schools became widely discussed by politicians and businessmen. On one hand, ExecEd-type business schools (especially private ones) favored faculty only with business experience at the expense of academic qualities (not surprisingly, the first 33 schools with state-recognized MBA programs had been asked to have undergraduate programs in their portfolios). On the other hand, business schools at state universities often had faculty that were too academic and old-fashioned. However, the approach-to-quality issue – especially in respect to international standards – varied a lot at Russian business schools and in certain aspects reflected alternative paths and tough decisions that they had undertaken in the period of deep and rapid socio-economic transition. Moreover, with this type of action, Russian providers of business education were not only influenced by path-dependence effects, but also in many cases by the lost opportunities of the 1990s to 2000s, to reinvent their economics and management programs in line with global trends.

This strategic decision-making of the educational institutions' leadership along the lines of change and continuity resulted (with certain generalizations) in three modes of behavior in the fast-growing national market for business education. First, the vast majority of Russian providers of degree programs in management continued in paternalistic (and thus reactive) mode, waiting until changes in state regulations forced them to move towards a Master in Management, thus recognizing ECTS and internationalization as a new concept and institutional value. Also, only roughly 10 per cent of these actors developed MBA programs, which is more evidence of little appetite for innovation in the Russian business education industry. Second, most of the institutions with strong brands built in the Soviet period followed a rent-seeking path, and did little in departing from 'teaching machines' and moving towards international standards (they rarely show any interest in international accreditations). Ultimately, this was leading to the relative decline of many 'old brands' of large traditional universities which specialized in economics, finance and trade. Not surprisingly, the new leaders were emerging from those who followed the third (proactive) path, characterized by priority investments (also from tuition revenues) in international-level graduate programs, faculty development and research capabilities. Such leading business schools were born in-house in the 1990s at the St. Petersburg, Moscow and Urkutsk Universities, and at ANE, or as independent institutions such as the Higher School of Economics (HSE) and the New Economic School (NES). Only this innovative mode supported business schools' legitimacy in the top Russian universities, and in becoming prototypes or even locomotives of the Bologna reforms of the 2000s in the national university system.

The differentiation trends among Russian business schools were quickly developing in the 2000s, with strong evidence of these in (a) price differentiation, and (b) international recognition of the leaders. If in 2000 tuition for MBA programs averaged \$4–5000, by the end of the decade the gap had grown nearly fivefold (the range being Rb200–900,000, or \$6.5–30,000), while price leaders faced no elasticity effects. By 2008 104 schools were accredited and, as RABE President Leonid Evenko described it, 'offered programs called MBA' (Evenko, 2009: 3), 58 schools had licenses to issue an MBA degree, but only 20–25 schools enrolled in each cohort (or even annually) 20+ participants. There were no full-time MBA programs in an international sense (quite similar to other CEE and BRIC countries), with the 'MBA' being differentiated from EMBA in price and participants' caliber, but not in delivery mode, and even sometimes not much in design and content.

In the 2000s, the best Russian business schools also received international recognition. As of April 2010, while still no Russian school had EQUIS or AACSB accreditation, eight schools were granted AMBA, and three also got EPAS, with 12 Russian schools as members of EFMD and six of AACSB. This was big progress in the global visibility of Russian schools, but these achievements were within a group of only 10–12 top ones, and all from Moscow and St. Petersburg, though business schools operate in 20 major cities.

Parallel to this 'organic' differentiation, in 2006, under the National Priority Project in Education, the Russian business elite joined with the federal government to build (including major investments in new campuses) two world-class business schools, based on alternative models. The Moscow School of Management Skolkovo was founded by 14 private companies and businessmen as a greenfield project with an 'entrepreneurial' model that focused on advances in the practice-based approach, and it soon successfully launched MBA, EMBA and ExedEd programs. The 'research-based' model was followed by the Graduate School of Management (GSOM) which resulted from a reorganization of the St. Petersburg University SOM and developed as a full-range (Bachelor, Master, PhD, EMBA and ExecEd) school. The platform of the successful school (est. 1993) permitted

St. Petersburg University GSOM to quickly expand its high-quality programs; it is the Russian member of CEMS, PIM, GMAC, GRLI and GBSN, and is marked by EdUniversal as the best Russian B-School and the second best in Eastern Europe. The two schools are benchmarks for developing further Russian management education.

Phase 3 – Maturation as opportunity (late 2000s – present). By the time of the 2008–9 economic crisis, Russian business education industry was reaching its maturation (Evenko, 2009). This crisis for Russian business schools was a test of both their viability, and their potential to recognize and seize new development opportunities. In 2009 (as compared to 2008), there was an overall 25 per cent drop in enrollment (and revenues) at business schools, and if this trend continues, quite a few schools may need to exit from, merge or reconsider their business models (the schools which suffered the least were those with diversified portfolios). At the same time, there are several major context changes from which business schools can benefit strategically.

First, there is major unmet market opportunity in Russia for management education. In 2008, about 5000 MBA degrees were granted by Russian schools, with the total number reaching 25,000. This is very low output for an economy of Russia's size: its annual demand was estimated by McKinsey as being 30–50,000 MBA degrees, and Roland Berger in 2008 projected that the Russian business education market may double by 2015 (Evenko, 2009; Milov, 2008). Additionally, there is generally little trust available from the business community for most Russian management schools, grounded in quality concerns for their students' selection, faculty professionalism, and programs' design and delivery methods. Executive education for major Russian companies is rarely done at local schools, and a few hundreds of Russians only will apply annually for MBA and EMBA programs abroad.

Second, in 2008–10, some innovative state regulations were introduced to support Russian higher education's move towards international standards. For Russian business schools interested in it, the introduction of the national citation index (RINZ) can be of great value, thus granted publication in refereed journals as the criteria for research excellence; Federal Educational Standards of 'Third Generation' for Bachelor and Master programs in Management (the mechanism for transfer to Bologna principles); and of specialization in management for doctoral programs.

Third (but not least), Russian business schools should consider becoming the main supplier of a modern managerial workforce to support the global competitiveness of the national economy and its transformation from resource-dependent to innovation-driven – these intentions (in line with 'modernization' policies) have been strongly articulated in recent years by Russian political and business leaders. There is growing interest from business in upgrading management education in the country, proven by examples such as its active involvement in two projects of world-class business schools; its creation in 2009 of the Business Education Committee of ARM; and the recent launch of corporate universities at major Russian companies.

In turn, leading Russian business schools have to dynamically adapt to these changes in their environment. Such frequent arguments which explain their development limits as low purchasing power and a shortage of qualified professors are, to a large extent, misleading. The real core issue is their ability to absorb institutional features of the modern professional management school, and thus to transform their business models.

BUSINESS MODELS' PLURALISM IN RUSSIAN MANAGEMENT EDUCATION

After 20 years of Russian management education's evolution, the controversy around the notion and values of the 'business school' remains an important issue. As of the late 2000s, there were about 150 RABE-member schools, representing 45 cities and 34 regions of Russia as well as foreign countries, and in total about 900 (public and private) higher education institutions were delivering some degree programs in economics and management. These providers operate on business models of a large variety, which is explained, at least partially, by differences in organizational path-dependencies and market niches. The most frequent are 'vocational schools' (as described in the famous Gordon and Howell and Pierson 1959 reports on the state of US business schools) and 'teaching machines' models. The 'vocational' types (and many 'teaching machines') usually have a very low capacity to produce new knowledge and no systemic connections with business; they are mostly commercial-oriented, overemphasize the 'specifics of doing business in Russia', are reluctant to follow global trends in management education, and lag behind the actual needs of Russian firms (especially industry leaders). Also, these providers often do not have such organizational identities of a business school as sufficient full-time faculty, career centers, library and IT resources, etc. The business rationale for these 'schools' is in positioning in low-price segments, or in capitalizing on market distortions (false signaling effects) when the demand for education is high in the absence of a national professional accreditation system (only accreditation by the Ministry of Education and Science) and reliable rankings for Russian business schools. It is important to stress that such providers are institutionally far from being professional business schools and usually have low-quality programs, and are in a Russian context often represented by both private schools and units at public universities. Possibly the only difference between such private and public 'enterprises' in management education is that at state universities there are at least some formal limits for such versions of 'teaching machines', described by RABE President Leonid Evenko as a 'private theatrical concern' when groups of professors and instructors are assembled ad hoc to serve a particular audience of students or participants (Evenko, 2010). Today, the leaders (in private schools, some are [co]owners) of such providers are still less occupied with building business schools as institutions and more with running commercially reasonable programs under the label of a 'business school'.

While in the late 2000s the Russian management education landscape was in large part populated by schools with such outdated (in respect to the needs of the country) business models, there were still 25–30 business schools based on much more advanced principles. Due to the heterogeneity of their organizational nature, these schools could be clustered in the following three ways:

- Schools at top research universities (i.e. at St. Petersburg State University, Moscow State University, HSE, Urals University).
- Private schools (i.e. Skolkovo, Mirbis, Sinergia, IMISP, Urals-Sibirian Insitute of Business [USIB]).
- Schools at (economics, technical, etc.) universities/academies (i.e. at ANE, Financial Academy, Plekhanov Russian Economy Academy, State University of Management, Perm and Irkutsk State Technical Universities).

By many other key organizational and operational criteria, such as product portfolio, full-time faculty, research activities, corporate and international academic ties, business models' typology of these schools is more likely to fit a dual typology of 'research-based' *vs.* 'entrepreneurial' models. In Russia, as well as in Central and Eastern Europe in general (for an excellent analysis of business education in the region see Larcon and Hmimda, 2008), this mainly develops at historical institutions and relies on a faculty of researchers in business-related sciences, while also used at private and sometimes state institutions but in all cases relying heavily on professionals and practitioners. In real life – especially in a country of Russia's scale and scope – this dichotomy is not 'black and white'. A private school like Mirbis may intend to develop towards what it calls a 'business university' or under the umbrella of one institution there may be units following alternative models, such as ANE with its 14 business schools.

While for this leading group of Russian business schools there is obviously no universal model for success (the arguments of some advocates for the entrepreneurial model as the most promising for the Russian market [see Mau and Seferyan, 2007] are not convincing), there are certain shared ways for reaching internationally comparable and (highly) competitive positions. For the schools interested in such positioning, (a) the competition – in Russian and international markets – will not be on programs/products but on business models, and (b) for both research-based and entrepreneurial models – irrespective of whether the school is private or public – there are at least four areas where they have to improve in order to achieve international competitiveness.

First, the best Russian schools need to prioritize faculty development and strike the right balance of rigor and relevance in accordance with their business model. This does not mean that faculty's intellectual contributions are not expected in an entrepreneurial one. However, the recent global debate on 'rigor and relevance' is wrongly interpreted at many Russian schools as an argument against building strong research capabilities/culture (as measured by publications in refereed journals) which, in fact, they never tried to develop before. Also, high-quality practice-relevant research is only now coming onto the agenda of Russian business schools. The majority continue to neglect organized research as a source of competitive advantage: only in 2005 and after heated discussions did the RABE board establish its research committee which had never developed a research agenda for member schools. But some schools, i.e. NES, HSE and St. Petersburg University GSOM (which also produces most of the Russian cases registered at ECCH, and publishes the top Russian-language research publication, *Russian Management Journal*) take research as a priority, have faculty published in international refereed journals, and are designing international-level PhD programs (some other schools offer the DBA).

This lack of a research culture limits the potential of many schools in thought leadership (and thus forces them to compete directly with consulting firms), and has direct implications for the shortage of high-quality faculty for Russian management education. On one hand, there is a popular naive assumption that 'professional businessmen could be successfully converted into business school faculty' (Milov, 2008), which seems to be an easy solution compared to investing in faculty development programs. On the other hand, few Russian faculty members are active in the international job market, though some have recently been contracted at international faculties part-time and as visiting scholars.

Second, top Russian business schools have to systemically internationalize, especially through international professional accreditations. As success stories show (see Katkalo, 2009), such accreditations may be used for 'modernization through internationalization', when considered as a mechanism for permanent quality improvement. Such internationalization may also result in innovations for the Russian higher education system, i.e. through the introduction of a required semester abroad in Bachelor and Master programs, and English-taught programs that provide a platform for large-scale international student mobility on an ECTS basis, which, in turn, can become the driver for cultural change across an organization. Russian business schools are slowly becoming more interested in international accreditations, both encouraged by the first recipients of AMBA and EPAS, and intrigued by the related new reputational opportunities, within business circles in particular.

Third, much is to be done in developing schools' stakeholder relations, especially in systemic business connections (still certainly innovative in Russia). Several aspects of these need major advancement:

- Involvement by business in programs' design and delivery. This is key given the global move from teaching to learning partnerships between schools and companies; and the growth in action-learning, life-long learning, learning on the job, and corporate universities.
- Fund-raising, which requires a new societal culture of donations (the Law on Endowment Funds was passed in late 2006), expertise in relationships with stakeholders, certain autonomy for a business school when it is a university unit.
- An institutional infrastructure to support stakeholder relations (Advisory Boards, Alumni Associations and Career Centers are still quite rare in Russian business schools).

Fourth, Russian schools that look for long-term relations with leading companies and sustainable market positions have to develop (internal and external) management systems that are in line with modern international standards. This relates both to administrative routines (student selection, quality control systems, faculty policies, etc.) and organizational capabilities for a dynamic adaptation to market changes and for integration into the global management education industry, which is today at a crossroads with even top international schools rethinking their ways of doing business(Datar et al., 2010).

Given this and the fact that leading Russian business schools (both private and at state universities) successfully evolved mostly as 'ventures in education', they are now challenged not only to build administrative systems but also to incorporate within them mechanisms for proactive adaptation, thus resulting in what are known as 'dynamic capabilities' (see Katkalo et al., 2010). These schools have to develop the internal mechanisms for change in order to be prepared to train managers not for the country's transition 'from socialism to capitalism' but for its move towards a knowledge society. This ability to transform their business models (both 'research-based' and 'entrepreneurial') into world-class ones is critical for them to contribute to the nation's competitiveness in the twenty-first century.

FUTURE TRENDS IN RUSSIAN MANAGEMENT EDUCATION

As for now, Russian business schools, except for the few leading ones, are not yet the institutions of influence in society that they are in the USA and Europe. This may change as

Russian schools continue to develop into more sophisticated institutions with a bigger focus on graduate studies and thought leadership, integration into global management education and a contribution to solving key issues in society as their important strategic imperatives. Future trends in Russian management education are related to these three dimensions of its further maturation.

First, by 2020, Russia will probably still have no more than three or four business schools with internationally strong brands, but it is very likely that in the 2010s the concept of the Graduate School of (Business) Management, as it is known worldwide, will become more common in Russia. Several institutional developments support this prognosis.

- In 2011 Russian higher education will complete its transfer to the Bologna system replacing the traditional five-year specialist degree with Bachelor and Master programs, and in the economics and management fields 17 specialties will be substituted by five areas of multilevel programs in Economics, Management, Business Informatics, Public Administration, and Statistics. This will lead to a major growth of the pre-experience (general and specialized) Master's segment in Russian business education, and to subsequent questioning (as elsewhere in Europe) of the role of the full- and part-time MBA. A parallel and interesting case is emerging in graduate education for professional managers in the public sector, where both the pre-experience Master in Public Administration and post-experience MPA (an abbreviation for the same title) programs were officially introduced in 2010.
- In the late 2000s, a stratification of Russian universities started with the government granting (by Federal Law) special statuses to the Moscow and St. Petersburg Universities, selecting 29 others for the status of 'national research universities', and creating eight 'federal universities'. It is likely that most of these top universities will develop (indeed some already have) Graduate Business Schools.
- The introduction of the management field to the list of doctoral programs in 2010 by the Ministry of Education and Science may result in PhD-type programs in management at top schools.

Second, Russian business schools will gradually increase their global presence through dual degree and jointly designed and delivered (Executive Education) programs, international student exchanges, professional accreditations, etc. Partnerships and alliances with (top) international business schools will become a must for any Russian school with strong strategic ambitions. The benchmarks here are the alliances formed by St. Petersburg University GSOM with HEC-Paris (including dual degree master and EMBA programs), CEMS global network (CEMS MIM program) and Duke's Fuqua School, and Skolkovo's with MIT's Sloan School, Fundacao Dom Cabral, and the Indian School of Business.

Third, Russian business schools will continue to increase their contribution to society, particularly on issues of public management, business and society relations, and the development of an innovation-driven economy in Russia.

Among key drivers for the expansion of degree and non-degree public management development programs are the recently accelerated professionalization of public administration (i.e. the pioneering cases of appointing city managers), and health care and education system reforms. Major institutional change in education for public administration was implemented by President Medvedev in late 2010: the Academy of Public Service (the main national provider of such training) became the unit of ANE, which is known for its higher quality of management programs. Also, public administration programs were and are among the priorities for other top providers of management education, i.e. the Moscow and St. Petersburg Universities, and HSE. At these and several other schools, new programs were also recently launched in Health Care Management, and Educational Institutions Management. It is quite likely that building capabilities for international-class programs in public management will remain at a handful of leading business schools that will consider it as part of their strategic agendas, and, probably, none of these (except for Skolkovo) will come from among private ones (this is also due to the need for serious investment in new programs and relatively lower revenues compared to those received for the MBA).

Thus, the growing awareness of corporate social responsibility (CSR) by Russian business schools (following the same trend in national business) should not always be tested through their interest in turning social workers into managers. More important here is the recognition of CSR as a special course and as a conceptual aspect for core courses for programs aimed at developing professional managers for the twenty-first century. Courses, textbooks and research projects in CSR have already been developed at a few top schools, and the CSR course is a required one in the new federal standard for the Bachelor in Management. An important impetus for these developments was created when in September 2010 EABIS, for the first time, held its annual colloquium and PhD conference in Russia (co-organized with St. Petersburg University GSOM).

The most challenging area for Russian business schools' contribution to society is the recently initiated transformation of the national economy into an innovation-driven one. To start with, given that about one third of Russian undergraduate education is currently in economics and management, business schools may contribute significantly to reforming Russian universities, and some schools already are proven laboratories for innovation and creativity. However, the main contribution to society will come from graduate schools of (business) management which are also recognized as thought leaders. An effective partnership of business, government and universities/business schools is critical for success in further developing such schools in Russia. For graduate business schools to become suppliers of the key human capital that will drive a national strategic change for an innovation-based economy, they need both to secure long-term support for their development (including a new generation of faculty) from other parties to this alliance, and to turn their own business models into world-class ones. Only through this systematic effort can Russian business schools realize the expectations that society has of them, and achieve international compatibility and high competitiveness.

REFERENCES

Datar, S.V., Garvin, D.S. and Cullen, P.G. (2010) *Rethinking the MBA: Business Education at a Crossroads.* Boston, MA: Harvard Business Press.

Evenko, L.I. (2009) *Razvitie rossiyskoy programmy MBA v 1999–2009 gody: sversheniy i problemy* (The Development of Russian MBA Programs in 1999–2009: Achievements and Problems). *Biznes Obrazovanye (Business Education),* 2: 3–11.

Evenko, L.I. (2010) *Dva desyatiletya RABO: puti i pereputya* (Two Decades of RABE: Paths and Crossroads). *Biznes Obrazovanye (Business Education),* 2: 3–11.

Gordon, R.A. and Howell, J.E. (1959) *Higher Education for Business*. New York: Columbia University Press.

Katkalo, V.S. (2009) Using EPAS to Drive Internationalization. *Global Focus*, 3(1), Special Supplement: 7–8.

Katkalo, V.S., Pitelis, C.N. and Teece, D.J. (2010) Introduction: on the nature and scope of dynamic capabilities. *Industrial and Corporate change*, 19(4): 1175–1186.

Larcon, J.-P. and Hmimda, N. (2008) Business Education in Central and Eastern Europe. In T. Durand and S. Dameron (eds), *The Future of Business Schools: Scenarios and Strategies for 2020*. New York: Palgrave Macmillan.

Mau, V. and Seferyan, A. (2007) *Biznes obrazovanye na rubezhe vekov: vyzovy vremeni i tedentsii razviniya* (Business Education at the Turn of Centuries: Challenges and Trends). *Ekonomicheskaya Politika (Economic Policy)*, 4: 35–72.

Milov, G. (2008) *Udvoit' za sem' let* (To Double in Seven Years). *Vedomosti*, September (3): A7.

Pierson, F.C. (1959) *The Education of American Businessmen*. New York: McGraw-Hill.

Puffer, S.M. (1981) Inside a Soviet Management Institute. *California Management Review*, 24(1): 90–6.

5 THE LEGITIMACY AND FUTURE OF BUSINESS SCHOOLS IN TURKEY

Barış Tan

Koc University, Turkey

In the recent global economic crisis, the moral position of business in society – and related to this discussion, the legitimacy of business schools and the role of managers – have each received considerable attention from all over the world. In fact these three actors (enterprises, business schools and managers) have greater responsibility for a sustainable and value-oriented society.

In this section, the legitimacy, challenges and future of business schools are discussed by using the case of Koç University that was established by the Vehbi Koç Foundation in Turkey. I argue that business schools that educate future leaders in a responsible way by using an innovative curriculum and also advocate the responsibility of business in society play an important role in the development of a country towards a sustainable and value-oriented society.

This case may be of interest to readers for a number of reasons. First, Turkey is a country located at the crossroads of Europe and Asia, and it has a growing economy, a number of important challenges and a young population. The future sustainable growth of the country and its stability depend on the education of its future leaders.

Second, the establishment of Koç University is a good example of a public–private partnership. The Vehbi Koç Foundation that was established by the founder of the largest business group in Turkey has contributed to society by establishing the second privately funded university in Turkey. A contribution in the form of establishing a university is expected to have a multiplicative effect on its graduates, research and teaching programs in the future.

Third, our experience shows that a business school that has strong links with business and educates future leaders of the country can have a positive effect in instilling a culture of social responsibility. All the concerns that are related to the social responsibility of business operations are especially important in emerging and rapidly growing countries such as Turkey.

INFLUENCING DEVELOPMENTS IN A SOCIETY THROUGH EDUCATION

The effect of providing an education that emphasizes the importance of social responsibility starts with the students when they are at the school, and it will then be multiplied when graduates assume leadership responsibilities and make decisions that are in line with the values rooted in their education.

The future sustainable growth of a country and its stability depend on how well it educates its youth to lead its business, economy and political system in a responsible way and on how well it creates an environment for new businesses to be developed and value to be created.

Perhaps it is useful to recall that the topic of corporate social responsibility (CSR) includes a range of quite distinct, broad issue areas: from labor rights to human rights to environmental concerns, and from philanthropy to corporate governance to ethical business practices such as avoiding corrupt business payments (Garriga and Melé, 2004). All of these issues are very important for the present and, more importantly, for the future of an emerging country.

Achieving the goal of having graduates who possess a sense of social responsibility will contribute to the transformation of society when they become leaders. These leaders will manage their organizations by assuming their responsibility to all stakeholders in areas related to labor rights, human rights, environmental concerns, ethical business practices, corporate governance and philanthropy.

A business school can – and indeed must – have a profound effect on the future of a society. The legitimacy of the business school in this environment comes from this responsibility, its role in shaping the future and its contribution to society.

Providing an education that will contribute to the welfare of the country and all humanity, educating future leaders in all organizations who will be socially responsible and therefore committed to the highest ethical standards and to the values of democracy, and influencing the intellectual, technological, economic and social development of the country, will bring legitimacy to a business school and ensure its future.

In addition to educating future leaders about CSR matters, business schools should also be the advocates of these issues in society. Leading a discussion on corporate social responsibility in the society and playing an active role to influence the transformation can be a genuinely important responsibility for business schools. All the concerns that are related to the social responsibility of business operations are especially important in emerging and rapidly growing countries such as Turkey.

It is not possible to separate developments at business schools from developments in the environment in which they operate. In the Turkish case, factors such as the European Union membership process, economic developments and the emergence of privately funded universities affect the role of corporate social responsibility in this context.

TURKEY AND THE NEED FOR QUALITY EDUCATION FOR FUTURE DEVELOPMENTS

Turkey is located at the crossroads of Europe and Asia. With a population of 72.5 million, it faces significant opportunities and challenges.

Since the 1980s, Turkey has gone through a major economic transformation. With an export-oriented state policy, its economy has enjoyed high growth in many sectors. Today, Turkey has the 17th largest economy in the world and the 7th within the 27 European

Union (EU) countries (International Monetary Fund, 2010). The inflation rate is stable after a long period of high inflation and the economy is growing steadily.

On the other hand, Turkey has also experienced a long period of high inflation, major economic crises and fluctuations. The economic reforms that were put in place following the major economic crises of 2001 have been effective in the transformation of the banking sector, in the stability of the money and foreign exchange markets, and in providing a substantial growth environment. Partially due to these reforms, the financial sector was not adversely affected during the 2008 crisis. Since that crisis, the discussions have been related to globalization, regulation, the effects of global financial players on local economies, the need for sustainable growth, and unemployment, which are all related to considerations of corporate social responsibility.

Turkey was declared a candidate for full European Union (EU) membership in 1999. Since then, the country has been implementing a comprehensive reform process to meet the membership criteria. Following the decision of the European Commission that stated that Turkey had met the Copenhagen Criteria, the accession negotiations started in 2005. The prospect of European Union membership has accelerated the change process in the country. This change is affecting the economy, as well as the legal and education systems. In addition, Turkey set objectives in all areas for the year 2023 that will mark the 100th year of being a republic. These objectives and the EU membership process have a direct impact on higher education.

Furthermore, the accession negotiation for possible EU membership introduces new challenges for the institutional framework. In this environment, legislative framework areas that are covered in corporate social responsibility such as labor rights, human rights, environmental concerns, philanthropy, corporate governance and ethical business practices are reviewed and revised. Educating future leaders on these issues is of the highest importance for future developments.

Turkey has a very young population with a growth rate of 1.5 per cent. There are around 20 million youth between the ages of 10 and 24. It also has the largest youth population of all 27 EU countries (Republic of Turkey Prime Ministry, 2011). The share of this group in the population is expected to increase in coming years and to reach its maximum in 2020 (World Bank, 2007). If Turkey finds an effective way to provide a quality education to its young population who will join the workforce, and if this education improves productivity and growth, this demographic change will introduce new opportunities for the Turkish economy.

The demand for university education in Turkey is very high. There are currently 8 million university graduates in Turkey. Turkey plans, as a state policy, to have 15 million university graduates by the year 2023 (Higher Education Strategy of Turkey, 2007). Currently, there are a total of 141 universities, consisting of 94 state and 47 foundation universities. With the new universities that are expected to be approved by the parliament in coming years, it is likely that the total number of universities in Turkey will reach 200 in the next decade. However, opening new universities is not sufficient in itself to reach the targets unless qualified faculty members can be appointed to teach in these universities.

In addition to providing access to higher education, the type of education given at the universities is very important for the future. Educating students who will lead their organizations in a responsible way is vital for Turkey. In this environment, universities play a special role in educating future leaders.

PUBLIC–PRIVATE PARTNERSHIP IN EDUCATION AS A MODEL FOR EMERGING COUNTRIES

The establishment of foundation universities in Turkey is a good example of a public–private partnership that has a positive effect on society. A contribution in the form of establishing a university is expected to have a multiplicative effect on its graduates, research and teaching programs of the future.

Private universities are referred to as foundation universities in Turkey in order to emphasize their non-profit status that is required under the law. Foundation universities were established in 1986 with new legislation that allowed foundations to open universities under restrictive conditions. Bilkent University in Ankara, founded in 1989, was the first such foundation university, and Koç University, founded in 1993, was the second. In 1996, Sabancı University was established by the Sabancı Foundation.

Koç University was founded by the Vehbi Koç Foundation. Vehbi Koç was the founder of the Koç Group which has 113 companies operating in the automotive, durable goods, food, retailing, energy, financial services, tourism, construction and IT industries. The first trading company that was established in 1926 grew to form the Koç Group which became Turkey's largest industrial group in terms of revenue, exports, share in the Istanbul Stock Exchange and number of employees, and was ranked 172nd in the *Fortune Global 500*. The Vehbi Koç Foundation was established in 1969 as the first major foundation in the country. Since its establishment, the foundation has been very active in the fields of education, culture and health, and as recognition of its activities the Koç family received the Carnegie Medal of Philanthropy in 2009.

Koç University provides an education to 4200 students in a wide range of programs including business, economics, international relations, social sciences, sciences, law, engineering and medicine. Notably, 60 per cent of the students are on a full or partial scholarship. The full scholarship equivalent leads to a ratio of 40 per cent of all students being fully sponsored by the Foundation. The scholarship covers tuition fees, accommodation and a monthly allowance.

The university offers undergraduate programs in business administration, a full-time MBA program, an Executive MBA program, a Master of Science in Finance, a CEMS Master in International Management program, and a PhD in Business. In order to educate its students on issues concerning social responsibility in the broadest sense, Koç University introduced several courses at different levels. These courses include an ethics course in the undergraduate core program, elective courses on Corporate Social Responsibility, Management of Non-profit Organizations, Corporate Governance, as well as courses on Human Rights and Labor Rights. Ethical reasoning is one of the main areas of knowledge in the liberal arts core program for undergraduates. Functional courses in finance and accounting also cover topics related to ethics and professional conduct within the scope of several courses. All of these courses are open to all students in all areas. In addition, several conferences on Corporate Social Responsibility, Sustainability, and Corporate Governance have been organized jointly with the leading associations working in these areas. Furthermore, Koç University is setting a good example to society, not only by demonstrating its commitment to these values but also in the way it utilizes resources, shows great concern for the environment and undertakes initiatives to promote greater environmental responsibility.

An example of the effect of this kind of education on the students is the Koç Volunteers student initiative at the university. Since 2003, Koç Volunteers has been organized as a student club with members who would like to work on social projects. It is the umbrella student organization for all volunteer activities. These include various continuous and short-term projects such as the Little Hearts Project, which supports the development of 2–7-year-old children in state orphanages; the Thinking Children Project and the KUYAT Koç University Summer Workshop, which support the education and social lives of students in Sarıyer and its vicinity, near the university itself; the KET Education Team, which provides educational support to secondary and high school students in the region; awareness activities that run projects for disabled people; and the Teeth Care Project, which provides dental care education to primary school students. These projects contribute immensely to the personal development of students. They enrich their team building, organization, communication and leadership skills. These projects also develop students' capabilities to be socially responsible leaders in the future. Each year, approximately 400 participate in the activities of Koç Volunteers. More than 1000 of the Koç undergraduate alumni have taken an active part in Koç Volunteers since 2003.

We expect the contribution of these students to society to be multiplied when they become the leaders of society itself. Today, Koç University has around 5000 alumni, and 3250 of them graduated from the undergraduate and graduate programs of the School of Business. Even though it has been only 15 years since the very first graduation, a number of Koç graduates have already assumed leading positions in various corporations and organizations.

The establishment of a university by a foundation that is financially supported by a group of companies is not unique to the case of Koç University in Turkey. Sabancı University was also set up by a family-run foundation and is financially supported by the Sabancı group of companies, which form a leading business group in Turkey. In the examples of Bilkent, Koç and Sabancı, their foundations make significant financial contributions to the universities each year. The mission of these universities reflects the foundations' objective of contributing to society by educating its future leaders. As a result, social responsibility is inherently built in to the very fabric of these universities at their establishment.

Most of the foundation universities, including Koç, Bilkent and Sabancı, have generous scholarship programs. As a result, the foundation universities that have the financial resources to offer scholarships are accessible to talented students from all over Turkey who could not otherwise financially support their education. The establishment of Bilkent, Koç and Sabancı also played an important role in bringing qualified researchers back to Turkey. For example, Koç University has recruited close to 200 faculty members from abroad.

It is fair to say that the foundation universities emphasize corporate social responsibility in their programs more compared to the state universities in Turkey. Koç University signed the United Nations Global Compact at a ceremony where Kofi Annan was present in November 2007. Currently, eight universities have signed the Global Compact in Turkey and seven of these are foundation universities. By signing the Global Compact, these universities pledged their commitment to contribute to the objective of increasing the knowledge and understanding of corporate citizenship with their research, educational resources, learning know-how and infrastructure. The Principles of Responsible Management Education (PRME) were also adopted by Koç University and Sabancı University and have become an important part of all the programs. All the current PRME academic participants from Turkey are foundation universities.

Other families and foundations also began to invest in education in Turkey, and the number of foundation universities increased rapidly. Kadir Has University, founded in 1997 by the Kadir Has Foundation, and Özyeğin University, founded in 2007 by the Hüsnü Özyeğin Foundation, are also examples of this development.

Although discussions regarding state versus private higher education still continue in Turkey, given the high demand for higher education in general and the even higher demand for quality education, the foundations' contributions to the Turkish education system, with scholarship programs, are regarded positively throughout Turkish society. Since not all the foundations have the same financial resources, the sustainability of scholarship programs, and maintaining the quality of faculty and programs, may become important issues in the future. Namely, if a foundation cannot provide the financial resources to support a university, relying on tuition income as the main source may limit the resources that can be used to support scholarships, faculty development, and scholarly and other activities.

The developments outlined above can provide a model for other emerging countries that have young populations and a great need for quality education. Since 2000, a number of business schools have been formed and financially supported by businessmen or companies in countries such as India, China, Russia and Germany (De Almedia, 2010). In this model, it is very important to reflect a contribution to society in the mission and make sure that students are educated with a broad understanding of the needs of society and the role and responsibility of business.

In the Koç University model, special attention was given to positioning the university as an independent entity that could be financially supported by a foundation that would then be supported by an endowment and by a group of companies. The broad academic disciplines of the university and the liberal arts core program provide an education that allows students to understand the role of business and the responsibility of managers in society. The legislative structure in Turkey also determines the restrictive conditions for a foundation to establish a non-profit university.

A NEED FOR INNOVATION IN BUSINESS EDUCATION

Innovation is a major challenge in business education. There is a great need for innovation in the curriculum, content and delivery of business education programs. Globalization leads to the harmonization of business education programs. Although it is essential to benchmark these programs and provide a business education that will prepare students for positions anywhere in the world, various business schools can develop innovative programs that will contribute to education in different ways.

There can be new approaches for business education stemming from business schools located in emerging countries that focus on areas that are especially important for those countries. For example, in the discussion of CSR in Turkey or in a similar country, topics such as labor rights, human rights, corporate governance and ethical business practice are as important as the discussion of environmental concerns and philanthropy.

Assuming a role in intellectual, technological, economic and social development implies an interdisciplinary approach in business schools. Confining the activities of a business school to simply functional areas will not be sufficient to assume this role. An interdisciplinary approach that combines business, economics and political science, as well as other fields, will serve the needs of emerging countries.

In the model of Koç University, the Business School is a part of the university. This provides the possibility of pursuing an interdisciplinary approach and of including a liberal arts core in business education.

Providing business education with an interdisciplinary approach can be accomplished over a longer time period. Considering the time, the distribution of students and the participation rates in undergraduate and graduate programs, undergraduate business education may play a more important role in the future, especially in emerging countries. This education should be accessible to all students regardless of their intended area of study. In other words, providing an education to all students that is built on the values of social responsibility is very important for a society. Business school can play a significant role as a driver of this change.

THE FUTURE FOR BUSINESS SCHOOLS

Emerging countries such as Turkey will go through a period that has challenges and also opportunities for the future. The transformation that takes place in developing countries includes the transformation of all organizations, including private businesses, governmental and non-governmental organizations.

In order to provide employment opportunities to the young and increasing population and to increase the standard of living in the country, the economy must sustain high growth rates. While internal dynamics and increasing globalization have helped the economy to enjoy high growth rates in Turkey, the recent financial crisis has shown that this growth is prone to interruptions due to both external and internal factors.

In a country like Turkey, there is a great need to educate future leaders who will lead organizations in a responsible way. This need is not only for business leaders but also for leaders of governmental and non-governmental organizations.

In this setting, all the areas covered in corporate social responsibility, including labor rights, human rights, environmental concerns, philanthropy, corporate governance and ethical business practice, are equally important for a business school education.

These developments are expected to transform business education from an education that is designed to deliver technical expertise in functional areas to a broad education that has foundations in various areas. The future of business schools in this environment will depend on how they will address this need.

CHALLENGES

The demand for higher education in Turkey is expected to increase rapidly in the coming years. The net enrolment rate in higher education in 2007–08 was 20 per cent in Turkey which is low by international standards. Given the increase in attendance rates at primary and secondary schools, a corresponding increase in the number of students who will demand higher education in coming years is expected. Furthermore, in order to reach the national objective of having 15 million university graduates by the year 2023, the number of students who graduate from universities each year must be doubled to reach a level of a half a million students each year.

The major challenge for business education in Turkey and other similar countries is the shortage of qualified faculty members. This is a challenge for all academic disciplines in Turkey, but the need to improve the situation in the social sciences in Turkey is the greatest. While the overall ratio of students per faculty member in all areas is around 30 in Turkey, the ratio for the Applied Social Sciences, which includes business administration, economics, international relations and law, is around 70. The number of students in these areas is 45 per cent of the total university population while the faculty in these areas is only 18 per cent of the total faculty population. In addition to the need to increase the number of faculty members, increasing the quality and assurance of quality is a very important challenge for Turkey.

Another key challenge is innovation in the curriculum, content and delivery of business education programs. There should be new approaches for business education stemming from business schools located in emerging countries that focus on areas such as social responsibility, entrepreneurship, development and business in society that are especially important for these countries.

Public–private partnerships may also introduce challenges for business schools. The model of establishing standalone business schools financed by business groups must be balanced by making contributions to society, with educating better people for a better world an important part of their mission (De Almedia, 2010). In the Turkish case, the legislative structure ensures that only foundations can establish universities under restrictive conditions. These conditions include expectations regarding the financial resources of the foundations, the non-profit status of the foundation universities, approval of the degree programs by the Higher Education Council, and receiving a decree from parliament.

Regardless of these challenges, a business school can and must have a profound effect on the future of a country by educating future responsible leaders to lead its business, economy and political systems, by helping in the creation of an environment for new businesses, and by advocating the values and role of businesses and managers for a sustainable and value-oriented society. The legitimacy of the business school then comes from this responsibility, its role in shaping the future and its contribution to society.

REFERENCES

De Almedia, E. (2010) Business of Education. *Global Focus*, 4(1): 38–42.

Garriga, E. and Melé, D. (2004) Corporate Social Responsibility Theories: Mapping the Territory. *Journal of Business Ethics*, 53(1–2): 51–71.

Higher Education Strategy of Turkey, Turkish Higher Education Council, 2007.

International Monetary Fund, World Economic Outlook Database, April 2011: Nominal GDP list of countries 2010.

Republic of Turkey Prime Ministry Investment Support and Promotion Agency Reports (2011) Available at: www.invest.gov.tr

World Bank (2007) *Turkey – Higher Education Policy Study Volume I: Strategic Directions for Higher Education in Turkey*. Report No. 39674 TU, Human Development Unit Europe and Central Asia Region, June.

6 EUROPEAN BUSINESS SCHOOLS AND GLOBALIZATION

Lluis Pugès

An interesting question arose some years ago when we met to create the Global Alliance in Management Education (CEMS, formerly the Community of European Management Schools). There are various schools of thought in the management training field. The USA was considered the intellectual leader in the sector and there was talk of the Japanese style of management given Japan's rapid economic growth. The question was: 'Is there a European alternative to the American/Japanese management models?' and if there was an alternative, what were its salient features? Perhaps we should now add a further question, namely if there is such a thing as a European management model and – if so – is it not in our interests to foster it?

The Europe Union has grown a great deal since and it therefore seems a good time for those working in the management education industry to ask the question again.

When other countries joined the European Economic Community (EEC), we recognized the dangers of limiting our horizons to Europe and of thus adopting a parochial approach to management, and saw the need to broaden the concept of globalization. That is why we conceived CEMS as a three-stage process: (1) setting up centers in EU countries; (2) setting up centers in other European countries; (3) forging links with centers in the rest of the world.

This vision was wholly accepted by the four founding members and was made clear from the outset by including European business schools from non-EU countries in the first stage of the CEMS process.

THE INCLUSION OF UNIVERSITY INSTITUTIONS OF VARIOUS KINDS AND FROM DIVERSE CULTURES NECESSARILY MEANS TAKING ON ALL ASPECTS OF THE GLOBAL CHALLENGE

The foregoing points should be borne in mind in the discussion on the future of business schools and CEMS that follows.

If we understand management as a complex human activity, it seems only natural that managers' backgrounds will affect the way they 'manage'. From this view arises the question that has been discussed at so many planning meetings for the CEMS network: 'Does Europe have a special way of running companies?'. So far, the answer has eluded us.

If we accept that the concept of management does not exist in a vacuum, it seems obvious that European culture and history may influence our behavior, how we analyze problems, identify solutions and carry out decisions.

As Europeans, we tend to consider all the issues arising from globalization. Our cultural birthright helps us to perceive relationships that others might easily miss.

Clearly, Catholicism and Greek and Roman culture have shaped a majority of our historic events. This legacy was subsequently leavened with influences from Northern and Eastern European countries to shape what we now call European culture. This pot-pourri has shaped our ways of thinking and acting, which differ from those found on other continents. This may sometimes render our decision-making slower and less efficient, and make us wonder whether it is worth discarding our management models in favor of others. However, it is all too easy to slavishly imitate exotic models and discard European-grown principles that might usefully complement them.

These issues all have a bearing on the questions asked earlier: Is there another way of managing companies and organizations? Is there, in fact, a European management model? Asking these questions should not be seen as challenging other management systems but rather as a desire to broaden and round off a part of the European cultural tradition that is less evident in other business models. The aim here is to globalize the management concept when drawing up training programs.

A PARTIAL FAILURE AND A GLOBAL SUCCESS

Most European business schools have drawn heavily on American literature and the case study method. Thus, even though the classrooms of Paris University date back to the Middle Ages, their style and workings have been adapted to follow the pattern set by American business schools.

The consequences have been positive in terms of greater productivity and system efficiency but negative in other respects because we have gradually focused more on results than on seeking new paths for knowledge.

Business schools have exacerbated this trend by taking a more results-based approach to the education they impart. Individual values suffer when the focus is on reaching ever-more ambitious (numerical) targets instead of pausing to think about how such objectives are met.

It is not my intention to criticise the morals of the education system but rather to draw attention to the bias in management training. The problem is that we often fail to see the wood for the trees. The individual's complexity has been picked apart by the desire to reach even higher targets, forcing us to aspire to true market competitiveness and assuage stakeholders' economic demands.

Perhaps this focus on results means we have had to accept the consequences of a crisis that is of a social and ethical nature as well as of an economic kind. Sportsmen are driven by a desire to reach ever-higher goals. Unfortunately, in the business world the relentless drive for ever-bigger profits led to financial dumping in which dodgy debts and derivatives were eagerly snapped up. The present crisis owes much to financial wizardry and a risible failure to grasp the nature of the instruments being traded.

Given this state of affairs, it is not surprising that questions are asked about the role played by business schools and whether they act in good faith. Are they providing the right training for tomorrow's company and organizational managers?

Attempts to answer this question stem from a desire to improve programs, specialize in growth areas and better prepare our students for the future.

Examining processes throws up a wide range of technical responses, which all aim to meet current demands. However, something has been left out here. Companies are not only responsible for efficiency but also for the way they achieve it and the consequences of their actions.

This challenge is now being posed in more tangible terms. We cannot forget who we are and the culture from which we spring but neither can we ignore other ways of thinking and acting. In other words, we cannot afford to stick to our old ways if we want to globalize our activities. However, as I see it, our reaction is both piecemeal and unsustainable.

Something similar occurs when we talk of social responsibility. We think more about our principles and our way of seeing things than about the needs and thought processes of other cultures.

Evidently, we cannot condone child labor but the cold fact is that many families are forced to resort to this practice in order to survive. Our way of seeing things makes us strive to end child labor but it ignores the survival of people who live on the edge. It is not a question of defending the system but rather of understanding the situation so that reasonable alternatives can be found. Change cannot be achieved without a prior, deep-rooted understanding of the current state of affairs.

Often, we fail to heed the demands of globalization because we are too wrapped up in defending our ideas and practices. We are swift to condemn what we disagree with but slow to ask why others see things differently.

Our criterion of social responsibility does not always square with the way other cultures see the issue. In this context, trying to impose our own cultural preferences and ways of thinking on others is counterproductive. The understandable negative impact of such an approach is swiftly felt in the remotest corners of the world, for we live in an age of instant communication.

But not all hope is lost. In my view, we have a new opportunity to redefine and complete the aims of business schools.

We cannot forget that our aim is to train managers who will shape tomorrow's global society in general and the corporate sector in particular. A global world is not one in which an infinite number of languages mix but rather one in which various ways of living and thinking are pitched against the problems facing each nation and society.

Looking at this panorama should make us realize the complexity of what we need to tackle. We cannot yet again make the mistake of believing that organizations' priorities only refer to the improvement of profitability. To do so would simply mean falling into the contradictions that have sometimes led to the very business school ethos being questioned. We must not allow history to repeat itself.

Neither can we afford to ignore the fact that real management training is needed to secure the economic and social development that we all yearn for.

Putting the topic of globalization in these terms increases the distrust between people, making it harder for them to work together to achieve harmonious, sustainable social development.

Needless to say, the confrontation between systems spurs competition, which can yield positive results and create advancements. However, we can sometimes become so blinded by this intrinsic desire to overcome our competitors that we do not recognize the potential allies within them, and we ignore the opportunities for learning from a different system. In a world of economic recession, this can be devastating. For this reason, innovation, seeking areas of influence and widening the reach of our schools are not only advisable – they are also vital for survival in today's world.

However, we must not think of ourselves as knights in shining armour who can simply set up shop somewhere and boost regional productivity. To understand this, it is worth reflecting on what is happening in some countries that eagerly accepted multinational investments and then found themselves at odds with their erstwhile 'saviors'. The globalization and internationalization of European companies must be done with care, respect and, most importantly, knowledge.

Many times, we choose to blame the new governments of those countries that have been affected by large investments by multinational organizations for the maladies of the managerial and financial worlds. We say they are ungrateful and populist. This may be true in some cases, just as it is true that certain government policies will deter future private investment. Too often, governments resort to institutional lending on far too soft terms, and for some reason they avoid tackling deep-routed structural problems. However, it is much too simple to blame the new governments for all these problems.

One should also ask oneself why governments react in this way. To what extent have new investments ignored the conditions and needs of local populations? To answer this, we must go beyond results and look at how the investments were made.

Results are not only determined by efficiency and greater social welfare through job creation. They are also determined by the socio-cultural setting in which a company operates. Work habits are not the same everywhere and neither are people's needs. Cultural factors affect results and therefore have to be understood and discussed with local politicians.

Environmental requirements will also shape a region's future, however the issues can be seen from various points of view. The drive for economic development is not always in tune with environmental needs.

The natural question that arises is this: who should set the priorities? Here, one should not overlook the fact that sometimes those who make the decisions will have little or nothing to lose. We should not take decisions without bearing such factors in mind but we often ignore these or blithely dismiss them as irrelevant.

The matters that need to be considered here are much wider in scope than are usually covered by the case studies given in business schools.

It is also true that one cannot specialize in everything and this fact affects the decisions made by managers, whether for good or ill.

For all these reasons, we must be very cautious in choosing the globalization paths and in deciding what to teach in our management programs.

In CEMS globalization projects, we are making great efforts to find new associate members and to forge alliances with business schools and centers around the world.

Yet in doing so, we may be making the same mistake all over again. The size of our network is important but, first, we must ask ourselves why we want to grow, and then analyze how we will go about it. If we merely focus on the number of contacts, it will be hard to find the right answers to the questions concerning the 'how' and 'why' of what we do.

What is the purpose of our program? Why do we need worldwide support? Are we really helping our students understand and work with everyone on the planet?

Are our students aware of this objective? Sometimes it seems doubtful, given the way new members are determined and in what conditions the union is created.

It is easy to make the same mistake when it comes to learning. The most important thing is not to cover a vast range of knowledge but rather to ensure that the meaning of what is taught is thoroughly grasped and that its full consequences are understood.

Right now, business schools face a big challenge and also have a big opportunity. We must touch on everything in embracing globalization but we cannot know each and every topic that will crop up in our careers. Given this dilemma, we must think long and hard about the best way of meeting the challenge of globalization.

A RENEWED OPPORTUNITY

Earlier, we noted the cultural keys to our behavior patterns. The great challenge and opportunity is to ensure our training programs provide the cultural keys to all mankind.

Clearly, we cannot embrace all the themes or consider their cultural impact in detail but we can discover some of the strands that unite mankind. That is why we must whet students' appetite for and grasp of universal features. While knowledge of management sciences is required for this purpose, we also need to be open-minded and transcend our cultural horizons if we are to appreciate this universality.

Europe is the cradle of a great culture that has shaped every aspect of science and the modern world. Maybe we now need to return to our cultural roots in meeting current globalization needs if we are to give society what it wants and needs.

The breadth and depth of European culture (with all its great artists and thinkers) widens our intellectual horizons and makes us eager to sip at the well of knowledge and learn from Nature and her ways.

As I see it, this is the most fertile approach to understanding others and sharing our knowledge and experience with them. Keeping an open mind does not rule out holding one's own beliefs but it does help in grasping how others think, live and feel.

Understanding other cultures will help us to globalize our professional activities. Posing questions and suggesting solutions is a very different kettle of fish when seen through African, Asian or Muslim eyes. Failing to look beyond results will only make it harder for us to understand the culturally determined paths that people take to get results and accept them as their own.

It is thus a question of alternating academic education in the management field with training that feeds the mind and heart. Only thus can we hope to get to grips with a complex and odd world. History, Literature, Philosophy, Music and Art in general enrich the spirit and foster creativity. These disciplines give great insights into other cultures and help us see the same problems in different lights, shedding light on fiscal, social and personal development.

Professional and personal experience over the years may enrich our technical knowledge. Keeping an open mind and taking an interest in other ways of living and behaving should be part of business training from the outset and a key part of professional development.

That is why I believe that training centers should foster this cultural dimension as a way of helping us to work with people from distant cultures, allowing us to learn from them, and them from us.

Another consequence of such an approach for training centers and CEMS would be a shift in our quest for partners abroad.

Instead of roping in as many centers as possible, the focus would be on finding the partner that provided most value to the project and complemented what we already offer. Again, it is the quality, not the quantity, we must focus on. It is a question of adding on new ways of seeing and analyzing issues and thus of providing added value.

Globalization understood in these terms becomes a challenge and an opportunity to gain a better understanding of universities' role in and contribution to society. It should greatly enhance our training of tomorrow's movers and shakers.

FINAL REMARKS

In a globalized world, European management schools can contribute to a better understanding and enrichment of the students that form their classes. It's not about trying to find a way to 'manage' what is different from that which can be learned in other continents, but about expanding the teaching system to include those values and knowledge that traditional European culture has developed over the centuries.

This cultural package helps expand the horizon of our thought and enhance our ability to understand and comprehend different ways of thinking and acting. Globalization unites us with people and institutions whose origins and ways of thinking and deciding may be completely dissimilar to our ways. If we are not able to understand and accept this diversity, it will be hard to be professionals who are ready to collaborate with them.

We cannot, on the other hand, forget the professional duties that go with managing people and knowledge. Hence, our current battle must aim to find the union between both necessities. Forgetting the cultural aspects has in the past created grave economic and social problems. Management schools now have a battle to fight – and also a great opportunity. We must engrave onto the minds of our participants that all aspects are important in our professional activity, and that in order to meet all our needs we must understand, listen to and value all that others can contribute. To this effect, we could remember the classic saying 'Nihil Humanum a me alienum puto'– nothing that is human is estranged from my interests.

CEMS, with its efforts and wish to increase globalization, should carefully evaluate why it wants to increase the number of centers in its network. What can be learned from a new ally? And what can CEMS, as a European network, offer the new member?

Students use this enlarged network for their benefit. It is not only about offering them a new opportunity in a new center and in a new country. It is also about widening their cultural horizon so they can learn and assimílate the profound principles of globalization.

This is where the global challenge lies. It is an opportunity in which Europe, and the CEMS as a European association, may lead. The European cultural capacity that in so many historic moments has initiated and pioneered cultural changes, allows us to confront this new, challenging and universal era of globalization with optimism and great expectations.

7 CSR, BUSINESS SCHOOLS AND THE ASIA PACIFIC CONTEXT

Juliet Roper

APABIS and Waikato School of Management, New Zealand

Taken from the perspective of the very diverse Asia Pacific region, this chapter looks at the challenges of integrating sustainability and CSR issues into business school curricula. In particular, it considers the contexts – micro and macro – that shape such challenges. Where does the pressure for change come from and why? For example, it is widely held that European corporations are putting pressure on European business schools to change their curricula. While it may be that such corporations independently require the need for change in their own practices, it is also true that CSR is mandated in EU policy, with a flow-on impact on European business. In contrast, many countries in the Asia Pacific do not have governments that are taking leadership positions in this area. Thus businesses in the region may not experience the same degree of direct pressure to reform – and consequently are less likely to pass this pressure on to business schools. This hypothesis is supported by research into the sustainability practices of Asia Pacific businesses, as well as by the reported experiences of business schools.

INTRODUCTION

Much has been written about the need for businesses to become more responsive to their complex social and environmental externalities, rather than remain singularly focused on profit. Further, business schools are repeatedly charged with the responsibility to produce graduates who are both aware of such externalities and equipped to work with them in a responsible manner. This chapter takes a look at some of the motivations and barriers associated with the integration of CSR/sustainability in the curricula of business schools in the Asia Pacific region. Context is all important. While some organizations, be they in education or business sectors, may embrace notions of CSR because of internal factors such as CEO and/or employee values most will do so because of external drivers, including governmental, competitor and consumer pressure. In the absence of such pressures, why change? And what are some of the barriers to taking a proactive role in change?

Matten and Moon's (2004) survey and analysis of teaching CSR in European business schools provides a useful basis for a comparison with Asia Pacific counterparts. Their findings suggest that the most prominent future drivers for teaching CSR include the business sector as future employers of business school graduates as well as accreditation and ranking requirements. Further, they suggest that interest in graduates who are well versed in issues of CSR stems from the increase in 'company communications; company organizational structures; company reports and audits; new business coalitions; new consultancy firms; portfolios of traditional business consultants; government policies; and media coverage' and that the demands imposed by these trends place pressure upon companies to acquire a new skill set (p. 324). This demand was found to be reflected in the fact that the majority of CSR teaching in European business schools occurs in executive and short courses, rather than in the more academic programs. Whereas the corporate sector was seen to be the most likely driver of CSR education in the future, individual academics had until then been the prominent drivers.

If companies are now beginning to exert pressure on business schools to deliver graduates with competencies in CSR, what pressures have been placed upon them to bring about such a change in attitude? At a micro level, for example, the direction will come from inspired leaders driven by the opportunities that come with competitive advantage, or by their own personal convictions. At the macro level, influences may include the national or supra-national regulatory environments or consumer pressures that are transferred globally through supply chains, as well as social norms and traditions. Different contexts will exert differing pressures upon businesses to adopt CSR. The form that CSR takes will also differ. And those pressures will, in part, determine the uptake in CSR teaching by business schools.

Baughn et al. (2007) discuss the differences between European countries and their regulatory approaches versus the more voluntary forms of CSR to be found in the USA. Germany, Holland, Norway, Denmark, Sweden and the UK all have some sort of CSR code or reporting requirement. Many other European countries have voluntary systems but with incentives, accreditations, etc. to increase the uptake of the measures. The pan-European government, through the EU Commission, identified sustainable development as a key policy initiative through which to strengthen the competitiveness of its internal market. To encourage business attention to focus on social and environmental concerns, the European Parliament has also introduced policies that allow a consideration of CSR criteria in awarding government contracts to companies (see also Spidla, 2006; Fombrun, 2005). It is thus little wonder that it is predicted that companies will increasingly pass this pressure on to the business schools that educate their future employees.

THE ASIA PACIFIC CONTEXT

If we take the view that firms must be responsive to the particular institutional – economic, regulatory, etc. – contexts of the nations in which they operate (Baughn et al., 2007; Wright et al., 2005) we can better understand how issues such as CSR will vary, especially across such a diverse region as that of the Asia Pacific. We can then, in turn, view how such pressures may or may not affect the demands placed on business schools by employers.

Anecdotal evidence, coupled with analysis of business practices, suggests that CSR in both concept and practice in the Asia Pacific context is very different from that of Europe. That said, it is extremely difficult to generalize here because the region is vast, diverse and changing rapidly. A country's economic development is directly related to CSR activities (Baughn et al., 2007; Welford, 2005), yet even within individual Asia Pacific countries there is huge diversity in levels of education, income and business practices.

China and India are generally recognized as the two most rapidly emerging economies of the world, but these are certainly not exempt from poverty. Singapore, Japan, Taiwan and Hong Kong all have long established industrialized economies. New Zealand and Australia, both products of colonial Britain, are primarily Western in their outlook and practice. Further differences in CSR activities occur through cultural differences, which include long-held traditional perspectives on the role of business and other institutions in society.

The notion of CSR is predominantly Western in origin, at least as applied in current contexts. Along with the closely related term, sustainability, its meaning is contested. Some will, for example, maintain that a focus on the 'social' in CSR is at the expense of the environment. Others will argue that 'sustainability' excludes the social in its predominant attention to the environment. For many, however, both will serve as umbrella terms that address social, environmental and economic issues in a long-term view. This is the meaning generally ascribed to the term in the context of broad discussion in this chapter. While these variables of meaning are often discussed, there are more local applications that are less well acknowledged. This is especially important in the Asia Pacific context, with the region comprising many of the world's less economically developed countries and increasingly subject to Western values, including those embedded in Western understandings of CSR.

A COLLECTIVE WORLD VIEW

The societies of most Asian and Pacific countries have for a very long time adhered to a highly collective world view, in contrast to the individualist perspectives of the West that have accompanied the neoliberal economic systems that predominate there. Thus it is interesting to ask how a call for CSR that springs from failures of individualist-driven notions of free markets is applicable to societies for whom individualism is anathema and where CSR, albeit under other names, may well already be integral to company performance. While answers, of course, will again depend upon the local context, it is also interesting to note the changes in local context, especially under the influence of expanding global markets.

One pervasive example of embedded collectivism is that which stems from Confucian philosophy, found throughout Eastern Asia though adhered to in varying degrees. Confucian principles have guided family and commercial life, and especially relationships, in China for two and a half thousand years. Their dominance in business dates from the time of the late Ming Dynasty (1368–1644), when scholars increasingly sought careers in business (Cheung and King, 2004). Neo-Confucian practice by these scholar merchants was underpinned by the privileging of virtue over profitableness, with the two held in balance with each other. This tradition is still deeply ingrained in Chinese social and cultural life, and hence thinking, particularly in mainland China (Redding, 2002).

The influence of Taoism in Confucian thinking integrates the concept of yin and yang – balance and harmony. The freedom of individual behavior is constrained by social norms that dictate that that behavior will be humane and will not violate the requirement of a consideration of others in societal relationships. The key Confucian precept is the value and respect of people. Applied to business this means all stakeholders but especially employees, as the hierarchical nature of Confucian loyalty will place the latter as closer to the 'family' than external stakeholders. Thus while unspoken, many of the fundamental principles of CSR have been culturally embedded and in practice in some Asian countries a great deal longer than in their Western counterparts. Whereas Western firms are returning to notions of CSR in the wake of corporate scandals and changed public expectations, the irony is that Confucian ethics have been a part of business practice and the national culture for thousands of years. Given that Asian – especially Chinese – business students are brought up with Confucian ethics, it can be argued that demand for CSR in business school curricula will not be strong. A counter argument is that as Western notions of CSR are adopted, that will change.

Interestingly, countries such as Japan and Taiwan which have followed Western economic priorities and have long competed in a free market have the least evidence of residual Confucian principles in business practice. Warner and Zhu (2002) discuss differences in the the development of human resources policies and trends between China and Taiwan as a result of economic reform. Both countries began with Confucian principles, but Taiwan, which has competed in a free market environment for longer than China and with much less governmental intervention, has gone further towards the Western model. Nevertheless, collectivism has not been replaced as the cohesive force for society in these countries.

In contrast, and as already noted, New Zealand and Australia are Western in outlook and practice. Their economies are largely based upon free market principles, including individualism. Interestingly, a business for social responsibility (BSR) movement that was introduced to New Zealand in the 1990s was supplanted by the terminology, and associated organizations, of 'sustainability'. A detailed study of the movements showed that the more socially oriented perspective of BSR proved to be less influential than the demonstrably environmentally-oriented term 'sustainability' which is now dominant in public discourse, government and company policy documents (Allen, 2009).

India's social and cultural history also has strong religious traditions that foster benevolence and community values. However, suggestions are that while the country's economy has developed so extraordinarily rapidly, emphasis has transferred more to individualism and profit generation, especially amongst the wealthy. CSR remains an important aspect of business life in India, with around three quarters of corporations claiming CSR policies and practices (Chambers et al., 2003). That said, Balasubramanian et al. (2005) find that while CSR is a concern of Indian corporations, it is not actually widely integrated into corporate practice. The discrepancies between these reports could be a matter of interpretation of CSR itself.

Although the term 'CSR' is now in common usage in many Asian countries, the meanings associated with it vary greatly, especially in contrast with Western perspectives. CSR is generally seen as complying with local law – which in many cases means a very low requirement (Tsoi, 2010). Further, for many companies in Asia, CSR is seen as philanthropy, rather than being directly relevant to company practices. Balasubramanian et al. (2005) indicate that this is so in India where financial support underpins CSR activities. While this remains the case, there is little likelihood that companies will exert pressure upon business schools to incorporate the concept in their teaching.

What then are the institutional influences at play in the Asia Pacific region? And how do these affect business schools and what is the role of Asian Pacific business schools in the future? Typically, the motivation for change in company practices – especially towards greater levels of CSR – comes from governments, consumers, NGO activism, and individuals within firms including employees and managers. While local influences are likely to be stronger, globalization increasingly means that such influences are being felt across national borders. The remainder of this chapter looks at how these influences play out in the Asia Pacific, first for companies and then how they might in turn impact upon business schools.

POTENTIAL DRIVERS OF CSR FOR BUSINESS

Most governments of Asian economies have economic growth as the mainstay of their policies. However, while such economic growth in wealthier countries is now accompanied by pressures from civil society, government regulations and new technologies to encourage the 'greening' of business, in poorer countries the pressures are far less evident (Utting, 2002). In many developing countries governments, especially undemocratic ones, are less likely to be responsive to external pressures and so companies, in turn, are less obliged to work for legitimacy in the form of social capital (Prasad, 2004). Indeed, it is for this reason that it is suggested that some global companies will locate where regulation does not interfere with their environmental and social practices (Gonzalez-Benito and Gonzalez-Benito, 2010).

There are, however, countries in the Asia Pacific region that have regulated for CSR. For example, in 2006 the Malaysian government introduced the Bursa Malaysia CSR Framework by which it required all publicly listed companies to disclose their CSR activities. The framework stresses that CSR goes beyond a compliance with laws and aims to bring sustainable value to society. One commentator informally related the move to a desire by all Prime Ministers in Malaysia to leave legacies, with that of the 2003–8 incumbent being 'Integrity'. For example, he established the Institute of Integrity Malaysia, the Malaysian Anti Corruption Commission, the Witness Bill 2008 (for Whistle Blowing), and the Anti-Corruption Act in 2008. The current Prime Minister is championing 'National Unity', although the CSR/ethics initiatives are still in place. Government-linked companies (previously government utility companies such as power, water, airlines, telecom, highway, ports, etc.), privately owned but still very much controlled by the government, have to adhere to what is called the 'Silver Book' that sets out the guidelines for community development, the environment and employment relations. While international companies in both Malaysia and Singapore are much more likely to follow sound environmental practices than local ones, these are restricted to a few areas. Taken as a whole, the degree to which such regulation is effective remains doubtful (Perry and Singh, 2002; Prasad, 2004).

The impacts from the internationalization of companies should not be underestimated. On one hand, it can be argued, amongst other things, that market globalization carries with it an individualistic view of society, that unscrupulous companies may relocate to areas of least environmental and employment regulation, and that local producers suffer from the opening of national borders to unrestricted trade. On the other more positive hand, the demands of civil society over issues such as fair trade, employee welfare, and environmental responsibility – especially in the case of transnational issues like global warming – are responded to by global companies who will pass the responsibility along their supply chains. As local companies are integrated into global corporations, there is little doubt that environmental and social proactivity increases. The larger the corporation, the greater the impact of external stakeholders (Gonzalez-Benito and Gonzalez-Benito, 2010).

Levels of activism in the Asia Pacific are very much determined by the particular country's politics and level of economic development. The less pluralist the political system, the less tolerance is given to activism (Sriramesh, 2004). However, the internet has long since been established as a means of international activism, with the ready exposure of social and environmental transgressions. The garment industry is a prime example here where local manufacturers are forced to comply with social policies imposed by multinational companies who are forced by activists to take responsibility for practices throughout their supply chain. Nevertheless, at a local level, the impact of consumer pressures for attention to CSR is less evident across the Asia Pacific region than in the West. Research conducted by Tsoi (2010) found that CSR is adopted in Asia if it is required by European and US clients, but Asian consumers do not appear to be concerned about the social responsibility practices behind the products they buy. She reports an absence of strong media, consumer and public pressure in Hong Kong and mainland China and suggests that moving CSR forward in Asia will require public sector involvement.

Growing requirements for CSR reporting can also exert pressure on companies to examine their CSR practices. As with other CSR trends, the incidence of sustainability and CSR reporting in the Asia Pacific is considerably less than in Europe or the USA, with some notable exceptions such as Japan. Even in New Zealand and Australia, reporting levels are low (see, for example, Milne et al., 2001). It is interesting that there are no New Zealand companies signed up to the UN Global Compact. Foreign-owned companies operating in Australia voluntarily report at a rate more than twice that of Australian-owned companies. Even government departments have low reporting rates.

While a low level of reporting does not necessarily reflect corporate – or government – performance, the fact that it is unreported suggests that the pressure to demonstrate corporate activity is not strongly felt, or is not considered important enough to prompt action. If that is the case, then what motivations or pressures flow from the government and corporate sectors to business schools that are ostensibly charged with producing graduates for the governments and corporations of the Asia Pacific? And if CSR is not currently high on the employer agenda, what role do business schools play in changing that agenda?

BUSINESS SCHOOLS

Business schools in Asia arguably reflect their context, which includes their business counterparts' economic focus and lack of motivation to engage with issues of sustainability or CSR. However, as for governments and corporations, there is clear evidence to suggest that CSR is rising on the business school agenda and that business schools also face comparable pressures of internationalization, reporting and accreditation. So far, the source of most of these pressures comes from beyond the region, but as they grow and are responded to, so too does the nature of the local market in education change.

Participation in the United Nations' Principles of Responsible Management Education (PRME) by Asia Pacific business schools reflects the region's low levels of engagement by the corporate sector in the parallel UN Global Compact. Of 291 participants in the PRME, only about 11 per cent are from Asia Pacific countries. Many countries in the region are not represented at all, only one is based in New Zealand and only two each are from Pakistan, Vietnam, the Philippines and Japan. The low levels of participation are probably an indication of the low profile of the PRME.

There are, however, other voluntary standards that are growing in currency, reflecting the fact that, like companies, Asia Pacific business schools are also open to globalization and the competition that goes with that. European and USA-based accreditations become more attractive, and arguably more important, in the competition to attract international students, with the largest markets for these being China and, increasingly, India.

The European Foundation for Management Development (EFMD) has memberships that span 80 countries. Of these, 14 are in the Asia Pacific region. EFMD owns and administers the international business school accreditation, EQUIS. The link between the EFMD, EQUIS and the teaching of CSR in business schools is that the EQUIS standard now explicitly states that 'corporate responsibility will be evidenced not only in the School's approach to the education of future managers, but also in its own behavior within its environment'. This is just a small part of the requirements for accreditation, but it is significant. As of February 2010, from a total of 122 business schools with EQUIS accreditation, only 18 are from the Asia Pacific, with three of those also having campuses in Europe. As yet, some students may not understand the importance of these accreditations but we are seeing more Chinese universities going for EQUIS (and for other accreditations such as AACSB) so it will not take long for its recognition to spread.

These international accreditations provide a quality mark. When a business school does not appear in the international B-School rankings, accreditation is a good substitute. If students seeking international qualifications ask their own university about the accreditations, they will certainly be advised to attend a school which is ranked or accredited. Thus, indirectly, accreditations have a role to play in bringing about change in business school curricula.

From the USA, the Aspen Institute's Beyond Grey Pinstripes is well established internationally as a ranking for business schools that is based upon teaching and staff research in CSR and sustainability related topics. While the vast majority of their top 100-ranked business schools still come from the USA, 17 now come from Europe and the UK, and four from Asia Pacific countries. Beyond Grey Pinstripes focuses only on MBA programs, but still stands to be a more broadly significant influence as schools aspire to be ranked. The University of the South Pacific, for example, is currently incorporating a range of sustainability and CSR-related courses into its MBA program.

CSR Asia's 2009 report 'The Future of CSR' places educational institutions as 8th in a list of the top 10 institutional types that are influencing CSR – up from a placing of 10th in 2008. Of note is the fact that in 2009 governments and politicians moved into the top place, up from 3rd. This does indicate that regulation will be increasingly brought to bear upon corporations to improve their CSR performance, and that the demand for graduates with CSR expertise will grow. While global corporations are not currently hiring business school graduates because of the CSR/sustainability training they have had, what influence can business schools that teach CSR have on the corporate sector? Given that most change initiatives come from those in leadership positions, it's not likely to be directly through new graduates. Of course, such influence may percolate from passionate junior staff, or from a more senior MBA graduate, or even through the graduate who enters politics and can influence national policy. This is not to underestimate the influence that can be possible through business schools' teaching of sustainability and CSR issues. Rather, while the influence may not be immediately evident, it should be seen as a long-term strategy: eventually these young graduates will become a generation of CEOs.

As CSR is becoming a more highly considered issue than it has been (Tsoi, 2010), business and governments will increasingly seek to ensure their legitimacy by adopting CSR programs. Evidence of this already happening can be seen in the growth of interest in organizations such as the Asia Pacific Academy of Business in Society (APABIS) and CSR Asia. APABIS has a commitment to helping business schools integrate CSR into their curricula, and is facilitating an internship program by which students of its academic members can witness at first-hand the CSR activities of its corporate members. Corporate and government sector interest will result in increasing demand for professional development in CSR, including through MBA programs. Customer demand, and a need for their own legitimacy in a global market, will see business schools incorporating CSR into their teaching.

Although it is widely seen as desirable that business schools embrace notions of CSR and sustainability in their curricula, there are some caveats to be raised here. As stated, business schools, like companies, increasingly have to cater for an international market. Through accreditations and through pressures that are likely to be brought to bear through multinational corporations with bases in the West, the conditions and expectations of the international market are likely to be driven by European and US perspectives, values and requirements. If business schools all teach CSR according to those perspectives, they stand to suffer from the homogenizing process that globalization has brought to many sectors. Cultural, political, economic, social and even environmental differences have a bearing on how CSR is understood, and how it plays out in local contexts. If business schools can drive CSR and also remain relevant within their cultural context, they will play an important role in seeing CSR grow as a positive influence throughout the Asia Pacific region.

REFERENCES

Allen, C. (2009) The caring face of business? A study of the discursive construction of the New Zealand Business for Social Responsibility. Unpublished PhD, University of Waikato, Hamilton, New Zealand.

Balasubramanian, N.K., Kimber, D. and Siemensma, F. (2005) Emerging opportunities or traditions reinforced? An analysis of the attitudes towards CSR, and trends of thinking about CSR, in India. *Journal of Corporate Citizenship*, Spring: 79–92.

Baughn, C., Bodie, N. and McIntosh, J. (2007) Corporate social and environmental responsibility in Asian countries and other geographical regions. *Corporate Social Responsibility and Environmental Management*, 14: 189–205.

Chambers, E., Chapple, W., Moon, J. and Sullivan, M. (2003) *CSR in Asia: A Seven Country Study of CSR Website Reporting.* Nottingham, UK: International Centre for Corporate Social Responsibility. RP-9.

Cheung, T.S. and King, A.Y.-c. (2004) Righteousness and profitableness: The moral choices of contemporary Confucian entrepreneurs. *Journal of Business Ethics,* 54: 245–60.

Fombrun, C.J. (2005) Building corporate reputation through CSR initiatives: Evolving standards. *Corporate Reputation Review,* 8(1): 7–11.

Gonzalez-Benito, J. and Gonzalez-Benito, O. (2010) A study of determinant factors of stakeholder environmental pressure perceived by industrial companies. *Business, Strategy and the Environment,* 19: 164–81.

Matten, D. and Moon, J. (2004) Corporate social resonsibility education in Europe. *Journal of Business Ethics,* 54: 323–37.

Milne, M., Owen, D. and Tilt, C. (2001) Corporate environmental reporting: Are New Zealand companies being left behind? *University of Auckland Business Review,* 3(2): 24–36.

Perry, M. and Singh, S. (2002) Corporate environmental responsibility in Singapore and Malaysia: The potential and limits of voluntary initiatives. In P. Utting (ed.), *The Greening of Business in Developing Countries: Rhetoric, Reality and Prospects* (pp. 97–131). London: Zed Books, in association with UNRISD.

Prasad, B. (2004) Globalisation, free trade and corporate citizenship in Pacific Forum Island Countries: How relevant is the United Nations Global Compact? *Journal of Corporate Citizenship,* 13(spring): 65–76.

Redding, G. (2002) The capitalist business system of China and its rationale. *Asia Pacific Journal of Management,* 19: 221–49.

Spidla, V. (2006) Corporate Social Responsibility: The European perspective. *Ethical Corporation,* April.

Sriramesh, K. (ed.) (2004) *An Anthology of Public Relations in Asia.* Singapore: Thomson Learning Asia.

Tsoi, J. (2010) Stakeholders' perceptions and future scenarios to improve Corporate Social Responsibility in Hong Kong and Mainland China. *Journal of Business Ethics,* 91: 391–404.

Utting, P. (2002) Introduction: Towards corporate environmental responsibility. In P. Utting (ed.), *The Greening of Business in Developing Countries: Rhetoric, Reality and Prospects* (pp. 268–91). London: Zed Books, in association with UNRISD.

Warner, M. and Zhu, Y. (2002) Human resource management 'with Chinese characteristics': A comparative study of the People's Republic of China and Taiwan. *Asia Pacific Business Review,* 9(2): 21–43.

Welford, R. (2005) Corporate Social Responsibility in Europe, North America and Asia: 2004 survey results. *Journal of Corporate Citizenship,* 17(spring): 33–52.

Wright, M., Filatotchev, I., Hoskisson, R. and Peng, M. (2005) Strategy research in emerging economies: Challenging the conventional wisdom. *Journal of Management Studies,* 42(1): 1–33.

Part 2

TOWARDS A NEW LEGITIMACY FOR BUSINESS SCHOOLS IN GLOBAL SOCIETY

8 BUSINESS SCHOOLS IN SOCIETY: THE DISTINCTIVENESS OF DIVERSITY

Dean of Research and Acting President Alan Irwin, Vice-President Dorte Salskov-Iversen and Professor Mette Morsing

Copenhagen Business School, Denmark

'Business and society have been pitted against each other for too long.'

(Porter and Kramer, 2011: 64)

In the wake of the most recent financial crisis, and at a time when companies are regularly accused of causing social and environmental problems, business certainly faces many challenges. As Porter and Kramer rather dramatically put it: 'The capitalist system is under siege' (2011). In calling for a move towards 'shared value' creation, they simultaneously call for changes in business school curricula – especially in the direction of 'broadening' what is taught so that, for example, business and government courses cover the economic impact of societal factors as well as the effects of regulation and macroeconomics. Undoubtedly, business schools are central to the creation of the new social, environmental and economic conditions. One might reasonably describe business schools as one of the most important laboratories in which the future is being built. In these circumstances, a pressing question emerges: how are business schools to create and shape knowledge advancement and dissemination so as to provide the greatest societal benefit ? As we will suggest, this question is in turn inseparable from the larger question of business schools' place in society. While business school scholars would agree on the importance of these questions, there is no agreed approach as to how to meet the challenges.

Porter and Kramer surely have a good point when they argue that economic and social progress should connect strongly. In that way also, 'success' for a company can only be defined in terms of our wider sense of societal and environmental development: how can a company 'succeed' if not in terms of social benefit? It follows from this 'business in society' perspective that business schools will at least partially be held accountable for the consequences of managerial action and for the social and environmental impact of economic development. We in the business school world are certainly being urged to encourage and take responsibility for future steps to improve public and private decision-making and for the direction of economic activity. Business schools internationally are responding to the current lack of trust in business, but this also necessitates some deep reflection on the aims and purposes of business school teaching and research.

In this chapter, we argue that, since the late 1950s, business schools have emphasized two key stakeholders – the business and the academic communities – and that this has created a separation of business schools into either a 'business' or an 'academic research' focus. The Carnegie report from 2011 (Colby et al., 2011) indicates that this separation still presents challenges to business school education. Practice-oriented as well as research-oriented business schools have failed to prepare their undergraduates for their responsibilities to society. Practitioner-oriented business schools are directed towards providing local relevance and the tools to promote business performance and here research is often sponsored via consulting for corporations. Meanwhile, research-oriented schools are driven by academic competition to generate knowledge that is aimed primarily at enhancing academic prestige and standing. Of course, in reality many business schools have juxtaposed these two directions with often-mixed results – exemplified by the frustrated faculty question to the all-demanding dean: do you want me to focus on A-journal publications or on assisting the local business community?.

We would like to challenge both of these extremes as we would advocate a business school model that is able to articulate its contribution to practice and theory whilst also addressing societal needs. Thus, and in a word, our answer to the question is 'both'. We would argue that the business of business schools is the continuous consideration of how to stimulate the advancement of knowledge with societal relevance through theory, reflection, empirical research, education, practice-orientation and dissemination. This is not a quick fix. It is a long road that requires stamina, curiosity and innovation. It also means taking the proposition that business schools are the laboratories of future society extremely seriously.

In the following section, we will provide a few general reflections as we consider the previous oscillation of business schools between practice and theory. Following this, we will sketch out how the Copenhagen Business School (CBS) has tried to build a model that is able to engage in the Business in Society challenges of contemporary society, operating always with the broad organizing principle of academic diversity. Along the way, we will emphasize one of the key requirements: the inspiration, empowerment and mobilization of academic colleagues.

GENERAL REFLECTIONS ON PRACTICE AND SCIENCE

In the late nineteenth and early twentieth century, prominent businessmen in many countries began to lay the foundations for commercial colleges and what later became business schools. These institutions served the purpose of teaching practical skills to business people that were based on experience rather than theory. With their strong influence and personal engagement in the establishment of local business schools, respected individuals such as Mr Stanford and Mr Wharton in the USA and Mr Tietgen in Denmark embodied this development (Roos, 2009). However, in the mid-1950s business schools faced severe criticism of their experience-based teaching, and the Gordon-Howell report from 1959 concluded that more systematic research, theory, mathematics and ethics were needed in the classroom. Subsequently, business schools began to change tack, driven by a new type of knowledge generation which appealed more to academic peers than business folk. Professors began to focus on publishing as their main activity rather than teaching and practical relevance.

Recently, the shift towards publishing and away from teaching and practice has created much criticism from within business school scholars themselves (e.g. Kotter, 1996; Pfeffer and Fong, 2000; Ghoshal, 2005; Khurana, 2007; Adler and Harzing, 2009; Mintzberg, 2004). Minnesota professor Andy Van de Ven in his book *Engaged Scholarship* (2007) argues that business schools should encourage an engagement with larger society. In his seminal paper, Sumantra Ghoshal has raised a strong critique of business schools' detachment from practice and the way they have 'professed that business is reducible to a kind of physics in which even if individual managers do play a role, it can safely be taken as determined by the economic, social, and psychological laws that inevitably shape people's actions' (Ghoshal, 2005). Nancy Adler and Anne-Wil Harzing (2009) in a similar fashion have expressed their concern about the scholarly decoupling from society. They emphasize that it is time to approach business school tasks from the perspective of the company and society, and not from the academic career system. Adler and Harzing question the closed assessment systems of academic journal publications, operating as they see it far from business practice, and rendering products of little relevance for managerial practice. As Harvard Business School professor Rakesh Khurana puts it: '... *many of the discipline-trained scholars joining business school faculties were not intrinsically interested in the business ... Fewer [younger faculty members] were motivated in their research by a desire to examine the real problems that managers faced ...*' (Khurana, 2007). These scholars claim that business schools don't fulfill their principal role to '*support scholarship that addresses the complex questions that matter most to society*' (Adler and Harzing, 2009: 73). The consequence is that business seems often to find business school research irrelevant (*Financial Times*, 2011).

While the current critique of business schools offers an important stimulus to self-reflection, we believe this self-reflexive exercise is an integral part of the development of any business school, not least for those claiming to be 'research-driven'. On a continuing basis business school deans and professors have to inquire about the role of our work and our institutions in contemporary society. Business schools have an obligation to contribute to society in a number of ways, and while we all like to think that we already do, we also have to acknowledge that we might benefit from again asking ourselves 'how and in what ways?' Rarely, if ever, will we face a situation in which all business school stakeholders are convinced that we are doing enough and that we are doing the right things. Such concern, questions and skepticism ought to stimulate our thinking about 'business schools as usual'. Business schools must generate research and education of a high quality and relevance, while also acknowledging that the premise for such quality and relevance relies on our ongoing attention to how we may best contribute to society – and an intellectual humility as knowledge about the 'business of business' is not only generated in the business school world but also among practitioners themselves. In that sense, the co-production of knowledge should be seen both as a responsibility and a substantial opportunity for business school scholars.

In the following we will discuss how CBS is developing a way of taking our societal contribution seriously without losing its focus on research excellence and high educational standards. We do not claim that CBS always and in all decisions stays within this framework. But we do suggest that (like the concept of democracy) such a framework is necessary as an ideal type: it is strived for, if never fully realized. The difference between the status quo (who we are as a business school today) and the ideal type (what business school we would like to be) serves as an important resource for our unending but energizing efforts (Thyssen, 2009; Christensen, et al., 2008). This means that the difference of course should be minimized but never closed, would mean the end of movement and change. On that basis, if the difference begins to close, the ideal type should be redefined in order to ensure a constructive dynamic.

THE BUSINESS OF BUSINESS SCHOOLS – A FRAMEWORK

As a simplification, we can say that business schools are obliged to contribute to society within five broad areas: **theory** to advance knowledge, empirically-based **research** to generate new insight in business and economic practice, **education** for managers and future managers, the development of **practice-oriented** guidelines, and (not least) the **dissemination** of results and participation in public debate .

Put very simply, the legitimacy of business schools was once associated with how business schools contributed to society concerning experience-based education. Later, this depended on theory-development as the main mark of esteem. We argue that today's business school legitimacy depends, and certainly **should** depend, on a visible and balanced contribution to all five dimensions. Narrow business school obsessions with either teaching local business practices or nurturing A-publications alone turned them into self-contained and self-absorbed units. To develop and sustain legitimacy in contemporary society, business schools need to develop excellence in all five mentioned areas. Many scholars have described this as both an ideal and a practical way of operating (as in Andrew van de Ven's (2007) account of 'engaged scholarship' or Andrew Pettigrew's (2001) highly-influential advocacy of 'double hurdle' research).

This certainly does not mean, as McKelvey (2006) has pointed out, that business schools should lose academic quality and bend to all business managers' whims, ideas and biases – thus ending up as hostages to business people whose intellectual curiosity may not always be extensive (McKelvey, 2006: 823). Nor does it mean that scholars should not test and stretch themselves against the best international research in their field. The CBS way of addressing and integrating societal realities is developed out of a strong belief in the importance of bringing relevance and citizenship into the core of business school identity and thereby influencing managerial practice.

In using these terms we do not mean to moralize in the sense of preaching a particular set of values of business to society. Instead, we have in mind a way of engaging in research, education and outreach programs that take an interest in contributing to business development with respect to business-in-society challenges. Put at its simplest, the CBS Business in Society strategy is about recognizing the vital role of business in shaping and (at least

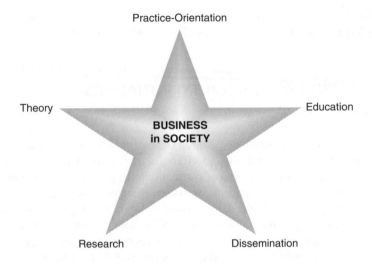

Figure 8.1   Key dimensions of the business of business schools

potentially) improving society. From a business school perspective, this means bringing knowledge and ideas to business firms and organizations – and to society as a whole. However, and very importantly, we can neither be relevant nor make a contribution in terms of global citizenship if we do not also espouse the scholarly values of intellectual rigour, serious reflection, critical scrutiny and open-mindedness. To be relevant does not mean to be lacking in excellence or originality. For business schools to serve as global citizens, we must challenge existing work practices and ways of thinking (as cases such as global warming and the international debt crisis strongly suggest). Equally, the quality of our activities must be underpinned by research excellence and a commitment to judging ourselves by the highest international standards.

The dynamics of business schools' societal engagement take place in an interaction between the business school (both staff and students) and its stakeholders. The challenges for society and business are many and will vary over time. CBS cannot engage fully in all of them. As a business school we must identify, select and prioritize those societal challenges that address our core competences: where do we as a business school see a need and the potential to contribute and where we can make a difference; what are our main competences and where can we have a real and relevant impact on society? Very importantly, and again this is deep in the CBS ethic, also reflecting our roots in Danish Society, such choices cannot simply be made in a 'top-down' fashion. Good university governance, and good scholarly engagement, requires that strategy should be a matter of local as well as 'corporate' action: intellectual curiosity and the energy to engage cannot simply be dictated from above. It is especially important that we recognize the crucial value of difference and plurality within our institution. As the 2009 *festschrift* for Finn Junge-Jensen, the long-serving CBS President, put it: the distinctiveness of diversity (Molin and Irwin, 2009). One of the significant challenges for modern business schools therefore is both to inspire and empower academic colleagues within a broadly-agreed direction. Here, 'shared governance' has more to offer than centralized models of university management and administration. At CBS, we often use the language of 'loosely coupled systems' to characterize our generally-emergent (or 'organic') approach to strategy-building (Molin and Irwin, 2009).

CBS BIS (BUSINESS IN SOCIETY) INITIATIVES – MAKING A CHANGE

CBS is by international standards a very large business school (or as we sometimes refer to it: a business university) in the small, welfare society of Denmark. Currently, we have around 18,000 students. Expectations of our contributing to society are high. Since the early 1980s, CBS has built a reputation for encouraging cross-disciplinary research and education to address society's need for managers with a comprehensive and critical understanding of society. What happened at CBS can also be seen as a response to developments in the broader social sciences, variously referred to as the linguistic turn, the cultural turn, postmodernism and social constructionism. This implied a shift in emphasis away from a narrow focus on economy and politics towards the processes and practices of meaning-creation, and a more holistic and critical investigation of the social. Knowledge generation across disciplines and practices is by no means an easy task. In her research on the complex conditions for knowledge generation to produce insightful knowledge on sustainability, CBS professor Susse Georg suggests that such knowledge transfer entails transgressing not only disciplinary but also organizational and cultural boundaries (Georg, 2004).

While primarily located in the social sciences themselves, many business schools and in particular the curricula of their flagship programs – notably the MBA and the Executive EMBA – have generally remained insulated from such developments. Important counter-discourses from within the business school environment such as Business Ethics, Corporate Social Responsibility, Sustainability, Stakeholder Theory, The Triple Bottom Line, and Critical Management Studies thrived on the margins but rarely in the core courses, in the leading business school journals and conferences, and interactions with practitioners.

Of course, CBS is strong in the 'classical' business school areas such as finance, accounting, marketing and economics. But CBS has for more than 25 years also recruited researchers from, among others, philosophy, information technology, anthropology, political science, psychology, sociology, geography, communication studies, law and history. Importantly, we invited these researchers to help us challenge and innovate business and management studies not from off-side but from within, working centre-stage with colleagues from the classical business disciplines. In that way, CBS has been in the 'business in society' business for a very long time (Pedersen and Haarder, 2009), even if that focus has become more explicit since 2009. Thus, CBS's decision to play a strong role in co-founding the Academy of Business in Society (EABIS) in 2002 is a clear indication of our deep-seated dedication to Business in Society issues.

Starting in 1984, this plurality of competences has also resulted in the creation of a number of innovative, interdisciplinary degree programs (BSc and MSc) such as philosophy and business economics , mathematics and business economics , law and business economics, language, culture and business economics, and psychology and business economics, politics and business economics, sociology and business economics, among others. The presence of a diversity of disciplines has enabled us to address a much broader range of social phenomena – indeed societal challenges – than would be possible when applying only the classical business school lens.

In many ways, CBS's embracing of academic diversity, stressing context, critique and cross-/interdisciplinarity as a means to stay atuned to society is echoed in a new Carnegie report, *Rethinking Undergraduate Business Education: Liberal Learning for the Profession* (Colby et al., 2011), which adopts a very clear Business in Society approach to business education. It does so in response to concerns about the failure of business education to prepare undergraduates for their responsibilities in society and business practice. Business leaders, the report notes, emphasize the important role of liberal learning but most liberal arts courses are poorly integrated with the business curriculum. According to the report, the challenge ahead is to integrate the Liberal Arts and practical training into business education.

As already noted, any business school – no matter how large – cannot and should not engage in all societal challenges. Following a discussion led by previous President Johan Roos, at CBS two grand societal challenges are under particular discussion. The first generation proposals address current business and societal concerns and opportunities, and they build on CBS competences in the areas of Sustainability and Public-Private Partnerships. Our plan is that these initiatives will serve as a point of departure for strategic attention and development for a period of three to five years, during which time other Business in Society (BiS) initiatives will hopefully emerge.

The first BiS proposal is concerned with how the sustainability agenda is both influenced by and is influencing business, environmental and societal development. Here, there is a strong connection between local industrial competences and leadership, governmental regulations and a significant global challenge – building on a Scandinavian citizenship model in which the state, unions and management collectively negotiate how to address and create new standards for sustainability. The second proposal concerns public-private relations as a way of mobilizing new actors to explore and solve pressing policy problems – drawing on the Danish 'welfare' tradition as a laboratory of practice but also asking much larger questions about the relationship between private capital and the state. Each of the two BiS proposals is working to deliver research, education and outreach activities grounded in business-society relations (Van de Ven, 2007).

While CBS encourages scholars to deliver basic as well as applied research, the new BiS initiatives are being developed to investigate specific problems and opportunities with real implications for improving societal development. In this way, they also serve as a counterpoint to our already-established world class research environments which primarily stress academic excellence rather than application. Each new BiS initiative will systematically develop a strategy for how to work both internally and externally in terms of generating public interest, questions and relevance. The plan is to include a network of significant contributors and challengers of the platform across disciplines, but also to encompass and encourage education for managers and future managers, the development of practice-oriented guidelines, and (not least) the dissemination of results and participation in public debate. Most importantly, while many of the other business school activities in which we engage will focus on research, education or outreach, the idea is for the new BiS initiatives to seize the moment and contribute to all five of the business school tasks presented in Figure 8.1.

The thinking behind the proposed new initiatives is that they should engage in grand societal challenges in which businesses have a stake, and that they should be willing to take on cross-disciplinary research, education and outreach. In practice, this means that CBS's BiS initiatives should integrate a number of CBS internal and external colleagues across disciplines and ideally engage cross-disciplinary teams of economists, sociologists, anthropologists, geographers, philosophers, political scientists and management scholars. Along the same line of thinking, our aim is to reach out to colleagues from other academic institutions and from other disciplines in order to experiment and add knowledge as part of our basic quest to explore how business may better contribute to complex societal challenges. As at least the case of Sustainability suggests, the challenges and opportunities of 'business in society' cannot be addressed without building strong links with disciplines outside the traditional business school repertoire, even if these are enlarged to include the broader social and human sciences. Science, technology, engineering, industrial design and medicine are also highly significant for future societal development and business schools need to play their part in a wider dialogue over the future direction and purpose.

FUTURE CHALLENGES

The potential opportunities for business schools of working within a 'Business in Society' framework are clear. Very importantly, these opportunities include not only a heightened sense of societal relevance and a renewed citizenship contribution, but also the intellectual challenge of examining (and as necessary unraveling) the institutional, cognitive and disciplinary processes which have led to the strange situation of 'business' and 'society' being (as Porter and Kramer put it) 'pitted against each other'. Whilst 'application' is often ranked in the academic pecking order below 'theory', conceptions of 'double hurdle' research and 'engaged scholarship' in many ways turn this order on its head: topics such as sustainability and public-private relations deserve the very best thinking and the most innovative practices.

Strategic direction at a business university like CBS cannot simply be carried down from the mountain top. Already, terms like 'emergent', 'loosely coupled' and 'organic' have been employed in this context. Debate, disagreement, reflection and transparency are our life blood – even if, once again, we often fall short of the ideal. 'Business in society' is a call not just for business schools to examine the practice of others but also to engage our stakeholders in this conversation whilst looking deeply at the ways in which we ourselves work, including the manifestations of citizenship and their relevance within our own institutions. From a CBS perspective, the call cannot only be made from on high but must also engage with the practices and processes on which the university depends. Within the business school world, 'business in society' needs to be less of a slogan and more of a provocation, a stimulus, a matter of institutional practice and a serious intellectual challenge. Only in this way can we move forward.

And yet, despite the endorsement of powerful voices such as Porter and Kramer and the most recent Carnegie report, a Business in Society approach to business education and research still has a long way to go before it is fully part of the mainstream, with many stakeholders – including some faculty and students, recruiters, businesses and ranking institutions – questioning the underlying rationale. This road ahead requires a willingness to face the costs and risks of such an approach: student enrolment, faculty recruitment, employability, research and publications, funding, accreditation and ranking. Despite the recent commotion and contrition, a turn towards context, critique and the cross-disciplinary will require a strong commitment and risk-preparedness from all those involved – including the corporate community and our students. Let us not shrink from these challenges.

ACKNOWLEDGMENTS

Our thanks for valuable comments on earlier versions of this paper go to the CBS Vice-Dean of Education Sven Bislev and the CBS UNPRME coordinator Jonas Eder-Hansen.

REFERENCES

Adler, N. and Harzing, A. (2009). When knowledge wins: Transcending the Sense and Nonsense of Academic Rankings, *Academy of Management Learning and Education*, vol. 9, no. 1, 72–95

Christensen, L.T., Morsing, M. and Cheney, G. (2008) *Corporate Communications: Convention, Challenge, Complexity*. London: Sage Publications.

Colby, A., Ehrlich, T. and Sullivan, W.M, (2011), *Rethinking Undergraduate Business Education: Liberal Learning for the Profession*. Boston, MA: Jossey-Bass

Financial Times, 25 April 2011: Bent Schiller: Academia strives for relevance (http://www.ft.com/cms/s/2/4eeab7d4-6c37-11e0-a049-00144feab49a.html#axzz1Kkc49v8t)

Georg, S. (2004) Research collaboration – The challenges of transgressing boundaries. In R., Fincham, S. Georg, and E.H. Nielsen, (Eds), *Sustainable Development and The University. New Strategies for Research, Teaching and Practice*. Howick: Brevitas (2004), 14–34

Ghoshal, S. (2005) Bad management theories are destroying good management practices. *Academy of Management Learning and Education*, 4 (1), 75–91

Khurana, R. (2007) *From Higher Aims to Hired Hans: The Social Transformation of American Business Schools and the Unfulfilled Promise of Management as a Profession*. Princeton: Princeton University Press

Kotter, K.P. (1996) *Leading Change*. Boston: Harvard Business School Press.

McKelvey, B. (2006) Van de Ven and Johnson's Engaged Scholarship. Nice Try, But … *Academy of Management Review*, 31 (4), 822–829.

Mintzberg, H. (2004) *Mangers Not MBAs: A Hard Look at the Soft Practice of Managing and Management Development*. San Francisco, CA: Berrett-Koehler Publishers.

Molin, J. and Irwin, A. (Eds) (2009) *The Distinctiveness of Diversity: CBS – A Case in Point*. Copenhagen: Copenhagen Business School.

Pedersen, O.K. and Haarder, B. (2009) Partnering with society at large. In J. Molin and A. Irwin (Eds) *The Distinctiveness of Diversity: CBS – A Case in Point*. Copenhagen: Copenhagen Business School, 59–73.

Pettigrew, A.M. (2001) Management research after modernism. In *British Journal of Management,* 12, Issue Supplement, 61–70.

Pfeffer, J. and Ting Fong, JC. (2004) The business school business: Some lessons learned from the US experience. *Stanford Research Paper no. 1855.*

Porter, M.E. and Kramer, M.R. (2011) Creating shared value. *Harvard Business Review.* Jan-Feb: 62–77.

Roos, J. (2009) *Inaugral Lecture,* Copenhagen Business School (August 25, 2009).

Thyssen, O. (2009) *Business Ethics and Organizational Values: A Systems-theoretical Analysis.* London: Palgrave.

Van de Ven, A. (2007) *Engaged Scholarship: A Guide for Organizational and Social Research.* London: Oxford University Press.

9 DESIGN SCIENCE AS A REFERENCE POINT FOR MANAGEMENT RESEARCH

Michael Barzelay and Saul Estrin

London School of Economics, United Kingdom

Sustained appraisals of the product and process of management research have now become cogent arguments for a change in business schools' identity, mission and activity. A sensible response to this context is to take a closer look at proposals for academics to follow a design science approach to doing research. This chapter puts forward the view that design science should be a reference approach for management research. In doing so, we try to make the case that the design science approach has been implicitly followed in the management field, so that the issue is whether or not to exploit this underlying competence.

In the history of the management research and education which is centered in business schools, one finds periodic critical examinations of its identity, design logic and features. Recent years have seen contention about the implications business schools should draw from real-world management failures and the global economic crisis. The issues being actively discussed are no less fundamental than institutional identity, the teaching enterprise, the research culture and forms of engagement with professional practice. Each of these issues had previously been the subject of discussion: now, as a consequence of the responses to world-level political and economic events, they have come to be framed as part of the same interconnected problematic (Boland and Collopy 2004).

Perhaps the most thoughtful, credible and bold critic of the current academic enterprise in business schools is that of Jeffrey Pfeffer from Stanford's Graduate School of Business. In an invited essay for the *Academy of Management Journal* (AMJ) entitled 'A Modest Proposal: How We Might Change the Process and Product of Managerial Research', Pfeffer (2007) develops the evaluative argument that the management research enterprise centered in business schools is underperforming in crucial respects; by way of remedy, Pfeffer also develops a policy argument that medical and engineering schools should be regarded as the models that business schools should emulate.

Whatever one may think of Pfeffer's specific suggestion, it is difficult to reject the argument of a major strategic rethinking of business schools as an institutional 'site' for management research is overdue. We accept that it is stimulating to consider medical and engineering schools as institutional models. However, Pfeffer's essay stops short of identifying approaches to management research that would play a part in remedying the predicament faced by business schools today.

Surely one approach to management research that should be considered is that of design science, a term that has long been part of commentary on management research, going back at least to Herbert A. Simon (1996). The terminology of a design science has recently come to the fore again, as indicated by the interest shown in two statements in European journals by Joan Ernst van Aken (2004, 2005). Pfeffer's argument should be filled out by taking the design science idea seriously, not just as a feature that could become common to business, medical and engineering schools, but also as an underexploited existing competence of our field. This revision of Pfeffer's position is meant to play the same role in the debate: to accomplish a strategic rethink of the business-school-centered academic enterprise of management, while the legitimacy issue remains unresolved.

THE ARGUMENT FOR A STRATEGIC RETHINK

Pfeffer's *AMJ* essay is a chained evaluative and policy argument. The evaluative argument is that the management research enterprise is underperforming. The policy argument is to rethink and realign the business school model, with medical and engineering schools playing the role of reference models. Pfeffer's evaluative thesis is supported by two lines of argument. One is that the scientific archive built up in elite management journals is vulnerable to critique on the basis of the standards for an empirical science. Another is that management researchers cannot be credited with the initiation of major practice innovations. In this second respect the standard of adequacy invoked is the reputation of engineering and medical schools, especially the latter:

> As evidence-based medicine has grown, the practical issues of treatment, diagnosis and the understanding of disease processes have influenced the research – even the basis science, in some instances – that gets done. In turn, advancing scientific understanding has been implemented in practice and in the drugs and devices that help to deliver care. The link between science and practice is closer, as it seems to be in engineering and computer science, as well, but I don't see any less academic legitimacy for these fields. (Pfeffer 2007: 1343)

In sum, 'it is possible to be both relevant and rigorous, to serve the scientific enterprise while doing work that informs policy and practice' (Pfeffer 2007: 1342).

The specifically institutional assessment focuses on the features of business schools that limit the performance of management research. Singled out for discussion are career pressures: 'The structure and processes governing both the careers of academics and the pre-publication review of their work limit the influence of management research on practice, social policy, and even the terms of public discourse about organizational issues' (Pfeffer 2007: 1335). The collateral effect of career pressures is that 'the competition for status that is part and parcel of the academic career process in management discourages collaborative research efforts and the building of the sort of laboratories that one sees in the physical sciences and medicine'. Collaborative research is seen as an effective mode of research. Pfeffer concludes: 'We should be conscious of the extent to which we may be trading work arrangements that might produce more useful and innovative knowledge for arrangements that make assigning individual credit easier' (2007: 1343).

These assessments operate as reasons for a strategic rethink and realignment. Pfeffer states: 'It is clear from considering other areas of research within business schools and other professional schools, that we have a choice as to what role we want management research to play and how to construct that role' (2007: 1336). His essay also proposes a way to conduct this rethink, once the need is acknowledged and the opportunity seized. The remainder of this chapter suggests an avenue for so doing.

WHAT IF THE MANAGEMENT RESEARCH ENTERPRISE BECAME A DESIGN SCIENCE?

Pfeffer's position can be usefully compared with the idea that the management research enterprise should see itself as a design science. This idea has been retrieved in recent years (Hevner et al. 2004; Romme 2003; Van Aken 2004, 2005). Judging by citation records, the environmental habitat (Heath and Seidel 2005) for this notion is such that it might well stick.

The design science idea boasts a distinguished pedigree that can be traced back to Herbert A. Simon. Various projections of the concept were set forth in three editions of his *Sciences of the Artificial*, published between 1969 and 1996. In a chapter, entitled 'The Science of Design: Creating the Artificial', published in all three editions, Simon took up the issue of the mission of professional schools and the role that a design science could play in their research and educational activities. His main contention was that academics in professional schools should develop and teach a science of design:

> *The intellectual activity that produces material artefacts is no different fundamentally from the one that prescribes remedies for a sick patient or the one that devises a new sales plan for a company or a social welfare policy for a state. Design, so construed, is the core of all professional training; it is the principal mark that distinguishes the professions from the sciences … The older kind of professional school did not know how to educate for professional design at an intellectual level appropriate to a university; the newer kind of school nearly abdicated responsibility for training in the core professional skill … The professional schools can reassume their professional responsibilities just to the degree that they discover and teach a science of design, a body of intellectually tough, analytic, partly formalizable, partly empirical, teachable doctrine about the design process. (Simon 1996: 111–13)*

Recent attempts to revive the design science idea pay homage to Simon's rhetoric of identity and values for professional schools, including business schools. In Van Aken's words:

> *The term design science is used here to indicate that the mission of (academic) research in such a field is to develop scientific knowledge to support the design of interventions or artefacts by professionals and to emphasize its knowledge-orientation: a design science is not concerned with action itself, but with knowledge to be used in designing solutions, to be followed by design-based action. (Van Aken 2004: 226)*

The most significant point of continuity is to conceive of managing as designing interventions and artificial systems. The entailments of the conceptual metaphor (Lakoff and Johnson, 1980) that 'managing is designing' include a recognition that responding purposefully to challenges requires creativity and judgment, which, in turn, can be aided by knowing how to use formal knowledge about the domains of problems and solutions that managers consider relevant to the design task.

Van Aken's writings play a particularly useful role by conceptualizing what counts as knowledge within the design science approach to research. His heavily adjective-laden expression is that knowledge within a design science takes the form of grounded and field-tested heuristic technological rules. In his own words: 'The solution concept embedded in the rule is a well-tested, well-understood, and well-documented general solution, which should be used as the basis for the design of a specific variant of it for a specific case' (2005: 23).

Van Aken's discussion develops a distinction between the original meaning of techno-logical rules, attributed to Mario Bunge, and Van Aken's extended sense of the term. Bunge (1967) defined a technological rule as an instruction to perform a finite number of acts in a given order with a given aim. Van Aken considers Bunge's algorithmic conception of a technological rule as unsuitably restrictive and widens its meaning: 'To me a technological rule is a chunk of general knowledge linking an intervention or artefact with an expected outcome or performance in a certain field of application' (Van Aken, 2005: 23). Heuristic technological rules encompass all technological rules, apart from the algorithmic ones. They do not lay out the steps to be taken to accomplish a given goal: they are more approaches for practitioners to consider in working out the specific design of an interven-tion or artefact. Approaches specify an intervention logic that guides but does not deter-mine the choice of an intervention or artefact's features.

What qualifies a technological rule (whether algorithmic or heuristic) to be considered knowledge? Roughly speaking, a grounded rule bears a validating relationship with prevail-ing knowledge about the natural and/or social worlds. A field-tested rule bears a validating relationship to the analysis of how heuristic technological rules have been applied to actual interventions and artefacts.

More could be said here about Van Aken's account of a design science; several issues help to elucidate the idea of design science-oriented management research, as an avenue to pur-sue within a strategic rethinking of business schools. One is the difference between social science, viewed as an enterprise to achieve valid contemplative knowledge, on the one hand, and a design science, viewed as an enterprise to achieve valid and useful technological rules, on the other.

At the risk of digression, it's worth pointing out that the idea of a design science is not identical to that of evidence-based management. Certainly, the idea of evidence-based management would be clearer if the distinction between algorithmic and heuristic techno-logical rules was brought to the forefront of that discussion.[1] A close look would show that a design science approach stems from a different intellectual tradition – and has a different view of the knowledge–practice relation – than the idea of evidence-based management, in either Pfeffer or others' versions (e.g. Barzelay and Thompson 2009).

In sum, current formulations of the design science can play the role of a 'solution' within the strategic rethink of business schools, whether focusing on research or on the combination of research and professional education.

CAN THE DESIGN SCIENCE IDEA GAIN TRACTION?

Is the current understanding of a design science really a 'solution' in a strategic rethink of business schools? There may be reasons to be doubtful here if we consider the argument in Heath and Heath's recent popular book *Made to Stick: Why Some Ideas Take Hold and Others Come Unstuck* (2008). The Heath brothers' design principles for sticky ideas are SUCCESs; simplicity, unexpectedness, concreteness, credibility, emotion, and stories. Some of these principles are reflected in Van Aken's improved account of design science. The presentation of technological rules as a paradigm for research knowledge satisfies the principle of simplicity. Perhaps the reference to Simon enhances credibility. However, neither concreteness nor stories characterizes Van Aken's message. Regarding absent concreteness, it is easy to pay mere lip service to the design science idea, as has recently been done by Denise Rousseau, a prominent advocate of evidence-based management (Hodgkinson and Rousseau 2009). Regarding absent stories, it's hard for anyone to imagine what it would really mean to follow the design science conception of management research. The implication is that Van Aken has left rhetorical work to be done. In what follows, we try to implement the sticky ideas principles of concreteness and stories by discussing studies that can be cast as examples of the design science approach to management research.

It is perhaps not surprising that the design science approach is alive and well in the operations management field. After all, particular manufacturing systems are concrete examples of Simon's 'artificial systems'. A self-styled design science approach to manufacturing management is presented in an admired textbook on the subject, *Factory Physics*, by Wallace Hopp and Mark Spearman (2008). Indeed, parts of two chapters are given over to explicating a general conception of designing artificial systems, in which research plays an enabling role, mainly as an aid to intuition.

What about the strategy field? One would be hard pressed to think of a more influential work in this field – and perhaps any within management – than Porter's (1985) *Competitive Advantage*. We have chosen to illustrate our argument with Porter because most people reading this chapter are likely to be aware of his work. More importantly, in substance but not presentation, it seems to us about as good an example of the design science approach as one can find outside its natural habitat of operations management. As such, it helps to make our general point that quite a lot of existing work already fits our call to the field.

In the book, Porter was effectively mute about what kind of approach he brought to his subject, leaving the impression that it was solely an application of industrial organization economics, just like his earlier *Competitive Strategy* (1980). It was almost a decade later that Porter allowed himself to be drawn out on the approach taken. The account he gave in 1994 provides a telling clue, as he likened the content of *Competitive Strategy* to an expert system:

> *The approach was to build frameworks ... Frameworks identify the relevant variables and the questions that the user must answer in order to develop conclusions tailored to a particular industry and company ... In this sense, they can be seen almost as expert systems ... If managers can understand their competitive environment and the sources of competitive advantages, they will be better able to search creatively for favorable positions that are different from competitors', assemble the needed skills and assets, configure the value chain appropriately, and put in place supportive organizational routines and a culture that reinforces the required internal behavior. (Porter 1994: 439)*

Table 9.1   A stylization of Porter's Competitive Strategy as design science

Design science of management	Porter, *Competitive Strategy* (1985)
Disciplinary conceptions of social process and structure	The selection, blending and adaptation of industrial organization economics
Theoretically grounded intervention approaches to be followed in designing artificial systems for a kind of practice situation	The competitive advantage approach to strategy analysis and design
Case-oriented research to understand the causal processes affecting the functionality of particular artificial systems and interventions under field conditions	Harvard Business School cases that are presented as illustrative evidence for particular facets of the competitive advantage approach
Generalizing research arguments playing the conceptual role of field-tested heuristic technological rules	No exact counterpart

It seems fair, then, to suggest that Porter's *Competitive Strategy* sets out a system of heuristic technological rules, which would make it an example of a design science approach to management research. To be precise, it formulates and justifies heuristic technological rules about stylized managerial challenges covering corporate and business strategy. One such challenge is to analyse and synthesize solutions to questions of which industries to enter and exit and the heuristic rule is framed in terms of the goal to earn high profits. The synthesis is a qualitative decision rule, though the remainder of the analysis is about the five forces framework rather than design in the full sense.

To maintain continuity with our interpretation of Van Aken's argument, we offer the following abstract characterization of this important reference point in the management literature (see Table 9.1). In Porter's strategy analysis framework, the artificial system that managers construct or improve is a business (product- or service-creating enterprise). The business's internal composition is conceived as a nested system of activities, nested in Porter's jargon, within the business's overall value chain. Interdependencies across value activities at the same level and nesting relationships across levels are important characteristics of the 'inner environment' of the business. A business's goal is to achieve and sustain above-average profitability, compared to rivals' in its industry. A business's performance relative to the goal depends on what happens over the long run along the interface between the business and its environment. The concept of 'industry' plays the conceptual role of environment, standing for entities such as rivals and suppliers, as well as the competitive process.

As can be immediately seen, this conceptual set-up has the same conceptual structure as chapters within Simon's (1996) *Sciences of the Artificial*. Simon wrote: 'Fulfillment of purpose or adaptation to a goal involves a relation among three terms: the purpose or goal, the character of the artefact, and the environment in which the artefact performs' (1996: 5). Further, a business is seen as a hierarchic system of activities, which is consistent with Simon's abstract default model of a hierarchically ordered artificial system (1996: 184).

The design problem arises because the competitive process has a tendency to frustrate attaining and sustaining above-average profitability in an industry. The way to adapt the business to this challenge is to formulate and implement a competitive strategy, a never-ending task that can be aided by understanding and using the expert system presented in Porter's *Competitive Strategy*. The expert system provides a template for devising an analogue world that can then be used to develop reality judgments and instrumental (policy) judgments about the real world of a particular business in a particular environment.[2]

Competitive Strategy provides heuristic technological rules about doing strategy analysis and making strategy choices. One such heuristic rule is to partition the strategy choice issue into two sub-issues, choosing a competitive position and configuring the value chain. The distinction builds on the background conception that a business is a complex artificial system whose performance relative to goals depends on what happens along the business–industry interface. Choosing a competitive position corresponds to the issue of deciding how the artificial system, as a whole, is to be adapted to the environment, given the goal. In *Competitive Strategy*, ideal-type or generic competitive positions correspond to differentiation, cost leadership and niche strategies. In Porter's words:

> Given the pivotal role of competitive advantage in superior performance, the centerpiece of a firm's strategic plan should be its generic strategy. The generic strategy specifies the fundamental approach to competitive advantage a firm is pursuing, and provides the context for the actions to be taken in each functional area. (1985: 25)

The heuristic technological rule, to borrow Van Aken's term, is two-fold: (1) to choose the best option, given prevailing conditions within the artificial system and foreseeable conditions in the industry environment; and (2) to stick to the choice, unless strategy analysis in the future results in the conclusion that a different choice of position would be better.

Once the competitive position is designated, lower-level features of the business need to be designed. Their functional role is to enabled establishing and safeguarding the business's competitive position. Given this functional role, the value chain's required performance characteristics can be inferred, as can be seen from Porter's discussion of configuring a value chain for cost leadership. In this kind of case, the derived requirement to be fulfilled by the value chain is a path of costs lower than industry rivals' – in a phrase, a cost advantage. The heuristic technological rule to be followed in choosing features of the value chain, for the sake of achieving cost advantage, is a two-tier list of driving mechanisms, with the top-tier including that which controls scale, learning, capacity utilization, discretionary policies, location and institutional factors (1985: 100–6). (Porter calls this heuristic technological rule a set of 'generalizations' about how controlling cost drivers can lead to a cost advantage.) When the overall requirement is seen as sustainability of the competitive position, the solution concept in the heuristic technological rule involves the same kinds of driving mechanisms listed earlier, but with more specificity. The heuristic technological rule is to seek a cost advantage through a combination of interrelationships, linkages, proprietary learning and policy choices to create a proprietary product or process technologies. Illustrative evidence for this component of Porter's design science is taken from the experience of Gallo wines, the topic for a Harvard teaching case study.

Thus, Porter's *Competitive Strategy* has the same conceptual structure as Herbert Simon's projections of the design science concept in the field of business management. We can think of three reasons why this claim would be unexpected, upon first encounter. The first is that Porter didn't reveal the indirect sources of his approach, even in the 1994 account that introduced the expert system analogy.[3] A second is that *Competitive Strategy* has been used by its critics as a foil to offer contrasting (and competing) views of how the strategy field should be developed. A third is that commentators, like Pfeffer and Van Aken, have effectively air-brushed Porter and, for that matter, Harvard Business School, out of the history of the business-school-centered management research enterprise. All three reasons provide a basis for reflection on whether the idea of the design science approach is likely to stick. If it doesn't, it wouldn't be due to the absence of a simple, concrete and credible message. It could however be due to the watered down and selective way in which stories are told within our 'community of practice'.

CONCLUSION

In this chapter, we have built on Jeffrey Pfeffer's courageous argument that the management research enterprise is underperforming, a judgment that plays a pivotal supporting role in his call for a strategic rethink of business schools and an emulation of medical and engineering schools. We have sought to show the mutual relevance of Pfeffer's policy argument and Van Aken's slightly earlier proposal for management research to be modelled as a design science. This argument conceives of managing as designing interventions and artificial systems, with the management research enterprise providing coherent bodies of grounded and field-tested technological rules, mainly of a heuristic sort.

For this proposal to become a reference point in a strategic redesign of business schools it needs 'stickiness', by which we mean that the idea of a design science has to stick around for long enough for researchers to work out how it can become widely adopted and practised. This can come from more 'concreteness' and better 'stories'. For example, the theory of the design of business strategies has a counterpart in the theoretical accounts about the design process: 'top-down design'. Some would argue that Porter must favor a top-down approach to designing business strategies in the real world. We would argue that Porter is actually working out an analogue world of formal, explicit, expert knowledge about the conditions for success. The fact that 'theory' has a similar conceptual structure as top-down design processes does not mean that following a top-down process is the way to formulate strategy that meets the conditions for business success. One thought leads to the other only if one fails to make a distinction that is crucial to design practice – distinguishing the analogue and real worlds.

Thus, we find at the moment a wide variation across management fields, with a design sciences approach highly visible in areas like operations management, but shrouded in others, as we saw with Porter. One suspects that small amounts of further, imaginative archaeological work, even restricted within the precincts of organizational studies (for example, Daft and Lengel 1986), would expand the catalogue entries considerably. This suggests that our field could usefully exploit its own competencies in pursuing the kind of identity shift and realignment that currently we are rightly pondering in management research and education. These further studies could confirm what we hypothesize here: that design science does offer an overarching intellectual framework for management, addressing the issues raised in the introduction of institutional identity, an engagement with professional practice, research and teaching. If this is the case, a major research and teaching agenda opens up for business schools in exploring the consequences.

ACKNOWLEDGMENTS

The authors gratefully acknowledge comments from the editors, Chrisanthi Avgerou, Daniel Beunza, Jonathan Liebenau, Costas Markides, Alec Morton, Daniel Shapiro, Fred Thompson and Sid Winter, as well as valuable research assistance from Jorge Betzhold Valenzuela. Any omissions and errors remain our responsibility.

NOTES

1. What Pfeffer seems to admire most in evidence-based medicine is its algorithmic technological rules and their implementation in the context of professional bureaucracies.
2. This framing of the expert system idea, delineating analogue models from the real world, is patterned on Hopp and Spearman's (2008) explication of the role that their book can play in scenarios where managers and engineers construct or improve manufacturing systems. The terms 'reality judgment' and 'instrumental judgments' are standard in the field of policy making, set out nicely in Vickers (1983 [1965]).
3. This fact might be attributed to the academic and organizational culture of Harvard Business School and to the somewhat elusive development of the field of business policy at that institution during the 1960s and 1970s. For an illuminating discussion, see Rumelt et al. (1994: 10–16) and Porter (1994: 424–7).

REFERENCES

Barzelay, M. and Thompson F. (2009) 'All Aboard? Evidence-Based Management and the Future of Management Scholarship', *International Public Management Journal*, 12(3): 289–309.

Boland, R.J. and F. Collopy (eds). (2004) *Managing as Designing*. Stanford, CA: Stanford Business Books.

Bunge, M. (1967) *Scientific Research II: The Search for Truth*. Berlin: Springer Verlag.

Daft, R.L. and Lengel, R.H. (1986) 'Organizational Information Requirements, Media Richness, and Structural Design', *Management Science*, 32(5): 554–71.

Heath, C. and Seidel, C. (2005) 'Language as a Coordinating Mechanism: How Linguistic Memes Help Direct Appropriate Action'. Working paper presented at the Academy of Management Meetings, August.

Heath, C. and Heath, D. (2008) *Made to Stick: Why Some Ideas Take Hold and Others Come Unstuck*. London: Random House/Arrow Books.

Hevner, A.R., March S.T., Park J. and Ram S. (2004) 'Design Science in Information Systems Research', *MIS Quarterly*, 28(1): 75–105.

Hodgkinson, G.P. and Rousseau D. (2009) 'Bridging the Rigour–Relevance Gap in Management Research: It's Already Happening!' *Journal of Management Studies*, 46(3): 534–46.

Hopp, W.J. and Spearman M.L. (2008) *Factory Physics: The Foundations of Manufacturing Management*, 3d edn. Boston, MA: McGraw-Hill.

Lakoff, G. and Johnson M. (1980) *Metaphors We Live By*. Chicago, IL: University of Chicago Press.

Pfeffer, J. (2007) 'A Modest Proposal: How We Might Change the Process and Product of Managerial Research', *Academy of Management Journal*, 50(6): 1334–45.

Porter, M.E. (1980) *Competitive Strategy: Techniques for Analyzing Industries and Competitors*. New York: Free Press.

Porter, M.E. (1985) *Competitive Advantage: Creating and Sustaining Superior Performance*. New York: Free Press.

Porter, M.E. (1994) 'Toward a Dynamic Theory of Strategy', *Fundamental Issues in Strategy: A Research Agenda*, in R. P. Rumelt, D. E. Schendel, and D. Teece, Boston, MA: Harvard Business School Press, 423–62.

Romme, A.G. (2003) 'Making a Difference: Organization as Design', *Organization Science*, 14(5): 558–73.

Rumelt, R.P., Schendel D.E. and Teece T. (1994) 'Fundamental Issues in Strategy' in *Fundamental Issues in Strategy: A Research Agenda*, ed. Richard P. Rumelt, Dan E. Schendel and D. Teece. Boston, MA: Harvard Business School Press, 9–47.

Simon, H.A. (1996) *The Sciences of the Artificial*, 3d edn. Cambridge, MA: MIT Press.

Van Aken, J.E. (2004) 'Management Research Based on the Paradigm of the Design Sciences: The Quest for Field-Tested and Grounded Technological Rules', *Journal of Management Studies*, 41(2): 219–46.

Van Aken, J.E. (2005) 'Management Research as Design Science: Articulating the Research Products of Mode 2 Knowledge Production in Management', *British Journal of Management*, 16: 19–36.

Vickers, G. (1983 [1965]). *The Art of Judgment: A Study of Policy Making*. London: Harper and Row.

10 THE NATIONAL ROLE OF CONTEMPORARY BUSINESS SCHOOLS IN RESPONSE TO THE FINANCIAL CRISIS

Thomas M. Begley and Patrick T. Gibbons

University College Dublin (UCD) Business School, Ireland

The scale, depth and duration of the world financial crisis have shaken the foundations of the capitalist model. In particular, the corporate and managerial emphasis on the primacy of creating shareholder value has been seriously undermined. Among institutions associated with capitalism, business schools have attracted much comment from within their own walls (e.g. Podolny, 2009) and from respected commentators outside academia (e.g. *Financial Times*, 2010).

While the legitimacy of business schools and their activities is explored throughout this book, our purpose is to address the specific challenges facing business schools from the financial crisis and in particular to consider how business schools in smaller countries are adapting. In assessing the role of prominent business schools in smaller countries, we must position these countries in relation to issues of market dynamics, risk and global trade. Essentially, smaller countries are highly exposed. As observers more than shapers, their inability to influence international financial markets and economic policy subject them to additional risk considerations. As they compete in a global industry, business schools in smaller countries are acutely aware of their country's vulnerability. They see an opportunity as well as a felt responsibility to offer education and expertise in order to better position their country to deal with present and future challenges.

Prominent business schools in smaller countries have never been able to ignore national stakeholders. Such schools are often closely observed domestically. They may be regarded as the country's standard bearer in the international arena. Their reputation reflects well or poorly on the country so its place in global rankings is carefully noted, along with a subsequent movement up or down. With many alumni among the country's citizens, a symbiotic relationship can exist. The school benefits from its graduates' accomplishments and prominence; graduates benefit from the school's accomplishments and prominence. This circle is not always virtuous. A well-known national columnist wrote a piece on the financial crisis that essentially blamed our school's undergraduate programs for the banking sector's mismanagement because several of its executives were our alumni. He failed to note the many graduates who led companies in other business sectors and yet others who were among the authorities attempting to pick up the pieces. One, for example, headed the agency that persuaded international markets to buy Irish bonds at a time when the viability of government finances was in serious question. After our initial negative reaction to the column, we decided to take it as a compliment that he attributed so much power to the school!

THE SCALE AND NATURE OF THE CRISIS FOR BUSINESS SCHOOLS GLOBALLY

Commentators such as Paul Krugman have claimed that specific theories taught as part of standard economics or finance courses at business schools, such as market efficiency, have contributed to the crisis. Fully supported by the tenets of market efficiency, banks, regulators and the body politic relied extensively on self-regulatory and self-correcting mechanisms to handle market dislocations. This phenomenon occurred as financial institutions adopted advanced, quantitative modelling techniques to estimate 'value at risk'. However, those exposed were not sufficiently informed that such ideas remain hypotheses rather than accepted wisdom. In discussing these hypotheses in finance classes, business school academics may have avoided deeper considerations of how knowledge itself is developed in the social sciences, which could have provoked more reflective and critical thought on, and less blind acceptance of, what we purport to know.

Even before the financial crisis, the basic model of business education had attracted much criticism. For example, questions were asked about whether the circular process of knowledge generation permitted sufficient independence of thought by business academics. In simple terms, business school researchers co-produced knowledge with practitioners, which the practitioners then implemented, which the researchers then researched. Critics within the academy were harsher in their judgments than those outside. Pfeffer and Fong (2002) found little that associated the grades earned on MBA programs with career success and questioned the impact of business school research on managerial practice. Since the crisis, the search for scapegoats has included business schools. One argument holds that they transmitted values based on a view of the capitalist system that emphasized shareholder value to the exclusion of other stakeholders.

Moreover, the speed and systemic nature of the credit crisis have raised questions about whether business school instruction adequately attended to the importance of considering risk. Risk is at the heart of all decisions about the future, where assumptions are required about stakeholder interests and the major parameters that inform decisions. While a more formal, mathematical treatment of risk is typically a centerpiece of finance classes, it is rarely treated intensively by other subject areas. In fact, one of the critical challenges to business school education is that its treatment of subject areas as very discrete creates a silo mentality among students. The absence of systemic, holistic approaches toward business issues may help create false, erroneous and only partial diagnostic skills among students.

Finally, business schools may have paid insufficient attention to the inter-connectedness of a world economy where trade, foreign-direct investment and portfolio investment are underpinned by the monetary system. If nothing else, the crisis has highlighted the fragility of that system and provoked more academic thinking on the profound repercussions of the perturbations within it.

THE SCALE AND NATURE OF THE CRISIS IN SMALLER COUNTRIES

Much attention has focused on the financial and fiscal crises afflicting Portugal, Ireland, Greece and Spain, the so-called PIGS. The first three of these countries are small. The nature and causes of their crises are somewhat different to the situation faced in larger countries, particularly the USA, where much of the debate on the role of business schools has been conducted. The crisis in Ireland resulted from exuberant 'vanilla' lending by banks which fuelled ever-more outlandish land speculation. Meanwhile, a government lulled into complacency by finances bolstered by a sizable tax on property transactions channelled its overflowing coffers into pay rises, particularly in the public sector, that outpaced the rate of productivity growth. In both Portugal and Greece, the correction of very large fiscal deficits, in the context of a currency union is likely to reduce real incomes dramatically.

Although these crises may seem somewhat removed from the activities of business schools, their consequences profoundly affect businesses in these countries. More important even than the question of how business schools might have contributed to the crisis is the other question of how they can incorporate the lessons learned into curriculum development.

These lessons may be particularly salient to business schools in smaller countries, particularly those that have been affected dramatically by the financial crisis, because they operate in a more limited organizational field. While, in larger countries, the role of business schools as a category can be questioned, in smaller countries it is easier to associate responsibility with, and possibly scapegoat, specific institutions. By their very nature and impact on the local economy, these institutions are clearly identifiable and their response is highly salient among local publics and stakeholder groups. Moreover, given the scale of the calamity that has befallen some smaller countries, the institutional legitimacy of the business school as an entity may require defence. In the next section, we examine the reasons for this somewhat symbiotic relationship, which revolves around perceptions of business school responsibilities to their home countries, from both their own perspectives and those of country business and political leaders.

HOW ARE BUSINESS SCHOOLS IN SMALL COUNTRIES RESPONDING?

In exploring how business schools in smaller countries were responding to the crisis, we identified, contacted and distributed a questionnaire to the deans/directors of CEMS member schools in countries with a population of about 10 million or less. We decided to focus on CEMS member schools as each represented the leading institution in its country. CEMS's history as of European origins prior to global expansion meant that 11 of the 12 countries (Portugal, Belgium, the Czech Republic, Hungary, Sweden, Austria, Switzerland, Denmark, Finland, Norway and Ireland – listed in size from largest to smallest) in the sample were from Europe, with the 12th being Singapore. We received written responses from eight of the 11 schools surveyed and engaged in oral discussion with a 9th, along with follow-up oral discussions with three respondents to the survey.

Their positions as heads of schools made deans/directors especially appropriate respondents to discuss the institutional pressures on their schools. The questionnaire consisted of a series of short, open-ended questions focused around three themes. The first theme asked whether they believed their schools had a responsibility to address the particular needs of business and others in their own countries and, if so, how. The second theme asked whether the government and business sectors expected their schools to address these needs. A third theme asked if their schools had been blamed for the financial crisis and whether the crisis had affected their approach towards education.

All respondents reported a belief that, amidst larger internationally-oriented responsibilities, their school had a particular responsibility to its home country. They saw themselves as contributors to their country's development in several ways. The five most frequently mentioned were:

1. Educating the next generation through undergraduate and graduate degree programs (mentioned by all nine).
2. Conducting research and analysis, offering advice on public policy, and media engagement (eight).
3. Educating and developing managerial talent through executive education and consulting (seven).
4. Responding to the needs of sectors important to the country's economy (seven).
5. Encouraging academics to serve on corporate, government and non-profit boards and lend their expertise to task forces, review groups and professional associations (five).

These activities may take place in business schools in larger countries as well. However, they bear qualitative differences in the smaller country context. In the next section, we expand on the responses received to our survey.

EDUCATING THE NEXT GENERATION

First and foremost, our respondents cited their responsibility to educate the next generation of leaders through the programs they delivered to undergraduate and graduate students. Through this activity, they served as supply lines of talented students who later went on to assume senior leadership positions. Extending the activity further, one respondent reported that his school took in more students than they wanted because the country's need for educated manpower was so great and apparent. Many deans/directors cited the central involvement graduates of earlier years had in the senior ranks of their country's business and government sectors.

For several reasons, respondents also welcomed the opportunity to educate international students. Most simply, they enjoyed the multi-cultural mix. Beyond that, some viewed it as a means to draw in talented students who might stay in the country after graduation and contribute to the workforce. Further, they saw international students who left the country after graduating as potential ambassadors for both school and country. These graduates often became important contacts globally, especially if they returned to their home countries and connected the school to local networks.

Finally, recruiting international students helped schools to educate students from their own countries by exposing them to different cultures, mindsets and business practices. Paradoxically, an important way to contribute to their home country was to become very international. Since the requirements of business in the twenty-first century were global, they needed to globalize their schools. Internationally savvied graduates contributed to their country's ability to compete in global markets. In summarizing his school's stance, one respondent somewhat jokingly referred to his school as part of the country's foreign office.

In places like Singapore, Ireland and emerging economies in Central and Eastern Europe, these contributions helped to ensure that multinationals with subsidiaries in their country were happy with the quality of the local workforce. Global markets are unforgiving. As the cost base increases, lower-skilled manufacturing and service work migrates to lower-cost countries. Higher-cost countries need to attract industries with higher value-added jobs, which in turn necessitates employees with higher levels of education. Universities generally, and business schools as a component part, are becoming more central to long-term economic health. While this phenomenon is true across larger as well as smaller countries, in larger countries, the responsibilities to develop an educated workforce are diffused across many providers; in smaller ones they are much more concentrated. A country's top business school can receive closer scrutiny for the quality and quantity of its educational offerings.

RESEARCH, PUBLIC POLICY AND THE MEDIA

A second area of contribution is in conducting research and analysis, offering advice on public policy, and providing media commentators. As a focal point, these schools are often the first places those in need of research, analysis, policy advice and consultancy will go to. Their experts are regularly sought out for help and are more likely to be known personally by government officials and corporate executives. As a result, their research projects and teaching interests are more likely to relate to important areas of country need. A striking difference to many senior academics who move from larger to smaller countries is the opportunities available to connect with high-ranking public and private sector executives and to serve as media commentators. While these opportunities can appeal to some, others used to working in relative obscurity from the public eye can find them discomforting.

Media commentary, in particular, often requires academics to step beyond the bounds of their own research to offer opinions and advice from a broader perspective. The odds are higher that an academic will be asked to comment in smaller countries. Our school, for example, has faculty members in banking, corporate governance, leadership, marketing, finance, industrial relations, entrepreneurship and strategy, amongst others, whose views are regularly sought out by national outlets.

During the heart of the financial crisis, some academics in finance and economics became minor celebrities as the daily media coverage brought an attendant need for experts to interpret what was happening. Beyond that, some academics will thrust themselves into the middle of hotly contested issues. In one instance, as the government prepared a plan to set up a 'bad bank', several finance and economics faculty signed a letter to the editor of the country's leading daily newspaper to oppose it. While ultimately their stance did not prevail, at the time the letter stirred national controversy and was a significant blow to the credibility of the government plan.

EXECUTIVE EDUCATION

A third way in which our respondents saw their schools contributing to their country was by way of an extension of their educational mission to include experienced managers and executives. Professors engaged in consulting for businesses and government. Executive education wings at the schools delivered market-responsive programs to private and public sector organizations. These wings often encountered a limitation to their reach. Since none of the respondent schools was in the 'top 10' in the global rankings, potential clients within their country engaged them for executive education to middle-level managers, professionals and high potentials but sent senior executives to the very top schools and hired them out to key programs. Three factors came into play:

1.   Projects sometimes required broader delivery capabilities than the school had.
2.   Some companies sought affiliation with a premier global brand.
3.   Executives preferred relative anonymity. Locally, they were sure to recognize the companies if not the participants themselves and might therefore be reluctant to fully disclose major company issues or expose personal development needs.

RESPONDING TO THE NEEDS OF SECTORS IMPORTANT TO THE ECONOMY

As a fourth way of contributing, all but two responding schools reported developing specialized expertise in sectors of central importance to their country's economy. In a visible way, they strove to take the country's specific needs into account in developing and implementing school strategies. Two respondents referred specifically to their use of think tanks for national economic policy. In one, from Western Europe, the institute had existed for a long time. In the other, from Eastern Europe, the school was in the process of establishing one because the financial crisis had revealed the country's vulnerability due to insufficient economic expertise to anticipate the crisis, to foresee its effects, and especially to offer good advice on how to respond to it.

Another school, located in a former colonial power, sought to develop in-depth knowledge on the conduct of business in former colonies where its language was still spoken and historical links remained strong. In our own case, we established a center for global finance because this key sector of the Irish economy needed to replace the high-volume transaction-processing operations it was losing with functions requiring more complex financial and technological capabilities. These mission-driven initiatives work best when both the school and the sectors it is addressing share a perception of need.

CORPORATE AND CIVIC ENGAGEMENT

The fifth and final area where the majority of responding schools reported contributing nationally was in their academics' participation on corporate, governmental and non-profit boards, in public review groups and task forces and in professional association governance and activities. When any of these groups seek academic representation, they look first to the country's top business school. At our school, this category of activity is not required for promotion but can aid a candidate's case.

From the individual academic's perspective, media commentary, public policy input and civic engagement are double-edged. While they may gain the contributors much national recognition, they often detract from academic careers. Time commitments reduce investments in their own research and local issues of pressing concern do not always mirror global trends in their disciplines. Research conducted with a focus on a smaller country runs the risk of rejection by those international colleagues who view the findings as too limited to apply to a broader world stage.

EXPECTATIONS OF BUSINESS AND GOVERNMENT

The previous discussion focused mainly on a small country business school's perceived responsibility to its country. We also asked whether the business and government sectors expected these schools to respond to country needs in the five areas identified earlier. Most respondents were public and received governmental financial support. Funded at least partially by taxpayer money, they reported a diffused sense of expectation that they would provide high-quality education in relevant areas. The one private school in our group expressed a similar view but from a different position. Ironically, in its case, without the built-in legitimacy of a public school, it had to work hard to demonstrate the importance of its service to the business community and society at large in order to motivate continued support.

An even more diffused sense prevailed regarding business and government expectations for the other four services provided by business schools. Research and commentary, executive education, responding to key sectoral needs, and serving on boards and other public-serving bodies all went into the mix for what the top business school is expected to do, though 'counted on' or 'looked toward' may be more accurate than 'expected'. In arguing that smaller countries can only support one business school of international standing, a respondent stated that this situation gave such schools special responsibilities. Larger countries usually have several leading business schools. If one or more do not provide the services desired, students and businesses will simply turn to others. Without such options in smaller countries, the best school needed to step up to the mark.

A recent situation illustrates the role top business schools play in smaller countries. Portugal's two best business schools, Nova Lisbon and Catolica, are staunch rivals. Their close proximity only serves to heighten the competition. The Portuguese government and leading business figures wanted a Portuguese MBA program to be placed among the top 100 in the *Financial Times'* annual ranking to enhance the image of Portuguese business internationally. Concluding that neither school could easily achieve such international acclaim by itself, they strongly pressured them to develop a joint MBA program. Prominent companies combined to put up €1 million to fund the program and solicited help from the MIT Sloan School. The two schools agreed to cooperate, as one observer commented, 'because they thought it was in their best interest but also because they were well aware that saying no would be something that Portuguese business would not understand or take lightly'.

REGIONAL SCHOOLS

'Regional' schools in larger countries can play a role similar to that of prominent schools in smaller countries. They can be champions for a specific geographic area and their contributions may be carefully tracked. Their primary role generally is to represent their region compared with schools in other regions within the country, though nothing prevents them from seeking international prominence as well. Business schools in large state universities in the USA often occupy this position; most *grand ecoles* in France also do because they are closely connected to, indeed governed and financially supported by, their area chamber of commerce. Ironically, many *grand ecoles* seek to decrease the percentage of students who come from their home region, viewing a broader base of appeal as an indicator of quality.

CONCLUDING THOUGHTS ON PERSONAL CONNECTIONS

Frank Rhodes, the former President of Cornell University, observed: ' universities, I believe, must not only adapt to contemporary forces but also sometimes resist them; they must both conform to the wishes of their various publics and patrons and also sometimes confront them' (2002: 242). Rhodes' quote highlights a major challenge for prominent business schools in smaller countries. As central purveyors of business education, they can readily connect what they teach and who they teach with specific levels of business preparedness and with particular individuals they have educated. The skills of their graduates are more visible than in larger countries and their failings need only take a short route back to them.

The columnist mentioned earlier may have been inspired to blame us because the most visible symbol of the excesses of the Celtic Tiger was a banker who was an alumnus of the school. In fact, he served a term on our corporate board of advisors and, as a prominent, highly successful executive at the time, we were happy to have him. Despite the many counterweights we cited previously and the fact that he had graduated 40 years earlier, we still gave pause for thought. Our discussion of business school culpability in the financial crisis was not distant and conducted in the abstract – it was up close and personal.

Rhodes' quote may also point toward a particular challenge in smaller countries: close connections to high-level business circles mean that criticisms of actors within those circles are also criticisms of individuals and companies whom senior school personnel are likely to know. The challenge of speaking up in those circumstances is greater. Paradoxically, given the paucity of alternative sources, the need to speak up may also be greater.

Business schools are currently being asked to increase their awareness of and commitment to societal service. For many schools in larger countries, a diffused sense of responsibility motivates their efforts toward society, and the international sphere is often central to their missions. Prominent schools in smaller countries, on the other hand, incorporate a strong responsibility to their home countries into their missions. They often have high profiles within their countries, especially in the business community, and represent their countries on the international stage. Most deans of schools in larger countries do not wake up in the morning asking what they can do that day to contribute to the development of their country's economy. Deans of schools in smaller countries are much more aware of their school's ongoing contributions to their country's future workforce and of offering intellectual leadership on the business and larger economic issues of the day.

FUTURE CHALLENGES

Prominent business schools in smaller countries are emblematic of the business environment in those countries. The content, pedagogical approach and value systems they deliver are particularly salient to the local business community. Given their schools' prominence, business school leaders must navigate three critical tensions. The first is the tension between service to the business community and critical detachment from it. Business is a vital supporter of business school aims and objectives, yet business schools, embedded in larger universities, must maintain distance to guarantee their dispassionate inquiry. The second is balancing locally appropriate content, tools and techniques with approaches used in other countries or those which are globally dominant. While many students will be employed in the home country others will seek international careers and many international students will return home. Balancing the curriculum to serve both career choices requires careful design and appropriate delivery. The third tension involves the ongoing debate between rigor and relevance. In smaller countries, there is typically a desire to see an immediate impact from research conducted by business schools. Pressure can exist to focus on the quotidian concerns of managers, while faculty reputations and promotion prospects will usually depend on publication in international academic journals where the questions and issues are less susceptible to immediate, unequivocal answers.

The successful navigation of these tensions is vital to the legitimacy of business schools in smaller countries, both for their reputation within the country and for their standing amongst their peers globally.

REFERENCES

Financial Times (2010) 'Risk and returns of the MBA diploma', Editorial, 4 January, p. 12.

Pfeffer, J. and Fong, C.T. (2002) 'The end of business schools? Less success than meets the eye', *Academy of Management Learning and Education*, 1: 78–95.

Podolny, J.M. (2009) 'The buck stops (and starts) at business school', *Harvard Business Review*, June: 62–7.

Rhodes, F. (2002) *The Creation of the Future*. Ithaca, NY: Cornell University Press.

11 BUSINESS SCHOOLS – FROM CAREER TRAINING CENTERS TOWARDS ENABLERS OF CSR: A NEW VISION FOR TEACHING AT BUSINESS SCHOOLS

Thomas Bieger

University of St. Gallen, Switzerland

In the recent past, and in the perception of many, business schools developed into training centers for future careers with a strong focus on income and profit maximization. Consequently, there was also a strong emphasis on functional knowledge, methodologies, and more and more on skills. If the new self-understanding of business schools should not primarily be one of a training center for functional specialists but rather one of an institution which helps to improve organizations and companies in their functionality for society, a more systemic and integrated perspective on teaching is needed. This has not only consequences for teaching but also for the curriculum and the reference models used. Even more, there are consequences for faculty management, incentive structures, program management, student selection and expectation management.

Many traditional business schools in the last millennium were founded by trade associations *Wirtschaftskammern* or *chambre de commerce,* as an instrument for contributing to the development of business in a certain industry and/or region by training excellent graduates and developing knowledge for decision makers within companies and governmental institutions. Through globalization, business schools today face global markets for students, professors and recruitment. By their nature, these markets are all non-transparent to a high degree. Information instruments like rankings or accreditations therefore attract growing interest from all stakeholders and reference groups.

In the ambition to optimize their future careers, students look for schools with the highest rankings and best recruitment and salary prospects. Recruiters look for schools with the best students and top talents. Faculty is interested in the best research opportunities to maximize their publication potential and by this their market value as academics. These ambitions lead to a 'virtuous cycle' of mutually strengthening forces (see Figure 11.1). Students can expect the best teaching and recruiters leading graduates at universities with the very best professors. Professors can expect the best teaching possibilities at schools in which international

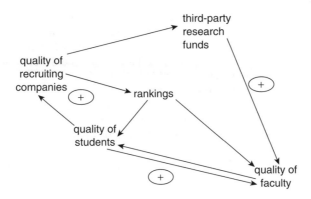

Figure 11.1   The success dynamics of modern business schools

corporations have a strong interest as recruiting universities – which makes access to third-party research funds easier – and where they have the possibility of recruiting PhD candidates and research assistants from superior students. Companies are interested in access to excellent research results and top graduates. Moreover, leading professors desire to share their latest research results with top students and companies to foster joint knowledge creation in a learning community. So what is wrong with business schools?

In the general debate, business schools are criticized because of (cf. among others Zsolnai and Tencati, 2009):

- Their contribution to knowledge creation through research (cf. Pfeffer and Fong, 2004). Business schools have been criticized for a long time for their lack of scientific foundation and their underdeveloped research compared to other disciplines (Starkey and Tempest, 2005). For about 20 years, top business schools have therefore put an emphasis on research and ranking agencies consequently on research output (Kerr, 2001). Still, rigor in many sub-disciplines and national research cultures is an issue. The efforts to develop a more paradigmatic scientific work favor axiomatic research, which because of the closed models, is hardly able to provide relevant results for the complex issues of real life (cf. Lorange, 2008). Therefore, research at business schools often lacks relevance and rigor. As a consequence of the growing competition between discipline-based scientific communities, management is going to be increasingly divided into sub-disciplines (cf. Mitroff, 2004). A narrow disciplinary research focus reduces the relevance even more since real issues of management and society are mostly based on complex systems requiring a broader, interdisciplinary approach.
- Their basic concepts, models and theories (cf. Ghoshal, 2005) based mainly on a mechanistic and economic view of human nature (Mitroff, 2004). In search of a Newton-like paradigm, closed, axiomatic models are favored. Models which influence the students most tend to be very one-dimensional with the single target variable of profit maximization, and explain human decision-making as being poorly monetary driven. In the words of Ghosal (2005: 76): 'By propagating ideologically inspired amoral theories business schools have actively freed their students from any sense of moral responsibility'; or of Starkey et al. (2004: 1523): 'There are also important questions about the models and values of management that emanate from the business school.'

- Their graduates are seen as purely career-driven and salary maximizing. Graduates show insufficient practice in the field because the models taught lack critical thinking and because research is driven by axiomatic and sub-disciplinary approaches (Mintzberg and Gosling, 2004; Pfeffer and Fong, 2004; Starkey et al., 2004). At the time when the first business schools were introduced and even today in many parts of Europe, they had no right to select students. Due to changes in the admission scheme (Kerr, 2001), business schools will more and more apply standardized admission tests like GMAT – which allow for an additional form of ranking based on the scores of admitted students – and in this will favor a special type of analytical thinking which fits optimally with the axiomatic research conducted by these schools.

Obviously, the economics of business schools can have negative side-effects. A special type of research – axiomatic research (cf. Lorange, 2008) – is favored because of the mechanisms of scientific communities, rankings, models applied and students selected. As a result, this system with its specific incentive schemes also works in favor of a shift of emphasis and resources from teaching to research (cf. Kerr, 2001; Besancenot et al., 2009). Some question the value of a business school education when the teaching is based on wrong models or irrelevant research and there is a neglect of teaching quality. If the value of the education is questionable, the sole value of a business school might be the selection of students, as an important pre-selection function for recruiters and universities in search of research-oriented future faculty (Pfeffer and Fong, 2004).

As always, the criticism might be too harsh and overemphasizes bad examples, but nevertheless it shows certain dangers. If business schools just teach standardized disciplinary models, they degenerate into pure selection machines and branded service platforms for students, professors and recruiters. In this, they become exchangeable. They also become subject to powerful net economics which will ultimately lead to a consolidation of the industry. Business schools could react to this consolidation by using traditional business strategies like developing new markets, products or a reconfiguration of the knowledge development and teaching value chain through cooperations, strategic alliances or outsourcing strategies (cf. Friga et al., 2003). However, through the loss of teaching quality and the fragmentation of knowledge production and dissemination, they would lose their most important functions: to develop knowledge and solutions for society and to train graduates who were capable of handling real-life issues. They have to develop value for society and companies based on non-transferable resources by being a place of knowledge creation and exchange (Starkey et al., 2004).

VISIONS OF A NEW BUSINESS SCHOOL

THE BUSINESS SCHOOLS AS TRADITIONAL UNIVERSITY DEPARTMENTS – A ROUTE BACK?

Some advocate that business schools could trace a way back to their roots by (re)developing into ordinary university departments and behaving more like a traditional academic entity (Pfeffer and Fong, 2004; Starkey et al., 2004). Closer cooperation within the disciplinary boundaries would strengthen academic rigor and academic independence. Critical thinking and tough academic standards would also attract and challenge the brightest students.

However, universities are also exposed to competition. Due to a lack of other measures and rankings in many fields, 'excellence initiatives' are implemented based on an evaluation of universities using broad sets of criteria. As a result, bureaucratization is increasing and a control culture is growing within universities (Starkey and Tempest, 2005). One could argue that business schools have already overcome this stage because they already apply relatively simple, widely recognized standards of comparison. Business schools in most cases already have a sound tradition of more or less close cooperation with the 'real world' of management, while traditional universities often lack industry contacts because they focus on basic research.

Therefore, the vision of developing business schools into traditional university departments seems not to be too attractive, whereby some elements like a stronger focus on developing critical thinking and reducing the emphasis on an instrumental recipe-type of content have to be considered for the future.

THE BUSINESS SCHOOL AS A LEARNING SPACE

Many advocate the importance of developing the business school into a learning (Andersen and Rask, 2008) or knowledge (Starkey and Tempest, 2005) space. Students, professors, companies and other organizations work jointly on issues and develop new knowledge by bringing teaching and relevant research together. Many approaches have been brought forward to improve teaching at business schools, such as:

- Internationalization of business schools and in this including more relevant issues and ideas (Crosling et al., 2008).
- Involving managers in business education (Andersen and Rask, 2008).
- Introducing new courses, for example in business ethics or business history (cf. Warren and Tweedale, 2002).
- Introducing critical thinking pedagogy (Smith, 2003).
- Introducing business skills laboratories (Blaylock et al., 2009).

Developing business schools into a learning space requires the commitment of professors and students with broader interests and motivations. Through this strategy, powerful mechanisms and synergies can be activated. In dialogue with companies and through applied research, current issues and actual topics can be identified. These can then fuel ideas for basic research. The results of such basic research can in turn inspire seminars and cooperation projects with students and practitioners which can lead to new mandates for applied research projects.

Joint learning involving not only students and researchers, but also managers, politicians and other stakeholder groups is a fundamental ingredient if business schools want to fulfill one of their primary goals: to deliver answers to current issues and questions in society. The role of business schools in management research can be seen at both ends of the 'knowledge value chain' (consisting of the elements – identification of problems and issues, basic research, development of tools and instruments, implementation/transfer). Business schools have to contribute through their insights into long-term developments or explanatory models to cope with the complexity of today's systems based on basic research as well as to work on current questions of companies and society that have been identified through applied research and transfer projects.

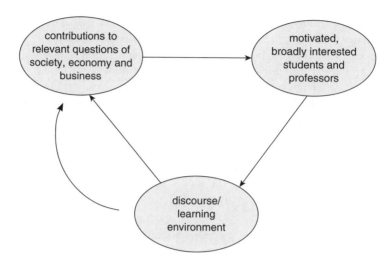

Figure 11.2 The virtuous cycle of research and development and learning in a transformational business school

The development of business schools into interdisciplinary and transdisciplinary-learning spaces is facing several challenges, among others:

- Bringing top professors' interest back to teaching and a discourse with the practical world.
- Providing a culture which allows and rewards a balance of applied research, basic research, teaching and working in interdisciplinary teams.
- Balancing an integrative, comprehensive perspective on management and disciplinary soundness in a time of continuous differentiation into new sub-disciplines.
- Implementing new teaching formats.

All these changes require the transformation of traditional business schools. On the other hand, they enable business schools to contribute to the transformation of society and the economy. Ultimately, business schools would develop into organizations which as learning spaces create value for society in the form of research results on current issues and graduates being able and willing to handle complex questions and act in a responsible manner. Contributions to the practical world, i.e. in the form of management concepts, would also motivate and attract excellent students and professors. This further strengthens the discourse and learning environment (see the virtuous cycle of research in Figure 11.2).

The changes in business schools cannot be achieved simply through new incentive schemes and governance structures in the sense of a transactional leadership. Rather, they require a transformational leadership fueled by vision, inspiration and decisive action (Burns, 1978; Bass and Bass, 2009. By developing into learning spaces, business schools themselves, through their graduates, professors and research output, can become important elements of transformational leadership in society. Therefore, this vision of a business school will be called 'the transformational business school'.

TEACHING IN A 'TRANSFORMATIONAL' BUSINESS SCHOOL

In the aftermath of the financial crises, the CEMS schools in different workshops (academic directors in their spring meeting, April 2009 in Monterrey, Mexico; the Executive Board in May 2009 in Prague) worked on the question of how reforms of business schools' teaching and innovations in the CEMS MIM program could address the management problems identified in the financial crisis. These approaches were motivated by the conclusion that one of the main reasons for the financial crisis of 2008 onwards was a too narrow focus by all actors and a lack of knowledge about the side-effects and systemic impacts (cf. *Der Spiegel*, 47/2008) of new (financial) instruments and measures. Regulators did not understand the impact of new financial instruments in the real world, bankers did not understand the impact of their newly structured financial products on other markets, and managers did not understand the impact of bonification schemes on social cohesion and the political climate.

The ambition of business schools therefore should be to provide, in the sense of a learning space, broader contextual teaching which allows for the inclusion of systemic side-effects and strengthens ethical thinking. A list of possible measures to strengthen corporate social responsibility (CSR) by 'University Social Responsiveness' has been identified. Such measures touch the different levels of teaching (see Figure 11.3) – teaching material (e.g. by

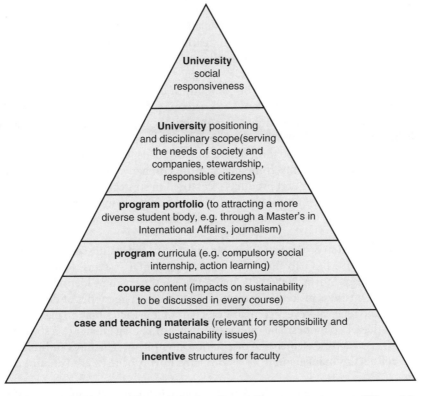

Figure 11.3   Towards a learning space: implementing measures on different layers of teaching

Source: based on discussions within the Academic Committee of CEMS including integrative aspects in case studies), single teaching modules (i.e. by including examples or speakers which represent broader values than just economic), courses (i.e. by including systems approaches), programs (i.e. by positioning them in the context of issues of business and society or including integrative and critical thinking abilities as selection criteria) and the university as a whole (i.e. by including non-business or economic departments and programs that provide a contextual view on management and have the potential to attract a more diverse student body).

INTEGRATIVE MANAGEMENT MODEL AND CONTEXTUAL STUDIES AS ELEMENTS OF A TRANSFORMATIONAL BUSINESS SCHOOL

A transformational university functioning as a learning space requires an integrative, interdisciplinary and transdisciplinary teaching approach to enabling a systemic view on society, economy and management. In addition to the above-mentioned measures and ideas, an integrative model of management as an analytical reference model can enable an integrative systemic view and facilitate the integration of contextual disciplines.

The systems approach based on an integrative management model has had a long tradition in teaching at the University of St. Gallen. It goes back to research conducted by Ulrich and Krieg (1974) as pioneers in teaching management in German-speaking Europe. The basic model sees the organization or company surrounded by different environments: the socio-political, economic, natural and technological environments with which systemic interrelations exist. The company or organization itself depends on and is constituted by groups of stakeholders like customers, collaborators, capital owners and suppliers as well as government and state, competitors and the general public (for example, inhabitants in the neighborhood of the company site). The traditional St. Gallen Management Model identified different levels of management. Management policies define the general goals of the company and the company value system. Management strategies deal with markets and products structured in strategic business units, as well as the development and use of strategic resources and cooperations. Operational management thereby deals with business decisions with a shorter reach such as staff selection and sales management.

The latest generation of the St. Gallen Management Model still sees the enterprise as a complex system with links to the different environmental systems. However, it takes a process view (Rüegg-Stürm, 2009). The main processes that can be identified are management processes, business processes and support processes. The modes of development are optimization and renewal – every company or a part of it in each situation places an emphasis on one of these two modes. The integrative issues of management are resources, values and norms. The structural elements of orientation are strategy, structures and culture. These elements define 'the management' of a company, how processes are run and decisions are taken.

It seems clear that there is no perfect management model. However, like all models it can help to provide an overview, to prioritize, to structure and to integrate and by this enable communication and discourse. As with all models, there is the danger of blind-spots. Therefore, it is important to reflect on the model, its perspectives and origins when introducing it to students but even more so in the later stages of a study's progress.

To enable an integrative view on management as part of society and the economy, all Bologna programs at the University of St. Gallen consist of a compulsory minimum of 25 per cent credits in contextual studies. In the first year, there are compulsory introductory courses in important subjects linked to management and the social sciences in general, such as Theories of State and Economy, European History or Sociology of the Organization. In the second and third year of Bachelor studies, students can choose from roughly 150 courses with an applied and interdisciplinary content, such as Transformative Leadership in Action, Corporate Social Responsibility (CSR) – Case Studies on Companies' Responsibility in a Global Context – or Conflicts between Politics and Economics. The courses are structured into the three groups of competencies: Leadership Abilities, Critical Thinking and Cultural Awareness. At Master's level, courses are also structured into the aforementioned three categories. Students can choose from approximately 120 courses that cover issues such as Gender and Economics or Organization and Morale.

To raise awareness of the importance of an integrated perspective on management and to motivate students for their contextual studies, an integrated case study is the main element of the compulsory introductory week for all Bachelor programs. The cases should address all three environments of sustainable management and allow for the involvement of professors from the School of Humanities and Social Sciences. Examples of cases from recent years are 'Intercultural Conflicts and Cooperation' and 'The Challenge of a Sustainable Energy Supply'.

St. Gallen's tradition and its current strong focus on contextual and systemic views date back to its specific history and financial conditions. It was founded in 1898 as a trade school and has always included those subjects considered necessary for success in trade such as technical understanding and foreign languages and cultures. Due to its liberal political system, it received early on the right to establish independent research institutes which in an entrepreneurial manner raised third-party money. Today, with 50 per cent of its budget coming from private sources, the university has the highest share of non-governmental money of all the public universities in German-speaking Europe. This provides its academics with a certain independence from rating and ranking systems – and encourages teaching and research with a strong link to the real world.

The perceived usefulness of contextual studies is assessed through regularly conducted graduate surveys. The management model is introduced in the first-term core courses in management and serves as a reference model for all other courses. It is also an element in the final examination at the end of the first year. The approaches are widely accepted among faculty and most of the student body. However, and especially with the recent growth in the number of students, some implementation problems have appeared:

- The share of new faculty that has not been part of the development process of the St. Gallen Management Model increases because of the growth and renewal of faculty. Hence, the implementation of the model in the classroom is challenged.
- Because of the ongoing standardization of curricula, there is pressure from new faculty and especially Master's students coming from other universities to reduce contextual studies and increase the weight of core courses.

CONCLUSIONS

All the aforementioned measures can help to introduce a more integrated perspective in teaching and to bring business schools closer to becoming learning spaces. There are two main elements that can serve as a basis for many other measures: an integrated management model as a reference model in teaching, especially in the first, introductory part of studies, and the inclusion of contextual studies as a compulsory part of all programs. As can be shown in the example of the University of St. Gallen, the implementation of such approaches requires the motivation and continuous commitment of the faculty and leadership in the university.

School vision, strategic program development, learning goals, a reference model of teaching and the curriculum structure are interlinked elements. A sole adjustment of one element, for example the development of a reference model in management without an underlying vision of its role in teaching, is not sustainable. The introduction of a new program or a major program reform based on a new vision can be a rare opportunity to really move forward.

To ensure the development of contextual studies, to preserve their independence and diversity and to avoid over-convergence with management subjects, it makes sense to organize it under an independent unit. In St. Gallen, the School for Humanities and Social Sciences was strengthened for this purpose and mandated with the management of contextual studies as an independent program unit. Program management often has an interest in reducing contextual studies to make room for more traditional, often more short-term oriented content. Not surprisingly, the finance programs most strongly advocated a reduction of contextual studies right before the financial crisis in order to have the opportunity to include more quantitative, axiomatic elements.

Challenges for the development and implementation of the vision of the business school as a learning space include faculty development, adjusting the culture, and balancing applied and basic research as well as disciplinary and interdisciplinary initiatives and required innovations. Major success factors are a broadly accepted vision and a culture that rewards the internal contribution to program management and content development. If business schools want to develop their own profile based on content and teaching qualities and avoid turning into exchangeable deliverers of selection and standardized teaching, they have to overcome these challenges.

REFERENCES

Andersen, P. and Rask, M. (2008) Taking Action: New Forms of Student and Manager Involvement in Business Education. *Marketing Intelligence and Planning*, 26(2): 145–65.

Bass, B. and Bass, R. (2009) *The Bass Handbook of Leadership: theory, research and managerial applications*. New York: Free Press.

Besancenot, D., Faria, J.R. and Vranceanu, R. (2009) Why Business Schools do so Much Research: A Signaling Explanation. *Research Policy*, 38(7): 1093–101.

Blaylock, B., McDaniel, J.L., Falk, C.F., Hollandsworth, R. and Kopf, J.M. (2009) A Borrowed Approach for a More Effective Business Education. *Journal of Management Education*, 33(5): 577–95.

Burns, J.W. (1978) Leadership, Moral Development and Citizenship Behavior, *Business Ethics Quarterly*, 5 (1): 43–54.

Crosling, G., Edwards, R. and Schroder, B. (2008) Internationalizing the Curriculum: The Implementation Experience in a Faculty of Business and Economics. *Journal of Higher Education Policy and Management*, 30(2): 107–21.

Friga, P., Bettis, R. and Sullivan, R. (2003) Changes in Graduate Management Education and New Business School Strategies for the 21st Century. *Academy of Management Learning and Education*, 2(3): 233–49.

Ghoshal, S. (2005) Bad Management Theories are Destroying Good Management Practices. *Academy of Management Learning and Education*, 4(1): 75–91.

Kerr, C. (2001) *The Uses of the University*. Cambridge, MA: Harvard University Press.

Lorange, P. (2008) *Thought Leadership Meets Business: How Business Schools can Become More Successful*. New York: Cambridge University Press.

Mintzberg, H. and Gosling, J. (2004) The Education of Practicing Managers. *MIT Sloan Management Review*, 45(4): 19–22.

Mitroff, I. (2004) An Open Letter to the Deans and the Faculties of American Business Schools. *Journal of Business Ethics*, 54(2): 185–9.

Pfeffer, J. and Fong, C.T. (2004) The Business School Business: Some Lessons from the US Experience. *Journal of Management Studies*, 41(8): 1501–20.

Rüegg-Stürm, J. (2009) *Das St Galler Management-Modell*. In R. Dubs, R. Euler, J. Rüegg-Stürm and C.E. Wyss (eds), *Einführung in die Managementlehre, Vol. 1*, 2nd edn. Bern: Haupt.

Der Spiegel (2008) *Das Kapitalverbrechen. Anatomie einer Weltkrise, die gerade erst begonnen hat, Der Spiegel*, 47. Hamburg: Author.

Smith, G.F. (2003) Beyond Critical Thinking and Decision Making: Teaching Business Students How to Think. *Journal of Management Education*, 27(1): 24–51.

Starkey, K. and Tempest, S. (2005) The Future of the Business School: Knowledge Challenges and Opportunities. *Human Relations*, 58(1): 61–82.

Starkey, K., Hatchuel, A. and Tempest, S. (2004) Rethinking the Business School. *Journal of Management Studies*, 41(8): 1521–31.

Ulrich, H. and Krieg, W. (1974) *St Galler Management-Modell*, 3rd edn. Bern: Haupt.

Warren, R. and Tweedale, G. (2002) Business Ethics and Business History: Neglected Dimensions in Management Education. *British Journal of Management*, 13(3): 209–19.

Zsolnai, L. and Tencati, A. (2009) *The Future International Manager*. Basingstoke: Palgrave Macmillan.

12 THE FUTURE OF BUSINESS SCHOOL RESEARCH: THE NEED FOR DUAL RESEARCH METHODOLOGIES

Muel Kaptein and George S. Yip

Rotterdam School of Management, Erasmus University, The Netherlands

Throughout the 100+ years of the existence of business schools, the role of research has steadily increased relative to business schools' original primary role of teaching. Indeed, at the top schools, or perhaps at least the top 100 schools in the world,[1] and certainly in all CEMS schools, the time spent on research is close to or exceeds that spent on teaching. Certainly, the ambitions and energies of most regular (as opposed to adjunct) faculty mainly focus on research rather than teaching. We know that fact from personal experience at schools including Harvard, Stanford, UCLA, Georgetown, Cambridge, the London Business School and the Rotterdam School of Management (abbreviated in the rest of this chapter as RSM), as well as from interactions with our colleagues at other top US, European and Asian schools. It is 'publish or perish' not 'teach or perish', so we certainly need to question the past, present and future contribution to society of business school research. A full discourse would well exceed the length of this chapter. Therefore, we will focus on how the unique position of business schools seems to have generated extreme angst about rigor versus relevance in research. Consequently, we will describe the way RSM has dealt with this dilemma by integrating a business-society dimension in business research. We hope to show in this chapter the necessity and feasibility of dual research methodologies at business schools.

ANGST ABOUT RIGOR AND RELEVANCE

Why have business schools been so conflicted about rigor and relevance in research? Quite apart from external criticism, business schools are regularly criticized from within for their lack of relevance in research. One of the more prominent recent critiques argues that business schools have lost their way by focusing on 'scientific' research (Bennis and O'Toole, 2005). On the other hand, many believe the opposite: that a lack of disciplinary rigor is part of the problem of management research (Kilduff and Kelemen, 2001; Pettigrew, 2001). Pfeffer

(2007) argued that management research was bedevilled by the lack of a coherent and consistent framework or paradigm. A recent review of the rigor versus relevance debate is provided by Wensley (2007). So why is business research so conflicted?

WHAT IS DIFFERENT ABOUT BUSINESS SCHOOLS?

We believe that the problem with business research comes from a unique challenge faced by business schools compared with other academic fields. Business schools have two audiences: academics and business practitioners. Furthermore, because the academics are outside business organizations, we cannot directly participate in or easily observe what is happening inside these. In contrast, by just comparing ourselves to other professional subjects, a medical academic does research on the same human bodies on which doctors practise, a legal academic uses the same legal materials as does a practising lawyer, and an engineering academic researches the same bridge structures as may be built by a practising engineer. Other social sciences, such as politics or government, have similar but lesser challenges, as the practitioners of these topics tend to generate a large public record. When we move towards classic academic subjects such as literature and history, this separation between academics and practitioners is even less of an issue. Literature academics can themselves directly do the same thing as novelists and playwrights. History academics are in a position where the practitioners are usually dead, and are not changing history while the academics try to study them!

THE NEED FOR DUAL METHODOLOGIES

Even when business academics can gather data and conduct research on business topics, we face the additional challenge that the great majority of our output-tested hypotheses with probabilistic predictions, are generally not what managers can use. Managers are far more interested in pattern recognition. Does this configuration of external circumstances mesh with my particular configuration of strategies and actions to produce a successful outcome for my company? That is why managers much prefer to read articles in managerial journals, such as the *Harvard Business Review*, that are based on in-depth case studies where there are more variables than observations, rather than large-sample statistical studies with many more observations than variables. An inspection of the contents of the best managerial journals – the *Harvard Business Review, MIT Sloan Management Review* and *California Management Review* – as well as best-selling business books, strongly demonstrates the practitioner preference for pattern recognition in company examples. Furthermore, rather than wanting tested hypotheses, the practitioner will want to test the hypothesis on his or her own situation. Only when the hypothesis seems to fit the particular situation will the practitioner implement the recommendation from the hypothesis.

This preference of the managerial audience for case-based evidence raises a very challenging requirement for top business schools to conduct research with two different types of methodology, because it is not just a case of 'translating' academic research for a managerial audience. We can cite from personal observation the case of Michael Porter's conversion of industrial organization theory into his framework for competitive strategy. The second author of this chapter was Porter's second doctoral student as he worked on his book,

Competitive Strategy (Porter, 1980). Twenty or more years worth of industrial organization economics research, from Bain (1956) to Caves (1980), did not make the 'translation' to competitive strategy. Instead, after completing his own doctoral research within the paradigm of industrial organization (IO) economics (Porter, 1976), Porter required another six years (1974 to 1980) of case research to 'convert' industrial organization to competitive strategy. Furthermore, it is very telling that despite his doctoral thesis winning the Harvard University Economics Department's Wells Prize for the best economics thesis, Porter never published a managerial article from that work. He could not do so because his doctoral research methodology did not generate the sort of insights that were craved by managers.

Dual methodologies typically involve a combination of qualitative and quantitative approaches. Van Maanen (1979: 520) said: 'Qualitative and quantitative methodology are not mutually exclusive … moreover, no matter what the topic of study, qualitative researchers in contrast to their quantitative colleagues claim forcefully to know relatively little about what a given piece of observed behaviour means until they have developed a description of the context in which the behaviour takes place.' Another typical aspect of qualitative research is the use of case studies, a key part of managerial research. The link with theory comes from the ability of case research to generate theory. Eisenhardt (1989: 534) said: 'The case study is a research strategy which focuses on understanding the dynamics present within single settings.' Pfeffer (2007) also makes the case for academic research to become more relevant, partly by combining the output of different types of research. This can also come from expanding our definitions to encourage clinical, qualitative research and case writing.

So we are making a rather novel and potentially controversial case for using dual methodologies, although we first heard this argument from the late, and great, Sumantra Ghoshal. Indeed, Ghoshal was such a believer in dual methodologies that he studied for two business doctorates at the same time, one from the school epitomizing rigor (MIT's Sloan School of Management) and one from that epitomizing relevance (Harvard Business School). Using dual methodologies need not be done in the same publication or even the same research study but could be done in the same research program. Ghoshal further argued (in Moran and Ghoshal, 1999) that business school research could influence managers' behavior in both good and bad ways.

Understanding the differing roles of the two types of methodologies also helps explain why few individual management researchers will admit that their own research lacks relevance. (Just once, we witnessed a refreshingly honest but incredibly naïve, candidate for a full professorship at a top US school – when asked what was the managerial relevance of his research – reply, 'I have never thought about that'. He did not get the job!) Nearly all researchers think their own research is relevant because the subject is relevant to business or management. It would be astonishing if that were not the case. But true relevance comes only if the results are useable by managers. From our earlier arguments, applicability is mostly generated by a relevant methodology. That said, we are certainly not saying that all, or even most, business researchers must conduct immediately relevant research. The same researchers can make the conversion to relevance at a later time. Other academic researchers can make the conversion. Or practitioners, especially management consultants, can make the conversion.

The case for dual methodologies has also been made by those who developed the notion of Mode 1 and Mode 2 research approaches. Gibbons et al. (1994) argued for a new form of knowledge production which would be context-driven, problem-focused and interdisciplinary. It would involve multidisciplinary teams brought together for short periods of time to work on specific problems in the real world. Gibbons et al. labelled this 'Mode 2' knowledge production. In contrast, 'Mode 1' is academic, investigator-initiated and discipline-based knowledge production. The UK has gone so far as to provide major funding (over £20 million to date) for a national research institute, one of whose major objectives is to practise Mode 2 research by engaging with practitioners as co-producers of knowledge (see www.aimresearch.org; and Delbridge et al., 2006). This UK institute embodies the 'triple helix' model of the state, academia and industry combining to foster innovation (Etzkowitz and Leydesdorff, 2000: 111).

In the next section, we will present the way in which RSM has tried to implement dual research methodologies in its business school.

THE BUSINESS-SOCIETY DIMENSION OF RESEARCH

Business-Society Management (B-SM), which focuses on issues such as social responsibility, sustainability and ethics, is now an established field of research in its own right. The next challenge is to integrate the B-SM perspective into other traditional fields of business research. This section uses RSM as a case study to illustrate how this challenge can be approached and how RSM has tried to do both relevant and rigorous research. The current integration phase at RSM was preceded by three phases of B-SM research at RSM: specialization (1986–96), concentration (1997–2000) and intensification (2000–6). Our journey at RSM shows that integrating the B-SM perspective into other research disciplines could be achieved by first attracting a group of academics who would conduct research in B-SM. It also shows that boards of schools could use different instruments to foster this integration process.

THE ROTTERDAM SCHOOL OF MANAGEMENT

RSM is the business school of Erasmus University Rotterdam, which is located in Rotterdam, the Netherlands. Erasmus University was founded in 1913 and named after the fifteenth-century Dutch humanist and theologian Desiderius Erasmus Roterodamus. RSM currently offers a range of undergraduate and graduate programs, including a Bachelor, Master and PhD program, as well as in-company programs for executives and an international full-time MBA. Today, the school has 7500 undergraduate and postgraduate students, 250 senior researchers, 100 PhD students and 10 research centers.

PHASE 1: THE START OF RESEARCH IN BUSINESS ETHICS AND PUBLIC MANAGEMENT

Since its establishment in 1984, RSM has acknowledged the importance of society. The school was founded by eight Dutch-based multinationals, including Shell, Philips and Unilever, to address what they perceived to be a lack of suitable training and higher educational facilities for managers in the Netherlands. From its inception, the school was therefore aware of its responsibility towards business and society. Its first mission statement not only stated that RSM 'creates, disseminates and applies managerial knowledge', but also that 'RSM is guided by the future needs of business' and that through teaching and research 'RSM aims to contribute to a well-functioning society'.

Since its foundation, the business-society dimension has featured prominently in the teaching programs offered at RSM. In its first graduate program, for example, each student had to draw up a business plan for a starting company (first year of program), participate in two one-week simulations in which they had to run a company in a complex social environment (second year), conduct an eight-month research assignment on behalf of a company to solve a current issue (third year), and do an internship for three months at a company and write a Master's thesis which was socially and managerially relevant (fourth and final year). Furthermore, there were several company visits and guest lectures given by prominent business people, politicians and representatives of NGOs as well as case teaching and practical assignments.

Although explicit attention was paid to the societal component in the teaching programs, attention to the societal component in research was more implicit in those early days. One of the school's assumptions of the school was that by attending to society in courses, teachers would be stimulated to do socially relevant research. And by also attracting teaching staff with business and managerial experience, the societal focus would be guaranteed in research.

There were, however, two exceptional and explicit attempts by the school to encourage research into socially relevant issues. First, in 1986 the school created a teaching and research position in business ethics, located at that time in the methodology department. One philosopher was appointed to begin with and tasked with the assignment of conducting research into what we can expect from companies and their management from a normative perspective. Second, in the same period, a professor was appointed to a chair in Public Management with the aim to teach but also to conduct research into the way governmental and not-for-profit organizations could be understood and managed. This public management position was located at another department, which was the Department of Change Management.

Both areas, business ethics and public management, grew during the years that followed. In the mid-1990s, four people were employed in the field of business ethics, along with four people in public management.

PHASE 2: THE ESTABLISHMENT OF THE DEPARTMENT IN BUSINESS-SOCIETY MANAGEMENT

One achievement in the first 10 years of the school was the growing number of staff conducting research in the field of B-SM. At the same time, research was fragmented across two different departments and not treated as a coherent field of teaching and research. Business ethics research was also largely normatively oriented – what companies should do from a moral perspective – and not positively oriented – how ethics contributes to the success and good functioning of companies. This led to business ethics being viewed as a separate, standalone discipline and not an intrinsic and integrated part of other teaching and research in, for example, strategy, finance and marketing. Research in public management at that time was far removed from the other research programs of the school. Its main focus was on governmental and not-for-profit organizations, whereas the rest of the school focused mainly on the business sector.

To better encourage – rigorous and relevant – research in the field of B-SM, the school decided in 1999 to establish a separate department for B-SM, as one of its seven departments. The purpose of founding a department for B-SM was to bring all the people working in this field together. The Department of Business-Society Management was created and composed of the ethics staff and the staff from public management. People working in the field of corporate communication, until then positioned in the strategic management department, joined the department as the interface between business and society depends on the quality of communication between business and society.

The aim of the Department of B-SM was not only to develop Bachelor and Master programs in this field. The objective was also to combine research in this field to define new research topics, to develop new concepts and models, and to conduct more research of a socially relevant nature. By concentrating all this in one department, contact and interaction between its members was stimulated. Research also became more manageable because resources could now be allocated specifically to this domain and performance could also be better monitored. Having a separate department in this field clearly signalled the importance of B-SM to the outside world and attracted more attention from businesses and society (e.g. the media), which also made it easier to obtain funding for research and to collaborate with other parties. This led to a new phase.

PHASE 3: THE GROWTH OF THE DEPARTMENT OF BUSINESS-SOCIETY MANAGEMENT

Since its establishment in 1999, the Department of B-SM had grown to comprise 25 staff members as of 2006. The department started to offer courses throughout the education program, from the Bachelor program to the executive program. For example, the Bachelor course in business ethics was transformed into the course in business-society management and the number of lectures doubled. The department also introduced its own B-SM Master program. Since its start-up phase, the program has been attended by at least 60 national and international students each year.

New chairs were also created between 2000 and 2005 in the field of (1) international business-society management; (2) corporate sustainability; (3) business ethics and integrity management; and (4) volunteering, civil society and business. The number of PhD students in B-SM, along with the number of publications, increased steadily. Research by Chang, Fung and Yau (2009) shows that the school scored the best amongst all European universities with the most papers published in business ethics journals within the last 10 years and second amongst all universities worldwide (only the University of Pennsylvania performed better).

Aside from conducting rigorous research, another reason for establishing the department was to conduct research commissioned by or in cooperation with the business sector. To facilitate this objective, in 2001 the board of RSM funded the development of three research centers located at the B-SM department. These centers were in the field of international business-society management (SCOPE), business ethics (Ethicon), and communication (Corporate Communication Centre). To give some examples of the results: the corporate communication center developed an instrument to measure the reputation of an organization, which has since been purchased by many companies and which has helped the center to build up its database for academic research; SCOPE created a database of the societal strategies of the 200 largest companies in the world leading to multiple publications; and Ethicon worked closely with the Dutch employer association VNO-NCW, resulting in multiple booklets for managers on how to improve business ethics in practice, as well as with the advisory firm KPMG to create a database of business codes of ethics.

Efforts by the school to concentrate and intensify the research in B-SM were not in vain, as indicated by the results of the Aspen Institute's Beyond Grey Pinstripes ranking in 2005. The study showed that RSM was ranked 16th in the world of business schools and third in Europe with respect to teaching and research in B-SM.

PHASE 4: THE INTEGRATION OF B-SM RESEARCH INTO OTHER RESEARCH

Having a well-functioning department of B-SM in 2005 – in teaching and research as well as visibility in society – the question arose of how to integrate B-SM research into other traditional research areas. Socially relevant research should not be conducted solely by scholars specialized in the field of business and society, it is a responsibility of and a challenge to all scholars in the field of business and management. But how was this to be achieved? And how did RSM rise to this challenge?

Different, mutually reinforcing, processes were implemented. As in the preceding three phases, it was believed that cooperation in teaching would be a fruitful basis for researchers to interact with others, to recognize the relevance of others' research to one's own research, and to start conducting research together and develop new insights. On the one hand, the B-SM department started to offer courses outside its own area but still strongly related to B-SM, for example in the field of corporate governance, leadership, management skills, stakeholder management and institutions. On the other hand, it also started to teach courses together with other departments, for example in the field of corporate law, macroeconomics and intercultural management.

Next to integrated teaching, professors were appointed within the B-SM department with the explicit mission to work not only within the borders of B-SM, but also in close cooperation with other departments of the business school or even with other schools at the university and other universities. For example, in 2008 a professor was appointed in the field of 'corporate governance and normative responsibility' with the brief to work closely with researchers in the field of corporate governance in the Finance department. In 2005 a professor was appointed in the field of transition management, someone who holds a dual position at the B-SM department and the School of Sociology at Erasmus University, with the aim of studying the relationship between corporate and social sustainability. And in 2009 a professor was appointed to the B-SM department who also holds a position at the Duisenberg School of Finance, an academic research center in Amsterdam, in the field of Globalization, Sustainability and Finance.

Next to integrated teaching and dual appointments, RSM also decided to establish research centers in which people from different departments and schools could participate in order to further integrate the societal dimension within traditional research areas. The Erasmus Centre of Behavioural Ethics was founded in 2009 and it draws together researchers not only from the B-SM department, but also researchers in organizational and social psychology, and from other departments, schools and universities. The Erasmus Centre for Strategic Philanthropy, also founded in 2009, is a cooperation between the B-SM department and the Erasmus School of Economics (financed by a multimillion-pound grant from an entrepreneur). And, to give another example, the Erasmus Institute of Supervision and Compliance was founded in 2007, where researchers from RSM – and also B-SM – are carrying out research together with researchers from the Schools of Law and Economics in the field of the compliance of companies and its relationship with internal and external supervision.

Next to these new centers, more flexible, less institutionalized initiatives were also promoted during this fourth phase of integrating B-SM into other research fields. In 2008, a platform was created in the field of climate change. Led by a member of the B-SM department, people from different departments of RSM who are doing research into climate change are involved (e.g. staff from the department of logistics as well as strategy). On such a platform, people share their research, present research ideas and papers, and collaborate. The school has supported this platform through, among other things, the provision of technical assistance to develop and maintain a website, research assistance for combined research, and covering the costs of presentations from researchers from other universities.

RSM's efforts during this fourth phase yielded fruitful results. One of them was the rise in the rankings in the Aspen Institute's Beyond Grey Pinstripes report. From being ranked 16th in 2005, and 15th in 2007, RSM was ranked 7th globally and 1st in Europe in 2009 (for a combined ranking based on research, teaching and institutional support).

WHAT NEXT?

We can conclude that today at RSM the societal component is thoroughly acknowledged and included in research. This has been achieved via different phases – from specialization to concentration and intensification, and now integration. The degree to which RSM has succeeded cannot only be attributed to attracting the right scholars. It has also required the right conditions, conditions that motivate and stimulate scholars to work together and across disciplines. At RSM, such conditions have been created through, among others, the inclusion of criteria of cooperation in job descriptions, rewarding researchers who work together with other disciplines, and establishing an infrastructure which promotes learning and interactions among scholars.

One way in which RSM stimulates the societal orientation of research is by allocating financial resources to centers on the condition that these are matched with contributions from business and other societal players. This stimulates staff to consider current and anticipate future societal issues and needs and to translate and address them in research programs. It also stimulates staff to establish contact with practitioners. Some recent initiatives are quite successful in this respect. Together with other universities and societal actors, like employer and employee associations, RSM founded the Centre for Social Innovation, which gained extensive funding. And, in 2010, RSM was commissioned by the Dutch Ministry of Development Cooperation to establish alliances between non-profit organizations that were active in providing aid to developing countries.

Also of importance is that the school, led by the dean (who is one of the authors of this chapter), uses every opportunity available to emphasize that it exists only by virtue of the resources and opportunities society grants it. In the end, RSM can only survive if this investment by society yields meaningful returns. It is a privilege to do research on behalf of society but it also places a responsibility on researchers to create added value and to meet the needs of business and society. In this manner, RSM further stimulates the importance of the social dimension among its staff, the aim being not only that they conduct research into socially relevant issues such as environmental strategy or the marketing of environmentally friendly products, but also that their entire research output and the discipline within which they are working are socially relevant.

We do not want to suggest that the 'RSM way' is the only way to integrate business and society research into a business school. Nor do we want to suggest that RSM does not face problems and challenges in this regard. One of the problems that it faces is how financial revenues for externally-funded research activities should be distributed among involved staff. What is a fair reward and good incentive for staff to do externally funded research and other externally paid activities but without this becoming mere consultancy and without discouraging staff who primarily conduct fundamental research?

The biggest challenge is not only to develop new theories that do not simply add the perspectives from B-SM to the more traditional research fields, but also to integrate these perspectives and to develop completely different, rigor theories. While we do not have all the answers, we do feel that this way of integrating B-SM can and will make the difference.

Neither do we know what it will mean to have a separate department in B-SM. Perhaps we can do without it once the B-SM perspective is fully integrated into the other disciplines. But for the foreseeable future – in order to ensure the integration of the B-SM perspective and to expose researchers to new and in-depth knowledge of B-SM – we still need dedicated specialists from a dedicated, specialized department in B-SM.

CONCLUSION

The central idea of this book and also of this chapter is to discuss how business schools can make a positive contribution to society. As described in this chapter, a central dilemma for business schools is how to achieve both rigor and relevance in research. The unique position of business schools seems to have generated extreme angst about this dilemma. We have advocated in this chapter that to achieve both rigor and relevant research, dual research methodologies are needed.

To illustrate our argument, we have presented in this chapter the way in which RSM has dealt with this dilemma. In four phases, RSM has built up a position in business-society management which is regarded as the best in Europe and seventh in the world. Rigorous research was achieved by first investing in new research positions in the field of B-SM, then by combining resources in one B-SM department and expanding this department, and consequently integrating B-SM research with other research through, for example, close cooperation with other departments, schools and universities.

Relevant research was achieved through the objective of the B-SM research itself (i.e. the interface between business and society) and also through the way in which research is conducted. Businesses are involved in research projects not just by funding research, but also by defining the research agenda, providing data and, for example, allowing their best staff to do part-time research at RSM. But this also works the other way round: RSM is involved more in practice, by listening carefully to the research needs of businesses, doing research together with practitioners and, for example, allowing academic staff to work part-time in the business sector.

Dual research methodologies are, we believe, the way forward. To dispel the angst, we at RSM have described the dilemma of rigor and relevance as a dilemma at the level of research programs and not at the level of individual researchers or individual research publications. What we mean is that we do not expect an individual researcher to completely serve both worlds. It is more realistic to have a team of researchers who have complementary research capabilities and who are able to serve both worlds together. In that sense we do not search for the ideal type of researcher, but for the ideal type of research team.

The same applies to research output. We do not expect one research publication to fully serve both worlds. But the output of a research program should certainly serve both worlds, not just through papers published in top academic journals, but also through the publication of opinion articles in newspapers, press releases and press reports, popular books, and White Papers for practitioners.

In this sense, we strongly believe that the rigor and relevance of research can mutually reinforce one other. This does not *support* the legitimacy of business schools: it *is* the legitimacy of business schools. At least it is so for those of us at RSM. And at RSM we therefore apply a simple principle: no relevant research without rigor and no rigorous research without relevance.

NOTE

1. The UK's *Financial Times* provides several rankings of business schools' teaching programs, such as the MBA and the MSc, and within those statistics also provides a ranking of research based on an admittedly limited set of 40 journals selected by the FT. There is a moderate correlation between program and research rankings, with most schools within +/- 10 or +/-20 ranks on the two criteria. Casual inspection of the top 100 list for either the MBA rankings or the research rankings will confirm that the faculty of these schools are driven first by research and only second by teaching.

REFERENCES

Bain, J.S. (1956) *Barriers to New Competition.* Cambridge, MA: Harvard University Press.

Bennis, W.G. and O'Toole, J. (2005) 'How Business Schools Lost Their Way', *Harvard Business Review*, 83(5): 96–104.

Caves, R.E. (1980) 'Industrial Organization, Corporate Strategy and Structure', *Journal of Economic Literature*, 18(1): 64–92.

Chang, K.C., Fung, H.G. and Yau, J. (2009) 'Business Ethics Research: A Global Perspective', *Journal of Business Ethics*, published online.

Delbridge, R., Gratton, L., Johnson, G. et al. (2006) *The Exceptional Manager.* Oxford: Oxford University Press.

Eisenhardt, K. (1989) 'Building Theories from Case Study Research', *The Academy of Management Review*, 14(4): 532–50.

Etzkowitz, H. and Leydesdorff, L. (2000) 'The Dynamics of Innovation: From National Systems and "Mode 2" to a Triple Helix of University–Industry–Government Relations', *Research Policy*, 29(2): 109–23.

Gibbons, M., Limoges, C., Nowotny, H., Schwartzman, S., Scott, P. and Trow, M. (1994) *The New Production of Knowledge: The Dynamics of Science and Research in Contemporary Societies.* London: Sage.

Kilduff, M. and Kelemen, M. (2001) 'The Consolations of Organization Theory 2001', *British Journal of Management*, 12 (Special Issue): S55–9.

Moran, P. and Ghoshal, S. (1999) 'Markets, Firms and the Process of Economic Development', *Academy of Management Review*, 24(3): 390–412.

Pettigrew, A.M. (2001) 'Management Research after Modernism', *British Journal of Management*, 12 (Special Issue): S61–70.

Pfeffer, J. (2007) 'A Modest Proposal: How We Might Change the Process and Product of Managerial Research', *Academy of Management Journal*, 50(6): 1334–45.

Porter, M.E. (1976) *Interbrand Choice, Strategy, and Bilateral Market Power.* Boston, MA: Harvard University Press.

Porter, M.E. (1980) *Competitive Strategy: Techniques for Analyzing Industries and Competitors.* New York: Free Press.

Van Maanen, J. (1979) 'The Fact of Fiction in Organizational Ethnography', *Administrative Science Quarterly*, 24 (4): 539–559.

Wensley, R. (2007) 'Beyond Rigour and Relevance: The Underlying Nature of both Business Schools and Management Research', AIM Research Working Paper Series, No. 051, January. AIM Research, Warwick, England.

13 BUSINESS SCHOOLS' CORPORATE SOCIAL RESPONSIBILITY: PRACTICE WHAT YOU PREACH

Christoph Badelt and Barbara Sporn

Vienna University of Economics and Business, Austria

Economic growth and societal well-being are strongly related to a high degree of education in any society. Businesses play an important role in society as they are engines for innovation and entrepreneurship as well as necessary prerequisites for stable employment. At the same time, the fiscal and global economic crisis has revealed that some principles for successful business behavior have often been ignored. These include the consequence of actions on a global scale, the broader view on society *vis-à-vis* businesses, ethical and sustainable behavior, a systemic analysis of actions including social and environmental consequences, and institutional efficiency. Certainly, they have relevance for business schools as well.

Based on this, the key message of this chapter is that business schools not only have to teach but also live the principles outlined above. Students, faculty and external stakeholders should be able to clearly experience an ethical and sustainable view of the world. In order to illustrate what a modern, socially responsible and credible business school should look like, we consider the case of Austria and WU (Vienna University of Economics and Business). Therefore, the key hypothesis is that business schools have to behave 'entrepreneurially', referring to models of entrepreneurs in the history of economic thought (e.g. Schumpeter 1963) as well as to the recent debate on entrepreneurial universities.

Austria and WU are well-taken cases in point as they are able to illustrate some key messages. First, it is important to keep in mind that the context is one of a public system with many restrictions and legal regulations. Austrian universities – like WU – are thus subject to some coercive steering mechanisms. Second, responses to these specific pressures require a high degree of entrepreneurship in order to be successful. And, third, the means of management will differ when looking at private and commercially independent versus public and budget constrainted colleges and universities. The contribution of this chapter then should be that entrepreneurship under difficult circumstances can be sustainable, ethical and successful as result of applying academic teaching standards to university management practice.

AUSTRIA'S HIGHER EDUCATION MARKET AND WU'S LEGITIMACY

Austria is a somewhat unique market for higher education. In general, institutions are mostly publicly financed with some exceptions in the form of small private colleges and universities. Most importantly, Austria runs an open access and no tuition policy for universities only, i.e. students with a high school diploma can freely enter most academic programs of their choice (the few exceptions include medicine and psychology). As a consequence, in areas of free student admission, Austrian universities tend to be very large in terms of student numbers. In those fields, they have to deal with the problems of mass higher education, e.g. high drop-out rates, lengthy degrees, unfavorable student–faculty ratios. Business Education is one of the fields suffering from these problems.

WU is the second largest Austrian university as well as the largest university of economics and business in Austria and in the European Union. WU programs focus on business and management, as well as on social and economic sciences, with additional expertise in business law, languages and formal sciences. WU's size gives the university a strong market position, specifically nationally but also internationally. Its reputation spans from the business world to the international scientific community in the areas of management, business law and economics. In Austria, WU is the prime partner for companies in hiring graduates and for international programs. Given its unique position of being a very large business university (with approximately 27,000 students) in a relatively small country (with a population of approximately 8 million), WU trains approximately 50 per cent of Austrian business managers and experts. Consequently, many CEOs in Austria are WU graduates.

As a consequence, WU is highly relevant for the Austrian labor market with its strong market position. Its reputation extends across the border to neighboring regions where Austrian companies are highly active like the Czech Republic, Slovakia or Romania. International responsibility stems from the fact that most WU graduates have international experience and want to pursue an international career.

Austrian policy makers have understood that universities a only be competitive if could far-reaching institutional autonomy was established. A law was passed by Parliament in 2002 which guaranteed autonomy in programmatic, financial, organizational and personnel matters. In a nutshell, Austrian universities are free to design their own academic programs, to receive a lump-sum budget, to define their structure and process independently, and to hire staff at their own will and at individual contract levels. Especially when compared to German universities, the high degree of institutional autonomy has put Austrian universities at a relative competitive advantage and in many cases this has led to a rise in entrepreneurial behavior.

Contrary to the institutional level, and because of their public character, Austrian universities are facing severe restrictions on the policy front. Legal frameworks, as well as ministries and policy makers, have a strong influence on pathways for the development of universities. The cornerstones of these restrictions are regulations regarding admission and tuition fees. On top of these are budgetary constraints which hinder growth and development. For many years, Austrian universities have been systematically underfunded to meet the expectations of top-class universities.

Students at Austrian universities do not pay any tuition fees except when their study period is extended or they come from non-EU countries. Apart from that, students with a secondary school diploma have the right to enroll at any university and in most academic fields of their choice without tests or selection. These policies have led to an enormous expansion in student numbers and created a phenomenon of mass higher education in certain fields like business administration, i.e. resources and staff are often insufficient in proportion to the amount of enrolled students. This situation is slightly mitigated by the fact that, today, universities are allowed to regulate the access to programs on the Master and PhD levels, provided the program is taught completely in a foreign language. This enables WU to set up admission procedures for all English programs – the programs with which WU is most directly exposed to international competition.

Concerning WU's legitimacy on an international scale, internationalization means more than mobility. WU sees itself as part of the European Higher Education arena, and therefore has thoroughly implemented the Bologna architecture with comparable Bachelor, Master and PhD degrees. Programs are designed to guarantee both employability in the labor market and international experience. In this sense, WU aims to provide opportunities for its students and to act responsibly.

At the same time, WU's responsibility and commitment to internationalization is in clear contrast to society and its expectations which has created tensions as well as several management challenges. The commitment to WU's public mission has been challenged by the fact that student numbers have skyrocketed and have thereby created a totally unacceptable student–faculty ratio and drop-out rates. WU's wish to also provide top quality in an internationally competitive environment has been jeopardized by the fact that internally compatible policies have not been put in place. WU is still acting responsibly and was able to establish its international reputation through clear and visible indicators, namely accreditation and rankings. WU was the first large public university of business in a German-speaking area to be EQUIS accredited. Its Executive Academy has also been AMBA accredited. Consequently, WU's programs have been well ranked. The *Finanical Times* puts its Master in Management at 24th (out of 65) and its EMBA at 52nd (out of 100). Both students and faculty at WU profit from a solid reputation.

As has been outlined above, WU is in a complex environment with divergent expectations. In order to meet these challenges successfully, it has committed itself to the idea of being an entrepreneurial university, thereby identifying opportunities quickly and in this way improving the institution's position. Within this, WU has started an organizational development process which focuses on creating efficient and effective new structures and innovative, state-of-the-art academic programs. The guiding principles accompanying the process include output orientation, efficiency and innovation, service orientation, a spirit of competition, and the will to develop strategies in a constructive institutional climate. The underlying values in the process have been sustainability and social responsibility.

BUSINESS UNIVERSITIES AS ENTREPRENEURS – THE CASE OF WU

Successful business schools have to practice what they preach. This is particularly true for the concept of 'entrepreneurship'. Other than much of the course material which applies purely to cognitive knowledge, entrepreneurship represents an attitude, i.e. successfully turning opportunity into action. Pursuing this goal does not imply a naïve tendency to 'commercialize' universities (see for example, Sporn 1999; Rhoades and Sporn 2002; Badelt 2004: 25), although tendencies can be observed and have been criticized (for example, Bok 2003). As was mentioned in the introduction to this chapter, the use of entrepreneurial behavior is especially relevant for public universities which have to serve society as a whole under difficult circumstances. The interchangeable use of the concepts of entrepreneurialism and commercialization may be one of the reasons why in everyday usage 'the term entrepreneur can have a positive as well as a decidedly negative semantic aura' (Mautner 2005: 112).

In colloquial use, entrepreneurial actions are identified as having a profit orientation. Thus, entrepreneurship seems to be entirely based on economic values and it is claimed that those who promote entrepreneurship are simply believers in profit-making and 'tough' management. Yet it should not be ignored that entrepreneurial theories have some very useful instruments to offer, such as the search for new opportunities and innovation, the orientation towards necessary change, or the will to provide socially relevant products and services. It would be helpful if a more differentiated discussion on this topic would dominate the discourse.

For this chapter, the meaning of the 'entrepreneurial university' can best be understood if one of the key sources of entrepreneurship in literature is considered: Schumpeter's 'Theory of Economic Development' (Schumpeter 1963). According to Schumpeter, entrepreneurship is characterized by certain attitudes of individuals. Entrepreneurs are those individuals whose function is 'to carry out new combinations of means of production' (p. 74) – which is seen as the 'fundamental phenomenon of economic development'. In our current language, this simply means that an entrepreneur is characterized by their ability and willingness to be 'innovative'.

The innovative power of an entrepreneur may refer to the production of a 'new' product or service, to a new qualitative dimension of service which has been produced before, to the introduction of new means of production, or to a change within an organization or organizational structure (pp. 81–94). Therefore, it is no coincidence that the more recent literature even defines 'entrepreneurial universities' by the innovative power of a university (see, for example, Clark 1998, 2004; Mautner 2010: 85–96) or views entrepreneurial governance structures as one of the key elements to becoming a 'world-class university' (Salmi 2009: 26–31). Other sources describe the 'entrepreneurial university' by the attitude of decision makers towards taking risks or being ready for change (see, for example, Barnett 2003).

If universities and business schools wish to practice what they preach, they need to apply this in a twofold fashion, i.e. through institutional functioning as well as research and teaching. Many of the following principles have often been ignored in the past. Also, they especially revolve around the notion of sustainability and corporate social responsibility. WU can serve as an example to illustrate this.

First, given the pivotal role of universities in society, business schools have to be the center and driving force for innovation through their research and academic programs. They should assist in developing and applying technological innovations and they should also be centers for social innovation, at least in the area of higher education and research (see also Lorange 2008: 83–9). To give a few examples, business schools must be the first to adopt new learning strategies, socially relevant content and state-of-the-art learning technologies; they should be and have been the frontrunners in the change process to internationalize their educational programs, for example – in Europe – by implementing the Bologna system (i.e. the three-tier study architecture) and also by setting up truly international degree programs or international research networks.

WU has fulfilled this task within its Austrian environment: through its active role in the CEMS program, through its pioneering role in the implementation of Bologna, through its E-learning system, and also by setting standards *vis-à-vis* outside stakeholders: for example, WU set up a career center at a time when job placement in Austria was officially a monopoly of the state and when literally no other university in the country was even thinking of setting up an institution of this kind. WU also built up an alumni network much earlier than most universities in the German-speaking area.

At the same time, WU has established different programs, hired faculty and built departments focusing on sustainability and social responsibility. On the one hand, WU is home to a newly created department of socio-economics which looks at the practical implication of economic behavior in the context of society as a whole. Topics covering sustainable development, environmental economics, ageing, social policy and urban planning are among its focus areas; and the highly renowned Wittgenstein Center for Demography and Global Human Capital has been awarded to a WU professor by the Austrian Science Fund.

On the other hand, WU programs also engage students and faculty in socially important projects, e.g. the volunteering program enables students to help disadvantaged youth groups. The speaker series 'open minds' creates a platform for a very critical discourse on relevant topics such as the financial crisis or Darwinism in the economy.

Second, given the challenges of a globalized world, business schools have to practice and teach global thinking, i.e. the worldwide effects of behavior have to be considered. At WU, this is reflected not only in regular course programs, for example by including courses on economic behavior and society in the introductory year of all Bachelor programs, but also, as mentioned earlier, through various specializations at Master level – for example, in matters of sustainability, the role of nonprofit enterprises, the long-term implications of demographic changes or issues in developing countries. Third, in their internal administrative procedures, business schools have to combine traditional 'rationality' with so-called 'soft skills'. Thus, decisions are made on a truly rational basis but also reflect a deeper understanding of the social relationships which need to be understood if decisions within organizations are to be influenced or improved. WU has again implemented this principle (and in this way practices what it preaches) in the way that change processes have been orchestrated and managed at the university. When WU switched to full institutional autonomy in 2002, it became necessary to change the complete organizational structure. A broad change process was set up involving most faculty members and a significant portion of administrative staff. As a result, WU's strategy and structure were decided based on a consensus by key 'players' inside the organization. Formal decision bodies like the Rector's

Council, the University Board and the Senate then followed those recommendations from the larger group and made decisions in a legal sense.

Fourth, a business school has to implement internal efficiency in order to be a legitimate institution that is educating future business leaders (i.e. to practice what it preaches). It is obvious that measures of efficiency have to be different from those of commercial enterprises, because of the complexity of measuring the output of a university. While output measures are not always easily defined, this should not be taken as an excuse not to work on indicators of performance, to discuss them internally and to finally use them for reporting or as a means of accountability *vis-à-vis* external stakeholders (e.g. the business world, the state, the taxpayer). At WU this has been done, for example, through a comprehensive system of course evaluations, regular research evaluations of departments and the provision of 'activity reports' for each faculty member annually describing their research output, contributions in teaching, participation in WU's self-governing bodies and services to the community.

FUTURE CHALLENGES

Both the national institutional environment and the challenges following on from globalization define the agenda for the future work of business schools. If corporate social responsibility and sustainability are to be taken seriously, business schools have to find answers to a number of questions where innovative solutions are necessary. In most cases, new forms of compromise are needed in matters which – at first sight – seem to be tradeoffs. Three examples demonstrate the case in point: responsible business management; a sustainable model for business schools; and a redefined public mission.

First, business schools have to be able to show their students as well as the general public how short-term business interests can be combined with sustainability for society. It is expected that businesses will analyze the external effects of their decisions on society, both regarding the physical environment and social implications. Accordingly, assessment and evaluations should be part of the standard decision-making procedures of management. This implies that businesses should be pursuing profit maximization goals but at the same time calculating the true costs of their actions. It should be a prerequisite that business managers understand the implications of their actions on employment, poverty, social tensions, etc. Business schools have to apply the same principles to their decisions as well, for example in admission policies and in their support for underprivileged students, and also when designing their educational programs. These programs have to enable future decision makers to integrate analyses of that kind in their everyday work life. If business schools succeed in doing so, sustainable and socially responsible offerings will evolve.

Second, a sustainable model for business schools in society is necessary. Schools should define themselves as truly academic institutions and not just as training sites for the short-term interests of businesses. Business schools in Europe have learned to deal with this tension, especially in the process of implementing the Bologna reforms. In practice, business schools have been challenged by designing curricula which will lead to the employability of graduates and still provide a broad academic education. In the last few months in several European countries, remarkable student protests against the Bologna reforms have illustrated that schools may have sacrificed many elements of a broad academic education.

Curricula were criticized for being too narrow, providing too few choices and forcing students too much into structures in which they found themselves only serving business interests instead of having a fair chance of personal intellectual development. In order to develop a sustainable model, universities and colleges of business have to refocus on their core function of contributing to the creation and dissemination of knowledge.

A third kind of challenge affects public business schools in Europe, especially those which operate under strict legal restrictions regarding admission policies and tuition matters. These schools have to find ways to provide top-quality research and education given large student numbers, tight budgets, limited space and unfavorable student–faculty ratios. In order to be socially responsible and sustainable, these schools have to find ways to manage different expectations and limitations successfully, e.g. through the application of entrepreneurialism in their functioning.

WU has reacted to these challenges by creating a new organizational structure based on their strategy to become a leading business university in Europe. This structure differentiates between different markets, programs and stakeholders: undergraduate school; graduate school; research centers; executive academy. Bachelor programs are organized for large cohorts, employing modern E-learning technology and working with tutors and student support services tailored for large class sizes. With this, WU serves its public function and the political goal of 'mass education'. At the same time, the portfolio of Master's and doctoral programs is designed around the school's strengths in research, thus attracting excellent students from all over the world. WU's executive academy acts as a separate 'profit center' which complements the school's academic profile. The academy offers MBA programs in WU's core fields, and also engages in in-house training for corporations, thus creating revenue by engaging in commercial activities. Last but not least, WU's research centers demonstrate the university's expertise in scholarship in interdisciplinary and issue-based matters. Both companies and society at large profit through the many findings. As the WU case shows, this model could be a sustainable way for business schools to move forward in a very volatile environment.

The social responsibility of business schools is an important topic to consider. It involves questions about sustainability and the role of these institutions in society. This chapter has tried to illustrate how the notion of an entrepreneurial university can help to implement some important changes. Of course, adopting the idea of an entrepreneurial university is not sufficient to completely manage the challenges of the business school, although it is difficult to consider any challenges where the attitude of entrepreneurship would not be helpful. Hence, it is a possible basis on which to truly demonstrate that business schools can actually practice what they preach.

REFERENCES

Badelt, C. (2004) *Die unternehmerische Universität: Herausforderung oder Widerspruch in sich?* Wien: Picus.

Barnett, R. (2003) *Beyond All Reason: Living with Ideology in the University.* Buckingham: Open University Press.

Bok, D. (2003) *Universities in the Marketplace.* Princeton, NJ: Princeton University Press.

Clark, B.R. (1998) *Creating Entrepreneurial Universities: Organizational Pathways of Transformation.* Oxford: Pergamon.

Clark, B.R. (2004) 'Delineating the Character of the Entrepreneurial University', *Higher Education Policy* 17(4): 355–70.

Lorange, P. (2008) *Thought Leadership Meets Business.* Cambridge: Cambridge University Press.

Mautner, G. (2005) 'The Entrepreneurial University', *Critical Discourse Studies*, 2(2): 95–120.

Mautner, G. (2010) *Language and the Market Society.* New York: Routledge.

Rhoades, G. and Sporn, B. (2002) 'New Models of Management and Shifting Modes and Costs of Production: Europe and the USA', *Tertiary Education and Management*, 8(1): 3–28.

Salmi, J. (2009) *The Challenge of Establishing World-class Universities.* Washington, DC: The World Bank.

Schumpeter, J.A. (1963 [1934]) *The Theory of Economic Development.* New York: Oxford University Press.

Sporn, B. (1999) *Adaptive University Structures: An Analysis of Adaption to Socioeconomic Environments of US and European Universities.* London: Jessica Kingsley.

14 THE ROLE OF HIGHER EDUCATION INSTITUTIONS IN THE FIELDS OF ECONOMIC AND SOCIAL SCIENCES: HAS IT BEEN CHANGED BY THE ECONOMIC DOWNTURN?

Guido Tabellini

Bocconi University, Italy

At this time, it is certainly important to participate in the global debate on the role of higher education institutions in society and to understand whether and how this has changed in connection with the economic crisis.

I strongly believe that the role of business schools and academic institutions in the fields of economic and social sciences in fostering human progress is not fully appreciated. In approaching such a debate we should proudly support our conduct and, simultaneously, avoid an apologetic approach.

BUSINESS SCHOOLS AND GLOBALIZATION

In recent years, the world has become much smaller due to the process of globalization. The progress made in information technologies, the spread of the internet, the lower costs of transportation and increased mobility have reduced distances at all levels. Globalization has reduced differences, has opened up the path towards development for a number of countries, and has helped to increase consumer benefits. Hence, it should be regarded as a positive factor within the process that has allowed us to fill such a gap and that has led to the substantial enrichment of those areas of the world that were once primarily facing poverty and few opportunities.

Both modern corporations and business schools have been drivers in fostering globalization, to be seen also as a direct result of the thinking patterns, the decision-making processes and the values taught and embedded in both the business scenarios and the education arena. As a representative of the latter, I think we should be proud of what we have contributed.

As it is for corporations, globalization is both a threat and an opportunity for business schools: a threat because it has embittered competition and an opportunity as the markets have widened, with the possibility of attracting talent from all over the world. To grasp such opportunities without the risk of being overwhelmed, we must ensure academic excellence.

In the field of economic and social sciences, which business schools belong to, excellence and progress are more difficult to measure than in the natural sciences. However, if we manage to shift the frontier of knowledge the return will be much higher than the mere spreading of already existing and familiar concepts.

I believe that the importance of my last remark is not always fully appreciated in the higher education scenario. We are often accustomed to believing that progress in the natural sciences and technology is the key driver of welfare. We think that discoveries in medicine, biology, physics, IT and in the field of energy (to name but a few) are the only possible means to contribute to and ensure a brighter future for mankind.

But it is not as simple as that. The role of economics and the social sciences is just as important in fostering human progress and must – in my opinion – be better appreciated. The capacity to organize groups into open and democratic societies, a respect for civil and human rights, and an understanding of how to run liberal economies are really fundamental. In the global economy, technology is not the scarcest resource. The poorest countries can often rely on state-of-the-art technologies but this does not necessarily mean that they will thrive. Their economic welfare, their political institutions and their ability to function as organized societies are often very weak and place them far behind their richer counterparts. What is often lacking is the presence of those institutions – both formal and informal – which will allow people to interact peacefully and contribute to the general welfare of the population.

What has led to the proliferation of these institutions was not only the gradual development of cultural habits and traditions. The predominant role was played by the spread of knowledge and values through the theories and concepts elaborated by economic and social scientists. And these values and theories have been intensively promulgated by universities that were independent of the ruling political powers. The possibility of progressing in modern societies very much lies within this heritage of values and knowledge and in its spreading within the community. It is, hence, also because of the role of economic and social higher education institutions that we now have thriving market economies based on a respect for laws, duties and rights.

In addition, in the most developed countries, the conservation of welfare is linked to the proper functioning of economic and political institutions. In these markets, the progress brought in by the social sciences is key to the success of institutions, to their evolution and adaptability to evolving circumstances.

The recent trends in economic and social sciences reinforce these remarks. In the evolution of sociology, the political sciences, managerial studies, economics and law (and so forth) empirical analysis and research has a very relevant role. There is a strong focus on the study of the behaviors of key decision makers (whether these are families, individuals, corporations, governments) and on their interactions. This evolution was of course made possible thanks to the proliferation of IT instruments that have made the gathering of behavioral data easier.

Today, good practices in the field of research are those with a close connection to the most relevant issues for society as a whole and those which guide key players in the real world. This is particularly true as far as political economics is concerned. In free modern economies, reforms are successful if these are implemented step by step and based on empirical analysis. For this reason, good economic research is preparatory for good economic policies.

Hence, educators and researchers in the field of economics and social sciences have had and will continue to have a huge impact on the world around them.

THE NEW CHALLENGES RAISED BY THE GLOBAL FINANCIAL CRISIS

Several publications and press articles have thoroughly discussed the threat brought to bear on the globalization wave by the recent economic downturn. Many have also asserted that such a crisis may be considered an outcome of modern and global capitalism.

I do believe though that not only is globalization not the cause of the crisis but also that such a slump will further accelerate the tendency towards a more open economy. Those countries fostering the paradigm of a global capitalism will develop at an increased pace. Hence, the lesson learnt from the downturn is that, unless major policy mistakes are made, the crisis will contribute to speeding up globalization processes even further.

If anything, the crisis has hurt the advanced world much more than emerging markets, and as a result the process of economic convergence will accelerate even more. Moreover, it is becoming increasingly evident that solutions to the global economic downturn can no longer be sought and implemented only at a local or regional level.

The first major challenge raised by the global financial crisis is no doubt the urgency to govern globalization through the implementation of supranational and intergovernmental institutions. With the shifting and broadening of global boundaries, entities such as the EU, WTO and IMF will need to play a different and more effective role.

Even though we in Europe are geographically distant from Asia – the continent which has been most impacted by globalization – many of our business schools lie in the heart of Europe, the area where most of the active international organizations have either flourished or been created. In respect of their traditions, technical competencies, perspectives and operational experiences, top EU schools are at the forefront in studying the challenges of European integration. Very often, we are also able to affect its evolution. In other words, many of our business schools may have a comparative advantage in generating ideas that might contribute to the solution of these global problems.

The recent financial crisis has also produced a combination of more technical and specific challenges concerning financial markets and institutions. They have to undertake both with financial market regulation systems and with the internal management systems/incentives of major banking/financial players. These challenges are now being addressed by governments and regulators throughout the advanced world. We have yet to see whether and how the new financial regulations and the reformed supervisory institutions will transform global financial markets. I strongly believe, however, that these difficulties will by no means undermine the principles upon which we have all encouraged and sustained globalization.

WHAT ARE THE MAIN PRIORITIES FOR BUSINESS SCHOOLS?

The first priority rests in what we are about to teach, in the academic contents we deliver.

To do this properly, we should draw on what the internationalization process has contributed. I expect to see – in the years to come – a progressive fall in disciplinary barriers. The emphasis on the empirical behavioral research of single units (individuals, families, corporations, etc.) has accelerated the convergence of different disciplines. This has happened because most of the methods of statistical analysis are common and also because it is evident that in order to understand the complexity behind social interaction an interdisciplinary approach is needed. The borderline dividing economic analysis, sociology, history, corporate and civil laws, political analysis and demography is fading. The most significant scientific contributions that are shifting the frontiers of knowledge are those that manage to exploit the ideas and intuitions coming from more than one discipline.

This trend will accelerate in the future. Business schools will be urged to teach how to manage extremely complex organizations. To do so, they will have to draw on a variety of disciplines – sometimes beyond the economic and social sciences – including psychology and other sciences.

The ultimate goal of research is not only to accumulate and create knowledge. It is equally important to convey such knowledge to younger generations, thus accomplishing our aim of being good educators. There is no contradiction between the goal of improving research activities, of giving them international visibility, and the goal of enhancing the quality of teaching. Conversely, these objectives are complementary – not only because research is a prerequisite to having international visibility and thus attracting talent, but also because good teaching implies the ability to deliver in class the most updated concepts and the ultimate results of research.

However, we need to transfer general knowledge and not only what can be applied in a particular context or in a particular timeframe. Good teaching methods must also focus on the learning process and not only on notions. Individual analytical skills, critical thought, active participation, curiosity and originality must be fostered. This can be better achieved if professors themselves are personally involved in and committed to moving beyond the frontiers of knowledge.

In this respect, a good example was produced in *The Economist* (29 July 2010, 'A post-crisis case study') about Harvard Business School (HBS), the apex of a vast global industry devoted to teaching business. After developing the 'case method' over decades – using case studies to teach students about real-world business problems and claiming to be the source of four-fifths of the case-study materials used in the world's leading business schools – it now faces radical innovations.

This is because of the lessons learnt from recent years that have been rocked by various crises, from Enron to the financial meltdown. On 1 July 2010, the new dean, Nitin Nohria, the first ever to have been born outside of the USA, took charge, promising a period of extraordinary innovation that would be able to restore faith in business in general and in business schools in particular, by improving 'competence' and 'character'. His primary goals are to draw faculty attention towards the analysis of the risks of smart financial techniques and to get faculty commitment in shaping students' characters and intellects, supporting a movement by students to implement something similar to the Hippocratic oath and stressing the importance of considering business people as members of a profession.

To give some detail, one of Mr Nohria's first acts as dean was to rethink the school's teaching methods. Since the 1920s, HBS students have pored over case studies of business decisions. The new dean wants them to take part in live case studies – to take themselves to the Midwest or Mumbai and spend time working for real companies. This answers one of the most persistent criticisms of business education: that it is too abstract. Mr Nohria wants his students to get their boots dirty.

None of these 'innovations' is entirely original. Most European business schools are already much more globalized than HBS. France's INSEAD has opened a campus in Singapore to put it at the heart of the Asian miracle. Many business schools started experimenting with 'live case studies' long ago: the late C.K. Prahalad was particularly successful at finding plum assignments in interesting Indian firms for his University of Michigan students.

Nevertheless, HBS plays a vital role in making good ideas stick. People listen when its star professors speak. Its case studies often become conventional wisdom.

In a quick and changing global world, a good understanding of how to manage people will be critical. Good management of complex institutions and organizations comprising a variety of backgrounds, individuals and motivation will also be key to success. As I said before, to get this right we will have to draw on a greater variety of disciplines. In addition, to overcome this challenge, we will also have to implement a more active way of teaching which will allow students to play a leading role in the learning process.

Academic institutions aiming at creating global citizens and the international leaders of tomorrow cannot only convey knowledge or develop analytical and critical skills. Universities must also contribute to shaping human beings, and to empowering students to make autonomous and responsible choices. To do so, we must also concentrate on the principles which drive behavior from a lifelong perspective, such as ethics, honesty, responsibility, respect for others and commitment. Internationalization is instrumental to this aim, as it helps young people understand the value of pluralism, appreciate and respect diversity, realize that the world is smaller than it seems and that it is inhabited by individuals with traditions, cultures, opinions and objectives that are often different from our own and from each others'. At the same time, our research spirit should help us spread among students a passion for the search for truth, intellectual honesty, and our drive to understand the world and to act towards its improvement. This can be done by questioning the predominant ideas taken for granted by others.

However, transferring these values is much more difficult than delivering mere knowledge or competencies and not enough has yet been done towards achieving this goal by major schools. We should focus on delivering key elements to arrive at a shared code of conduct. But to do so, students must feel a sense of belonging to a community. They must be emotionally moved. They should emulate the behavior of esteemed individuals within the community. They must share the values and principles embedded in the identity of the institution. They must look at the years spent at the university not as instrumental to getting a career but as an unforgettable life experience. To reach these objectives, we need to carefully invest not only in research and teaching but also in all other aspects that would contribute to shaping the university. Among these are social interaction, cultural activities and all those occasions that enable our students to feel the spirit of living intensively within a community, and worthwhile knowing and belonging.

15 BUSINESS SCHOOLS IN RELATION TO THE ORGANIZATIONAL AND ETHICAL CHALLENGES OF SYSTEMATIC TRANSFORMATION: A POLISH EXAMPLE

Adam Budnikowski

Warsaw School of Economics, Poland

Some 20 years ago, Central and Eastern European countries began the process of systemic transformation, which consisted of a simultaneous transition from a non-democratic to a democratic system on the one hand, and from a centrally planned economy into a market economy on the other. This process was initiated in Poland, the first country in the region to have formed a non-communist government and to have adopted a market economy as well.

This systemic transformation also exerted a profound impact on higher education in Poland, including on the teaching of economics and management. The aim of this chapter is to present the author's point of view on the Polish experience in this field, primarily, but not exclusively, from the perspective of the Warsaw School of Economics (Szkoła Główna Handlowa – SGH).[1]

THE STARTING POINT: 1989–1990

In order to exemplify the shift away from dictatorship and towards democracy, reference could be made to a number of cases worldwide. In Europe, it was Greece, Spain and Portugal that experienced changes of the same sort several years ago. On the other hand, the transition from a centrally planned economy to adopting market mechanisms has been underway for several years now in China and Vietnam. And yet, neither before nor after that time can we find in the world's political and economic history a single example of when such a radical political or economic change has been implemented concurrently.

A cumulative changeover exposed countries undergoing the transformation to numerous problems in relation to the creation of laws and new institutions that were each necessary in order to make the democratic system and the market economy operate correctly.

This also involved overcoming various habits inherited from the old system, thereby impeding the creation of a new one. In Central and Eastern Europe (CEE), the process was further hindered by the economic backwardness of those countries compared with their neighbours in Western Europe. This was primarily a consequence of implementing in those states the principles of an ineffective, centrally planned economy for almost 50 years (1945–89). However, it must not be forgotten, which is often the case in the countries of Western Europe, that the unwanted economic and political system was imposed upon CEE countries as a result of the decisions made by the Allies in Yalta, which, in the case of Czechoslovakia (the first victim of Nazi Germany) and Poland (the first country to mount armed resistance against the aggressor), was simply treated as treason.

In the process of this systemic transformation, the countries of CEE had to face a number of challenges involving difficult moral decisions. As an example, reference could be made to the scope and form of settling scores with those people who had cooperated with the communist authorities and the secret police, the issue of responsibility for crimes committed over those years, or the scale of the re-privatization of assets nationalized under the rule of the previous authorities. It was very painful to have to accept the fact that a systemic transformation had resulted in previously non-existent phenomena, such as unemployment, which to a large extent involved workers from the institutions that had contributed most to the initiation of that same transformation, including the Baltic coast shipyards, the cradle of Solidarity.

Polish universities, including business schools,[2] also had to face similar challenges. It can even be said that the challenges they had to cope with were of a special character. After all, in 1945–89 such universities trained specialists, more or less successfully, for a centrally planned economy. On the other hand, the graduates and employees of such universities had an enormous impact on the transition from a centrally planned to a market economy. An example of such a graduate and employee of the SGH is Professor Leszek Balcerowicz, Deputy Prime Minister and Minister of Finance in the government established in 1989, the first non-communist government in Poland since World War II. Here is a person whose contribution to the transition from a centrally planned to a market economy in Poland has been equal to that made by Lech Wałęsa in relation to the change in the political system.

The initiation of the market transition launched another crucial factor to change the current conditions of business schools. It was a need for economic education on the part of the Polish people which resulted in a tremendous rise in the number of those willing to study economics and management. The growth in demand for economic education was accompanied by a rise in the significance of a business university diploma and much clearer interdependence between individual success or financial position and the acquired knowledge (see Zaidi and Sulejewicz, 2009: 85–100).

In 1990, at the beginning of the systemic transformation in Poland, economists were educated at five state-owned business schools located in the four most important academic centers in the country, i.e. in Warsaw, Cracow, Poznan, Wroclaw and Katowice, the capital city of Upper Silesia. Furthermore, economists were also educated, though on a smaller scale, in the economic departments of several other universities. It should be pointed out that four out of five business universities were founded in the early decades of the previous century as private business schools. Even at that time, all of these enjoyed the full range of academic rights.

At the end of the 1940s, all five business schools were taken over by the state. The direct consequences included a loss of academic freedom, the abolition of tuition fees and, more importantly, the loss of curricular independence, as well as the necessity of accepting the imposed academic authorities.

THE BEGINNINGS OF CHANGE AND THE HERITAGE OF THE PAST

The systemic transformation begun in Poland in 1989 and 1990 was accompanied by the adjustment of business schools to the new conditions. Just as with the whole system of higher education in Poland, business schools underwent this process quickly and relatively painlessly. The process, however, posed quite serious organizational and ethical challenges.

The first of these, one which even the academic community in those universities was probably only partially aware of, was the question of whether or not and to what extent the universities wished to return to the style used in the period preceding World War II, or at the end of the 1940s, or in other words, whether the universities should undergo re-privatization. At SGH, for example, this issue was raised almost exclusively during unofficial conversations and even the most ardent proponents of a radical shake-up who gathered around Solidarity had never presented a comprehensive proposal for such changes.

Such an approach by the academic communities of business schools must have raised doubts. This approach implied that the community, being in fact the driving force of the economic transformation in Poland, had effectively rejected those principles in their own workplace. Today, we can only suppose that this did not result from conformism. The reason for such an approach should be attributed instead to the general belief that state higher education, and in particular its relatively general availability, was one of the few achievements of the previous system. It was also rather obvious that this very model would be the easiest to accept for a wide range of social groups.

On the other hand, the academic community of business schools had started to change, in a determined way, the basic operational principles of such schools as well as their academic curriculum. The former were implemented in a top-down fashion through changes to the legal regulations governing all Polish universities. Therefore, in all business schools, just as in other universities, autonomy was considerably increased; fully democratic rules for electing the academic authorities, including the rector and deans, were introduced; and the freedom to build the curriculum was considerably expanded. The minister responsible for higher education became to all intents and purposes a supervizing authority.

It is worth stressing that the organizational changes at Polish business schools were implemented without major retaliatory actions. Some rectors and deans who had held their positions under communism lost these. This was done, however, as part of a regular electoral procedure. On the other hand, the group of people actively transforming the universities included former members of the communist party. It was symptomatic that only one out of five people elected to the position of the rector at the Warsaw School of Economics between 1989 and 2010 had never been a member of the communist party. Interestingly, systemic changes were not accompanied by depriving lecturers (who had connections with the former regime) of the right to practice their profession. SGH employed, for example, on a full-time basis until his retirement, a professor who had headed the council of economic advisers to Edward Gierek, the first secretary of the communist party (PZPR) in the 1970s.

There could be a lot of hypotheses put forward to explain such behavior. Undoubtedly, all of these would be related to the recent history of Poland.

Many groups within Polish society never accepted the system which was imposed upon them after World War II. This was reflected in recurring rebellions (in 1956, 1968, 1970, 1976 and 1980–1) which were usually bloodily suppressed. As a consequence, since the beginning of the 1980s, academic authorities, including their party structures, were rather reluctant to become involved in any activities that bore the features of political cleansing. This process could also be observed at SGH, including during the period of martial law imposed in 1981. In this period some people had their right to practice the profession of university teacher suspended and some were removed from their positions of dean and vice dean. Yet some active members of the communist party also acted in a completely different way and protected their colleague professors who were actively participating in the Solidarity movement.

The reason why transformation at Polish business schools was not accompanied by retaliatory actions against staff members who had cooperated with the former regime was undoubtedly the policy of the first non-communist government. Thaddeus Mazowiecki, who was Prime Minister at that time, was in favor of the so-called thick-line policy which separated the present from the past and actually gave an emphasis to the swift implementation of changes, rather than settling scores from the past.

It has to be pointed out that the issue of responsibility for the past appeared again on the agendas of Polish universities in 2007 due to the legal requirement obliging a major part of professorial staff (who were of legal age prior to the period of transformation and are currently holding managerial positions) to submit their statements regarding possible co-operation with the secret police operating in Poland under the rule of communism. Even though the obligation to submit such statements was widely discussed throughout the country, the process of submitting the statements at business schools was relatively uneventful. This was the case at many universities, including SGH, where the rectors, despite being authorized to inspect the statements, resigned from exercising the right, while ensuring that these were forwarded directly to competent state bodies.

Media reports revealing the names of those people who had allegedly cooperated with the communist special services aroused more intense emotions. In the case of SGH, such a situation took place following the publication of an article that put forward such accusations in relation to one of the professors.

CURRICULAR CHANGES

The transformation made it necessary for all business schools to implement rapid curricular changes. The situation for the Polish universities of economics was much better in this respect than in most countries of CEE. This was mostly the result of historical factors, including the special status of such schools under communism, as well as the manner of exercising power by communists. First of all, when compared with other CEE countries, Poland was a country whose economy during communism had included the greatest number of (as it was said before 1989) relics of a capitalist economy. This primarily applied to agriculture, which was privately owned in three out of four cases, as well as to a relatively large number of shops, and even small-scale production facilities. This, combined with economic migration, exposed the majority of our society to the operations of market mechanisms.

Compared with other countries in the region, except for the Stalinist era at the end of the 1940s and the beginning of the 1950s, censorship was much more lenient and the ideological propaganda much less insistent. The authorities also had to take into account the opinions of the Catholic Church, an independent institution which was also deeply rooted in Polish national tradition. The Church criticized the communist authorities openly only in exceptional circumstances, but it epitomized the system of values which served as an alternative to communism.

The aforementioned circumstances were reflected in the specific features of the curriculum implemented at Polish business schools during communism. Let me refer to some examples here. With the exception of the Stalinist period, Polish business schools did not offer lectures in Marxist philosophy but simply in philosophy. Lectures on economics were removed from the curriculum for the sake of lectures on the political economics of capitalism and socialism, and yet, a university graduate would still be awarded a Master's degree in economics. Neither microeconomics nor macroeconomics were taught, and yet that student had the opportunity to study many basic issues related to those disciplines while also studying the history of economic thought or international economics. Furthermore, some departments preparing students for doing business on foreign markets offered classes in market analysis and marketing.

Compared with the other countries of CEE, Poland ensured much easier access to foreign economic literature. As a rule, students did not encounter any obstacles while trying to access older foreign literature available in libraries; economic literature brought from abroad did not arouse the reservations of customs officers; and some examples of Western literature were even translated into Polish. As an interesting aside reflecting the spirit of the age, one could also refer to the fact that Polish was the only language of the CEE into which the famous *1st Report to the Club of Rome – the Limits to Growth* (Meadows et al., 1972) was translated immediately after its publication in the 1970s.

The possibility of maintaining contacts with Western academics was a vital element influencing the academic curriculum prior to the systemic transformation. This included, in particular, scholarships abroad and occasionally the possibility of studying in another country. The number of such opportunities increased at the beginning of the 1970s, due both to the relaxation of passport policy and the scholarship policy of many Western countries, in particular the USA. To give an idea of the scale of such trips, reference can be made to the fact that at the beginning of the 1990s, at some departments of SGH, almost all the professors of about 40 years of age would spend at least one year at one of the top American universities as part of a scholarship.

As a result of the aforementioned circumstances, top business schools in the country found it quite hard but relatively manageable to prepare a new educational offering. Due to the existing regulations, the curriculum was prepared with the participation of the Ministry of Science and Higher Education, which established the so-called minimum curriculum while leaving a wide scope to the discretion to particular universities, which were expected to add the final touches. Due to the aforementioned relative openness of the Polish academic community to Western science, preparation of the curriculum did not encounter any serious obstacles. An insufficient number of personnel to teach particular subjects did not pose a problem either.

In the case of some disciplines (e.g. international economics or marketing), preparing a new curriculum meant introducing only small changes to the subjects that had already been taught. Preparing lectures in relation to narrow fields was more difficult, as in a centrally planned economy there was no application for them. Moreover, due to Poland's absence from the international capital markets, such subjects had not previously been included at faculties preparing staff for jobs in international trade (e.g. the evaluation of investment projects or capital markets).

It is worth mentioning, however, that aid from Western countries was a significant support for Polish business schools. In the case of SGH, we had, for instance, the involvement of American and Canadian universities in the joint MBA programs together with SGH. These programs played an important role, not only in educating staff managing the Polish economy but thanks to the joint lectures delivered by Polish and foreign lecturers, they also became an important instrument of adaptation for the modern methodology of teaching management in Polish universities.

Although the implementation of curricular changes did not encounter serious obstacles, this obviously does not mean that in individual cases the shift occurred without any reluctance. This was especially true of definite leftist, though not communist, views. It can be supposed that, for some lecturers, the adaptation problems were due not to ideological factors but simply to a poor education, with no command of English or age.

Polish business schools also solved, relatively quickly, the problem of textbooks. At the beginning of the period these were mainly books by Western authors which were then translated into Polish. This offer was quickly extended to include books by Polish authors, which covered the whole spectrum of interests in economics and management sciences.

State business schools in Poland also managed to make up fairly quickly for any deficiencies in the knowledge of foreign languages. This process took a different form at each university, but all of them had some experience in the field as at during communism some departments had prepared students for foreign co-operation. The curriculum for these studies, which included an intensive course in two foreign languages, offered future specialists the opportunity to develop a language fluency. The only major difference was that the prominent position for Russian was overtaken by English.

It is worth stressing that by deciding to adopt such a solution Polish business schools offer their students, free of charge, the possibility of acquiring skills, which in the case of many universities of the same type in Europe is undertaken by students individually. It is to be noted, however, that this solution, justified as it was in the fledgling years following the transformation, is now questioned more and more frequently because of the related costs which universities must incur.

THE SOCIAL STATUS AND SOCIAL RESPONSIBILITY OF PUBLIC BUSINESS SCHOOLS

The systemic transformation fundamentally changed the position of public business schools. The progress of this transformation made it more and more obvious that economic success, besides the efforts of the whole nation, also depends on the level of knowledge of economics and management acquired by graduates from the leading business schools in the country, as well as the standards represented by the professors at these universities. This opinion was reinforced by a number of factors. One of them was a common association of Leszek Balcerowicz, the father of the Polish transformation, with SGH. Another was appointing professors and business schools and university department staff to the positions of Finance Minister, the Governor of the National Bank of Poland and members of the Monetary Policy Council – the body responsible, together with the Central Bank governor, for the monetary policy of the country – as well as one commissioner of the European Union. However, the factor that strengthened the position of business schools to the largest extent was the professional success of subsequent generations of graduates who, since the very beginning of the transformation, have been the most sought after 'product' on the Polish labor market, and who after Poland's accession to the European Union with no hesitation at all entered the competition within the Union marketplace alongside graduates from the best European business schools.

Together with the strengthening of their position, business schools began to pay more and more attention to corporate social responsibility (CSR). This was reflected, for instance, in missions undertaken by business schools as well as other universities which had not been customary before the systemic transformation. The Warsaw School of Economics undertook its first mission in 1992, and its present one in 2009.[3] On the other hand, the interest of the Polish people in missions accomplished by Polish universities is reflected in the relatively numerous rankings of universities published annually by several Polish magazines and looked forward to by both universities and the whole society. It must be underlined that the highest recognition is given to the ranking that has been prepared most professionally, with the use of the highest number of criteria and the participation of numerous experts.

NEW CHALLENGE: TUITION FEES AND PRIVATE SCHOOLS

One of the consequences of the systemic transformation that Polish business schools have had to face has been the issue of tuition fees and the related co-existence of state-owned and private business schools.

The new constitution, which came into effect in 1997, includes a clause stating that education at university level is free of charge. It soon became apparent that this only refers to state-owned schools, and only and exclusively in relation to full-time studies. State universities have been given the right to charge fees, but only to cover the costs of teaching part-time as well as post-graduate students. These fees, also as a result of a relatively slow growth in state subsidies, started to constitute approximately half of the revenues of many state-owned universities, business schools included.

The aforementioned limitations on tuition fees do not apply to private universities, which had not existed in Poland for many years but restarted their activities in the early 1990s on a large scale. In most cases these were established by foundations, companies or private individuals. A considerable majority of newly founded schools were business schools operating under a variety of different names. Supposedly, there were two reasons for this: the demand for business specialists mentioned above and the relatively low costs of education, especially when compared with technical, medical and natural science schools.

It was thanks to private universities that Poland experienced a real boom in the higher education market, with the direct consequence of a huge increase in the number of students as well as the number of university graduates. In the academic year 1992–3, which was directly after the start of the systemic transformation, there were 124 universities in Poland, including 18 which were non-public. In comparison, in the academic year 2008–9, these amounted to 458 and 326 respectively. The growth in the number of universities was accompanied by a rise in the number of students from 403,000 in the academic year 1990–1 to 1,930,000 in the academic year 2007–8.

On the other hand, the existence of such schools poses a number of problems concerning the regulations for the employment conditions of staff within the higher education system.

Under the effective legislation, an academic employed by a state university has the right to do another full-time job, on the condition that they inform the rector about it. They may even have more full-time jobs, provided these are also approved by the rector. These second, third and possibly further full-time jobs may include work at universities, including private ones.

The legal requirements created a unique situation on the university professors' job market, particularly with respect to economics and management experts. Due to the huge demand for academic staff created by newly founded private universities, thousands of academics employed by state universities have received job offers from one or several private schools, which only occasionally come from state universities. Due to the profile of the majority of private schools, the demand is directed primarily towards the five major public business schools and several economic and management departments at universities, and to a smaller extent to departments of law and political science.

The scale of the problem is reflected by the fact that the job at SGH for more than one third of lecturers is not their only full-time employment, and more than 5 per cent work full-time in two other workplaces. These other jobs are, in the great majority, at private universities.

This kind of situation brings specific and measurable benefits to a number of entities. In the past, for private schools, an inflow of staff from public universities was their only chance to commence operations. Even today, after 20 years of operation, the majority of private schools would not be able to operate purely on the basis of the staff employed exclusively by them. The possibility of holding two jobs is also an opportunity for professors employed by state universities. To begin with there is the opportunity to increase their income considerably, in many cases up to seven times.

Undoubtedly, the state also benefits from the possibility of employing academics at two or more universities. The main advantage of such a situation is the possibility of increasing the number of students without incurring significant costs.

The situation gives rise, however, to a number of doubts of an ethical nature. First of all, it is difficult to accept the fact that in working at two or even more workplaces, selling the same services (in this case, educational services), a lecturer in fact contradicts the basic rules of a market economy under which working for competing entities is not allowed. It is difficult to imagine that a professor teaching the same subject (e.g. marketing) at two or three different universities will follow a completely different curriculum in each case.

Another serious danger in relation to the possibility of concurrent employment at two or more universities is the excessive concentration by a considerable number of Polish economists on the teaching aspect of their jobs. Considering the fact that this situation has existed at Polish universities for almost two decades now, some academics, in particular economists and management specialists, have developed an approach to their jobs which might best be described as a 'flight into teaching'. They are losing their sense of mission, the core of which involves combination of research and teaching students. By concentrating only on the latter, they have become well-qualified lecturers who neither conduct research nor publish anything. From the point of view of long-term public interest, this should undoubtedly be considered a substantial loss.

AN INCOMPLETE TRANSFORMATION?

Based on this overview of changes in Polish business schools, it may be concluded that their transformation has been successful. Such an opinion is legitimate in light of an impressively huge rise in the number of students who can study economics and management, the implementation of considerable changes in the curriculum, the establishment of hundreds of private business schools, and the introduction of new specializations at many state-owned universities.

On the other hand, it is relatively easy to point out the circumstances which can make optimistic conclusions less obvious. First, in the last two decades, Polish economic and management studies have not managed to bridge the 20-year gap in scientific research separating them from the top European and American academic centers. During this time, no Polish academic has won such worldwide renown in those fields as compared with the renown that Oskar Lange or Michał Kalecki enjoyed. A visible consequence of this is the absence of Polish business schools from the so-called Shanghai ranking list.

A long list of reasons responsible for this state of affairs can be enumerated. One of them is undoubtedly the persistently underfunded science in Poland resulting from the policy of various Polish governments over the last two decades. Another reason is connected with the regulations permitting concurrent employment in several workplaces. As stated above, this entices a considerable number of academics away from doing research.

From the current perspective, it can also be said that, even though during the first years of the systemic transformation, holding many job contracts was somehow justified, subsequent governments have been more and more concerned about this. Preserving the system of several job contracts is a pre-requisite for the existence of many private business schools, and their existence offers a considerable number of young people a chance to study without incurring considerable expense as a result. Furthermore, creating sources of additional income for public university professors lowers the costs of maintaining such universities, and, as a result, free full-time studies may still be offered without incurring additional expenses, which also makes it possible to comply with the constitutional requirement of providing free higher education.

One consequence of this policy is a slow development in terms of scientific research. A much more dangerous consequence however is the resultant ethical ambiguity. On the one hand, the state is more and more involved in protecting a void constitutional provision with regard to free higher education, and on the other hand, most students, in particular students of economics and management, are paying tuition fees. Furthermore, to put it mildly, it is an imperfect part of our educational services as a price has only been placed on educational services of the lowest quality offered by weak private schools, whereas top-quality services, provided almost exclusively by state-owned universities (with the exception of a few good private schools), are subject to free of charge distribution in the form of a recruitment process.

In recent years, there have been some new factors which might force Polish universities to introduce changes aimed at completing the transformation of Polish business schools. External factors include demographic changes resulting in a decrease in the number of people interested in studying, which in turn endangers the position of many private universities. In response to the new circumstances, the authorities of private universities demand that the state should also include private schools in the system of subsidies provided to state universities. At the same time, and despite increased supervision by the Ministry of Science and Higher Education, in some private business schools teaching standards and requirements towards the students are being lowered to reflect the rule that the collection of tuition fees is the most important issue.

Interestingly, state universities also want changes to the organization of higher education. Last year, they contributed to the creation of two drafts concerning a considerable restructuring of the system of higher education in Poland. They put forward the idea of a gradual introduction of tuition fees for higher education in all universities. The rectors of the five state-owned business schools adopted the most determined stance here. They suggested that a true educational market should be created, even if it was only to include business schools at the beginning, so that state universities should have an equal right to collect tuition fees, receive public subsidies and have the freedom to run their staff-related policies. To prove that this is not only a demand by rectors seeking additional financial means, let me refer to an article published in one of the recent issues of *Gazeta SGH* by one of its students. The title of the article is 'Down with communism, or why all studies should be paid' (Jedlewski, 2010).

THE EUROPEAN DIMENSION OF THE SYSTEMIC TRANSFORMATION IN POLISH BUSINESS SCHOOLS

The process of systemic transformation taking effect in CEE in the last two decades has coincided with the involvement of the countries of this region in the major trend of European integration. This has resulted both from the economic interest of these countries and, what cannot be ignored, the desire to participate in the creation of the new economic and political order in Europe. Because of their limited sovereignty, countries in this part of the continent could not participate in the process at the very beginning.

The academic community of business schools in Poland also took part in this process. This was reflected by the introduction of research into the problems of economic integration and the consequences of association and, soon after, into EU membership. At the same time, there was a process of including lectures on European integration in the curriculum. Both these processes advanced rapidly, among other reasons, due to the opportunity given to Polish scientists to participate in the research and didactic programs co-financed by the European Union.

In SGH, it is both Jean Monnet chairs that play a particular role in the dissemination of the idea of integration. The first of these, which was also one of the first in Poland, was founded in 1997, while the other was founded in 1998. For Polish students, the opportunity to participate in numerous international exchange programs was of the utmost importance, with the most significant EU-funded programs being TEMPUS, SOCRATES and presently ERASMUS. A lot of SGH students have participated in these – in the academic year 2008–9, there were 260 foreign incoming students and 400 SGH outgoing students.

Together with the progress of the process of systemic transformation and the related changes in the Polish business school system, there were more and more important forms of international cooperation in which Polish business schools performed as rightful entities within the European academic community. For SGH, a breakthrough event came with admission to CEMS in 1998. This gave new opportunities to the staff and students, allowing them to cooperate with the best universities on the continent and indirectly encouraging them to try to achieve a higher position in the *Financial Times* ranking.

On the whole, the example of the Warsaw School of Economics seems to indicate that in the future Polish business schools, as well as universities in other European countries, will not want to be universities on the domestic scale only. Instead, they will seek a share of the whole European educational market. Despite certain limitations resulting from smaller funds for higher education (when compared to richer countries) as well as the smaller scope of their national language, these universities will certainly not want to confine their offering to Bachelor studies which will prepare their graduates to study in the best Western European or American universities. The course of changes in these universities in the last two decades indicates that this is possible. However, the pre-requisite seems to be, first of all, a change in the legislation that will make a complete transformation of the Polish higher education system a possibility.

NOTES

1.   Readers interested in a comprehensive approach to the discussed problems are referred to Zaidi and Sulejewicz (2009) and Morawski (2006).
2.   In this chapter, the term *business schools* will be used with reference to state universities and non-public universities of a similar profile. It should be remembered, however, that at state universities, which is not often the case in non-public universities, there are departments that teach economics and management.
3.   The Warsaw School of Economics is the oldest university of economics and management in Poland. As it seeks to impart a European dimension to its academic activity, SGH combines over a century's tradition with engagement in the contemporary world and the pursuit of future challenges. In its educational endeavors, the School seeks to provide students with the latest knowledge, solid working skills and a sense of responsibility to society. In its research activities, the School is guided by a respect for the truth and usefulness within society. The School conducts both its educational and research activities in the field of economics and managerial sciences drawing on the achievements of other social sciences. Graduates of SGH, equipped with the latest general and specialized knowledge, are making a significant contribution to the economic, social and political life in Poland and abroad. Together with academic and administrative staff, students and representatives of milieus connected with the School, they create the image of SGH, promoting its achievements and realizing its mission.

REFERENCES

Jedlewski, Ł. (2010) 'Down with communism, or why all studies should be paid', *Gazeta SGH*, February, pp. 14–16.

Meadows, D.H., Meadows, D.L., Randers, J. and Behrens, W.W. (1972) *1st Report to the Club of Rome – The Limits to Growth*. New York: Universe Books.

Morawski, W. (ed.) (2006) *Historia Szkoły Głównej Handlowej w Warszawie 1906–2006 (History of the Warsaw School of Economics 1906–2006)*. Warsaw: SGH. Available at: www.nauka.gov.pl/szkolnictwo-wyzsze/dane-statystyczne-o-szkolnictwie-wyzszym/

Zaidi, M.A. and Sulejewicz, A. (2009) *Beyond MBA: Management Education in Transitional Economies*. Warsaw: Warsaw School of Economics.

16 THE NEW RIGOR: BEYOND THE RIGHT ANSWER

Judith Samuelson

Aspen Institute of Business and Society Program, USA

When top executives from Goldman Sachs, JP Morgan Chase, Morgan Stanley and Bank of America appeared before the US Congress early in 2010 to answer questions about the financial crisis that had rocked markets and impoverished so many institutions and families, the reaction ranged from disbelief to outrage. Commissioner John Thompson addressed the CEO of Goldman Sachs: '… you said that there were products … created that served no purpose … To what extent did those products that had no purpose contribute to this problem?' A long exchange followed, highlighting complex and sometimes troubling questions about the fundamental purpose of the firms, their activities and how executives view their role in society.

A few months later, executives at Google re-routed all traffic from Google China to Google Hong Kong, the latest development in a four-year narrative pitting their 'do-no-evil' principle against their quest for market share and profits. Not unlike the deliberations in the Congressional hearing room, the questions at the heart of Google's exit from China come in shades of grey, not black or white. Should the company have entered China at all? Do democratic values and rights seep into the landscape when we pry open new markets, like modern-day capitalists claim? Or does the mere presence of the big brands help validate the actions of corrupt or anti-democratic regimes?

These are not new questions, but a broader range of actors is now interested in the answers. Fundamental concerns about the legitimacy of business are growing. The critical path for companies is already complex and is getting more so. Thus, one thing is clear: to succeed in the global economy business leaders will require new kinds of management processes and analytical frameworks. Their decision rules will need to be more rigorous, and open to a wider set of measures and realities than in the past. The old decision rules and assumptions won't do. In fact, a new definition of rigor is needed.

THE NEW RIGOR

To many, proof of rigor is an excel spreadsheet, a Monte Carlo simulation or research that comes with the appropriate p value. And indeed these can be extraordinarily powerful tools.

But from our vantage point, business education cannot be considered rigorous until educators see that all managers, even those steeped in shareholder primacy, must make important choices based on the perspectives they bring and values they apply to each decision. The point is to make these assumptions and perspectives explicit – and more encompassing of relevant stakeholder views. In doing so, important risks and opportunities will emerge.

The implications for business schools are now appearing. In this chapter, we explore a 'new rigor' that replaces *Homus economicus* with a professional stance devoted to a larger purpose – where morals, ethical reasoning and careful judgment truly matter. This new rigor is characterized by the depth of the discussion around questions that are fundamental to the role of business – questions concerning the purpose of the firm and its discrete activities, about its interdependence with the context in which it operates, and about our collective notions of what constitutes success in business. Because the new rigor is anchored in inquiry, it is inherently context-specific. This chapter will therefore point to numerous 'teachable moments' in MBA training where new or deeper questions can be asked, rather than point to a singular definition of the new rigor.

It imparts analytical frameworks and conceptual skills that look far outside the gate rather than only at the enterprise level, to explicitly incorporate multiple perspectives, and to deeply consider – rather than deeply discount – the future. It is also characterized by a renewed commitment to inquiry, by the opportunity to challenge the fundamental assumptions of the MBA canon, and by instructing students in strategies to give voice to personal and institutional values.

So what's the bottom line here? We think it's time to put the lynchpin for all business decision rules – short-term financial profit maximizing – into context. Profit maximizing is a two-dimensional analysis in a three-dimensional world. Business schools are an appropriate – and necessary – place to rethink the paradigm.

Relevant educational content and pedagogy that contributes to or even exemplifies this new rigor were once limited to the ethics classroom, but now go by many names: corporate responsibility, social impact management, social entrepreneurship, sustainable development and values-based leadership. To succeed in exploring this new rigor, faculty and administrators can leverage the core strengths of the school – there is no one formula or approach to enhancing the MBA. However, to help prepare our graduates for their careers, the new approach needs to be integrated throughout the MBA core curriculum rather than positioned as an introduction or capstone to what MBAs now view as the courses that actually matter.

At its best, the new rigor can embrace pragmatic elements of business management, like risk management and financial value creation; however, it can also explore new growth opportunities at the intersection of financial success and social and environmental progress. In a world of extraordinary challenges – climate change, poverty, the HIV/AIDS crisis, looming water shortages – we believe business has both the potential and the responsibility – even the self-interest – to unlock solutions to our most complex problems. In fact, activists today observe the sheer scale and reach of our largest companies, greater than most nation states, and understand that it is business that has the capital, the distribution systems, the talent to take these issues on, and increasingly, the motivation to act.

As we consider these core questions about the role and purpose of business, it causes us to rethink the role and purpose of business education. And though the concept of new rigor is arguably applicable to a range of business school activities, we focus in this chapter on

MBA programs, where we have the deepest expertise. Since our founding in 1998, the Aspen Institute Business and Society Program has advocated for change in business education and corporate practice. Given our location, our broadest networks are in the USA and our focus within business education is on the MBA, the second most popular graduate degree in the USA. Our MBA-related work includes survey research on the state of management education[1] and how it influences student attitudes about the role of business.[2] We convene networks of researchers and administrators, support research consortia, make innovative teaching materials more broadly available and build bridges between the academic and business worlds.

At times, our position outside academia allows us the freedom to think more expansively than those on campus who are bound by the constraints of the tenure system, independent departments and disciplines and the market demands of students, rankings and recruiters. In fact, along with the World Resources Institute, we jumped in the deep end of the pool, creating an alternative ranking of global schools to promote a new perspective on what matters in MBA education. Later in this chapter, we utilize this research to offer up examples of the exciting curriculum innovations we believe are bringing new rigor into the MBA classroom. But first, I have some thoughts on the challenge that faces business schools.

THE ROLE OF THE BUSINESS SCHOOL

Just as there is great potential in the power of business to be a force for good, there is enormous – although largely untapped – potential in management education to produce leaders who are capable of stepping up to occupy this historic role. The most-often cited gaps in MBA training – among them, a global perspective, leadership development, creative and innovative thinking, a nuanced view of the roles and responsibilities of business leaders and an understanding of the limits of markets and models (Datar et al., 2010) – are evidence of this untapped potential. Yet business schools, as academic institutions, are uniquely positioned to be intellectual hubs of research, teaching and dialogue on the role of business and its leaders today.

Business schools claim to train business leaders who create value for society[3] yet it is hard to recall a time when business education was under greater scrutiny or more thoughtfully criticized, particularly by those within academia itself. Especially in the wake of the financial crisis, critics have raised important questions about the footprint made by the MBA on individual firms' performance – and on broad macro-economic conditions.

These new critiques revive long-standing concerns about graduate management education. Some critics – including many voices within business – claim that business education has grown irrelevant and ineffectual within the practice of business (Mintzberg, 2004; Bennis and O'Toole, 2005). Other criticisms take a different tack. Rather than ineffective, the MBA is decried as tragically too effective at indoctrinating business managers with ideas that actively destroy both economic and social value (Ghoshal, 2005).

At the Aspen Institute, our chief concern is that the dominant theory and organizing principle of MBA education – short-term profit and share price maximization – introduces what amounts to a false rigor, one that is chilling in terms of teaching, research and the classroom discussion about the true costs and potential benefits of business activity, about the non-financial measures of business success, and about the most important questions and practices where business and society intersect.

In the 1950s, the Ford Foundation was also concerned about the effectiveness of business education. Over a decade, it invested $35 million in business schools, over $250 million in today's dollars (Ghoshal, 2005: 77), intent on 'professionalizing' what, regardless of the original intent (Khurana and Khanna, 2007), had become the more narrow vocational and specialized industry training of the 1930s and 1940s (Gordon and Howell, 1959). But the Foundation's investment yielded unintended consequences – among them, an overemphasis on technical training and quantitative methods, and an infrastructure made up of journals and tenure processes that contributed significantly to the disciplinary 'silos' we see today.

BUILDING A BETTER MBA

For over a decade, the Aspen Institute has worked with business school faculty and administrators on a wide range of teaching and research initiatives. We have been inspired by the commitment of individuals working within their discipline or institution to bring about change in MBA education. We have carefully tracked the curricular innovations that educate future managers in the new rigor that our companies and our society require.

From 2003 to 2009, each of our biennial *Beyond Grey Pinstripes* surveys documented significant growth in academic practice areas that prepare students for social and environmental stewardship. What follows is a sampling of the coursework that we believe merits attention. Information on the coursework we highlight in this chapter, summarized in Table 16.1, is all drawn from our *Beyond Grey Pinstripes* survey, 2009–10. Though many of the topics here aren't new, what is exciting is that the faculty use some familiar themes as a way to offer students new chances to think about their future professional roles and to integrate vital new questions and decisions rules that are more likely to capture the wide spectrum of risks and opportunities of contemporary global business.

GLOBALISM AND INTERDEPENDENCE

Philip Bobbit, in *The Shield of Achilles* (2002), argues that our society is evolving from 'nation states' to 'market states': ... private businesses and their leaders will find they are given more public and political responsibilities'. However Kleiner adds: 'They are not trained to handle them; their leaders often do not seek them; and they are not comfortable being made responsible for them. But they cannot avoid them' (2004).

Today's management scholars are challenged to infuse their classroom discussions with an understanding and respect for the power that the next generation of business executives and leaders will wield in global social and environmental welfare. They can build leadership capacity by providing students with more exposure to global trends, especially those that rebound on the business environment, such as environmental changes, the rise of emerging

Table 16.1   Cited courses drawn from *Beyond Grey Pinstripes* data

Course Name	Course Type	Instructor	School	Country
Ten Years Hence	Elective	James O'Rourke, Carolyn Woo	University of Notre Dame Mendoza College of Business	USA
Globalization and Corporate Responsibility	Core	Andrew Spicer	University of South Carolina Moore School of Business	USA
Systems Thinking for Sustainable Development and Enterprise	Elective	Tom Gladwin	University of Michigan Stephen M. Ross School of Business	USA
Design Management	Elective	Roberto Verganti	Copenhagen Business School	Denmark
Human Resources Management	Core	Diane Bergeron	Case Western Weatherhead School of Management	USA
Social and Environmental Accounting	Elective	Marko Järvenpää, Matias Laine, Hannu Kurki	University of Jyväskylä School of Business and Economics	Finland
Corporate Finance	Core	Wei Jiang, Gailen Hite, Donna Hitscherich, David Beim	Columbia University Graduate School of Business	USA
Paths to Power	Elective	Jeffrey Pfeffer	Stanford University Graduate School of Business	USA
Employee Involvement: Strategies and Dilemmas	Elective	T. Mock	York University Schulich School of Business	Canada
Values and Crisis Decision-Making	Elective	David Austen-Smith, Timothy Feddersen, Steven Callander, Daniel Diermeier	Northwestern University Kellogg School of Management	USA

economies and demographic shifts. They can impart to students a deep understanding of the historical and emerging roles of the private sector, government and civil society – as well as how these roles intersect and vary across regions. As David Cooperrider and Jane Dutton remind us, they can teach management as 'a matter of world affairs'.[4]

The new rigor would equip students with the ability to think systemically – to anticipate the unintended consequences of their decisions, to look for unexpected causes of problems and to project far further into the future. For example, at the University of Notre Dame's Mendoza College of Business, a lecture course called Ten Years Hence invites eight experts into a dialogue with students on topics likely to affect business, including economic demography, biotechnology, religious fundamentalism, oil and peace, futurism and work, and more. At the University of South Carolina's Moore School, the core International

Management course is built around three different globalization scenarios, drawn from Shell's Global Scenarios for 2025.

Tom Gladwin's course at the Ross School at the University of Michigan on Systems Thinking for Sustainable Development and Enterprise exposes students to the art of systems thinking and related simulation tools. Students explore challenges such as population growth, poverty, climate change, freshwater scarcity, gender bias, megacities and political instability, and focus especially on the roles of industry. Understanding as Gladwin does both the emotional and cognitive impacts of delving deeply into gloomy statistics, he also talks with students about the role of courage, and challenges them to examine the assumptions that underlie other business courses and business practice, like the propensity to ignore externalities.

REIMAGINE GROWTH AND INNOVATION

Students pursue MBA degrees because they are drawn to the 'can do' attitude of business. They want to solve problems – important problems – and a growing number also want to transform the world, using their business skills to make the changes they want to see.[5]

Educators can leverage this interest to explore how an enterprise can have both an economic bottom line and create a social good. C.K. Prahalad at the University of Michigan and Stuart Hart at Cornell pioneered and popularized the notion of finding a 'fortune at the bottom (or base) of the pyramid' (Hart, 2005; Prahalad, 2005; Prahalad and Hart, 2002). Inspired by their vision, students examine ways to harness markets for social good, including rethinking the technology, product and service needs of the billions of global citizens with limited financial resources. Scholarly work is still needed to better understand both the market opportunities and the true societal costs and benefits in these markets,[6] however this approach is highlighting new ways to partner with local communities and bringing into the classroom parts of the world and a depth of challenges that are still largely off the radar for business school students.

While 'stakeholder engagement' is hardly new, it is no longer only about risk management or reputation and community relations; today it is viewed as a pathway to innovation and opportunity. GE's Jeff Immelt emphasizes 'external focus' and 'inclusiveness' among the company's five leadership traits (Brady, 2005). This was part of the original concept Ed Freeman (1984) proposed for stakeholder management as a 'strategic' approach to business, but it has only recently been used in that way by business. Inward-looking companies not only tend to miss important signals in the external environment, making them prone to crisis, they also don't produce iPods, Post-it notes or micro-loans.

Beyond emphasizing why business managers must remain open to external voices, business schools can train students in how to listen and how to shape business decisions based on what they learn. For example, Copenhagen Business School offers 'Design Management', to explore innovation that is rooted in social issues. In this course, students learn how to find 'key interpreters' in the socio-cultural context (firms in other industries, designers, architects, artists, suppliers, journalists, researchers, etc.) that can help identify people's aspirations for new products and meaning.

VALUING INQUIRY AND VOICE

We conclude our exploration of the new rigor required in business education with a focus on the skill set that managers will need to manage an enterprise and lead firms in an era of what Don Tapscott calls 'radical transparency' (Tapscott and Williams, 2003).

It's about skill, but also about attitude and expanded notions of 'what's my job?' In this era, firms need to take in perspectives beyond the gate, think long term and in a holistic fashion. This translates into employees and managers who are able to challenge the conventional wisdom about what matters most, and to bring values in from the parking lot and put them to use at the water cooler and in the boardroom. Nothing offers greater protection, or is more likely to identify important new opportunities for the company, than an engaged workforce with its collective antenna raised.

ASK NEW QUESTIONS

Successful business managers will seek the right questions, not just the right answers. Business schools have an excellent track record in training students to ask – and answer – technical questions like, 'Does the deal make the hurdle rate?' or 'How can a production process be optimized?' Some schools – and some courageous faculty – go further. They encourage a rigorous exploration of questions that don't always have right answers, but that help students discover the skills and perspectives needed to manage a company successfully for the benefit of both business and society.

Because the right questions are context-specific, educators serve students well – and enhance their readiness to manage along multiple dimensions – by encouraging a lifelong commitment to inquiry. Traditional questions are likely to underestimate the risks to reputations enabled by a highly connected world. They may miss the risk of market failures from external threats – as Monsanto missed consumer and farmer resistance to genetically modified seed, or as Google overestimated its ability to affect change in the China market. And they may fail to build a consciousness of the social and environmental impacts of business decisions, just like the effects of carbon emissions were ignored by industry for decades.

Although the traditional questions can help us with the all-important tasks of quantifying and executing, they are also less likely to help us break through convention and imagine bigger possibilities. And it's imagination and exploration that lead to exciting breakthroughs in new products and services at the nexus of business, society and a new market opportunity. As a starting point for moving inquiry to a new level, business schools can call on students to ponder three fundamental questions. These can be asked in the context of every business discipline and decision:

- First, what is the purpose, in both business and societal terms, of a company, business activity or financial investment?
- Second, what is the social context of a business decision or investment? Who needs to be consulted to assure a high-quality decision that stands the test of time? Are the rights of multiple stakeholders considered? What are the impacts of a firm's strategy on the quality of life in the community, on security, on safety?

- Third, how are performance and profitability assessed? Over what time period? What is being counted and what is not being counted? Do managers compute the cost of externalities? (Gentile, 2002)

These questions cannot be answered simply or conclusively, but we believe MBA training would be greatly enhanced by the asking. A broad dialogue that encounters multiple perspectives can prove invaluable. In a core Human Resources Management course at Case Western's Weatherhead School, for example, students deliberate fundamental questions including 'Can HR be ethical?' and 'Do organizations and organizational science really contribute to the welfare of the people working in the organization?' In a course in Social and Environmental Accounting at the University of Jyväskylä, students also consider how accounting may be part of the solution as well as part of the problem in social and environmental issues.

CHALLENGE ASSUMPTIONS

In Google's pre-IPO prospectus, founders Larry Page and Sergey Brin wrote: 'We believe strongly that in the long term, we will be better served – as shareholders and in all other ways – by a company that does good things for the world even if we forgo some short-term gains' (SEC, 2004: vi).

How can business educators equip students to think as critically about the interaction of capital markets and firms as the Google founders at least set out to do? An important step is deep inquiry into the underlying assumptions of the decision rules and frameworks that dominate business school classrooms today – among them, efficient markets and shareholder primacy.

The latter, at least in US-style capitalism, has become roughly (and some would say, inaccurately) translated in practice into a mandate to maximize shareholder value in the very short term. In extensive interviews with business school scholars in finance, economics, business law, accounting and strategy, faculty identify many 'teachable moments' that occur as they teach shareholder value maximization (Scully, 2004). Through these windows of opportunity, faculty can encourage students to question the implicit assumptions of the shareholder primacy model – and to examine the necessary conditions for its optimal functioning. For example, Columbia Business School weaves tough questions directly into its core Corporate Finance course. Professors ask: should maximizing shareholder value be a sole or primary objective of the corporation? Is this equivalent to maximizing the current stock price – and what if this involves manipulating the stock price? Is there a short- versus long-run distinction? As an example of the important role ethics faculty may play, these questions were derived as a result of a consultation process between core teaching faculty and experts in teaching ethics (Gentile, 2004). Faculty can take the lead by intellectually engaging students with such fundamental questions. For example, if the case for the shareholder primacy model is premised on the responsibility of government to attend to externalities, what is the appropriate role of business and the right balance when it comes to industry lobbying to reduce government regulation? When we speak of 'shareholders', how do we account for the fact that this is a heterogeneous group, with different time horizons, different tolerances for risk and different investment objectives? And instead of approaching the law as a bother and something to be managed, business faculty can intellectually engage students around questions such as 'exactly what does the law require of executives and directors when it comes to shareholder primacy?'[7]

GIVE VOICE TO VALUES

For any of these components of the new rigor to flourish, management education must first provide students with opportunities to practice giving voice to their values. Aspen Institute research shows that 50 per cent of MBA students believe their education is only 'somewhat' training them to manage values conflicts (Aspen Institute, 2008: 59).

More and more schools are experimenting in this domain. Students on Stanford's 'Paths to Power' elective reflect on what they are willing and not willing to do to obtain and exercise influence. In the 'Employee Involvement: Strategy and Dilemmas' course at the Schulich School at York University in Toronto, students experiment with new approaches to manage the quality of work life and the changing gender and ethnic composition of the workplace. The Kellogg School of Management at Northwestern University's 'Values and Crisis Decision-Making' course includes a one-week experiential component. Students are confronted with an ethical crisis and must resolve it. Each day, their task is further complicated as new information is received and integrated in real time.

Despite the notion that these courses are teaching 'soft' skills, these competencies are difficult to master and the stakes are high. Management educators can help students frame values conflicts, explore ways to address them and even help them practice scripts for speaking up. The moment of the implementation of ethics is the focus of Giving Voice to Values, a cross-disciplinary curriculum that has now been piloted at over 100 business schools. It is centered on a critical, if overlooked, question: what would I say and do in the workplace if I wanted to act on my values?[8] More courses posing such challenges are needed if students are to raise important issues as they rise up the ladder to greater levels of responsibility.

Nervous educators often object – 'Who am I to interject values in the classroom?' and 'What if students have bad values?' The first concern was fully explored – and fears about it allayed – by Harvard Business School in the noteworthy publication of their research *Can Ethics Be Taught?* (Piper et al., 1993). The latter question, of course, is so fundamental to the democratic experiment that it was explored in the Federalist papers. Yet just as the messy system of democracy proved superior to the stated ideals of communism or fascism, so, too, the messy reality of values in business is far better than a pretend world where values are cast aside. It is critical that we teach students that they have the permission, if not the obligation, to act on their values. They will not always agree with us or with each other. But they will be able to navigate these conflicts and invent the best mechanisms for change within their own firms and contexts.

CHALLENGES FOR THE FUTURE

When we began this work 12 years ago under the auspices of the Ford Foundation, we started by trying to support the small cadre of faculty and administrators who already believed in our goals. By strengthening their position, we hoped to build up a beachhead that might influence a larger 'movable majority' of business school faculty. Today, as our CasePlace.org website exceeds 50,000 users, and as a growing percentage of the schools in our *Beyond Grey Pinstripes* survey require a course in social or environmental issues, we know that change is coming.

Over the next five years, we expect a dramatic realignment in management education. The financial crisis has opened the door for fresh, scholarly inquiry about the very purpose of business and sparked debate about how key frameworks are communicated to students, especially in finance and economics classrooms – places where students receive the most powerful messages about business decision-making. Student interest in applying business skills to social problems is burgeoning. A number of high-profile graduate schools – Yale and Stanford among them – have recently revamped their curriculum to create more robust training for new business realities.

So, in pursuit of new rigor, what can business professors do differently on Monday morning? The answer, of course, is 'it depends' – on their institutional context, on their discipline, on their national regulatory environment and political economy. And yet, recalling the framework introduced earlier, they can more deeply engage students around questions of business purpose, context and metrics. They can welcome new voices and encourage students to question their decision models. They can introduce would-be entrepreneurs to business models that assume the need for longer time frames, multiple objectives and wider consultation. They can challenge MBA students to practice making decisions where the 'right' answer cannot be derived from a spreadsheet. And they can insist that students summon the courage and master the tactics for giving voice to their values.

Just as we expect business to expand horizons and listen to all legitimate stakeholders, we need faculty, especially ethics faculty, to consider new frameworks, ask new questions, listen to new voices and in particular build bridges across disciplines.

In other words, faculty can take some risks and help others do the same. They can celebrate successes in managing in the name of both financial and societal benefit. They can search for small wins that have the visibility and leverage to send a signal far and wide that change is not just possible but also inescapable.

When they do this, educators will find they are tapping students' deeply held aspirations for making a difference. Aspen Institute research shows that business students believe they can make a better job of serving all stakeholders – of serving society – than today's business leaders can (Aspen Institute, 2008). All educators have to do, the students say, is give them the tools to make that happen.

There is still much work to be done. For those institutions that make the leap, the benefits to students, business and our society will be enormous.

NOTES

An earlier version of this chapter was published in September 2006 in *Academy of Management Learning and Education*. Special thanks to Mary C. Gentile, Rich Leimsider, Nancy McGaw, Claire Preisser, Justin Goldbach and Matthew Kane for their substantial contributions to this chapter.

1. Since 1999, the Aspen Institute's Business and Society Program has administered *Beyond Grey Pinstripes*, a research survey and alternative ranking of global MBA programs. (1999–2006 surveys were conducted in partnership with the World Resources Institute's Sustainable Enterprise Program.) In 2009, 149 schools from 24 countries participated. Much of the information in this article about the state of business education derives from the data collected for *Beyond Grey Pinstripes* (Aspen Institute, 2009), available at www.BeyondGreyPinstripes.org. This site currently contains 1160 syllabi, information about 3700 courses and over 1000 article abstracts.

2. The Aspen Institute's Business and Society Program surveyed MBA students at leading international business schools in four surveys conducted between 1999 and 2007, designed to study the impact of an MBA education on student attitudes about the role of business in society and the messages students were receiving from business schools about values and behavior in business.

3. Harvard Business School's website states: 'we educate leaders who make a difference in the world' (www.hbs.edu), while Stanford aspires 'to develop innovative, principled, and insightful leaders who change the world' (www.gsb.stanford.edu). Statements like these appeal to a new generation of MBA students who are eager to participate in the business world in a way that contributes to something larger than the self.

4. Professor David Cooperrider, of the Business as an Agent of World Benefit (BAWB) Center at Case Western Reserve University's Weatherhead School of Management, employs Peter Drucker's famous quote about management in his classes and in his work at BAWB.

5. Net Impact, a network of over 15,000 business students and alumni, now has affiliated clubs at 120 business schools in the USA and around the globe. Their mission is 'using the power of business to improve the world'.

6. A promising start is the joint Oxfam–Unilever study of Unilever's operations in Indonesia (Clay, 2005).

7. These questions are explored in depth through the Corporate Governance and Accountability Project on the Aspen Institute's Business and Society Program. Many of the findings from this project are incorporated in business school teaching modules available on www.CasePlace. org, including: 'Investments and Returns: Who has Legitimate Claim on the Returns of the Firm?', 'What the Law Allows', 'Earnings Management: Causes, Techniques, and Transparent Financial Reporting', 'Market Failures' and 'Maximizing Shareholder Value: What are Shareholders' Interests?'

8. The Aspen Institute's Business and Society Program was a founding partner and incubator, together with Yale School of Management, for *Giving Voice to Values*. Dr Mary Gentile is both the principle author and director of the project, now housed at Babson College.

REFERENCES

Aspen Institute (2008) *Where Will They Lead? MBA attitudes about business and society.* New York: Aspen Institute.

Aspen Institute (2009) *Beyond Grey Pinstripes.* Washington, DC: Aspen Institute.

Bach, G.L. (1966) *Lessons from Business Education: Memo to Marshall Robinson.* New York: Ford Foundation Archives.

Bennis, W. and O'Toole, J. (2005) How business schools lost their way. *Harvard Business Review,* 83(5): 96–104.

Bobbitt, P. (2002) *The Shield of Achilles.* New York: Random House.

Brady, D. (2005) Bringing innovation to the home of six sigma. *Business Week,* 68, August.

Brandeis, L. (1912) Business: A profession. Speech given at Brown University commencement, Providence, RI.

Buell, B. (2005) 'Dean Joss envisions larger business school role in multidisciplinary graduate education'. Stanford University Graduate School of Business press release, Stanford, CA.

Clay, J. (2005) *Exploring the Links between International Business and Poverty Reduction: A case study of Unilever in Indonesia.* Oxford: Oxfam.

Datar, S., Garvin, D. and Cullen, P. (2010) *Rethinking the MBA: Business Education at a Crossroads.* Boston, MA: Harvard Business School Publishing.

Freeman, E. (1984) *Strategic Management: A Stakeholder Approach.* Boston, MA: Pitman (Harper and Row).

Gentile, M.C. (2002) *Social Impact Management: A Definition.* New York: Aspen Institute.

Gentile, M.C. (2004) 'Corporate governance and accountability: What do we know and what do we teach future business leaders?' Paper presented at the 4th annual colloquium of the European Academy of Business in Society (EABIS), Ghent, Belgium.

Ghoshal, S. (2005) Bad management theories are destroying good management practices. *Academy of Management Learning and Education*, 4(1): 75–91.

Gordon, R.A. and Howell, J.E. (1993) *Higher Piper Education for Business.* New York: Columbia University Press.

Hart, S. (2005) *Capitalism at the Crossroads.* Upper Saddle River, NJ: Wharton.

Khurana, R. and Khanna, T. (2007) *From Higher Aims to Hired Hands.* Princeton, NJ: Princeton University Press.

Kleiner, A. (2004) Philip Bobbitt: The thought leader interview. *strategy+business*, 34: 91–7.

Kotter, J.P. (1985) *Power and Influence.* New York: Free Press.

Mintzberg, H. (2004) *Managers not MBAs: A hard look at the soft practice of managing and management development.* San Francisco, CA: Berrett-Koehler.

Piper, T., Gentile, M. and Daloz Parks, S. (1992) *Can Ethics be Taught?* Boston, MA: Harvard Business School.

Prahalad, C.K. (2005) *The Fortune at the Bottom of the Pyramid: Eradicating poverty through Profits.* Upper Saddle River, NJ: Wharton.

Prahalad, C.K. and Hart, S. (2002) The fortune at the bottom of the pyramid. *strategy+business*, 26: 54–67.

Scully, M. (2004) *Summary of Interview Themes: 'Corporate governance revisited: What do we know and what do we teach future business leaders?'.* New York: Aspen Institute.

Securities and Exchange Commission (SEC) (2004) Google Inc.: Form S-1 registration statement. Washington, DC.

Tapscott, D. and Williams, A. (2003) Value and values in the age of transparency. Digital 4Sight Inc.

Part 3

BUSINESS SCHOOLS' ROLE IN SHAPING AND TRANSFORMING ETHICAL BUSINESS CONDUCT

17 RESPONSIBLE BUSINESS EDUCATION: NOT A QUESTION OF CURRICULUM BUT A RAISON D'ÊTRE FOR BUSINESS SCHOOLS

Carlos Losada, Janette Martell and Josep M. Lozano

Esade Business School, Spain

Numerous scholars, school stakeholders and the media have expressed their serious concern that most business schools are educating students with a limited and distorted comprehension of their role, one which does not include ethical and social responsibility considerations. Many critics insist that there is a need to scrutinize what actions business schools are taking to overcome these growing legitimacy concerns. The recent global crisis provides business schools with an extraordinary opportunity to undertake a critical reflection and a profound self-examination of their own practices to ensure that similar mistakes do not repeat themselves and that business schools contribute effectively to the education of socially responsible leaders. As Starkey and Tempest state, 'we need to consider a broader definition of the role of the business school as a force for achieving the good of business and of society' (2009: 577).

This chapter addresses the importance of developing an identity in business schools, in relation to ethics and social responsibility, one which transcends the curriculum.

There is a need for self-examination and answering fundamental questions such as: What is our purpose? What type of people and professionals do we aim to educate? What profile do we want for our graduates? What kind of business leader is necessary for the welfare of society? What practices must we implement to responsibly manage our own school? What new roles and responsibilities should our school adopt to serve society's future needs? The central objective of these reflections is to get across the message that educating students in responsible business is not a question of curriculum *stricto sensu* (what we teach as a business school). If we truly want to educate students in responsible business practices, the way the business school is managed must also be socially responsible. This has many specific and demanding implications.

Consequently, the current context demands that business schools ask themselves whether they are also socially responsible institutions. In other words, the introduction of new courses or the transversal integration of ethics and social responsibility in curricula is not the only concern because a school's social responsibility can no longer be limited to a question of program content. Based on the theoretical framework proposed by François Vallaeys (2008), who refers to universities' social responsibility as a system to manage a school's impact, this involves four essential processes: management, education, research and outreach (social commitment).

We feel that European business schools currently have the opportunity to lead the way towards becoming socially responsible academic institutions. As Mintzberg argues, 'innovation in management education is no longer being created in the USA but in Europe' (cited by Bradshaw, 2009: 10). In any case, European business schools cannot stop moving in this direction nor can they renounce doing so.

The subject of ethics in business school programs has inspired a significant number of articles and debates. From 2000–9, and with greater intensity since the collapse of Enron, several provocative articles have been published, and a wave of business ethics topics and corporate governance issues has been introduced in MBA programs and included in curriculum reforms (e.g. Cowe, 2000; Etzioni, 2002; Garten, 2005; Holland, 2009; Webber, 2009). The concern shown by the *Harvard Business Review* (2009) was reflected in a week-long online forum that was conducted to foster discussion among deans, scholars, MBA graduates, writers, HBR readers, business leaders and the public at large, specifically on how to 'fix' business schools.

In 2002, leading scholars in the Academy of Management debated on this organization's role in responding to the ethical scandals of the early part of the decade. They determined that the root cause was the overemphasis which US corporations have been forced to give to maximizing shareholder value in recent years without regard for the effects of their actions on other stakeholders (Waddock, 2004: 24). Research validates the idea that business schools have the power to profoundly affect their students' values. In 'Where Will They Lead?', the Aspen Institute's MBA survey on business and society, researchers found that, during their time at business school, many students' values will change; they will start business school stressing the importance of employee and customer well-being, but they will graduate focusing on shareholder value (Aspen Institute, 2001). This underscores the notion that in attending business school, significant changes can occur within students ... for better or worse.

The results of the 2003 MBA survey indicated that students were concerned about possible value conflicts and unsure about whether or not their business schools were adequately preparing them to deal with such conflicts. In fact, one out of five students said their schools were not preparing them at all (Aspen Institute, 2003). Five years after the publication of this survey, Nancy McGaw, Deputy Director of the Aspen Institute's Business and Society Program, concluded in her analysis of the 2008 survey that environmental issues were not very important for the majority of students and, as they progressed throughout their business school program, they felt less prepared to manage the value conflicts they anticipated having to face in the workplace (Aspen Institute, 2008). This is just one symptom.

What is failing? Why is the business school 'experience' so limited in terms of changing the behavior of participants and students? Why are there no major changes in executive behavior? What is missing? There are indeed several causes, but some very relevant ones are related to the legitimacy of business schools and to the real 'messages' (education) that the participants receive while they are at such institutions. These 'messages' and education are not exclusively related to the curriculum. We must look beyond this issue and deal with the uncomfortable question of how business schools are fulfilling all of their objectives.

The question we propose refers to business schools' identity and, as such, to the transformation they have to enact if they truly want to assume the challenge of their social responsibility, something which affects everything they do, all their processes, as well as their awareness and the willingness with which they address the issue. For this reason, if business schools want to demonstrate their commitment to social responsibility in the near future, they will have to talk about more than just their curricula. The persistent calls for action from stakeholders, repeatedly suggesting changes in management education, indicate that the introduction of new courses or the transversal integration of topics is insufficient because a school's social responsibility can no longer be limited to the curricula. Focusing on the program content is important but also insufficient, and it is therefore necessary to address how business schools are transmitting values because, ultimately, this is one of their primary responsibilities.

BEYOND THE CURRICULUM

For business schools to act responsibly, a day-to-day reality has to be created that breathes and develops management practices that are coherent with the values they preach. We need business schools to 'do business responsibly'.

This affirmation is as true in business schools as it is in any other area of human activity. Consistency between the 'theory taught in the class' and day-to-day practice in business schools is fundamental if we aim to provide an education that encourages responsible leadership. If this coherence does not exist, the business school will strengthen the cynicism of those who believe that social responsibility issues are questions of external reputation or marketing, while management and business reality is another matter.

Compared to other organizations, the responsible management of business schools is extremely demanding. If we aim to educate students about 'responsible business', the schools promoting corporate responsibility have to include it as part of their own core operations. As such, any business school that declares that it is teaching corporate responsibility has to ensure it assumes this responsibility in its own day-to-day practices across all its management subsystems and also ensure that this management is imbued with responsible practices.

We briefly explore what this can imply in the following chart. To systemize this analysis, we will examine a business school's value chain. In the chart, we identify all the relevant sets of actions (management subsystems) that should be reviewed if we want to develop responsible business schools, in order to create an environment that impacts on students' and executives' behavior.

EDUCATIONAL SUBSYSTEMS

Let us begin with the communication and commercialization of the business school's own programs, whether these be the MBA, Executive Education or undergraduate degree programs. The school's declared values in its commercialization policies, its publicity material and, in general, all the elements that make up its sales process provide the initial tests regarding the school's coherence. The proposal put forward to potential participants and the motives to which we resort to capture their attention and interest are the first key elements to identify if we are truly making a responsible proposal and one that is consistent with our values.

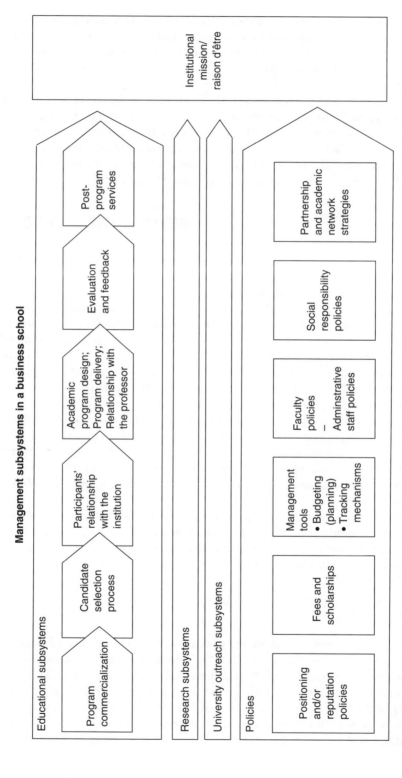

Figure 17.1 Areas that require decisions to be made which will define the identity and values of a business school

Appealing to economic success over the short term or promising a substantial and quick improvement of individual income upon completing the MBA is not the same as proposing an education which will help participants throughout their professional careers and provide them with diverse alternatives, emphasizing the development of their potential as persons and professionals. Elaborating publicity material that conforms to reality regarding what is offered by the educational programs and participants' future job placement is not the same as publicity which oversells or overpromises, making programs extremely attractive for potential participants but not congruent to their actual delivery. It is one thing to be appealing, and another to oversell.

Another management subsystem refers to the candidate selection process for any of the business school's programs. The need for coherence in this ambit clearly emerges in terms of the selection criteria used: if we talk about customization and adaptation, our selection process has to contemplate a high degree of candidate customization and knowledge. There are also elements within the selection process that refer to the business school's level of responsibility, for example: What exactly do we wish to measure during said process? And, what do we evaluate among candidates? The answers to these questions indicate the set of characteristics which we consider valuable for the candidates upon completing their programs at our institutions, though they go well beyond that which we preach in the classroom.

For example, the most renowned institutions in the world are obsessed with attracting students with the highest possible GMAT scores. A candidate with a score of 620 is clearly in an inferior position compared to those scoring 670 or 720. Prioritizing GMAT scores in the selection process implies, on the one hand, giving priority to the institution's position in the rankings and its prestige. At the same time, however, it also implies that what we fundamentally value in candidates is limited to their ability to successfully complete their studies. It also implies obviating that high GMAT scores, above 700, for example, tend to indicate, as shown in various neurological studies (Rock, 2009), that one part of the brain is highly developed (on average) at the expense of other intellectual skills which have probably been less developed. In fact, scoring over 720 on the GMAT exam may be an extraordinarily valid trait for a good analyst or consultant, but it is not necessarily the case for a good executive.

Essentially, do we want people who are highly prepared intellectually to complete their studies? Or, by contrast, do we want to offer society executives with other equally necessary competencies that are even more important today? These could include leadership skills, conflict resolution, the ability to face and overcome ambiguity, etc. The fact that a selection process or an academic institution does not value other attitudes and aptitudes is also a declaration of how school officials understand the institution's responsibilities. If we feel that a key characteristic in any executive is his/her entrepreneurial spirit, teamwork or dedication to service, for example, it would be logical for some measurement of these or other traits to be included in the selection process beyond the GMAT. Not doing so is indicative of how responsibility is seen within the institution. In other words, what we evaluate in the selection process is already an expression of the ideal executive model that we pursue.

The relationship between the participant and the academic institution is also particularly important. There are many types of possible relationships, but they can generally be classified into two categories: purchaser–client/supplier and partner relationships. Depending on the existing incentives and the culture established internally, the academic institution is declaring what type of relationship it favors in the educational setting. For example, business schools sometimes proudly declare that they aim to mimic the market, the goal being for the business community's consumer/supplier relationship to be applied to the educational area. This is a clear indication of how the institution understands its educational responsibility and the values and practices it transmits during the professional development process. A partnership-type relationship, by contrast, implies shared learning and experiences that enrich the relationship. It tells us something very different about how the educational institution regards its responsibility.

Analogous reflections can be made with respect to the quality of the education offered, how up-to-date it is and its importance within the curriculum. We have discussed this above, and it is not the main focus of this chapter (centered on what is 'beyond the curriculum'). However, we need to reflect once more on what is behind a demanding, relevant and up-to-date curriculum which sees business education from a holistic perspective. Similarly, the high level of demand (on others and ourselves) and the responsibility spread out amongst each and every member of the institution when designing the program and, especially delivering it is another element which students will learn through 'osmosis', potentially becoming, as a result, a reference or anti-reference for their own professional lives. For this reason, the relationship with the professor is especially important (what values are lived, established and favored in this relationship?).

This is not the same as the 'client/supplier relationship' in which quantification measures are used regarding the time spent with students rather than creating a relationship based on cooperation, a relationship in which the professor is sincerely interested in the student, where demand is accompanied by high standards, where there is a significant degree of customization, etc. In the end, the type of professionals favored by one or other form of relationship is different as is the style of leadership these executives will later put into practice. Through this relationship, it is possible to help students distinguish between areas where cooperation and the combination of individual wills is necessary and those areas in which it is absolutely essential to compete or compete fiercely. Through interpersonal relationships inside and outside the classroom, the institution also declares how it understands its institutional and educational responsibilities and what values it transmits to its program participants.

In this process, it is especially interesting to examine the evaluation criteria used when grading students' work and giving participants feedback. How we evaluate what they have learnt and some of the skills taught is a key element which reflects how the business school understands its responsibility. The famous Gaussian bell curve with grades A, B, C and D, where 10 per cent of students receiving the worst marks have to leave the program, reveals that the criteria and culture we favor among students are, basically, competitive and excluding. If that is what we in fact envisage, it's a good system, it's coherent and it can certainly educate people who are highly competitive and orientated towards individual success. At the same time, however, we have to be aware that, by doing so, we undervalue cooperation, teamwork and shared successes, establishing relationships to develop projects over the mid and long terms, and settings in which professionals can give the best of themselves.

Other systems may have different virtues and defects and, definitively, they may favor a different value proposition. For example, establishing high standards, where everyone can be successful and each individual fights against his/her own limits, making a true effort to succeed, favors a culture based on personal effort, one that encourages people to demand hard work of themselves and doesn't hinder (and even encourages) teamwork. Another alternative could be to combine different evaluation systems to transmit the message that both competition and collaboration are needed, but that we need to know where and when to apply them. The feedback students/participants receive on their work is also highly related to the evaluation system. This is a key moment in which the real value given to learning is 'declared', thereby manifesting what the professor feels regarding the participant and what he/she values in business education. In the end, students will remember the institution where they chose to study, its identity and responsibility by the evaluation system used, along with their relationship with faculty members. These are probably the key elements though they are generally not taken into consideration when talking about the values business schools transmit.

At the same time, we can also talk about the relationship established with students near the end of their program or after completing it. We refer here to post-program services or career service departments, responsible for training future executives on how to carry out work interviews, prepare their curriculum vitae, etc. These career services help orientate students' professional lives and suggest the criteria students should use when making decisions in this respect. During this orientation process, messages are sent which are key to the type of business education and executive profile each institution 'is set to launch on the market'. Here, as well, emphasis can be given only to the financial element, the individual project and the short term or it can introduce other criteria for students to make decisions on their careers. Analogously, the existence of an alumni association, its profile and services, though less important, is also indicative of the culture and values favored by the institution and, in effect, of the institution's coherence and commitment to its own educational proposal.

RESEARCH SUBSYSTEMS

The business school's research policy is another key element in terms of how it defines its responsibility. We need to mention a prior decision here, one which represents a pre-existing option regarding certain values that are difficult to compare. This choice refers to whether or not to provide complete freedom to professors to research all that they consider interesting from their respective departmental fields. At the other extreme, we find the option of specifically defining two or three basic research areas for the professors as, clearly, not all business schools can play an important role in every area of knowledge. Between these two options, there is also a large grey area encompassing numerous options and in which it is important to know how to allow for the freedom to research while establishing some priority or favored lines of research. In addition to the business schools' choice regarding one of these three distinct models, the criteria they use to prioritize these lines of research also reveal clues about how they understand their responsibility. What is valued? What topics do we favor and why are they prioritized? What link is there between the concrete research questions and a holistic and responsible view of business? The answers can range from carrying out research from which we can obtain resources to carrying out research on areas linked to a specific agenda in line with the business school's mission. At the extreme end of the first case, we would be talking about an institution that adapts to the market. The second case would reflect an institution which somehow attempts to transform social reality in accordance with its reason for being.

UNIVERSITY OUT-REACH SUBSYSTEMS

Another clear business school area of responsibility is its university outreach program or social projection, social commitment and connection to the society in which it finds itself. Becoming a part of this social reality implies great effort and realism, especially, if through this outreach program, the business school opens itself to debates on business, economic and social matters, relevant to both companies and society. Participating exclusively in academic or elitist debates where a certain business segment finds a favorable audience is not the same as allowing all the inhumane reality of the current economic situation and debates on crucial topics related to this reality to enter the business school. Furthermore, giving access to this reality in order to understand it, is not the same as letting it in to study and have an impact on it; nor is it the same as letting it in to understand it, have an impact on it and be affected by it.

As such, from the responsibility point of view, we feel that coherence in the decisions made in terms of research and the contribution the institution wants to make to society is also key as these are precise measures of this consistency. Are we guided by a business-as-usual approach and are we a forum where only those that already have forums and that already appear in the newspapers can speak? We could make an analogous reflection regarding the faculty's published articles and presence in the media. What topics are addressed? What appearances are prioritized? And what subjects and focuses do we propose to society?

POLICIES

Special attention has to be paid to business school policies regarding their positioning, reputation and how they are influenced by rankings. A lack of honesty and fair play in the data or a commitment to transparency is a capital question in creating the right internal environment in which business school responsibility can grow. Similarly, being a ranking-driven or a mission-driven organization creates a radically different culture. Being a ranking-driven school has numerous implications: centring on student job placement in specific industries and companies (i.e. international consultancy firms and investment banks), prioritizing GMAT scores in the selection process, etc. Here, the business school can be complacent, serving as one more actor in the system or, conversely, it can lobby transparently for the indicators used in these rankings to create appropriate incentives to improve the intrinsic quality of both the education and research carried out. The latter also includes working with other business schools that share this perspective to move positively in this direction.

The business school's policy regarding fees and scholarships is another area which reflects how it interprets its responsibility. Beyond reflecting on the segments of the population that the program is aimed at, the business school's positioning, its analysis of the competition and economic and financial needs, etc., the fees charged and the school's scholarship policy also manifestly reflect its responsibility policies. If the institution clearly and decisively wagers on an open, free and competitive social model in which everyone can contribute the best that they have, this has to be reflected in its pricing and scholarship policy.

If, by contrast, a meritocracy is significant, and the business school truly values talent, competition and equity while also being decisively opposed to maintaining the status quo which keeps society and the economy from progressing, it must offer an 'aggressive' scholarship policy aimed at compensating for the numerous inequalities and imbalances embedded within our society. Or seen another way: not having this scholarship policy indicates that the university institution, more than attempting to improve its management and practices, is reproducing (and, consequently, validating) the current status quo and refusing to serve as a factor for social improvement and transformation.

The business school's 'budgetary policy' is another area which reveals its level of responsibility. The budget serves to specify and, in fact, declare its priorities year after year. How funds (both current expenditures and investment) are distributed is essential in this sense. We can be dealing with an institution that gives special importance and credit to its facilities, attempting to make them as luxurious and select as possible for its participants, compared to another institution which prioritizes investing in talent, research and scholarships. Budgets also serve to define the balance between investing in the brand and its reputation and the priority the business school gives to educational content and research. Here is where we see up to what point the responses to the questions we have asked in this part of the chapter go from mere declarations of intent to having the resources to potentially become real policies that truly reflect the business school's values.

In terms of management tracking systems (versus planning systems), it is especially important to analyse what the institution measures, observes and monitors. The coherence between the responses to the questions presented thus far and management control panels and other management tools is crucial. We have to be able to clearly identify what we measure and observe and determine where we establish and prioritize actions when attempting to correct deviations. Focusing exclusively on some indicators (i.e. yield percent, the GMAT or profit and loss accounts) is not the same as also analysing, for example, the degree to which certain skills or knowledge are obtained or alumni performance 5 or 10 years after the completion of programs at the business school.

Upon reaching this point, it should be clear that policies affecting the faculty are pivotal to the discussion at hand. The business school's commitment and discourse on social responsibility is based fundamentally on its faculty policy. What factors do we evaluate when hiring faculty? How do we define the professional quality we seek? This will determine the dynamics of competitive processes. Once hired, however, what type of socialization system do we use? Do we leave new professors' adaptation to chance? Or do we have a mentoring or Cicerone structure in place? Does this process include some sort of reflection on the business school's values and mission? We also have to analyse our evaluation and retribution systems. What do we evaluate the faculty for every year? What criteria do we apply when promoting them? What academic contributions do we require? Do we tolerate the existence of various academic tracks (e.g. more focused on teaching, more on research, etc.)? How are each of these tracks treated within the institution? All this ultimately leads to another question regarding the behavior, attitudes and practices we aim to favor with our faculty policies.

An analogous reflection could be made regarding management, administrative and service staff in that they are also a relevant component within the educational process. To summarize with an example: the experience students can have in the business school itself when attempting to resolve their own conflicts and manage change is more important than a case study on conflict resolution. In general terms, how diverse academic services approach the different initiatives, problems or conflicts with participants is more important for the latter's education than a possible case study on managing conflicts or initiatives. It goes without saying how important the role played by business school management is in terms of its behavior, the objectives it sets and its management style. Through management, the organization's true identity and the culture it can promote are on the line, given that said behavior, objectives and management style can favor certain dominant values over others.

One question which often goes ignored relates to the business school's own social responsibility policy. This policy helps to define its identity. Its sustainability and diversity policies, the balance between personal life and work, its purchasing policies and accountability mechanisms, among others, all define the degree to which what the business school preaches is consistent with what it practices. If it is consistent, we thus have a responsible business school before us. Of particular importance are our answers to the following questions: What relationships are established between the business school and all the stakeholders, including alumni? Is the alumni association a select club that is difficult to join or is our network of alumni a tool to foment the desired behavior taught at the school? Is it a good means to refresh alumni's knowledge and skills and does it encourage all former students to develop and define their roles as agents to generate wealth responsibly?

The institution's social responsibility policy also affects its good governance system. What role does the management board play? What degree of transparency and accountability has the business school established? Is it expressly committed to the United Nations Principles for Responsible Management Education (PRME)? If so, does the business school have management systems in place to measure up to what point it is fulfilling these commitments?

Responsible management and commitment are factors which also affect the business school's policy regarding institutional relationships and, especially, its partnership relationships with companies. What companies does the business school associate with? A business school also defines itself by the links it establishes, whether with public or private institutions. Making it a priority to associate with market leaders is not the same as aiming to associate with 'challengers' or highly innovative firms. Accepting and prioritizing links with companies which survive, in part, due to specific protective trade policies is not the same as prioritizing links with export or import firms in a highly competitive market, etc. Through their preferred types of associations, business schools also define what they understand as responsibility. If we define ourselves as an institution which favors entrepreneurship, internationalization, innovation, etc., we would expect to see links primarily with companies that are entrepreneurial, that internationalize and that innovate. This does not imply that this option has to be exclusive or that it has to be a radical choice. Rather, it has to be perceived and lived and to posssess consequences. A similar reflection has to be made with respect to businessmen and others invited to give presentations, participate in seminars, etc., people who are presented at the business school as references. This last question has a direct effect on the dissemination of social responsibility principles: you cannot maintain a discourse and/or curriculum in which social responsibility plays an important role and then undermine this with a list of guests who have been invited on a preferential basis.

Similarly, the same could be said as regards the academic networks which are prioritized and favored or in terms of links with other business schools, universities and research centers. Not all academic partners are the same nor do they all reflect the same values, perspectives and commitments. If a business school opts for internationalization, this should also be observed in its sponsorship agreements. If an institution opts for pedagogical excellence, research or a certain mix of the two, the business school should also reflect this coherently in terms of its academic links. If it feels that the role of wealth generation and economic growth is important at the global level, it should have academic partners in developing countries within its networks with which it maintains truly mature, cooperative relationships that go beyond just sending a few PhD candidates to the other institutions, involving, instead, good professors who can especially train faculty in those developing country institutions.

CHALLENGES

To summarize, if the business school's raison d'être is to educate responsible executives, the level of demand required of the institution is very high. If the aim is to make a real social contribution, it is important to bear in mind that educating responsible executives implicates and involves the entire institution, well beyond its curriculum. This, of course, is not easy and constitutes a challenge. It is also true that this difficulty and demand can transmit some extraordinary and exceptional values to society. This would be especially true if these values were practiced by all business schools, though a first and extraordinary step forward would be for this to be the norm among the 50 or 100 best business schools out of the more than 10,000 around the world.

In effect, we do not transmit values or educate by what we say but by what we do and who we are. For this reason and given the new challenges that social responsibility development implies for business schools, throughout this chapter we have attempted to explore some of the elements which can help move us forward in this direction. Disseminating social responsibility principles is not only a question of curriculum for business schools; it is especially a matter of identity for socially responsible business schools. The future challenges are related to answering the above questions and resolving the dilemmas posed. The corresponding responses will determine whether our business schools serve to improve managerial practices or if they simply reproduce a given managerial culture, thus blocking any necessary improvements with the consequent high social cost this has for us all.

REFERENCES

Aspen Institute, Center for Business Education (2001, 2003, 2008) Where will they lead? MBA student attitudes about business and society. Available at: www.aspencbe.org/teaching/Student_Attitudes.html (accessed 3 February 2010).
Bradshaw, D. (2009) Deans fight crisis fires with MBA overhaul. *Financial Times*, Business Education section, 8 June, p. 10.

Cowe, R. (2000) Black hole in the MBA curriculum, *The Guardian*, 19 February.

Etzioni, A. (2002) When it comes to ethics, B-Schools get an F. *The Washington Post*, 4 August, B4. Available at: http://amitaietzioni.org/ documents/B399.pdf (accessed 6 May 2009).

Garten, J.E. (2005) Business schools: only a C+ in ethics. *Business Week*, 5 September. Available at: www.businessweek.com/magazine/content/05_36/b3949138.htm (accessed 3 May 2009).

Harvard Business Review Debate (2009) How to fix business schools, 30 March to 7 May. Available at: http://blogs.harvardbusiness.org/how-to-fix-business-schools/index.php?page=3 (accessed 22 October 2009).

Holland, K. (2009) Is it time to retrain B-Schools? *The New York Times*, 14 March. Available at: www.nytimes.com/2009/03/15/business/15school.html?_r=3andref=business (accessed 15 March 2009).

Rock, D. (2009) Strategy + business. *Organization and People*, 56.

Starkey, K. and Tempest, S. (2009) The winter of our discontent: the design challenge for business schools. *Academy of Management Learning and Education*, 8(4): 576–86.

Vallaeys, F. (2008) University social responsibility: a new philosophy of ethical and intelligent management for universities. *Educación Superior y Sociedad*, September, 13(2): 191–219. (A bi-annual journal published by the International Institute for Higher Education in Latin America and the Caribbean [IESALC] from UNESCO, Caracas, Venezuela.) Available at: www.redivu.org/docs/publicaciones/Revista_Educacion_y_Sociedad.pdf (accessed 22 April 2009).

Waddock, S. (2004) Hollowmen at the helm. *BizEd Magazine for Business Education*, July/August. Available at: www.aacsb.edu/publications/Archives/JulyAug04/p24–29.pdf (accessed 29 December 2009).

Webber, A.M. (2009) MBA's swearing in vain. *Forbes*, 19 June. Available at: www.forbes.com/2009/06/19/mba-swear-vain-intelligent-technology-webber.html (accessed 10 December 2009).

18 THE BUSINESS SCHOOL OF THE TWENTY-FIRST CENTURY: EDUCATING CITIZENS TO ADDRESS THE NEW WORLD CHALLENGES

Valérie Swaen, Philippe de Woot and Didier de Callataÿ

Louvain School of Management, Belgium

Today, CSR has become 'a vital part of the business conversation' (Pearce and Doh, 2005: 30) and is commonly used in the European business environment with no hint of irony: rates of CSR reporting by large companies have been consistently higher in Europe than in other parts of the world (KPMG, 2005). Some 90 per cent of European companies in the *Fortune Global 250* publish CSR reports, as contrasted with 83 per cent of Japanese companies and 35 per cent of American companies (Kolk, 2008). The emerging European view of CSR stands as a compromise between market pressure calls for innovation and competitiveness and the traditional European social model (Delbard, 2008). This view breaks with traditional European practices of active state intervention, 'by embedding the social dimension into civil society and self-regulatory market processes, with the state playing more of a facilitating and endorsing role' (Midttun, 2005: 160).

Crane and Matten (2004: 46) state that 'all levels of CSR play a role in Europe, but they have different significance, and furthermore are interlinked in a somewhat different manner [than in North America]'. More especially, ethical responsibilities enjoy a much higher priority in Europe, while European companies are less focused on discretionary and philanthropic responsibilities than their North American counterparts (Bennett, 1998; Palazzo, 2002). Moreover, European actors seem more inclined to focus on the impact of their activities and to point out those practices that are more closely linked to their production processes when trying to build a socially responsible image (Maignan and Ralston, 2002). Accordingly, European companies across industries have a tendency to converge on specific CSR issues they consider as strategic such as those more related to health, safety, environmental protection and energy consumption (Perrini, 2005).

On the other hand, in the last few years, a growing number of companies have faced strong and well-publicized accusations involving their socially irresponsible activities. For instance, Chiquita started to collaborate in 1992 with the Rainforest Alliance – an organization that militates for sustainable agriculture in tropical countries – on the 'better banana' project in order to certify its plantations according to social and environmental standards. And, in 1998, the *Cincinnati Enquirer* published the results of a one-year investigation accusing Chiquita of committing political, environmental and human rights abuses in Central America and depicting the company as having no societal conscience (Gallagher and McWhirter, 1998). The furniture manufacturer Ikea, which publicly claims to manufacture eco-friendly products, also became the target for repeated accusations from various non-governmental organizations (NGO), such as Greenpeace and Robin Wood, for failing to respect its environmental and human rights responsibilities (Bailly et al., 2006). Numerous companies have already faced crises involving their socially irresponsible activities and the number of such crises is expected to grow in the future (Strike et al., 2006). This expected growth could be partly explained by globalization, as firms 'may act irresponsibly, not out of malice or ill will, but because they have to stretch their resources and capabilities in order to coordinate and monitor subsidiaries' (Strike et al., 2006: 853).

In this context, some observers suggest that business schools are partly responsible for the recent business scandals and unethical executive actions which frequent the popular press (Henle, 2006), because they create a 'profit-first mentality' without any regard for moral considerations (Ghoshal, 2005; Giacalone and Thompson, 2006). Furthermore, Benn and Dunphy (2009) suggest that MBA programs do not adequately prepare students to deal with the challenges of sustainability issues in the workplace. Business schools are increasingly perceived as not up to the task of training managers and leaders for the challenges of the twenty-first century and sustainable development. One of the main criticisms bears on this disconnection from ethics and politics and the restricted and mechanical view of human beings and society that most management programs convey to the students (de Woot, 2005).

This chapter is structured as follows. First, we highlight CSR practices developed by European corporate actors through analysis of a set of 499 CSR initiatives gathered by CSR Europe, the leading European business network for CSR.[1] On that basis, we illustrate the challenges ahead in fostering CSR development in Europe and discuss what business schools can do to influence and promote responsible behavior. More specifically, we highlight the role of business schools in educating entrepreneurs, ethical leaders and statesmen. The main contribution of our chapter is notably to bring in personal competence learning as a central focus in CSR education.

INNOVATIVE CSR-RELATED PRACTICES PROPOSED BY EUROPEAN CORPORATE ACTORS

Maon and Swaen (2010) draw a relatively up-to-date picture of CSR-related activities adopted by corporate actors across Europe, by analyzing the 'CSR solutions database' posted on the internet by CSR Europe (www.csreurope.org/solutions). That database included 499 best practices implemented by 178 corporate actors originating from the 10 different industries constituting the Industry Classification Benchmark.[2]

Maon and Swaen (2010) classified those 499 initiatives according to four main themes: the type of concerns; the nature and type of CSR initiatives implemented; the type of stakeholders

Table 18.1 An analysis of 499 CSR initiatives gathered by CSR Europe

	N	%
Type of concerns*		
Social concerns – internal and organization-focused	231	46.3%
Social concerns – external and society-focused	305	61.1%
Environmental concerns	199	39.9%
Economic and commercial concerns	178	35.7%
Type of CSR initiatives*		
CSR-related awareness programs within the organization	90	18.0%
CSR-related products and services	78	15.6%
CSR-related processes and capabilities (training, sourcing, codes)	284	56.9%
Community and society involvement practices (philanthropy, employee volunteerism, expertise sharing)	242	48.5%
Type of stakeholders*		
Internal stakeholders		
Employees	246	49.3%
Managers	135	27.1%
Unions	22	4.4%
External stakeholders		
NGOs	232	46.5%
Local communities	208	41.7%
Business partners and suppliers	100	20.0%
Customers	87	17.4%
Public authorities	69	13.8%
Other businesses	45	9.0%
The media	15	3.0%
Impacts on strategy and culture		
Low	198	39.7%
Moderate	180	36.1%
High	121	24.2%

Source: Maon and Swaen, 2010

Note: * The subcategories are not mutually exclusive, which explains why the sum of the percentages can be greater than 100%

primarily impacted on or involved; and the potential impacts of the CSR initiatives on corporate strategy and culture.

As illustrated in Table 18.1, most of the CSR initiatives (61.1 per cent) were directly or indirectly linked to external social issues pertaining, for instance, to education, health or community. Internal social issues pertaining to the workers and the company's supply chain characterize 46.3 per cent of the solutions, while 39.9 per cent of the CSR initiatives are about environmental protection. Finally, 35.7 per cent of the CSR solutions are directly linked to commercial transactions or business concerns, such as in the case of sourcing practices and actions directly related to the marketing of products and services. Accordingly, CSR initiatives involve or affect both internal and external stakeholders. Employees/workers are the internal stakeholders who are most concerned by the CSR initiatives, while labor unions are the least concerned, reflecting to some extent the substantial degree of European unions' scepticism surrounding the CSR notion (Preuss, 2008). In reference to external stakeholders, civil society organizations such as NGOs, non-profit associations, and public and educational entities are most frequently involved in or affected by the CSR initiatives implemented, followed by local communities, commercial stakeholders such as suppliers and customers, and public authorities. On types of CSR initiatives, the development of CSR-related processes and capabilities constitutes the most frequent type of implemented initiative, followed by the development of community involvement practices. Conversely, CSR-related awareness programs within the organization and CSR-related products and services are much less frequent.

On that basis, Maon and Swaen (2010) distinguish between three main CSR approaches. The first one consists of focusing on discretionary actions with the objectives to contribute to local communities and improve quality of life, and to promote and improve human welfare and environmental stewardship in the external environment of the company. CSR is seen as a collection of discretionary practices (Carroll, 1979, 2004) that are peripheral to core business processes and activities. Companies adopting such an approach develop CSR initiatives through employee volunteerism programs, sensitization campaigns, philanthropic donations and sponsorship. CSR is seen as a way to enhance the corporate license to operate rather than as a potential opportunity to create or strengthen business value in the long run.

The second approach consists of focusing on business processes and competencies via the development of CSR management frameworks (including extra-financial measurement and reporting) and CSR-related skills within the company. This focus is supported by internal stakeholders and the development of cooperative relationships with business partners such as suppliers and – to some extent – customers. Companies adopting such an approach design and implement CSR-related initiatives aimed at measuring and limiting the negative environmental and social impact of their activities. This approach reflects some degree of integration of CSR-related concerns at the various levels of the organization. However, the CSR initiatives still mainly aim at risk reduction and business value maintenance through incremental improvements, rather than on value creation or a real change in corporate culture.

The third approach consists of focusing on business outcomes using the development of products and services with an apparent or indirect CSR dimension that meet specific stakeholders' expectations and desires. Companies endeavor to demonstrate that society's expectations matter by listening to external stakeholders' voice and opinions and by developing multi-stakeholder dialogue processes, with customers and secondary stakeholders such as NGOs and non-profit associations. Those continuous interactions with external stakeholders develop stakeholder confidence in corporate activities, products and services, and reduce the risk of green washing accusations. Companies adopting such an approach have a clear understanding of CSR-related market-driven trends and typically consider CSR as a value creator through 'improved community relations, legitimacy, and brand reputation' (Hart and Milstein, 2003: 62).

Those three approaches are not exclusive but should be considered complementarily in order for companies to develop constructive CSR programs and policies that meet society's expectations in a comprehensive way, in line with business objectives and imperatives: the development of CSR-related capabilities and technical competencies – that typically characterize the process-oriented, embedded approach – should ideally aim at supporting and fostering the development of innovative products and services value – that typify the outcome-oriented, embedded approach of CSR. Also, beyond their economic, legal and ethical responsibilities, corporate actors perform in a manner that is consistent with the philanthropic and charitable prospects of their environment and 'assist voluntarily those projects that enhance a community's quality of life' (Carroll, 2004), in line with the discretionary, philanthropy-oriented, disembedded approach of CSR.

Furthermore, despite the widely accepted viewpoint that the changes required to progress toward CSR require fundamental shifts in organizational culture (Doppelt, 2003; Lyon, 2004; Maon et al., 2010), the vast majority of CSR-related initiatives analyzed remain somewhat disconnected from the general strategic goals of organizations (Maon and Swaen, 2010). However, the literature also shows that in order to integrate CSR principles into an organization's long-term strategy and decision-making criteria, the organization must make the transition from an utterly economy-driven culture to a more value-laden culture (de Woot, 2005). That is, the organization must build on corporate values to create an organizational culture that promotes openness, does not focus solely on self-interest and adopts other-regarding sentiments (Jones et al., 2007).

Building on Maon and Swaen (2010)'s research, we could highlight five main challenges which most managers will be confronted with when they try to design and implement a CSR agenda, and to evolve from management of CSR to management by CSR:

- Evolve from a short-term profit focus to an enlarged vision of the company: most managers still adopt a perspective that is too focused on short-term profit, while the final purpose of a company should be enlarged to include economic, social and environmental progress (de Woot, 2005).
- Evolve from a 'best practice' perspective to a 'culturally embedded' perspective: most managers rely too heavily on best practice; in most cases, they are simply imitating what is successful elsewhere, instead of innovating their business models and taking into account their own values and organizational cultures.
- Adopt a more systemic perspective: most managers lack the ability to adopt a systemic perspective about business impacts and sustainability issues; they do not fully understand the societal impacts of their decisions and are not trained to solve dilemmas between the economic, social and environmental issues they are faced with daily. In the same vein, they express difficulties in collaboration and dialogue with their stakeholders, which is however essential in a CSR perspective.
- Question the system: most managers are unable to propose and implement a real strategic change by questioning the products and services they propose to the market; the processes they use to develop products and services; and more broadly the system in which they evolve.
- Reconnect brain (intellect), heart (emotional intelligence) and mind (spiritual intelligence): address the 'whole person' (Taylor, 2006).

THE ROLE OF BUSINESS SCHOOLS

For many observers, business schools are partly responsible for that situation, for two main reasons.

The most important reason is their imprisonment in the dominant profit-first ideology. This profit-first mentality taught in most business schools creates future managers who seek profit first, at any cost, without regard for moral considerations or social responsibility (de Woot, 2005; Ghoshal, 2005). 'The social responsibility of the firm is to maximize profit for the shareholder' – this famous statement by Milton Friedman (1970) has profoundly influenced business education by disconnecting it from ethics and politics, which is a serious flaw in training future leaders (de Woot, 2005). Business courses often encourage a view of human nature that does not inspire high-mindedness (Shiller, 2005). People are portrayed as nothing more than 'maximizers' of their own expected utility. This means that they are expected to be totally selfish, constantly calculating their own advantage, with no thought of others (Arnsperger, 2005; Mitroff, 2004). The raison d'être of most management schools is to equip their students to operate the existing system in an effective way without concerning themselves with its purpose or defects, or the dangers that it is presenting thus far. In this sense, the majority of professors are the clerics and celebrants of the 'single thought' or uniform thinking. They present a major obstacle to the establishment of a true culture of sustainable development. These schools defend an outdated model that is losing its legitimacy and that enlightened corporations are now questioning. Those business schools and their representatives may be outraged by business scandals but they very rarely discuss the fundamental flaws of the model. Management students tend to be trapped in the logic of means and to ignore the ends of the economic system. They learn how to make the system more effective and more efficient without reflecting upon its societal purpose or its raison d'être. Therefore, they do not develop any critical capacity regarding the system itself and this approach is a major obstacle to the establishment of a true culture of sustainable development (de Woot, 2005). Rayment and Smith's report on 'The Current and Future Role of Business Schools' – published in February 2010 – still insists on this cruel fact: 'Leaders of participating business schools did not convey the impression that steering business towards helping humanity achieve a sustainable future and tackle urgent global issues is seen by them as one of their main roles, either current or future'. There are very few, if any, business schools asking their students the ethical question of our time: 'What kind of world do we want to build with the resources, creativity and power available to us?'

The second reason for the unsuitableness of management schools is that, locked as they are into their ideology, they do little to prepare their students to face up to their social responsibilities and the real challenges of the twenty-first century: the evolution of human societies and a new form of contestation, the questionable legitimacy of economic and financial power, broadening the purpose of the firm, the ethics of foresight, new forms of societal debate, the use of precaution in the application of science and technology, and so on. Apart from globalization, the majority of important contemporary trends are omitted from the culture business schools promote. They pass on technical skills, tools, decision-making methods and organizational methods rather than values, independent thinking and ethical concern. One cannot criticize them for imparting professional knowledge, but one can question their essentially instrumental approach, given that their students are destined to drive an economic and technical system that is increasingly being challenged. More critical still, according to Mintzberg (2004), they do not even prepare their students for the profession of management, in the broad sense of professional leadership, but are content to pass on specialist skills, such as marketing, finance and production. Many have suggested that MBA programs focus too heavily on quantitatively based analytical techniques to the detriment of the 'soft skills', which are essential for managers (Simpson, 2006). Navarro (2008) also highlighted the fact that the curricula of top-ranked US business schools lacked multidisciplinary integration, which leads to the creation of functional silos within business school education. The business schools are mostly technical institutions oriented towards a logic of efficiency without questioning its purpose. They seek to promote a system that they view uncritically.[3]

It is, therefore, not surprising that they are resistant, as are many managers they have trained, to any fundamental change to the economic model and the ideology that underpins it. We should also not be surprised to learn that some recent deviation scandals were perpetrated by former students of those schools. In 2003, Sumantra Ghoshal (of the London Business School) argued that many of the 'worst excesses of recent management practices have their roots in a set of ideas that have emerged from business school academics over the last 30 years'.

ON THE ROAD TOWARD THE BUSINESS SCHOOL OF THE TWENTY-FIRST CENTURY: THE LOUVAIN SCHOOL OF MANAGEMENT CASE

The influence of business schools is vast. Not only do they train, retrain and recycle the majority of CEOs and managers of large companies, they also impose and widely promote their vision of the firm and their philosophy of management. It is their management culture that is transmitted, and their former students remain imbued with it as they rise in the hierarchy and take control of companies. Business schools produce the authors of the most widely read management texts, the gurus, wise men and consultants of every hue who besiege the firm.

The European Commission and the partners engaged in the European Alliance for CSR – 'The Responsible Business in 2020'[4] – strongly affirm that it is essential that business schools, universities and other educational institutions play a proactive role in mainstreaming CSR into traditional courses, in the curricula of future managers and graduate students, in executive education, and in other educational institutions. Business schools should go beyond some optional courses in CSR or ethics and completely revisit their values, their mission, their curricula and their pedagogy. The vision of the Louvain School of Management (LSM) clearly has the school heading in that direction.

THE LSM VISION AND OBJECTIVES

THE LOUVAIN SCHOOL OF MANAGEMENT[5]

The LSM has promoted a clear ambition – summarized in its slogan:'Excellence and Ethics in Business' – which is 'to train today's and tomorrow's managers in responsible decision-making within a complex socio-economic environment and to put human and societal

(Continued)

(Continued)

values at the heart of decisions'. The main objective of the LSM is to promote a responsible mode of management, open to new forms of dialogue and consultation by training responsible and professional entrepreneurs. The LSM is willing to develop the capabilities of students to be future generators of sustainable value for business and society at large and to work for an inclusive and sustainable global economy. The LSM tries as much as possible to incorporate into its academic activities and curricula the values of global social responsibility by offering educational frameworks, materials, processes and environments that enable effective learning experiences for responsible leadership.

Business schools could become major agents for cultural change if they addressed the main aforementioned challenges faced by the current economic system (a short-term profit focus; the best practice reflex; no systemic perspective; lack of questioning; lack of brain, heart and mind connection), through the training of (1) entrepreneurs – willing to launch innovative projects, to solve complex problems by adopting a systemic perspective and to change business norms; (2) ethical leaders – willing to motivate staff and to undertake cultural change for a more ethical and sustainable development; and (3) 'statesmen' – willing to adopt the role of concerned citizen and to participate in the design of a new political governance.

Accordingly, business schools should promote a renewed vision of the corporation for the twenty-first century in which entrepreneurship, leadership and statesmanship (de Woot, 2009; GRLI,[6] 2008) represent core elements. And they cannot succeed in isolation from each other; they have to collaborate together as well as with the most proactive companies, and to be part of the most advanced networks with respect to CSR, globally responsible leadership and sustainable development.

ENTREPRENEURSHIP

Spurred on by competition and technological advances, the successful company does not content itself with the production and distribution of goods and services. It constantly renews them, makes them evolve and creates new ones. If one monitors successful companies over a period of 5 or 10 years, it could be seen that not a single one had failed to adapt, transform or renew itself. Each one would have evolved and innovated, in their products, their markets, their procedures or their organization. This reality gives their actions a dynamic and creative flavour. Initiative and creativity constitute the backbone of entrepreneurship. Schumpeter (1949) highlighted this source of economic development. For him, the competition that really counted was the competition for new goods, new techniques, new supply sources, new types of organization. The driving force was mainly the individual entrepreneur, a rare character with specific qualities: the vision for potential progress, energy, an appetite for risk sufficient to implement things, and a power of conviction capable of bringing him the necessary support and resources.

Nowadays, it is not only the individual entrepreneur or businessman who creates innovation. The company has taken over a large part of this role and now ensures this type of progress in a collective and systematic way. The reality of economic and technical development is that of major innovations, often implemented at the start by individual entrepreneurs and rapidly relayed by large corporations acting as 'collective' entrepreneurs. Today, the names of Ford, Singer, Campbell, Solvay, Bekaert, Lafarge, Michelin and Renault no longer refer merely to the creator-individuals who founded them, but also to companies with collective capabilities that developed in themselves the qualities of the famous entrepreneurs who created them. It is on that role that they should focus in order to define their raison d'être and found their legitimacy.

The raison d'être of the company should be revisited and integrate the concepts of entrepreneurship, innovation, economic and technical progress as the main purposes of the firm. The purpose of the globally responsible business is to create economic and societal progress in a globally responsible and sustainable way (de Woot, 2009; GRLI, 2008). Educating future managers in this enlarged conception of the purpose of the firm instead of the traditionally taught profit-first ideology should avoid the aforementioned case of companies behaving irresponsibly and being driven only by profit.

Are business schools really training entrepreneurs? Do they develop the entrepreneurial capabilities of future managers, which include skills and competencies such as being able to develop a vision about possible innovation, to convince others to enter the new game, to take risks and to drive change? We should restore the pride in being an entrepreneur. Alongside courses in various techniques and tools (finance, marketing, control), students should be exposed to real entrepreneurs and innovators who can act as role models for them (see the LSM case below).

ENTREPRENEURSHIP AT LSM

The LSM has been delivering various courses in entrepreneurship and small medium enterprise (SME) management since the early 1990s. In 1997, at the engineering and law schools' request, an interdisciplinary program in entrepreneurship and firm creation, called CPME,[7] was launched in collaboration with the LSM. This CPME program is offered optionally to students in engineering, bio-engineering, law and management. It resulted from a desire to bring together students from different schools around one common entrepreneurial project, to adopt a collective, rather than an individualistic, view of entrepreneurship.

Furthermore, in the context of its mission of service to society, the LSM contributes to the socio-economic development of the Walloon region where there seems to have been a lack of entrepreneurial spirit. Indeed, the southern region of Belgium has been identified as a poor performer in terms of entrepreneurship and several of the leading local industries (steel, coal, textile, etc.) have experienced a steep decline since the early 1980s (*Global Entrepreneurship Monitor*, 2003). Its contribution to 'boosting entrepreneurship' in its environment was therefore perceived as a valuable objective for the LSM. As a result, the university has set up entrepreneurship support systems, working at three levels: managing intellectual property rights, financing new ventures and venture creation support.

ETHICAL LEADERSHIP

While Frederick Taylor recommended replacing the government of men with the administration of things, quite the opposite should be done today. Management – narrowly defined – consists, above all, of the administration of things: objectives, budgets, strategic analyses, plans, methods, procedures, etc. Leadership is the art of directing human reality: it is linked to motivation, communication, participation and the ability to convince people and to propose values that give sense and meaning to the economic drive of the company. If the company wants to give meaning to its activities, if it wants to give sense to economic progress by inserting it into other forms of human progress, the ethical dimension of leadership is essential to inform its choices and to guide its behavior.

Recent research conceptualizes and develops an 'ethical leadership' construct (Brown et al., 2005; Treviño et al., 2000, 2003) that is defined as 'the demonstration of normatively appropriate conduct through personal actions and interpersonal relationships, and the promotion of such conduct to followers through two-way communication, reinforcement, and decision-making' (Brown et al., 2005: 120).

A number of personal characteristics have been related to ethical leadership (Treviño et al., 2003): ethical leaders are honest and trustworthy; they are seen as principled decision makers who care about people and the broader society, and who behave ethically in their personal and professional lives. Ethical leaders make 'ethics an explicit part of their leadership agenda by communicating an ethics and values message, by visibly and intentionally role modelling ethical behavior, and by using the reward system to hold followers accountable for ethical conduct' (Brown and Treviño, 2006: 597).

To be an ethical leader requires putting ethics back into the consideration of strategies and behavior. The decisions made by ethical leaders rely both on an awareness of principles and regulations and on their personal consciences. As many of these decisions are dilemmas beyond the compass of regulations, the development of a globally responsible conscience is the most important foundation for globally ethical behavior. Guided by values, an ethical leader takes into account the consequences of his decisions and actions and assumes, as much as possible, responsibility for the future and for the society he creates. This responsibility becomes even greater as the capacity for innovation and power grows. This is the case with global business and the economic and technical systems it drives. This is also the case with leaders in companies as they seek to lead in a globally responsible manner. The major ethical question today is at another level to that of integrity alone. It is about knowing what kind of world we want to build together with the vast resources and enormous skills at our disposal.

For business schools, it is therefore essential to help the next generation of leaders develop an ethical leadership dimension. This will not happen through an intellectual approach only. Emotion and spirituality should be part of the learning process and that can only be achieved through a discussion and exchange of experiences engaging the 'whole person'. Governing people implies going beyond the simple intellect and to give way to the heart and mind. Experiential, presentational, propositional and practical ways of learning must be integrated into the future globally responsible leaders' curriculum. Students could, for instance, be confronted with a disorienting dilemma that combines both global and individual challenges, where the integration of multiple perspectives is paramount and where multiple stakeholders become part of the process. In those situations, students react not only with their rational minds, but with all of their senses and abilities (practical, affective, conceptual, imagination) – in a 'whole person learning' approach (Taylor, 2006). This enables globally responsible leaders to discover more of their inner dimension, to face the intended and unintended consequences of their decisions and to develop entrepreneurial learning processes (see the LSM case below).

ETHICAL LEADERSHIP AT THE LSM

For three years now, the LSM has offered a compulsory course on 'Corporate Social Responsibility' to all students involved in Master programs. This course aims at enabling future leaders to build and extend upon knowledge, questions, tools, values and behaviors, leading to a renewed vision of the human factor within enterprise and a reconsideration of the synergy between economic, social and environmental policies. In this sense, CSR is studied as a reflector of modern firms' self-awareness process in terms of responsibility and as a source of innovation in the face of challenges of competitiveness, sustainable development and world governance. This course aims to endow students with analytical references allowing them to identify organizations' values and their role, to highlight their strategic and philosophical backgrounds, to evaluate their pertinence and to sort out the various concurring positions. Analytical references give way to more personal questioning periods developed by students in terms of their own aspirations, perceptions and observations as citizens. All these elements foster personal change that in its turn creates transformation within organizations.

More specifically, as part of the final evaluation, students are asked to write their 'personal manifesto' which should help them better perceive who they are and what they want. Together with some experts and based on some pedagogical tools specifically designed for this course (questionnaire, video) by Noterdaeme and Maniquet (2010), students discuss their personal motivations – what do I really want? What kind of world would I like to be part of? Their impacts and responsibilities – am I aware of the impact of my decisions? Do I bear the consequences of my decisions? Their commitments – how far am I ready to go to defend what I believe in? Their motto – what is my *carpe diem*? These are elements that will influence not only their personal development but also the development of people and organizations with whom they will be interacting. This personal manifesto and the pedagogical tools associated with it represent one of the main innovations in CSR education at the LSM in the sense of 'whole person learning'.

In this respect, the course is addressed at future leaders concerned with giving more meaning to their citizens and a professional and spiritual engagement by repositioning human beings and their environment more centrally in the world.

STATESMANSHIP

Economic globalization advances much faster than global governance, escapes nation states and gradually imposes its logic on the whole world. This backwardness in politics with respect to economics leads to a kind of public helplessness in driving real development strategies and in democratically debating the societal issues of globalization. As Raymond Aron said, nation states have become too small for big problems and too big for small ones. If there is often over-regulation at the national level, there is virtually no economic regulation at the global level. The concept of sustainable development most faithfully translates, at the general level, the challenges facing twenty-first century leaders: broadening the purpose of economic progress, creating a political and ethical corporate culture, and mastering the process of collective change. To address those challenges, business leaders should participate more actively in the research and definition of the Common

Good and try to build it into their sphere of activity even if global governance is still in its infancy. Business leaders should also play a more responsible role in the emergence of a new culture of cooperation and debate that would replace the simple current 'lobbying' practices. To their role of entrepreneur and ethical leader, they should add that of states-man in the sense of adopting a role of concerned citizens and helping to construct new governance. In this sense, François Maon (2010) proposed a new conceptual model of CSR development integrating a permanent dialectical process with the different stakeholders. This model embeds a constant, and often conflictual, dialogue with stakeholders in the long-term development strategy of the corporation. It considers this new 'political' culture as a condition for corporate success and legitimacy. This is an interesting illustration of what corporate statesmanship could mean.

Business education should imply a realistic analysis of our economic system and searching to keep its dynamism and creativity while also reducing its defects, dysfunctions and devia-tions. Furthermore, dialogue, consultation and debate are needed in order to reintroduce the political dimension into economic decision-making. To deal with dilemmas and ambigui-ties, an openness towards the views of others and discussions with people with differing perspectives are vital. Dialogue enables people to understand and gain clarification together on what matters most in a specific context, from certain viewing points, in a certain balance, with certain negotiations. This involves more than intellectual capability. It calls for the capacity to work with internal contradictions and value conflicts while sustaining relation-ships with those engaged in the process (see the LSM case below).

STATESMANSHIP IN EDUCATION AT THE LSM

Each year on the CSR course, students have to develop concrete but creative CSR activities, politics and strategies for a corporate partner, taking into account the points of view of the different stakeholders directly and indirectly concerned with the project. For students, it notably involves carrying out different interviews, discussion panels and debates with man-agers and stakeholders having somewhat divergent perspectives on the project or the company, and finally to make sense of those viewpoints to develop a viable project from an economic, social, environmental and ethical perspective.

For students, this project is the opportunity to bridge practice and theory by getting out of the classroom and into real business situations, where they can apply some of their knowledge and know-how, but also experiment on how to work with contradictions and conflicting perspectives.

The LSM also encourages its students to attend the various conferences organized by the Hoover Chair in political and social ethics where key societal issues are permanently debated. Moreover, the Hoover Chair is currently hosting some of our PhD students who want to broaden the societal and political dimensions of their research work on business responsibilities.

The LSM participation in different international networks (notably the Global Responsible Leadership Initiative [GRLI], the UN Principles for Responsible Management Education [PRME] and the European Alliance for CSR) is another way to reinforce its states-manship mission.

COLLABORATION WITH OTHER BUSINESS SCHOOLS
AND PROACTIVE COMPANIES

Today's crisis brings our financial, economic and governance systems to an unprecedented moment of truth. The whole world is facing a strong socio-economical uncertainty and societal distrust, while the acceleration of climate and demographic changes is hurrying along a political, cultural and technological (r)evolution. The time has come for business schools to engage in innovating and sometimes unconventional partnerships with business, investors, governments, civil society, media, artistic and spiritual communities. Among other networks, the Global Responsible Leadership Initiative (GRLI) seems very promising, because it challenges company issues for the twenty-first century, the mission of business schools/learning institutions and the process for cultural change in organizations. This unique global community of action and learning – that was co-founded and supported by the United Nations Global Compact and the European Foundation for Management Development (EFMD) – represents a pioneering group of 60 business schools/learning institutions and companies over the five continents, including over 300,000 students and 1 million employees, that are engaged in developing the next generation of globally responsible leaders. A unique characteristic of the GRLI is that it seeks to maintain a balance between businesses and business schools/learning institutions, usually ensuring that each business school that joins does so with a business partner (see below for illustrations of some original partnerships developed at the LSM).

THE PHILIPPE DE WOOT AWARD – AN INNOVATIVE COLLABORATION BETWEEN DIFFERENT BUSINESS SCHOOLS AND PROACTIVE COMPANIES IN ORDER TO PROMOTE CSR

Every two years, the Philippe de Woot award aims to promote CSR by recognizing a Master's student (initially from a Belgian School of Management[8]) for a thesis constituting an original contribution to understanding and thinking on CSR. On the occasion of the award ceremony, an inter-university seminar is organized to discuss the ways in which CSR is addressed and taught in management schools, and how it can be improved. The award has been taken up by outstanding corporations (such as Bekaert, Belgacom, Colruytgroup, Delvaux, GDF Suez, GSK, IBA, ING, Lhoist, Umicore, among others) and personalities close to the business world. Their aims are to reinforce cooperation between the corporate and academic worlds in the CSR field, to enhance an inter-university approach on these matters and to raise this undertaking to a European level.

The first Inter-University Philippe de Woot award ceremony was held on 23 February 2010 in Louvain-la-Neuve. The award went to Marie Bertrand for her thesis entitled 'An Exploratory Study about Corporate Governance in Social Entrepreneurship' (supervised by Professor Frank Janssen at LSM). This thesis examines the governance mechanisms adopted in the social entrepreneurship sector. Although social entrepreneurship is benefitting from a growing recognition around the world, very little research has been conducted on the subject. Her research therefore aims to assess whether the various factors usually linked to

(Continued)

(Continued)

the phenomenon result in different management and governance mechanisms. The thesis helps in achieving a better understanding of the daily challenges and specific needs that this form of entrepreneurship brings in term of governance. Furthermore, it allows us to see how governance mechanisms can play a concrete role in the research of social innovation and social impact. And, finally, the study demonstrates the importance of having a good perception of the various operational issues at stake in the emergent field of social entrepreneurship, if we believe those initiatives should be proliferated in the future.

ACTION-RESEARCH PARTNERSHIPS WITH COMPANIES

- A 5-year partnership with GDF Suez has been established to understand what will be the brain and heart of future managers in relation to the growing importance of sustainable development and CSR. This project includes the design and implementation of original executive training with respect to CSR and the necessary personal change that in turn creates transformation within organizations.
- A 3-year partnership with Belgacom has been developed with three main objectives: (1) to develop the concepts and tools of a cultural transformation of Belgacom with respect to CSR and sustainable development; (2) to position Belgacom as one of the leaders in terms of CSR innovation in Europe and on an international level; and (3) to make Belgacom a real partner of CSR education and research at the LSM.
- Since 2006, the LSM has been an Institutional Partner of the GRLI. Within the last two years, the LSM has created an association with GSK Biologicals in order to unfold a strategic CSR agenda in this pharmaceutical company based on a complete auditing of GSK's CSR practices. This very fruitful collaboration organized in the context of the GRLI should definitely be repeated with other corporate partners. Within this framework, the LSM plays an active role in two major global research projects – The Corporation of the Twenty-first Century and The Business School of the Twenty-first Century – in order to assume its responsibility in creating a responsible future for business and business education.

CONCLUSION: THE LSM'S JOURNEY TOWARD SUSTAINABILITY

The culture at the heart of the LSM is based on a long European tradition of humanism, which has as its objective to form solid, free people, who are not only respectful of the talents of others, profoundly honest and tolerant, but also clear-sighted and dynamic. The LSM advocates 'savoir-être' as much as 'know-how' by training future executives who are conscious of their responsibilities, subscribing to a hierarchy of values which places the business world in its rightful place in society and is respectful of sustainable development for the progress of the largest number of people. The LSM particularly emphasizes human dignity, respect for the person and the common good. More specifically, it advocates an ethics of the future which exceeds traditional ethics and simple integrity. The different activities of the LSM in terms of education, research and partnerships together show its movement toward a more sustainable business school as an organization and as a role model for companies as well as for the next generation of leaders. However, we would be deluding ourselves if we believed that our school, as it stands at the moment, is at the end of its journey toward sustainability.

NOTES

1. CSR Europe was created in March 1996 on the basis of the European Business Declaration against Social Exclusion, initiated by former President Jacques Delors and business leaders.
2. Nevertheless, because of the nature of this dataset combined with the complexity of the organizational phenomena at stake, this study might not be fully and rigorously representative of the wide array of CSR-related corporate practices in the European context. Rather, this study constitutes an insightful endeavor that extends and nuances previous work (Albareda et al., 2007; Maignan and Ralston, 2002; Midttun et al., 2006; Welford, 2005) by offering an empirically grounded exploratory analysis of a contemporary organizational phenomenon.
3. Of course, there are some brilliant thinkers in those business schools' midst, but the latter are rarely representative of the culture of the schools. They are often swimming against the tide and have not yet succeeded in opening up most schools to social, political and human dimensions.
4. The European Alliance for Corporate Social Responsibility is an open partnership for enterprises to promote and encourage CSR. The Alliance was launched in 2006 as a joint initiative of the European Commission and the business community (see www.csreurope.org/pages/en/alliance.html).
5. The LSM is a newly formed business school grouping together four previously competing actors in the French-speaking part of Belgium: Brussels (FUSL), Louvain-la-Neuve (IAG from UCL), Mons (FUCAM) and Namur (FUNDP).
6. The Globally Responsible Leaders Initiative (GRLI) was co-founded and is supported by the United Nations Global Compact and the European Foundation for Management Development (EFMD). The GRLI's mission is to act as a catalyst to develop a next generation of globally responsible leaders. In doing so, it challenges the issues of the company for the twenty-first century, the mission of business schools/learning institutions and the process for cultural change in organizations. Today, the GRLI represents a pioneering group of 60 business schools/learning institutions and companies representing five continents, over 300,000 students and 1 million employees that are engaged in developing the next generation of globally responsible leaders.
7. 'CPME' stands for *Formation Interdisciplinaire en Création de Petites et Moyennes Entreprises* which means 'Interdisciplinary Education Program in SMEs' Creation'.
8. In a second phase, the Award will be extended to include other major European Schools of Management.

REFERENCES

Albareda, L., Lozano, J. and Ysa, T. (2007) 'Public policies on corporate social responsibility: The role of governments in Europe', *Journal of Business Ethics*, 74: 391–407.

Arnsperger, C. (2005) *Critique de l'existence capitaliste: Pour une éthique existentielle?* Paris: Editions du Cerf.

Bailly, O., Caudron, J.-M. and Lambert, D. (2006) 'Low prices, high social costs: The secrets in Ikea's closet', *Counterpunch*, 29 December. Available at: www.counterpunch.org/bailly12292006.html

Benn, S. and Dunphy, D. (2009) 'Leadership for sustainability.' In R. Staib (ed.), *Business Management and Environmental Stewardship*. Basingstoke: Palgrave Macmillan, 56–75.

Bennett, R. (1998) 'Corporate philanthropy in France, Germany, and the UK: International comparisons of commercial orientation towards company giving in European nations', *International Marketing Review*, 15: 458–75.

Brown, M.E. and Treviño, L.K. (2006) 'Ethical leadership: A review and future directions', *The Leadership Quarterly*, 17: 595–616.

Brown, M.E., Treviño, L.K. and Harrison, D.A. (2005) 'Ethical leadership: A social learning perspective for construct development and testing', *Organizational Behavior and Human Decision Processes*, 97: 117–34.

Carroll, A.B. (1979) 'A three-dimensional conceptual model of corporate performance', *Academy of Management Review*, 4: 497–505.

Carroll, A.B. (2004) 'Managing ethically with global stakeholders: A present and future challenge', *Academy of Management Executive*, 18: 114–20.

Crane, A. and Matten, D. (2004) *Business Ethics*. Oxford: Oxford University Press.

de Woot, P. (2005) *Should Prometheus Be Bound? Corporate Global Responsibility*. New York: Palgrave Macmillan.

de Woot, P. (2009) *Lettre ouverte aux dirigeants chrétiens en temps d'urgence*. Paris: Desclée de Brouwer.

Delbard, O. (2008) 'CSR legislation in France and the European regulatory paradox: An analysis of EU CSR policy and sustainability reporting practice', *Corporate Governance: The International Journal*, 8: 397–405.

Doppelt, B. (2003) *Leading Change Toward Sustainability*. Sheffield: Greenleaf Publishing.

Friedman, M. (1970) 'The social responsibility of business is to increase its profits', *The New York Times Magazine*, 33: 32–33, 122, 124, 126.

Gallagher, M. and McWhirter, C. (1998) 'Chiquita secrets revealed', *Cincinnati Enquirer*, 3 May.

Ghoshal, S. (2003) 'Business schools share the blame for Enron', *Financial Times*, 18 July.

Ghoshal, S. (2005) 'Bad management theories are destroying good management practices', *Academy of Management Learning and Education*, 4(1): 75–91.

Giacalone, R.A. and Thompson, K.R. (2006) 'Business ethics and social responsibility education: Shifting the worldview', *Academy of Management Learning and Education*, 5(3): 266–77.

Global Entrepreneurship Monitor (2003) Available at: www.gemconsortium.org/about.aspx?page=global_reports_2003

GRLI – Global Responsible Leadership Initiative (2008) 'GRLI Manifesto: A Call to Action'. Available at www.google.be/search?hl=frandq=GRLI+Manifesto percent2C+A+Call+to+Action percent2C+Brussels percent2C+2008.andmeta=

Hart, S. and Milstein, M. (2003) 'Creating sustainable value', *Academy of Management Executive*, 17: 56–69.

Henle, C.A. (2006) 'Bad apples or bad barrels? A former CEO discusses the interplay of person and situation with implications for business education (interview by Christine A. Henle)', *Academy of Management Learning and Education*, 5: 346–55.

KPMG (2005) KPMG international survey of corporate responsibility reporting 2005. Amsterdam: KPMG Global Sustainability Services. Available at: www.kpmg.com.au/Portals/0/KPMG percent20Survey percent202005_3.pdf

Kolk, A. (2008) 'Sustainability, accountability and corporate governance: Exploring multinationals' reporting practices', *Business Strategy and the Environment*, 17: 1–15.

Jones, T.M., Felps, W. and Bigley, G. (2007) 'Ethical theory and stakeholder-related decisions: The role of stakeholder culture', *Academy of Management Review*, 32(1): 137–55.

Lyon, D. (2004) 'How can you help organizations change to meet the corporate responsibility agenda?', *Corporate Social Responsibility and Environmental Management*, 11(3): 133–9.

Maignan, I. and Ralston, D. (2002) 'CSR in Europe and the U.S.: Insights from businesses' self-presentations', *Journal of International Business Studies*, 33: 497–514.

Maon, F. (2010) Toward the stakeholder company. Essay on the role of organizational culture, interaction and change in the pursuit of corporate social responsibility, Dissertation, UCL, Louvain School of management.

Maon, F. and Swaen, V. (2010) 'From Eastern dawn to Northern lights: a comparative analysis of CSR implementation practices across Europe', Academy of Management Annual Meeting, 6–10 August, Montreal, Canada, and Academy of Marketing Science Conference, 21–24 July, Lille, France.

Maon, F., Lindgreen, A. and Swaen, V. (2010) 'Organizational stages and cultural phases: a critical review and a consolidative model of corporate social responsibility development', *International Journal of Management Reviews*, 12(1): 20–38.

Midttun, A. (2005) 'Realigning business, government and civil society: emerging embedded relational governance beyond the (neo)liberal and welfare state models', *Corporate Governance: The International Journal*, 5: 159–74.

Midttun, A., Gautesen, K. and Gjølberg, M. (2006) 'The political economy of CSR in Western Europe', *Corporate Governance: The International Journal*, 6: 369–85.

Mintzberg, H. (2004) *Managers not MBAs*. Harlow: FT Prentice Hall/Pearson Education.

Mitroff, I. (2004) 'An open letter to the deans and the faculties of Amercian business schools', *Journal of Business Ethics*, 54: 185–9.

Navarro, P. (2008) 'The MBA core curricula of top-ranked US business schools: a study in failure?', *Academy of Management Learning and Education*, 7(1): 108–23.

Noterdaeme, J. and Maniquet, P.-Y. (2010) Guide for a personal manifesto for a responsible personal and professional life, Internal document, LSM.

Palazzo, B. (2002) 'US-American and German business ethics: An intercultural comparison', *Journal of Business Ethics*, 41: 195–216.

Pearce, J.A. II. and Doh, J.P. (2005) 'The high impact of collaborative social initiatives', *Sloan Management Review*, 46: 30–8.

Perrini, F. (2005) 'Building a European portrait of corporate social responsibility reporting', *European Management Journal*, 23: 611–27.

Preuss, L. (2008) 'A reluctant stakeholder? On the perception of corporate social responsibility among European trade unions', *Business Ethics: A European Review*, 17: 149–60.

Rayment, J. and Smith, J. (2010) 'Research Report: The Current and Future Role of Business Schools', Anglia Ruskin University, Cambridge and Chelmsford, England, February.

Schumpeter, J. (1949) *The Theory of Economic Development*. Cambridge, MA: Harvard University Press.

Shiller, R.J. (2005) 'How Wall Street learns to look the other way', *Herald Tribune*, 28 February.

Simpson, R. (2006) 'Masculinity and management education: Feminizing the MBA', *Academy of Management Education and Learning*, 5(2): 182–93.

Strike, V.M., Gao, J. and Bansal, P. (2006) 'Being good while being bad: social responsibility and the international diversification of US firms', *Journal of International Business Studies*, 37(6): 850–62.

Taylor, B. (2006) *Learning for Tomorrow: Whole Person Learning*. Oasis Press and GRLI.

Treviño, L.K., Brown, M.E. and Hartman, L.P. (2003) 'A qualitative investigation of perceived executive ethical leadership: perceptions from inside and outside the executive Suite', *Human Relations*, 56(1): 5–37.

Treviño, L.K., Hartman, L.P. and Brown, M. (2000) 'Moral person and moral manager: how executives develop a reputation for ethical leadership', *California Management Review*, 42(4): 128–42.

Welford, R. (2005) 'Corporate social responsibility in Europe, North America and Asia', *Journal of Corporate Citizenship*, 17: 33–52.

19 THE NEED FOR GOOD OLD PRINCIPLES IN FINANCIAL MANAGEMENT EDUCATION

Eero Kasanen and Robert Grosse

Aalto University School of Economics, Finland and EGADE Business School at Monterey Tec, Mexico

Financial crises have many acquaintances but no father. So far, the origin of the global financial crisis of 2008–9 has been traced back to China's politburo, greedy US bankers, naïve regulators and esoteric mathematical models. A crisis of this magnitude cannot be created by one factor alone but needs the coexistence of several contributing factors. The financial products created to match the global excess liquidity and the financing aspirations of the US housing market were complicated and massive enough to destabilize the global financial system. Likewise, the regulatory laxity was sufficient to permit an overextension of credit and inadequate risk evaluation and management.

It is fair to ask to what extent are the theories and values taught at business schools to blame for the creation of toxic financial products and the mismanagement of asset bubbles? After all, most of the 'Masters of the Finance Universe' have been educated at top business schools and economics departments. And it is important to note that we are pointing to two separate elements here: the first is the conceptual and empirical content of our curricula, and the second is the way in which values are incorporated (or not) into our teaching.

The academic community also has some explaining to do regarding why the crisis was not properly foreseen and why there were so few landmarks on the road ahead, as was pointed out by *The Economist* (cf. *The Economist*, 20 September 2008) during the peak of the crisis. Academics are not the only ones under the scrutiny of the general public. Underwriters of bankers' bonuses, financial market regulators and accounting standard setters will have their share of attention, too. Nevertheless, if we return to a classic work such as Kindleberger's *Manias, Panics, and Crashes* (2005), we must recognize that this crisis was not the first and will not be the last in the twenty-first century, just as in centuries before this one. Human nature and market behavior are such that financial crises are a recurrent, if not frequent, theme; and whatever changes there are in our teaching and/or thinking, we will not escape future episodes.

WHAT ARE WE TEACHING AT BUSINESS SCHOOLS?

Leading business schools around the world have a surprisingly uniform curriculum. Most highly ranked ones utilize the same set of standard textbooks and offer roughly the same portfolio of core courses. International accreditations and rankings ensure a consistent educational quality for the student, but also harmonize the content and delivery. To a certain extent, business schools are all in it together.

Broadly speaking, business schools are teaching the following issues worldwide:

- Analytical thinking (research methods, argumentation).
- Facts on how the world really works (cases, statistics).
- Theories for conceptual understanding.
- Tools for managing people, goods and money (models, frameworks).
- Values for the business management profession.

In our opinion, the leading business schools are pretty good at selecting smart students and then teaching them state-of-the-art theories, techniques, tools and the latest facts. At the same time, often implicitly, a certain value and belief system is transferred to these students. In times of economic crises and self reflection, it is useful to analyze more deeply whether some issues in the current theories and value system have to be readjusted. This would be consistent with the Argyris and Schön's (1974) logic concerning theory-in-practice.

That is, as existing assumptions about how the market (or business) functions become subject to examination, good managers and leaders need to be able to question those assumptions and practices, in order to develop strategies for succeeding in the re-defined world. Analyzing and challenging theories is not only an academic pastime but also an essential skill for sophisticated financial managers in an unforeseen market condition. An often-heard pragmatic comment provides a good example of the thought process: 'Let's start from the basic principles and figure out carefully what is really happening.'

Critical thinking capability is a good starting point for an ethical and prosperous business career. However, sharp analytical tools and factual knowledge are not enough. The real issue is to consider what we are actually teaching in the creation and development of a successful businessperson. This goes directly to the core of the management profession: along with technical skills, our graduates need to understand the creation of business opportunities, professional ethics, the management of people, the real organizational impacts of managers' actions, etc. No doubt sharp analytical tools are necessary but they are not enough. Critical thinking turns out to be a crucial capability and a good foothold for an ethical and prosperous career.

In the following sections, we will argue that, yes, certain curriculum issues need to be re-thought. But we will also argue that answers can be found in good old management principles.

GOOD OLD PRINCIPLES

OLD VALUES

Values are ever more visible in business education. Several leading business schools have undersigned the United Nations' Principles of Responsible Management Education

(PRME) (see www.unprme.org) and joined the UN Global Compact. By doing so, these business schools have committed themselves to teaching sustainable development, human rights and ethical business conduct. A business ethics course is a standard course on the modern business curriculum (though often not a required one).

However, in terms of professional values, probably the most influential educational part of the curriculum is the set of professional courses. These professional values, often implicit in cases or examples, are actually taught in finance, marketing or management courses. These principles are generally consistent with ethical behavior, argue against corruption and support competitive (not monopolistic) behavior. In finance, they also tend to assume efficient and perfect markets, and to ignore the inefficiencies and imperfections in order to focus on the conceptual structure of analytical tools, such as the capital asset pricing model, arbitrage theory and the Black-Scholes options model.

Even assuming, as is normally done in finance teaching, that a maximization of shareholder wealth and the efficient functioning of the invisible hand through markets, is theoretically sound, we have to be careful about what this means in terms of social values. Does economic theory really imply that any action increasing shareholder wealth is not only feasible but, even more strongly, should also be taken? Is it really the case that the only social responsibility of a company is to maximize wealth within existing legal boundaries? Certainly, Argyris and Schön (1974) would call for us to re-evaluate such a position.

One can argue that maximizing shareholder wealth actually requires placing a value on the goals and needs of external stakeholders (especially governments). This is because, in order to maximize wealth, the company needs to be around in the future to generate future earnings – and if the company alienates the government or another key stakeholder, it may lose its legitimacy and be forced out of business or otherwise penalized. Thus, maximizing the present value of future earnings demands that the company be around in the future, and that it therefore must comply with social/stakeholder requirements for acceptable behavior.

An alternative view of this same problem is that firms must try to maximize shareholder value subject to major constraints such as the legal and social norms that limit free-market optimizing behavior. While it may be problematic to identify exactly how a firm can pursue this goal, because the legal and particularly the social norms may not give clear guidance on optimal behavior, still the concept is clear and the difficulty is more in the implementation than in the understanding. One can argue that it is a constrained maximization problem of maximizing value while meeting social/legal constraints.

In addition, the wider social issues must still be addressed. Is the legal framework where the company functions developed enough? Practical examples abound of managerial situations where an aggressive maximization of shareholder wealth, with only scant regard for social or environmental concerns, would be technically legal in some circumstances. At the same time, basic principles of decency, fairness, human rights and sustainability will tell the manager that these actions would not stand within any professional ethical code.

It is exactly in these types of judgment calls that business schools need a serious discussion of a proper professional code. Business is, and should be, fiercely competitive. Managers sometimes need to be tough, sly and aggressive; while other times openness and generosity will do it. In all of these situations, a basic code of professional conduct should be adhered to. What this is is not crystal clear, but business schools should educate future managers to understand and honor real professionalism.

Let us explicitly mention a few good old principles that traditionally, and should also in the future, belong to the financial manager's professional code of conduct.

Trust – financial value is generated by future cash flows. The further into the future we aim, the more dependent that value will be on the trust between the economic agents. An extreme case here is life insurance, where a customer needs to trust the institution to act properly even after that customer is not there to look after his or her own rights. The whole idea of money, banking, insurance and financing is based on a sense of trust that the financial manager should embody. Two dictionary definitions of trust clarify this principle:

> *Trust is: firm belief in the reliability, truth, ability or strength of someone or something.* (The New Oxford Dictionary)

> *Trust is: the obligation or responsibility imposed on a person in whom confidence or authority is placed: a position of trust. (www.dictionary.reference.com)*

Diligence – financial products and deals are complex. The more sophisticated the transaction, the more a thorough analysis is called for. Financial managers need to be diligent when using the funds entrusted to them. A good example is provided by the standard procedure of 'due diligence' in mergers and acquisitions. Diligence is also one of the seven heavenly virtues, in contrast with the seven heavenly sins. The opposite of diligence is, by the way, sloth. A quote from an encyclopedia clarifies the meaning of the term:

> *Diligence is: a zealous and careful nature in one's actions and work; a decisive work ethic. (www.reference.com)*

Integrity – financial situations are delicate. To have a competitive edge and at the same take care of legitimate stakeholder concerns, such as in communication, requires close judgment calls. Professional ethics is not fair weather clothing only – it should always be worn with integrity, especially in stormy situations. Integrity applies at a personal as well as institutional level. The dictionary offers a good explanation:

> *Integrity is: steadfast adherence to a strict moral or ethical code. (www.en.wiktionary.org/)*

Global financial crises cannot be solved by financial managers' values alone – but trust, diligence and integrity will go a long way to avoiding toxic products that can poison the whole market. Sound professional ethics taught at university and through professional associations are a safeguard against excessive greed.

Social responsibility – after the excesses of individual and corporate greed, the general public will demand tighter rules and expect a more social set of values from the finance industry. The maximization of individual wealth, even if proven legal and efficient, will not suffice in an ethical sense. On a global scale, a large part of mankind lives without access to organized and well-regulated savings, loans and financial institutions. Also, the global financial markets are damaged by issues like systematic financial corruption, and the

underdeveloped legal protection of children and the environment. In these circumstances, finance professionals have to take the social consequences of their actions explicitly into account, as markets with imperfections and externalities cannot be trusted to blindly lead to socially desirable solutions.

A need arises here to justify financial deals and the structure of financial markets. This may be done in the future by argumentation based on concepts like:

> *Social responsibility: the principle that companies should contribute to the welfare of society and not be solely devoted to maximizing profits. (www.dictionary.reference.com)*

For example, aggressive option schemes used in start-up companies can easily be argued as necessary for the common interest of encouraging creative ideas, whereas huge no-downside incentives in established companies are not that easily linked to common interests.

This concept of social responsibility is a traditional ethical concept, but arguably somewhat new to mainstream finance thinking and textbooks. We looked at leading, widely used finance textbooks, and it appears that ethically they rely strongly on the real world markets' ability to turn individual wealth maximization into desirable social outcomes. More discussion is needed as to when and why, for example during financial crises, the wider social issues have also to be directly addressed within the finance profession.

OLD FACTS AND OLD LINES OF THINKING

A typical financial curriculum concentrates on learning the current theories, models, instruments, markets and issues. This is as it should be. There is a danger, however, that if one studies only issues that are of relevance to one business cycle, one loses sight of the issues that shape generations or even centuries. Business schools should make sure that students learn enough economic history to see clearly how new financial innovations like the limited liability company or derivative instruments have genuinely opened up new opportunities, and how accounting scandals or banking crises have caused serious systemic market failures.

Old facts are relevant, as human nature has not changed that much throughout time. As long as markets have existed, there has been a capricious market sentiment and greed fighting fear. Some effects can only be fully understood decades after. Probably, the full extent of the consequences of the current financial crisis will be seen only after the global regulatory system has been transformed. Financial patterns have long time spans.

Old theories and beliefs that have been influential are also worth studying, as the limitations of old concepts can hopefully help us better grasp the limitations of current concepts. If Ben Bernanke had not been a leading student of the Great Depression of 1929, it is easily imaginable that the US government's policy response to the 2008 crisis could have left the country in the grip of a new Depression. He clearly challenged the value of the pure market system, based on learning from the experience of the 1930s, and he, along with the leaders of the US Treasury, then made decisions that were based on a revised value structure.

USEFUL NEW THEORIES

Mainstream economic theory is the backbone of the current management curriculum. The axiom of rational economic man is the scientific standard against which deviations are defined. In many ways, critical studies of market efficiency or of the rationality of decision makers can be characterized as drilling holes in the ruling paradigm (or to paraphrase Argyris and Schön, adjusting theory to practice).

To us, the market and political reactions to the financial crises have pointed to two theoretical issues: (1) management education should utilize social psychology and ecology more thoroughly; and (2) maximization of the utility of one individual needs augmenting to take in a maximization of the utility of several individuals. These issues clearly fit under the heading of Behavioral Finance, which should be better incorporated into the core finance curriculum. (On the particular context of the 2008-9 financial crisis, see Grosse, 2010.)

There is a need to understand better how mass psychology and relative wealth rankings operate in the marketplace. It seems that we *Homo sapiens* are gregarious animals, both in general and also in the financial markets. Maybe financial players are closer to their biological relatives than we care to admit. Biology, after all, studies a very efficient and liquid market for food which includes us humans. This is not that far away from the market for financial assets, including agricultural assets.

SPECIFIC LESSONS FROM THE FINANCIAL CRISIS

The global financial crisis brought a handful of complications to the normally taught finance perspective in business schools. These complications can be categorized under four headings:

- The irrational exuberance of people involved in the market for US homes, where prices rose unsustainably for several years, and thus a bubble should have been evident.

Our finance curriculum typically does not speak to the issue of irrational behavior, even though we have experienced it on numerous occasions, for example in the decade before the latest crisis (in the instances of Long-Term Capital Management's crash in 1998 and in the dot-com crisis of 2000–1). We probably cannot teach students how to predict financial crises, but we certainly can teach them how to be prepared for such events that will definitely recur in the future.

- The markets' structural imperfections, most importantly the lack of short-term financing available to major investment banks when the bubble burst.

This phenomenon is one that we should have been teaching as part of our instruction on the operation of markets. It has nothing to do with values or beliefs, but rather with a possible breakdown in market functioning in times of panic. We experienced this in the Crash of 1987, when the stock market dropped dramatically, by 23 per cent of its total value, on Monday 19 October, with a subsequent rapid recovery. The New York Stock Exchange then implemented a 'circuit breaker' rule, to close the exchange for an hour or longer, for times when sharp market plunges (or spikes) of 10 per cent or more would produce enormous valuation changes that could be viewed as speculative and damaging. This phenomenon is the kind of exception to market functioning that we should teach as a matter of course, to temper our emphasis on the ordinary equilibrium-type functioning of the market.

- An inadequate regulatory oversight of the risk-creating behavior of mortgage lenders and repackagers, and of the valuations that were assigned to risky assets (especially to Collateralized Mortgage Obligations).

This aspect of the crisis may be viewed as a market imperfection, or as an institutional failure, or as a psychological feature of the securities markets. Whatever the label, the inability of regulators to understand the risks involved in the functioning of the mortgage market and the mortgage-backed securities market was part of the reason why the originate-to-distribute model produced such excesses. The fact that lenders sold their mortgage loans into the bond market, without paying careful attention to the risk involved in the original mortgages, may be viewed as part of the ethics problem that we finance instructors should be dealing with in our teaching. Even so, perhaps the skeptical reader should try teaching students that market-based incentives (namely to lend and sell off mortgages) should be ignored by bankers in order for them to act more responsibly as lenders. This is a very, very difficult idea to sell!

- An inadequate financial institution oversight over their own lenders' and analysts' activities that produced the assets that became 'toxic'.

Here it seems clear that we can provide much better instruction to our students about the risk issues involved in financial instruments and markets, and try to convey a sense that corporate responsibility requires paying attention to what otherwise becomes herd behavior without limits.

In sum, there are four key characteristics of the most recent global financial crisis that are relevant to understanding financial markets and to making decisions appropriately in those markets. Irrational exuberance is a feature of human behavior that has been demonstrated repeatedly over the decades and even centuries. We cannot eliminate it; but we can learn how to understand it better (and also to construct government policies to deal with future occurrences). Market structural imperfections are often ignored in our teaching, because the market generally functions well, and because the imperfections do not fit sufficiently with our modeling processes (for example, for options valuation). Perhaps the imperfections are not easy to model, but our teaching can certainly provide a more explicit consideration of such limits to competitive markets, and can alert our students to the likelihood of future shocks. Inadequate regulatory oversight is a problem that always exists when market participants are better informed than regulators; it calls for more adequate efforts by government to create mechanisms that provide better information to the regulators. This is outside of our scope in the finance curriculum. Inadequate financial institution oversight is squarely in our area of responsibility as finance instructors, and we need to develop both ethics and a social responsibility content in our curriculum as well as managerial content that will better serve financial institution decision makers.

BACK TO THE BUSINESS SCHOOL CURRICULUM

Financial crises, or no financial crises, business schools are drilling future financial managers day in and day out, teaching them accounting 101, economics 101 and finance 101. To add one isolated course of business ethics 101 will not change the curriculum alone. After all these ponderings, should something be truly changed?

At Aalto University School of Economics in Finland, and at EGADE Business School in Mexico, we have done, both by design and by accident, two things. There are quite a lot of courses available that deal with sustainable development, the base of the pyramid markets, corporate social responsibility, business ethics and other topics belonging to the realm of responsible management education, endorsed by the United Nations.

Aalto is also offering a wide variety of different theories of economic behavior, starting from hard core economics, through psychology to alternative economic communities. A student taking the full assortment will necessarily have to sort out both ethical issues and competing explanatory models before concluding on what to believe and why, or how to behave and why.

EGADE has established a Center on Corporate Social Responsibility and Sustainable Development, and this venture is introducing new knowledge via research as well as new course material through case studies and the insertion of key topics into existing courses. In addition, all university (including business) students in Mexico must dedicate a minimum of 240 hours during their period of study to social responsibility projects, from teaching low-income people about business to building low-income houses, to volunteering in hospitals and schools.

Based on the above reasoning and our experiences, we would recommend the following.

Professional ethical principles, with real-life cases and focused on managers, should be taught at the core of the professional courses. For example, a finance case course should include a couple of real contradictory ethical situations faced by a financial manager.

Management and market-oriented courses should draw upon several full-blown theories of human behavior like economics, psychology, sociology and ecology. Real managers and markets will not fully obey any one of these theories but more tools will give students a better handle on the issues.

Serious theoretical efforts should be focused on developing group behavior and relative wealth at the core of the behavior of the rational economic person in order to move on from the concept of individual utility. In the financial curriculum in particular, greater attention needs to be drawn to market imperfections and inefficiencies that have major implications for decision-making. Whether this is attacked from the perspective of behavioral finance or stakeholder management, or some combination of these, is not the issue; what is needed is a broader approach to understanding financial decisions than just the pure free-market analysis that is often presented.

REFERENCES

Argyris, M. and Schön, D. (1974) *Theory in Practice: Increasing Professional Effectiveness.* San Francisco, CA: Jossey-Bass.

Grosse, R. (2010) 'Bank Governance and the Crisis – A Behavioral Finance View', paper presented at the Wharton Conference on Corporate Governance and the Global Financial Crisis, Philadelphia, 24–25 September.

Kindleberger, C.P. (2005) *Manias, Panics, and Crashes,* 5th edn. New York: Wiley.

20 PRME AND FOUR THESES ON THE FUTURE OF MANAGEMENT EDUCATION

Manuel Escudero

UN PRME and Deusto Business School, Spain

Business school gatherings from 2008 to date have been characterized by soul-searching debates concerning what is wrong with business schools. Plenary sessions have not been devoted to technical problems, but to fundamental ones: are business schools to blame, in part, for the financial misbehavior that has required so much of taxpayers' bail-out money?

The Principles for Responsible Management Education or PRME (see www.unprme.org) – with more than 300 business schools as participants – is a good platform from which to observe that these are not uneventful times for business schools.

These principles were developed by an international task force of 60 deans, university presidents and official representatives from leading business schools and academic institutions. Under the coordination of the UN Global Compact, this task force developed a set of six principles which laid the foundation for the global platform for responsible management education. The principles were presented to several institutions within the sector – some accrediting bodies such as the Association of Advanced Collegiate Schools of Business (AACSB) or the European Foundation for Management Development (EFMD), other international institutions relevant in the sector such as the Graduate Management Admission Council (GMAC) or NetImpact, a business students' international organization, and other advanced international laboratories already working in the area of sustainability and business education, such as the Academy of Business in Society (EABIS), the Globally Responsible Initiative (GRLI) and the Aspen Institute Business and Society Program. All these institutions became founders of the initiative along with the UN Global Compact. The Principles were officially presented to the Secretary-General of the United Nations, Mr Ban Ki-Moon in July 2007, at the Global Compact Leaders Summit held in Geneva, and had around 40 business schools as its first participants. Acknowledging the potential benefits of the PRME, UN Secretary-General Ban Ki-Moon said during his closing remarks: 'The Principles for Responsible Management Education have the capacity to take the case for universal values and business into classrooms on every continent.'

The initiative grew rapidly, in terms of representation in international and regional associations, in number of business schools participating in the initiative and geographical spread. Thus, by the end of 2010, other important international associations, such as the Association of MBAs (AMBA), the African Association of Business Schools (AABS), the Central and Eastern European Management Association (CEEMAN) and the Latin American Council of Business Schools (CLADEA) were partners of the initiative. Also, 286 business schools were participating by February 2010 and 337 by the end of November 2010. In February 2010, its geographical distribution was as follows:

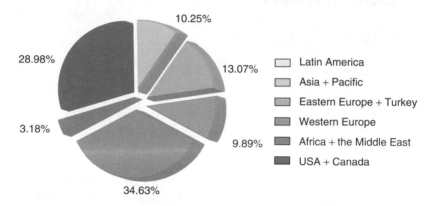

Figure 20.1   Geographical distribution of PRME, January 2010

From the vantage point of an international initiative such as PRME, how can we define the reaction of business schools to current times and dilemmas and characterize the present pathos of the sector?

   The financial crisis has acted as an additional catalyst for a process of redefining business education that was already in operation. It has added a note of urgency and perhaps may contribute to the acceleration of a pre-existing process of change. A generalized frame of mind is one of advocating an urgent adaptation to many changes in the landscape, of getting it right and updating and adapting business education to the new coordinates in the world. In sum, the mood is one of rethinking business education with a sense of imperative innovation.

   Business education is bracing itself for a new impulse and reorientation. Whatever the result, this is the time to initiate an enquiry into the future of business education. Here, briefly stated, are four theses about how this enquiry could proceed over the next few years.

THINKING ABOUT THE FUTURE BY LOOKING INTO THE PAST

The sector should start by being aware that it has its own history. Business education has been at a crossroads before: in 1959 the two Foundation studies (the Ford Foundation and the Carnegie Foundation Reports – see Gordon and Howell, 1959; Pierson, 1959) were a first attempt at redefining business education – with a long-lasting influence. Later on, in the mid-1980s, there was a second effort (Porter and McKibbin, 1988) which was perhaps a premonition of what we are dealing with now.

The first rethink of business education was a reactive move, based on a pressing need to reorient business education. The mood of the times, at the end of the 1950s, would probably be well defined by the position of Thomas L. Norton, dean of NYU's School of Commerce:

> *In my opinion, it is time for the American Association of Collegiate Schools of Business to revise its membership standard relating to the Business Base, sometimes referred to as the 'core' of business subjects. I believe that the present standard may well now be a hindrance than an aid to the improvement of college education for business. (Speech delivered at the Annual Meeting of the Middle Atlantic Association of Collegiate Schools of Business, 11 October 1957. Reproduced in Pierson [1959] – usually referred to as the Carnegie Foundation Report)*

Business education had been, from its inception in the latter years of the nineteenth century, at the forefront of the movement to carry higher education to a wide cross-section of the population, but it was time to rethink this effort: there was an increasing concern about whether business schools, both at the undergraduate and graduate level, were essentially different from other, more vocational strands of education such as trade schools, whether they were attracting students with an inferior academic ability than the average at college level, whether graduate business work ran a serious danger of being unduly narrow. The rapid growth of in graduate programs coupled with the proliferation of other alternative programs, such as night schools, special institutes, company training facilities, etc. increased the urgency of choosing between a rigorous academic or a highly vocational program (Pierson, 1959: 52–4).

The second rethink of business education took place in the 1980s (Porter and McKibbin, 1988). However, this new attempt was not a reactive but a proactive move. Indeed, in sharp difference to the first 'rethinking', there was not a pressing need to revisit business education: 'In marked contrast to the situation in the 1950s, we found no forceful push for systemic curriculum change emanating from business schools themselves'(Porter and McKibbin, 1988: 80).

In the 1980s, exercises of prognosing about the future mushroomed in all fields, from politics to economics or the social and cultural sphere.[1] At a time where everything seemed to be settled and stable, but also somewhat predictable and unsatisfactory,[2] the natural reaction was to be concerned about the future in the twenty-first century, to the extent that futurism was established as a mainstream exercise in numerous fields. Following the fashion of the times, this second rethink of business education tried to look towards the future.

There are several reasons explaining why, today, it is important to look to the past in order to enquire about the future:

- It gives us an optimistic historical perspective, very much in line with what business schools are about. Business schools are not strictly an academic 'ivory tower' but remain, by the very nature of their object of academic enquiry, in the uncomfortable intersection between the relevance of how business communities are evolving in the real world and the rigor of an academic endeavor. This explains why an academic sector that is, basically, very young (100 years old), has already undergone two systematic exercises of redefinition. Business schools are nothing but a reflection of the changing needs and nature of business, and sooner rather than later, business education changes as business changes.

- It might give us insights into what is happening now. The second revision of business education, the one that was enquiring into the future in the new century, has particularly highlighted the following emerging criticisms:

  o Too much emphasis on quantitative analytical techniques.
  o Insufficient attention paid to managing people, to the external (legal, social, political) environment, to the international dimension of business, to entrepreneurism and to ethics.
  o Does all this resonate with the current situation?

- Finally, our history provides us with the methodology used by our predecessors in order to rethink business education. The two revisions mentioned in this chapter followed a method which should be respected and emulated, based on a two-step methodology: first a thorough examination of the external environment (economic, demographic and societal variables), followed by an extensive empirical exploration of the internal or organizational variables within the sector of business education. The latter aspect encompassed both an extensive survey and a relevant sample of qualitative interviews.

Today, we are in a closer position to the first than the second attempt. Rather than a futuristic exercise as in the 1980s, we should get ready to react to a pressing current situation as in the 1950s. But this is where the similarities end. Rethinking business education in the 1950s was a response to the internal, infant and poorly defined state of business education and its institutions. However, today, and this is my second thesis, the urgency of rethinking business education is much more related to the changes around us, to how they are affecting business and, hence, business education.

THE FUTURE OF BUSINESS EDUCATION IS DIRECTLY RELATED TO CURRENT ECONOMIC, SOCIAL AND POLITICAL CHANGES

My conviction is that, first, a look at the external environment will suffice to give us a clear sense of the need for a new effort to rethink management and business education; and, second, that this look at the external environment affecting business education will also give us a clear sense of direction concerning where we need to go in terms of necessary changes.

Our biggest challenge now is to understand what is going on in the world, how this affects business growth and development and how, in turn, changes in business behavior will affect business education. I would propose that the three major (and self-evident) changes affecting business today are the following:

- Globalization.
- The IT revolution.
- Governance gaps.

We truly live in a new world, which emerged, approximately, at the beginning of the twenty-first century.

Globalization means that never before has the world been so integrated in terms of information, economic, financial and human flows. Today, most companies of all sizes serve supranational markets. Furthermore, around 77,000 companies have grown to become truly global corporations which not only operate in a global market but also organize their daily operations globally through outsourcing, branches and subsidiaries.

Globalization has been made possible by a complementary move toward more free market legal settings, labeled as deregulation and privatization – the sibling of deregulation. As a result, mergers and acquisitions have never before had the intensity they have had in this decade.

The technological base for this financial and corporate integration has been the microchip and the digital innovations. The delocalization and globalization of companies has also been made possible by instant communication through the internet, a giant leap forward in communications for global logistics and controlling systems.

The signal of the third crucial new process of this new world was the fall of the Berlin Wall. After the world had been divided into two blocks, we entered a new period of uncertainty concerning global governance: the option of going back to a unique 'hegemon' leading the world in technological, military and economic matters has turned out to be difficult and problematic, as a result of the slow but steady consolidation of the European Union and an increasing number of new political or economic regions which want their voice heard in the international arena (Mercosur, the African Union, Asean, etc.).

The difficulty for a unilateral regime is made even more problematic by the emergence of new potential superpowers, such as China, India and Brazil. One of the clearest outcomes of the meltdown of the financial and economic arrangements after 2008, is the evidence that, while we do not live in a multilateral system, we indeed live in a multipolar world. In this context, the seed of a multilateral governance system is germinating, but its growth faces difficulties. All things considered, the world's governance seems to be at a crossroads, caught between an old unilateral regime that has not yet died and a new multilateral order that has yet to emerge. In the meantime, traditional national political powers, as a result of the lack of effective global institutions, seem to be at pains to address and solve problems that have a global or transnational nature. Thus, governance gaps seem to be the only everpresent feature of a world unable to address many global challenges.

The consequences of these three linked new phenomena – globalization, the digital/internet revolution and governance gaps – are far reaching, and will shape the world in the future with many novel and unprecedented social and political processes. Among them, a central question for business educators is: have these new developments brought about the need to redefine the role of business in today's society? And, if so, should this affect the role of business educators and the content of their teachings? I believe this to be the case and my third thesis relates to this. I believe that today business is changing, and business education should change too, as a consequence of the impact on business of these three processes.

THE NEED FOR CHANGE IN BUSINESS EDUCATION IS ROOTED IN THE CHANGE OF BUSINESS TOWARDS A NEW PARADIGM OF VALUE CREATION

I believe that business education has to be rethought because businesses themselves and their role in society are changing.

With globalization, deregulation, mergers and acquisitions, corporations have attained a global decision-making power that they have never had before. There has been an unheard of shift in power, to the extent that, today, of the 100 largest economically measurable institutions – be they governments (GNP) or companies (turnover) – 51 are companies and 49 are nation states.

'Of the 100 largest economies in the world, 51 are corporations; only 49 are countries. Wal-Mart is bigger than 161 countries, including Israel, Poland and Greece. Mitsubishi is larger than the fourth most populous nation on earth: Indonesia. General Motors is bigger than Denmark. Ford is bigger than South Africa. Toyota is bigger than Norway.'[3]

This is not about economic or political power – it is about naked global power. In the same way that governments directly affect the lives and destinies of millions through their budgets or laws, the decisions of a global corporation as to where to establish a new plant, which companies to subcontract or where to downsize, affect millions of people.

This new situation poses unprecedented problems concerning the contribution of business to global governance. Surely, if current global governance arrangements are unable to deal with many global challenges, global corporations should enter the global agenda and help solve some of these problems. However, why should companies act as producers of 'public goods'? Their increase in power does not warrant, in itself, a change in their mission. However, this is only part of the story.

The other part is that globalization and the IT revolution have given birth to a new type of awareness in the world based on a new set of values. These values have been internalized by different actors: some multilateral institutions, a new generation of social and global organizations within civil society, and a new type of awareness in the citizenry. The decisive fact is the reflexivity gained as a result of universal access to all kinds of information and knowledge through computers, cell phones and the World Wide Web. Reflexive modernity, according to Anthony Giddens (1991), is the ability to ascertain the future consequences of human actions. He argues that, over time, society is becoming increasingly more self-aware, reflective and hence reflexive.

This newly acquired awareness has rapidly evolved into a values-based critical view of the state of affairs both in the global and local spheres. New multilateral institutions, new civil society organizations and the new citizen adhere to a very distinctive set of new values (Escudero, 2005). They believe in the need to stop climate change, in the need to respect human rights and in an economic and social convergence on a planetary scale. They are keen on more transparency in the working of social institutions and more accountability from public and private institutions.

The most important evidence concerning the existence of this global critical consciousness can be found in the proliferation of a new form of social organization, the nongovernmental organizations (NGOs) or civil society organizations. This new and truly universal pattern is, most likely, the most evident signal of the changing nature of today's society. Every society in the world has witnessed the impressive emergence of thousands of new civil society organizations, which scarcely existed 10 years ago.

But new civil society organizations or NGOs are no more than the tip of the iceberg. Underlying their existence, we can find a new citizen who is the most reflective individual in the history of humankind.

New global awareness of citizens, new global multilateral institutions and the emergence and proliferation of civil society organizations professing a common set of critical values, feed into each other and have dramatically changed the values landscape of our societies, giving place to the emergence of a new critical state of global conscience embodied in these new social (NGOs) and multilateral institutions – what I would like to call a new set of 'embodied' values.

This new set of 'embodied' values shed a very critical light upon corporations. This addresses the new power of the corporate sector, expecting more accountability and transparency, greater respect for human rights, decent labor and a more effective collaboration in the solution of global problems such as climate change, the eradication of hunger and the global provision of basic services, challenging the license of corporations to operate.

As a result, corporations, particularly multinational and large companies, have faced in these first years of the twenty-first century, a legitimacy crisis. Year after year, surveys measuring and ranking the trust of people in social institutions have consistently yielded the same result: the least trust-worthy institutions are political institutions along with large corporations and multinationals.

Corporations are reacting to their loss of legitimacy, enhanced by a constant stream of scandals starting in the late 1890s, by testing new ways of value creation which can be more compatible with the new set of universal values. This has been the origin of corporate social responsibility, sustainability or responsible corporate citizenship, a trend which started with the new century. It is not exactly a move towards self-regulation; rather, the new trend of corporate citizenship is being dictated globally by civil society, in a very innovative process of social regulation. Corporations are sensing that the business environment has changed and are readjusting to new ways of operating which can create values compatible with this new environment.

The need for a change in the role of business in society has been reinforced by four recent events:

1. From risk management to value creation, from morality to materiality – if the reaction of companies to their new environment in the new century was at the beginning reactive, defensive, a matter of avoiding risks and a move to again earn legitimacy or the license to operate, in the last few years the most advanced companies are finding that this new pattern of responsible behavior has become a source of new business models and value creation for the company. A growing number of leading firms are moving their citizenship into the commercial marketplace by producing 'green' products and services, reaching the world's poor through micro-lending and base-of-the-pyramid innovations, increasing access to health services, medicines, communications and other technologies, improving the nutritional value of foods and beverages, and exemplifying the business case for doing well for the company while doing good for society.

The issue we have to address as business educators is this: if the new trend of corporate sustainability has already evolved into a new proposition for value creation in the twenty-first century, we should be reporting this to our students, and preparing them to work in this new environment, where a new approach to smart risk management is evolving into a new scenario of value creation. Further, if we are supposed to train our students in business, we should change our own vision of the firm and its role *vis-à-vis* society in the twenty-first century, by adhering to a new paradigm or a new theory of the firm where companies set the limits of profit maximization in terms of the long-term sustainability of the company itself and the sustainability of society and the planet.

2. Financial markets and responsible behavior – as The Conference Board of Canada (Strandberg, 2008) summarized in a recent publication: 'Shareholders are perceived as the chief driver of CSR governance – particularly institutional investors with their quest for long-term value creation. The mainstream institutional shareholder community is starting to ask companies for greater consideration of social and environmental concerns.' Two indicators of this trend are:
   - The UN Principles for Responsible Investment, in which signatory investment firms sign on to embed environmental, social and governance (ESG) aspects into their assessment of companies and to engage actively with companies on these matters. There are currently over 560 signatories to the PRI and over US$20 trillion in assets signed up to the PRI's six principles.
   - The Carbon Disclosure Project, in which institutional investors with a current combined $57 trillion of assets under management seek information on business risks and opportunities, presented by climate change and greenhouse gas emissions from the world's largest companies (3000 firms in 2008).

Investors are becoming sensitive to the behavior of corporations because, in their view, companies that act in a responsible way have more guarantees of long-term higher returns and sustainable growth than the rest.

The relevant question for the community of business educators is, then, how to make a transition to responsible and sustainable finances, in turn providing our students with new analytical tools and capacities.

3. Business and the global agenda – the rapid development and growth of emerging economies is causing tensions to the supply of basic commodities such as energy. On the other hand, climate change has become an all-too-immediate threat caused by the constant growth of a carbon-based economy. Lastly, the escalation of international food prices indicates that agricultural supply is lagging behind the world demand for food.

All these recent events lead to the conclusion recently formulated by Jeffrey Sachs in his book *Common Wealth* (2008): humankind is pushing use of its basic resources to the limits. If we talk today about a food crisis today, tomorrow we may face a global water shortage, a new energy crisis or a generalized problem related to climate change.

In the light of these events, a new picture is emerging: a growing nexus between the desires of our reflective society to halt climate change or to boost shared global development, and the increasing awareness that we are entering a period in which the four pillars of human growth – climate, food, water and energy– are under increased stress, and demand smart global management. Global companies travelling along the new path of responsible behavior and value creation are already willing to sit at the table where these global problems can be averted by new global policies. Indeed, given the situation, new public–private dialogues conducive to new policies will shape the bulk of public and private investment over the next two to three decades.

But if this is part of the future landscape for private investment, we, as educators, should introduce into our education activities the real scenario of the global agenda, its challenges and its likely consequences for investment decisions and strategy over the next few decades.

4. The lessons of the recent financial crisis – the managerial model that has shown up its shortcomings in light of the financial crisis dictated that the yardstick for the success of CEOs was a narrow and short-term measure of shareholder value maximization. We have all been inspired by the pioneering work of Sumantra Ghoshal (2005) with his powerful posthumous critique of the prevailing model of managers and ensuing bad management practices based on agency theory, transaction costs theory and the 'negative approach' to economics defended by Milton Friedman's brand of 'liberalism'.

Ghoshal characterized prevailing theories taught in business schools in the following way: 'We have taught our students that managers cannot be trusted to do their jobs – which of course is to maximize shareholder value – and that to overcome "agency problems", managers' interests and incentives must be aligned with those of shareholders by, for example, making stock options a significant part of their pay.' He concluded: 'Combine agency theory with transaction costs economics, add in standard versions of game theory and negotiation analysis, and the picture of the manager that emerges is one that is now very familiar in practice: the ruthlessly, hard-driving, strictly top-down, command-and-control focused, shareholders-value-obsessed, win-at-any-cost business leader.'

As the *Financial Times* reported in 2009, Jack Welch, who is regarded as the father of the 'shareholder value' movement that has dominated the corporate world for more than 20 years, had said it was 'a dumb idea' for executives to focus so heavily on quarterly profits and share price gains. The former General Electric (GE) chief told the *Financial Times* that the emphasis that executives and investors had put on shareholder value, which began gaining popularity after a speech he made in 1981, was misplaced. Mr Welch, whose record at GE encouraged other executives to replicate its consistent returns, said that managers and investors should not set share price increases as their overarching goal. He added that short-term profits should be allied with an increase in the long-term value of a company. 'On the face of it, shareholder value is the dumbest idea in the world,' he said. 'Shareholder value is a result, not a strategy … Your main constituencies are your employees, your customers, your products' (Guerrera, 2009).

The shift towards a managerial model whose supreme goal is to balance the interests of a diverse group of interested parties or stakeholders seems to be emerging as a part of today's agenda, while the prevailing model and its underpinning theory of shareholder value has shown its devastating effects in the recent past.

The conclusion is clear: if we want to remain faithful to what business schools are about, that is, serving the business community as educators and thought leaders, we have to initiate a process of change. If the financial meltdown has presented us with the failure of prevailing approaches to management, we have to rethink management education, because businesses themselves are rethinking business along the lines of their own sustainable long-term growth and the sustainability of their social and ecological environment.

As *The Economist* put it very recently: 'You do not have to accept the idea that the business schools were "agents of the apocalypse" to believe that they need to change their ways, at least a little, in the light of recent events. [...] The real question is not whether business schools need to change, but how' (Schumpeter, 2009).

Indeed, after these two or three years of introspection by business schools, the question is not anymore 'why' we need to change (because of a number of extremely significant changes over the last few decades leading to a nascent new social contract between business and society), or even 'what' we need to change (our curricula, research and educational frameworks under the values of sustainability and the new role of business in society), but 'how'. In an attempt to answer this, here is what I would like to put forward as a fourth thesis.

BUSINESS EDUCATION HAS TO BE TRANSFORMED AT THREE LEVELS: TRANSVERSAL CHANGE AT THE SCHOOL LEVEL, INSTITUTIONAL CHANGES IN THE SECTOR AND INCLUSIVENESS AT THE GLOBAL SCALE AS THE UNDERLYING PHILOSOPHY OF CHANGE

The first condition for change is that business schools themselves initiate the process. Indeed, in the current situation, the competitive race to the top has been reopened. Winning schools will be those that are able to ignite the innovation of sustainability and technological and organizational change in their education offer and in their own organization. In order to achieve this, directors and deans need a clear vision, persistence and the ability to persuade. Education does not change because of the law, it is a change achieved by faculty members who update their teaching materials, their research and their methodologies. Here, the role of PRME as a learning community can play an important role.

The second condition for change is that the sector as a whole changes its institutional standards: its incentives for a less formal and more relevant research, its accreditation standards and rankings.

And the third condition for change is that the sector initiates a process of revision of business education, much like the one undertaken in the 1950s or 1980s. But for this process to be legitimate today, it has to be global and inclusive, and also has to be organized around a commonly accepted framework:

- To be global and inclusive – the past two revisions of business education, in the 1950s and the 1980s, were (logically) focused on the reality of business education at the time: the first one was based on the state of business education in the USA, and the second one on the USA and, to a lesser extent, Western Europe, the two regions of the world where the sector existed. Today, business education has gone global, and a new rethink of business education has to be inclusive of the reality of business schools not only in the USA and Western Europe, but also in Central and Eastern Europe, the Middle East, Africa, Latin America, the Pacific Region and Asia. If a sign of the times is multipolarity, this rethink has to be multilateral and global, giving a voice and place in the process to all regions and actors in the world.
- To be a common framework for change: the pressing problems of business schools today do not relate to the dilemma of specialization versus general approaches, the differentiation between vocational or academic training, or, in general, to problems related to the nascent nature of the sector. Business education is already a well-formed sector, facing, probably, its biggest challenge in its history: the challenge of a significant shift in the business environment and, hence, in the role of business, the theory of the firm and the approach to management.

In the academic environment of the 2000s, there was the need for a global call to facilitate the process of bringing business schools up to the new challenges and opportunities. The Principles for Responsible Management Education represent this call.

PRME is a voluntary engagement platform for business schools and management-related academic institutions. Academic institutions that have signed on to the PRME initiative have committed to work towards an implementation of the six principles as a long-term process of continuous performance improvement. The PRME initiative also functions as a learning network. PRME is a learning community where each participant reports publicly every 18 months on the progress achieved, so that everybody in the initiative can be inspired by such progress.

PRME unites the two characteristics required for the rethinking of business education in the twenty-first century:

- PRME already represents a global reality, where almost all the relevant associations from the USA, Latin America, Europe or Africa participate, and where a rapidly growing global community represents every corner of the world. Thus, PRME is a genuine global and inclusive initiative where all of us, together, can generate the collective effort and insight needed for change.
- The six principles of PRME focus on the crux of the matter: the need to place the new paradigm of sustainable and responsible value creation at the very core of business education.

Because of these two attributes, it is my belief that, with the emergence of PRME, the building blocks to facilitate progress and change for business educators have been already established, at a timely moment when the third revision of the future of business education is clearly needed.

NOTES

1. For instance, in the political domain there was a whole generation of 'Program 2000', as a prognosis of politics into the next century. I, myself, coordinated such an effort in Spain.
2. This was the background to the (in)famous thesis of Francis Fukuyama on the end of history. Also, it was a time of sociological dissatisfaction with the 'status quo' and, therefore, a time that saw the emergence of the (fake) new social movements.
3. See Global Policy Forum – Sarah Anderson and John Cavanagh – at www.globalpolicy.org/component/content/article/221/47211.html

REFERENCES

Escudero, M. (2005) *Homo Globalis: en Busca del Buen Gobierno.* Madrid: Espasa-Calpe.

Ghoshal, S. (2005) 'Bad management theories are destroying good management practices', *Academy of Management Learning and Education,* 4(1): 75–91.

Giddens, A. (1991) *Modernity and Self-identity: Self and Society in the Late Modern Age.* Cambridge: Polity Press.

Gordon, R.A. and Howell, J.E. (1959) *Higher Education for Business.* New York: Columbia University Press.

Guerrera, F. (2009) 'Welch condemns share price focus', *The Financial Times.* New York, 12 March.

Pierson, F.C. (1959) *The Education of American Businessmen.* New York: McGraw-Hill.

Podolny, J.M. (2009) 'The buck stops (and starts) at business school', *Harvard Business Review*, June: 62–7.

Porter, L.W. and McKibbin, L.E. (1988) *Management Education and Development: Drift or Thrust into the Twenty-first Century*. New York: McGraw-Hill.

Sachs, J.D. (2008) *Common Wealth: Economics for a Crowded Planet*. New York: Penguin.

Schumpeter, J. (2009) 'The pedagogy of the privileged', *The Economist*, 24 September.

Strandberg, C. (2008) *The Role of the Board of Directors in Corporate Social Responsibility*. Ottawa, ON: The Conference Board of Canada.

21 A PLEA TO BUSINESS SCHOOLS: TEAR DOWN YOUR WALLS

Robert Strand

Copenhagen Business School, Denmark

This past year, I attended a major business student conference focused on responsible business held at one of the most elite business schools in Europe. The campus was beautiful, the grounds were meticulously groomed, the buildings were stately, the conference halls for the discussions were plush, and when I ascended to an upper-floor terrace situated above the reaches of the security gates encapsulating the perimeter of the school – the views that greeted me were simply breathtaking. During the day, my business school colleagues and I dined on well-catered meals and in the evening many of us were treated to a wonderful multi-course meal at an elite restaurant in the city. And, from this well-fed vantage point, we, the privileged business students and the invited business elite, discussed how to promote responsible business to help make the world a more just and sustainable place. As I ate my many courses, drank my many glasses of wine, and participated in many conversations of global significance, a nagging little voice in the back of my head would occasionally question whether this was the best vantage point from which to consider what contributions we business students could make to society. Here we were, primarily all business students and business professionals, in an isolated atmosphere, discussing the challenges 'out there', well beyond the elegant sanctuary in which we were convening. I would contemplate this for a moment, and then have another glass of wine (they were free!).

In this chapter, I will explore this disconnection between business schools and society, what it means to those of us who are business students, and what we must do about it: tear down the walls that isolate business schools from society. From what I have seen, this kind of disconnection is pretty typical wherever business schools and their students are, by in large, disconnected from society's greatest challenges. It primarily remains only the business elite and people of power who are invited within the walls of our business schools, and it follows that many of us inside of those walls have the luxury of being ignorant of the greatest challenges of society.

A good question is this: why are business schools disconnected? The answer, at its core, is simply because they can be. Business schools are in a relative position of power. They receive large donations from affluent alumni and can count on ongoing support from the powerful corporations with whom they have a continued relationship. Now, with great power comes great responsibility, right? As I reflect upon the coursework I took as an MBA student in the USA, responsibility to anyone other than the shareholder was a topic that was left largely unexplored. So why is this?

Business schools have largely built their instruction on a perspective rooted in Adam Smith's (1776) classic *The Wealth of Nations*. As we have all read, Smith proposed that the butcher, the baker and the brewer did not produce goods out of altruism, but rather out of their own self-interest to feed themselves and their own families. Smith concluded that, overall, the result of this was positive as the necessities of life were better provided for by the butcher, the baker, the brewer and society at large through their self-interest rather than if benevolence was relied upon as the principal engine of production. Milton Friedman (1970) and others drew from this and, today, embedded in most business school coursework is the underlying premise that society benefits most when the modern-day corporation assumes a focus on one lone responsibility: to make profits. And while business schools may not explicitly teach business students to block their concern for anybody except the shareholders and the pursuit of profits, conspicuously missing from most business school curricula is any encouragement to consider areas that are outside of profit maximization strategies where the well-being of anyone other than the shareholders is explicitly taken account of. So the implicit message to those of us business students regarding their responsibility to others is: 'Don't worry about it. Just make profits and everything should work out'.

Now, before digging a bit deeper, it is important to highlight that profit, in and of itself, is a very good thing. IKEA founder Ingvar Kamprad (1976) rightfully pointed out that 'Profit is a wonderful word! … It gives us resources.' Not even the most diehard anti-business radical would bemoan a farmer for producing more food with less land and less water. But, regrettably, the word profit has become associated with the notion of greed run amok. This is most unfortunate and is cause for us to consider why Adam Smith and his lessons have failed us.

The simple answer is that Smith did not fail us; rather, it has been the failure of those drawing from Smith to consider the broader context of his offerings. Milton Friedman (1970), whose lessons serve as the foundation for much of the business school education (particularly in the USA), and colleagues have inappropriately cherry-picked from Smith's writings with a myopic focus on the sentiments within Smith's now famous line – 'it is not from the benevolence of the butcher, the baker, or the brewer that we expect our dinner, but from regard to their own self-interest' – without putting the statement within its context. This single line has been inappropriately used as a means to absolve businesspeople of the responsibility to consider anyone other than themselves and their shareholders. And it follows that business schools have, by and large, encouraged paying little attention to a responsibility to anything other than pursing self-interest and profits for shareholders.

So what is this broader context from which Smith's statement has been inappropriately plucked? Friedman (1970) and others have failed to focus on the significant detail that Smith's baker, butcher and brewer lived within the communities that they served and directly interacted with their stakeholders on a daily basis. So while it may be true that the baker, butcher and brewer produced goods out of their own self-interest, they also likely had a very strong incentive to take into account the interests of their stakeholders, as their personal reputations would suffer if they injured their employees, mistreated their suppliers, cheated their customers or polluted the environment of their community. And because these stakeholders were their neighbors, the baker, butcher and brewer were probably well informed about their stakeholders' perceptions of them. Moreover, given that the baker, butcher and brewer owned their businesses (or at the very least had a close connection with the owners) the longer term was more likely considered.

Furthermore, this myopic focus on self-interest fails to take into account the foundation upon which *The Wealth of Nations* was built, which was Smith's earlier offering in *The Theory of Moral Sentiments* (1759). Here, Smith described the natural tendency for people to take into account the well-being of others as a result of the simple act of seeing and interacting with them. For Smith, a concern for others arises from social relationships because people are social beings who develop empathy for one another. When we see a person who is happy or sad, we feel a degree of happiness or sadness ourselves irrespective of whether or not we have anything tangible to gain or lose from that person. It follows that because Smith's baker, butcher and brewer lived within the communities they served and saw their stakeholders on a regular basis, they developed relationships with them and would have a natural tendency to take their well-being into account. The relationship that develops between people who share empathy for one another is precisely the reason why community is so special – and important.

Fast forward 200 years, and the modern-day baker, butcher and brewer are corporations whose employees perform their daily activities within enclosed corporate offices surrounded by security guards and imposing metal gates. This serves to isolate businesspeople today from the communities in which they work. These corporate offices often have onsite cafeterias and health clubs designed for employee convenience but which further prevent those employees from getting to know the people just outside of the corporation's walls. This is further exasperated because many employees commute relatively long distances to work which, when taken together, results in limited contact between businesspeople and the local communities just outside of the corporation's walls. Moreover, the bulk of the corporation's suppliers are located thousands of kilometers away where there is little personal engagement. Thus, the corporation–supplier relationship becomes one that is solely about price, quality and deliverability with little consideration for the general well-being of the employees of the suppliers and the communities in which those suppliers operate. Additionally, the corporation's customers are spread throughout the world where any personal interaction between the corporation and its customers is through monthly sales figures and third-party surveys. And, finally, the shareholder – to whom Friedman states the businessperson is completely responsible – is not a person who lives in the community as the baker, butcher and brewer did. Rather, the modern-day shareholder is made up of a disparate collection of faceless institutions, indices with automatic buy/sell algorithms, and unknown traders spread throughout the world who are continuously buying and selling in an effort to maximize short-term gains.[1]

Therefore, the modern-day corporation is much less likely to naturally consider the impact of its actions on its stakeholders than Smith's butcher, baker and brewer. Diminishing the human element has unintentionally reduced the responsibilities that one would naturally take on by virtue of being part of a community and engaging with its members on a continuous basis. And while global supply chains and global financing were also in effect at the time of Adam Smith, consider if Smith had phrased his statement as 'it is not from the benevolence of the multinational global financier, the large cargo ship owner, or the industrial factory owner that we expect our dinner, but in regard to their own self-interest'. The statement would have lost its impact as these entities do not conjure up the image of community. Smith chose people whose faces we know and with whom we interact and share a sense of community. Thus, it is not appropriate to invoke such a narrow reading of Adam Smith as a means by which to absolve the corporation of its responsibility to consider anything other than pursing profits for the shareholder, and it follows that it is not appropriate for business schools to neglect encouraging business students to explore their responsibilities beyond the shareholder.

This is where business ethics becomes an important part of the discussion because central to ethics is the consideration of one's responsibility to the well-being of others (Beauchamp et al. 2009). Milton Friedman did imply that ethics was part of doing business in his much-cited piece 'The Social Responsibility of Business is to Increase its Profits' (Friedman 1970), but described 'ethical customs' as little more than a constraint on the businessperson. Moreover, Friedman suggested that executives who consider responsibilities to anything other than the interests of the shareholder are neglecting their responsibilities as an agent of the shareholder. Thus, Friedman argued for keeping ethics out of business. Given his immense influence, it is not surprising that, despite the current calls, ethics is not woven into the fabric of the business school curriculum. It follows that business students are not regularly challenged to consider the well-being of anyone other than the shareholders.

Sumantra Ghoshal (2005) declared that promoting Milton Friedman-based theories void of ethical considerations, where everyone and everything is out solely to serve self-interest, amounts to a self-fulfilling prophesy for a 'gloomy vision' of the world in which mistrust and the need for control are stressed. (In the same vein, Marglin [2008] put forth: 'thinking like an economist undermines community.') Therefore, Ghoshal challenged business schools and their professors to confront this blind allegiance to self-interest in our business school teachings, asking 'Why don't we actually acknowledge in our theories that companies survive and prosper when they simultaneously pay attention to the interests of customers, employees, shareholders, and perhaps even the communities in which they operate?' It is important to underscore that Ghoshal did not renounce the corporation pursuing profits, but rather rejected the notion that the corporation should pursue profits without simultaneously considering the well-being of others. Ghoshal rightfully argued that all parties would benefit when profits and the well-being of others were pursued in concert.

But in the aftermath of corporate scandals and a global financial crisis where government bailouts went to firms whose senior executives continued to reward themselves with excessive bonuses, one should forgive the people outside of the walls of business for questioning whether the interests of more than just the people within the corporate world were considered. And because of the walls that isolate our businesspeople and business students from the communities in which they are located, there is little opportunity for anything other than public skepticism to build. Moreover, if one did look inside the walls at the lessons being taught in our business schools, there would be little to see that would dispel this skepticism. Considering all of this, business schools have unwittingly put their legitimacy at grave risk in the eyes of society, and we the business students are in the middle of it all.

Joel Podolny (2009) recently charged that 'unless America's business schools make radical changes, society will become convinced that MBAs work to serve only their own selfish interests'. Correspondingly, Warren Bennis and James O'Toole (2005) pointed out in a not-so-subtle fashion that business schools had 'lost their way' and argued that this was due to a misalignment of incentives for how they went about educating their students and conducting their research, as much of it was completely disconnected from what was actually relevant for society. Bennis and O'Toole argued that business schools were 'graduating students who are ill equipped to wrangle with complex, unquantifiable issues' and called for 'the entire MBA curriculum [to] be infused with multidisciplinary, practical, and ethical questions and analyses reflecting the complex challenges business leaders face'.

These charges from the likes of Ghoshal, Podolny, Bennis and O'Toole amount to a call to tear down the walls that isolate business schools from society so that business school professors and students alike are encouraged to actively engage with the challenges of society. Searching for imaginative solutions to societal challenges also represents new opportunities and markets. Business strategists would recognize these opportunities as 'Blue Oceans' (Kim and Mauborgne 2005) and occasions for creating 'shared value' (Porter and Kramer 2011). But to realize these opportunities, business school students must escape from the confines of their schools, and engage with the communities outside their walls. And through this, that natural tendency of empathy that Smith described can kick in where business students further develop their concern for others and desire to help, and society at large can see business students as people who are concerned with the well-being of more than just themselves and their shareholders.

As Di Norcia and Tigner (2000) have described, ethics has historically been viewed as a constraint to economic benefit and Milton Friedman has been the poster boy for this view. But, paradoxically, Friedman's myopic focus on self-interest actually stands in the way of profits. Badaracco (2002) called for us to 'trust mixed motives' where the pursuit of self-interest and a concern for others are encouraged in concert, as this increases the likelihood of all parties benefiting as a result (see Stark 1993 for an additional discussion on the benefits of mixed motives). When businesspeople exercise a concern for the well-being of others and develop a strong curiosity for finding solutions to society's challenges, they are more likely to open their eyes to the 'Blue Oceans' and opportunities for creating 'shared value', and the results over the long run are scores of opportunities that would otherwise have gone unidentified. At the heart of identifying these opportunities are the need for awareness and a true concern for the well-being of others on the part of the businessperson. Thus, by putting ethics at the core of doing business, the likelihood of achieving profits over the long run is increased.

So how do we go about tearing down these walls to challenge those of us business students to imagine new and creative solutions to meet the challenges of society? One way is for business schools to facilitate exposing business students to the ethical dimensions of business and the impact on stakeholders beyond just the shareholders. A good way to do this is to get all of us, professors and students, physically outside of the confines of the business school. Two lone courses come to mind for me from my MBA program in which I was seriously challenged to consider my responsibility to anyone other than the shareholder, and these were the two courses that took me outside of the comfortable walls of my business school to explore corporate social responsibility (CSR) issues in Europe and sustainability issues in Central America. The business ethicist Dr Norman Bowie taught the course in CSR, and it was truly life-changing for my fellow students and me as it represented the first time many of us had been directly confronted with the challenges of society and asked what those of us in the business world were doing about it. We were asked pointedly by NGOs: 'What are you going to do about poverty? What are you going to do about depleting resources? What are you going to do about child labor or the safety of the workers in your supply chains? What is your responsibility regarding these issues?' Most of us business students found ourselves incredibly ill-equipped to respond. 'But those aren't our problems', I recall was a response by a fellow classmate. 'So who the hell's problems are they?' was the response fired back from an NGO member. It was the first time many of my fellow business students and I found ourselves critically challenging the business school teachings we had previously accepted on faith or out of expediency. Most of our business school teaching had largely revolved around templates and takeaways.

Through Dr Bowie's CSR course, my fellow students and I found ourselves making connections between events and people and organizations and challenges, and the whole cornucopia of messy issues outside of the walls of the business school and the corporation. Thus, it was for many of us our first taste in our business education of the development of reflexivity involving notions of connective thinking, critical thinking and self-awareness (De Dea Roglio and Light 2009). Reflexivity is core to CSR because CSR demands that business leaders understand the connections between their corporation and the broader world, actively engage with stakeholders outside of their corporate walls, think critically about the business decisions they make that affect the broader world, and develop self-awareness of their own behaviors and influence on others. The importance of developing reflexivity in business students is no secret (e.g. De Dea Roglio and Light 2009; Egan and Bendick 2008; Hedberg 2009; Schön 1983), but business schools have not appropriately addressed the issue. Rather than focusing on helping to develop reflexivity, they are largely following the approach of teaching instrumentally and arming with spreadsheets, templates and bullet points. We are not taught much about dealing with those tricky intangibles and a host of ethical dilemmas, and this is particularly true for MBA programs.

This standalone course raised my awareness (and that of my MBA colleagues) of those challenges in society which the business community could, and should, help to address. Installing a dedicated course, like Dr Bowie's, focused on responsible business practices in which reflexivity is stressed is part of the answer for MBA programs. But this lone awareness-raising course must also be coupled with a concerted and sustained effort to infuse responsible business across the business school curriculum. I have been privy to discussions at a number of business schools regarding whether to have both a standalone required course in responsible business (entitled 'Business Ethics' or 'Corporate Social Responsibility', for example) while also working to infuse responsible business throughout the curriculum. This can be met with resistance, where business schools that have established a standalone course may argue that this one course alone is sufficient, and schools without such a course may argue that responsible business practices are already integrated throughout their curriculum so a standalone course is unnecessary. In my experience and through my discussions with many other business school students, I have come to the firm conclusion that having just one without the other is not sufficient. We, the business school students, need an explicit course in responsible business to explicitly raise our awareness and interest in the issues related to ethics in business (Carroll 1987), and this is most effective when placed near the start of our business school education. Additionally, we need a continued revisiting of ethical and responsible business themes throughout all of our courses because, as Trevino and Brown (2004) put it, rarely do decisions come 'waving red flags', saying 'Hey, I'm an ethical issue'. Thus, we need to encounter ethical issues embedded within our fields as we will encounter them in this manner upon entering our careers in corporations. All of that said, establishing a standalone course in responsible business and embedding responsible business throughout the curriculum does not just happen – it requires a great deal of effort. And this is where we, the business students, can have a great deal of impact in affecting this change.

Enter Net Impact. As a long-time member of the organization, I have personally experienced how Net Impact and its members are taking on these challenges. Net Impact is an international nonprofit organization with a mission to inspire, educate and equip individuals to use the power of business to create a more socially and environmentally sustainable world. With over 15,000 members – the majority of whom are business school students – and a presence at over 150 business schools, Net Impact represents the world's largest organization of business school students who are actively committed to exploring open-ended questions related to what contributions business and business schools must make to society. I was first introduced to Net Impact as a student on Dr Bowie's course as some of my fellow students were actively involved on the leadership team of the Net Impact chapter at my business school. (And those Net Impact student leaders and I later went on to form a local professionals chapter of Net Impact that we have since worked to link closely with the student chapter at our former business school.)

Net Impact is the lone student organization co-convener with the United Nations Principles for Responsible Management Education (PRME), where PRME represents the largest formalized effort to integrate responsible business throughout business school curricula and research. Net Impact members are 'the foot soldiers for PRME' – there is a remarkable amount of activity in expanding responsible business course offerings and embedding the ideas throughout the business school curriculum, through Net Impact student members teaming up to drive forward PRME efforts at their school.

Net Impact has supported two long-standing initiatives in the Curriculum Change Initiative and the Campus Greening program, which represent two direct ways that Net Impact and PRME work well together to address many of the challenges discussed throughout this chapter. The Net Impact Curriculum Change Initiative is designed to empower Net Impact members to improve their MBA program by incorporating socially and environmentally focused classes, discussions and events into the curriculum. The Net Impact Campus Greening projects establish environmentally sustainable practices on campus, helping universities save money, improve learning conditions and increase efficiency. At many business schools, the percentage of Net Impact members is in excess of 30 per cent of the student body, which makes these forward PRME 'foot soldiers' a formidable army that has demonstrated a capacity to effect positive change at their schools.

In addition to impacting change regarding the business school curriculum and campus activities, Net Impact members are actively working to connect business schools and business students to society's challenges through Net Impact's Service Corps program and its Board Fellows program. Net Impact's Service Corps program provides an opportunity for members to use their business skills to help their community. Volunteers engage in short-term, part-time consulting projects related to marketing, business planning/operations and strategic planning. And the Net Impact Board Fellows program brings valuable business skills to nonprofits, while exposing Net Impact members to nonprofit management and governance. These are just a couple of examples of how Net Impact members are working to break down the walls around their business schools, and directly engaging with society's challenges.

Net Impact also produces its 'Business as Unusual' guide to facilitate prospective business students in their search for socially and environmentally sustainable business school programs. In addition to assisting prospective business school students, the guide also helps to facilitate business schools and current business students in comparing themselves against their peers and in developing more robust social impact curricula, career services and support for student activities. This hopefully helps to incentivize business schools to take these issues more seriously into account as business schools are being compared to one another.

Arguably, the most visible of Net Impact's activities is the Net Impact annual conference during the autumn of each year where over 2000 Net Impact members congregate to discuss responsible business. I have now attended dozens of sustainability/responsible business conferences, and this is undoubtedly the best and most engaging one out there through which I find myself rejuvenated and full of hope as a result of conversations with other business school students, practitioners, NGOs and others from within and outside of the business community. The Net Impact annual conference represents an opportunity for business students to explore how business can make a positive contribution to society, and provides business students with newfound ideas and the energy to go back to their respective schools to initiate grassroots efforts to better connect their business schools to societal challenges. Thus, Net Impact can be a very strong force in these efforts.

In this chapter, I have offered a few examples of ways to help tear down the walls around business schools. This has included discussions about innovative study-abroad programs focused on the topics of CSR and sustainability in which business school students explore responsible business far outside the confines of their familiar business schools. I also discussed the importance of establishing a standalone course in responsible business coupled with a concerted effort to embed responsible business throughout the curriculum, as exemplified by the PRME initiative and supported by the Net Impact business students through the Curriculum Change Initiative. Moreover, Net Impact members are also working to tear down the walls around business schools through such initiatives as their Service Corps and Board Fellows programs.

Beyond these offerings, I would also encourage all business school students and professors to seriously engage with their fellow students and professors from other schools at the universities in which their business school resides. As Freeman et al. (2010: 78) correctly point out '[no] one mode, and no single discipline, has a monopoly on insight'. We need not necessarily travel around the world to be exposed to different perspectives. The simple act of inviting non-business students from the schools of government, journalism, philosophy, creative arts, education, etc. to participate in our business school events can serve to bring new perspectives into the business school. Ideally, we should open up our business school classes to encourage a percentage of non-business students to enroll in our classes. Students from outside of the business school may well challenge the Milton Friedman notion that the only social responsibility of business is to make profits, and it would do those of us who are business students some good to grapple with these other perspectives. We could start by opening up and actively promoting the standalone course in responsible business (the course entitled 'Business Ethics' or 'Corporate Social Responsibility', for example) to a broader audience as this course is the one most likely to attract students from other schools – and the perspectives these non-business students would bring would prove invaluable.

We build walls around our business schools when we should be tearing them down. Those of us in such schools are in a privileged position to effect a change for the positive and we must demonstrate to society at large that we are taking more into account than just the interests of shareholders and ourselves. To do this, we must attempt to become much more connected and engaged with society's greatest challenges. The legitimacy of our business schools depends upon it. And most importantly, we can do a hell of a lot of good in this world by doing so.

NOTES

1. Some of these arguments regarding Adam Smith were developed, in part, within Strand (2009).
2. It is self-evident that the concept of 'shared value' is based in stakeholder theory, where the stakeholder theory literature has long explored the notion that the entrepreneur or manager creates value by capturing the 'jointness of interests' between stakeholders. Freeman et al. (2010) offers a comprehensive review of the rich stream of literature associated with stakeholder theory.

REFERENCES

Badaracco, J., Jr (2002) *Leading Quietly: An Unorthodox Guide to Doing the Right Thing.* Boston, MA: Harvard Business School Press.

Beauchamp, T., Bowie, N. and Arnold, G. (2009) Ethical theory and business practice. In *Ethical Theory and Business*, 8th edn (pp. 1–44). Prentice Hall, NJ: Pearson.

Bennis, W. and O'Toole, J. (2005) How business schools lost their way. *Harvard Business Review*, 83(5): 96–104.

Carroll, A. (1987) In search of the moral manager. *Business Horizons*, March–April: 7–15.

De Dea Roglio, K. and Light, G. (2009) Executive MBA programs: The development of the reflexive executive. *Academy of Management Learning and Education*, 8(2): 156–73.

Di Norcia, V. and Tigner, J. (2000) Mixed motives and ethical decisions in business. *Journal of Business Ethics*, 25(1): 1–13.

Egan, M. and Bendick, M. (2008) Combining multicultural management and diversity into one course on cultural competence. *Academy of Management Learning and Education*, 7(3): 387–93.

Freeman, R.E., Harrison, J.S., Wicks, A.C., Parmar, B.L., and De Colle, S. (2010) *Stakeholder Theory – The State of the Art.* Cambridge: Cambridge University Press.

Friedman, M. (1970) The social responsibility of business is to increase its profits. *The New York Times Magazine*, 33: 122–6.

Ghoshal, S. (2005) Bad management theories are destroying good management practices. *Academy of Management Learning and Education*, 4(1): 75–91.

Hedberg, P.R. (2009) Learning through reflective classroom practice. *Journal of Management Education*, 33(1): 10–36.

Kamprad, I. (1976) *A Furniture Dealer's Testament*. Inter IKEA Systems B.V.

Kim, C. and Mauborgne, R. (2005) *Blue Ocean Strategy*. Boston, MA: Harvard Business School Press.

Marglin, S. (2008) *The Dismal Science: How Thinking Like an Economist Undermines Community*. Boston, MA: Harvard University Press.

Podolny, J.M. (2009) The buck stops (and starts) at business school. *Harvard Business Review*, June: 62–7.

Porter, M. and Kramer, M. (2011) Creating shared value. *Harvard Business Review*, January–February: 62–77.

Schön, D. (1983) *The Reflective Practitioner: How Professionals Think in Action*. London: Temple Smith.

Smith, A. (1759) *The Theory of Moral Sentiments*. London: A. Millar, in the Strand.

Smith, A. (1776) *An Inquiry into the Nature and Causes of the Wealth of Nations*. London: Penguin.

Stark, A. (1993) What's the matter with business ethics? *Harvard Business Review*, May–June: 38–48.

Strand, R. (2009) The stakeholder dashboard. In C. Galea (ed.) *Consulting for Business Sustainability*. Sheffield: Greenleaf Publishing.

Trevino, L. and Brown, M. (2004) Managing to be ethical: Debunking five business ethics myths. *Academy of Management Executive*, 18(2): 69–81.

22 CORPORATE RESPONSIBILITY AND THE BUSINESS SCHOOLS' RESPONSE TO THE CREDIT CRISIS

Nigel Roome, David Bevan and Gilbert Lenssen

EABIS, Vlerick Leuven Gent Management School, Belgium and Grenoble Business School, France

The Academy of Business in Society (EABIS) was founded in 2001 by the deans of eight leading business schools in Europe together with senior executives from six global companies. It was supported by the European Commission (EC). EABIS's mission is to promote research and education on corporate responsibility and sustainability within the context of the evolving role of business in society. Its current membership of over 120 organizations includes leading companies, business schools, universities and affiliated organizations. There are some 75 academic members from Europe, the Americas, Africa, Asia and Australia/New Zealand. Most corporate members are global MNCs.

The origins of EABIS are European. European business school deans recognized the need for a more European view of CSR rather than adopting the US approach of adding business ethics courses in response to corporate scandals. There was also a distinct 'CSR' ('as a contribution to Sustainable Development', dixit EC) debate in Europe around the Lisbon Agenda (2007) launched in 2000. The European Commission provided over 5 million Euro to fund research projects in which EABIS plays a leading role. From these origins, EABIS has sought to define the field as Business in Society, going beyond business ethics and CSR, to encompass sustainability, corporate governance, and to span the interests of economics, strategic management, brand management and talent management.

With this orientation, EABIS was well positioned to consider the implications of the credit crisis in the context of the sustainability of global systems and the future role of Global Governance. The academic membership was growing outside Europe, especially in the USA and Asia, and EABIS re-launched itself as a global platform seeking to provide the knowledge and skills needed for today's and tomorrow's managers as they address issues of business in a more global economy and society. EABIS works closely with its strategic partner EFMD.

In this chapter, we consider business schools' response to the future of management education arising from the credit crisis of 2007 from the vantage point of the 'responsible corporation' and the changing role of business in society. However, it is not possible to discuss the future of management education without taking a longer perspective for the development of corporate social responsibility and the management curriculum in Europe in the lead-up to the crisis.

THE CONTEXT OF THE CRISIS

Our argument is simple. At the highest level of abstraction, the 'credit crisis' was generated by the way that leaders, managers and the staff of financial institutions thought about, governed, managed and conducted their activities. It resulted from a combination of factors – over-vigorous selling of sub-prime mortgages, the failure to assess that markets could fall as well as rise and thereby create toxic assets, the development of exotic derivatives that converted private risk into systems risk, the intensity of connections between financial institutions, and the pursuit of private gain through performance-driven bonuses, as well as the lack of corporate governance oversight, failures of self-regulation in business too big to fail, government regulation or both. This crisis was born in the way managers and business leaders understood their role and the ideas, and the technologies (tools, routines, structures, systems and procedures), through which their goals were realized. These ideas and technologies were often learned or reinforced through management development and education programs offered by business schools. Business schools may then take their turn to reflect on what happened and to react by considering what might need to be changed within their control or sphere of influence.

From the viewpoint of EABIS, the 'credit crisis' can be seen as a monumental example of managerial and corporate failure: a failure of good corporate governance and the poverty of management thinking and practice in the financial sector. However, our contention is that the credit crisis is simply a highly visible example of the failure of managers to address 'systems issues'. Indeed, this failure of management is endemic to the way managers conceive of the relationship between the business and economic, social and environmental systems of which they are part.

We start with the belief that corporate responsibility is about the way business leaders and managers think about and take responsibility for their actions and their consequences. While the field of 'corporate responsibility' is however broad and multi-faceted, the agenda is shaped in different ways in a variety of personal, national, institutional and cultural settings. This cultural and institutional shaping of norms and ideas equally applies to the way management education has developed and influences our perception of the role of business in society in a country of Europe or a region of the world.

Laid over this complexity are the powerful connections we have made in time and place through the processes of globalization (Giddens, 1986: 2068). For example, the spread of academic and managerial networks means that ideas and approaches constructed by individual researchers or practitioners in one setting are deployed in other settings, often with little questioning or scant attention being paid to their appropriateness in that context. Second, researchers view elements of the field of corporate responsibility through the lens of their own discipline and its traditions. They draw on experiences within their own cultural and institutional environment and there are strong perceptual filters derived, say, from their business school or their notion of the changing nature of business in society. These can blinker any understanding of underlying trends. Third, there is often a significant lag between events in business and society, the research undertaken on those events, the ultimate publication of findings, followed by their translation into education. Finally, there are those who might see a field synoptically and others who might research a small part of a field in great depth and detail. There are thought leaders and shapers, and there are then the many who exist some way off the leading-edge of ideas and practice. There is often a lag between the origins of theoretical and conceptual ideas and their adoption as routines in education or practice, and also a lag between the emergence of new phenomena and the response to them by practitioners or their study by academics. These lags can begin to assume great importance in a complex world going through rapid change. In the case of the credit crisis, the lag between formative events and their outcomes might have been at least 20 years. The same applies to the issue of climate change, while current concerns about resource scarcity and the competition for land for food and energy, water and minerals were identified over 10 years ago.

Even in such a complex context, weak signals will often arise well before major events draw wider attention to the need for action. If corporate responsibility is the business and managerial reaction to change in the social and environmental and business context, then we need to consider how business schools themselves have understood their contribution to identifying and responding to such change. We consider these ideas by developing a brief history of business education and the position of corporate responsibility. Without that background, any discussion of the response to the credit crisis makes little sense.

The next section provides a comment on the development of management education in Europe and the rest of the world. The relationship between some 'critical events' at the leading-edge of the changing interface between business and society in Europe is then charted. Particular attention is placed on the events and trends that shaped the evolution of corporate responsibility and its position in management education in business schools. The main trend discussed is the powerful effects of internationalized business since 1989, as this enlarged the scope and significance of corporate responsibility in the minds of managers in business and academics in business schools.

This period of internationalization of business, in which the complexity of management and the importance of corporate responsibility have grown beyond bounds, is so important that it is discussed in detail.

The history ends with the 'critical event', the 2008/9 credit crisis, and the questions it has raised about the contribution of business education to the crisis and the changes this might imply for the future of management education. Selected dimensions of this debate are outlined in the next section on the response by deans of business schools.

Conclusions touch on two issues – the future of management education and the position of corporate responsibility in the management curriculum – and our understanding of the European approach to the future of our increasingly connected economies and societies. We end with an overview of the direction that EABIS – the Academy of Business in Society – is set to take as the issues it was founded to address in Europe become matters of concern and interest to a broader international constituency of educators, researchers and practitioners.

MANAGEMENT EDUCATION, EVENTS, TRENDS AND CORPORATE RESPONSIBILITY

Management education has three distinct components: basic-level higher education for students without experience of business or organizational practice; post-graduate management education through MBAs and similar programs normally for those with first degrees and a minimum of three years' organizational experience; and the professionalization and skilling of practicing managers through management development programs. This chapter focuses primarily on post-graduate management and professional education, although it is evident that what students learn at undergraduate level or at school influences how they see the world.

Education to develop professional managers began in the developed economies during the period from 1880 to 1914. Schools of commerce were established in many industrial cities in Europe during this period: Birmingham, Brussels, Copenhagen, Helsinki, Leipzig, London, Manchester, Milan, Paris, St Gallen, Stockholm, as well as in the USA: at Berkley, Boston (Harvard), Chicago, (Hanover), New Hampshire (Tuck), Philadelphia (Wharton) and in Canada (Montreal).

Although schools of commerce were first established in Europe, it was the USA that promoted university-based management programs with the development of the MBA degree (Harvard, 1910). The MBA was introduced into European management education in 1957 at INSEAD, followed by IESE and ESADE in 1964. It arrived under the strong influence of Harvard and the experience of US business schools.

Other European countries followed with MBA programs in the mid-1960s: Smurfit Business School at University College Dublin, the London and Manchester Business Schools, the Rotterdam School of Management, HEC in Paris. Other schools in Western Europe soon developed MBA programs, from Scandinavia through to the Mediterranean, from Portugal through to Greece.

The IEDC-Bled School of Management was the first ex-communist bloc provider of the MBA degree in 1991. Other Central and Eastern European countries followed, with knowledge of the management curriculum arising from the USA and Western Europe. Space does not permit a longer elaboration. The formative period for the first generation of MBAs in Europe was 1957–75 and it focused on putting in place their curriculum, content and pedagogy. This was a period for action rather than deep reflection, when establishing the curriculum and the art of teaching management was far more important than the research credentials of faculty that have become so much more important today.

At this formative period in European MBAs, corporate responsibility arose mostly at the periphery of the curriculum, taking the form of ethics, and anti-trust and corporate codes of practice.

At the end of this period in the early 1970s, there were concerns about the scarcity of global resources (*Limits to Growth*, Meadows et al., 1972), coinciding with the UN's Stockholm Conference on Environment and Development in 1972, closely followed by the 1973 oil crisis. As an interesting aside, *Limits to Growth* was co-authored by the young Norwegian Jorgen Randers, a scenario planner interested in systems dynamics, who between 1981 and 1989 served as president of the Norwegian School of Management (BI). Currently, Randers is Professor of Climate Strategy at BI, describing his interest as corporate social responsibility: the corporate responsibility for contributing towards sustainability.

Next to corporate responsibility, we have the field of business ethics. In the USA, this field was laid out by philosophy, religious studies and the law. Subsequently, we have seen a wider commentary on business ethics from economists and strategists: for example, the arguments of Milton Friedman (1970: 52) and others on the social purpose of the firm and the contrasting arguments from Ed Freeman (1984), with his stakeholder view of strategy. At the same time, Archie Carroll (1979) developed his architecture for understanding responsibility from a US viewpoint. Outside of the USA, the debate between Friedman and Freeman was seen as that of a sterile contest of ideologies (Roome, 1997) with agency theory pitted against the ethics of responsibility. The debate between Friedman and Freeman was far more at home in the USA than Europe, but it became a source of much discussion in early classes on corporate responsibility around the globe. By contrast, European concerns about resource scarcity arising from the Club of Rome were taken up in strategy courses (see, for example, the work of authors such as Igor Ansoff, 1979) rather than in those on corporate responsibility. Ansoff's ideas about 'enterprise strategy' and its implications for business became less significant, even in European Business Schools, as MBA strategy courses focused more and more on ideas of competitive strategy (Porter, 1985, 1987). Ideas originating from the US model of the role of business in society became more widespread and this was accelerated by the process of internationalization witnessed during the 1990s.

The development of business school education around 1989 was fundamental to later developments. This period saw questions arise about global resource scarcity, the role of business in society and corporate environmental responsibility. At the same time, the agenda of management education became pre-occupied by the ideas of greater competition that followed internationalization. The outcome was a growing mismatch between the narrow focus and content of management education and the widespread impact of business practice on economic, environmental and social systems. Business schools promoted the evolving model of international business, giving scant attention to the capacity of economic or environmental systems to absorb business interdependencies. This did little to advance the skills that managers might need to address those systems issues. Business schools also contributed little that would be needed to understand or deal with the systemic problems of the credit crisis.

The following sections illustrate the poverty of the response by business schools in terms of curriculum change to the changing position of business in society. This is related through a series of 'signature events' in Europe and the world that have shaped our understanding of corporate responsibility as governance and management but which at the time failed to shape the business curriculum.

AWAKENING TO THE CHALLENGE

The first significant event in the recent history of corporate responsibility and the role of business in society occurred in 1981 in England, in a part of inner-city Liverpool called Toxteth. Prime Minister Thatcher was elected in 1979 and pursued a neo-liberal policy influenced strongly by the monetarist ideas of Milton Friedman. To control inflation, interests rates were raised, direct taxes were reduced and indirect taxes increased. Unemployment increased to 3 million with many factory closures. The UK entered its worst and longest post-war recession, until the credit crisis. In July 1981, there was a riot in Toxteth and other riots in the UK that same year. These were attributed to social problems and unemployment. The response was to address this through urban regeneration and rejuvenation campaigns that would lead to environmental and community benefits as well as job creation opportunities (Roome, 1988). A government minister was appointed, who drew together a 'task force' from public sectors, civil society and the private sector. Businesses and managers were expected to address these problems of social regeneration and environmental protection. Thatcher explicitly encouraged greater competitiveness but at the same time broke the long-standing divide between government as the sole agent of governance, and the private sector, as the engine of the economy. Key ideas at this time were partnerships and collaboration. Business managers had to learn how to contribute to shared governance and to bring their skills to the management of initiatives that focused on community and environmental regeneration as well as the spirit of enterprise.

Partnerships and collaborations emerged that involved businesses working with other sectors of society. Many of these projects are discussed by Carley and Christie (2001) in their book *Managing Sustainable Development* (see www.xfire.com/live_video/vortelol/).

These events may seem parochial to many readers but take a step back and you will recognize that the same processes have happened to many other European countries in the period since 1981. The monopoly role of the state in governance has been replaced by an emphasis on partnerships and collaboration across sectors to provide for the governance and management of the economy, society and the environment. The reduction of the role of the state and the selling-off of state companies, the stimulation and reward for enterprise, accompanied the advance of the neo-liberal agenda that fuelled globalization. Yet most business schools focused on the core issues of competitive business rather than on the more alien ideas of the managerial skills and competence required to contribute effectively to 'shared governance' or to understand the contribution of business to environmental and social concerns.

BROADENING OF THE CHALLENGE

As business went global, the resource and environmental issues anticipated by the Club of Rome were beginning to have impact. There was a growing debate about the environmental responsibilities of business in the Scandinavian countries, in Denmark, Germany and the UK for different reasons. Concerns were focused on a succession of global events from Bhophal (1984) to acid rain issuing from the UK coal-fired power plants affecting Scandinavia (1983/4), the combined effects of German and UK industrial pollution on the Black Forest (1984), the Sandoz pollution of the Rhine (1986), Chernobyl (1986), and the thinning of the ozone layer due to CFCs (1985–7). The environmental movement in Europe developed a greater confidence and membership, pressing governments for responses, while governments pressed business for cleaner and more transparent operations.

The move toward more unfettered markets caused business to ask for more 'space' to innovate through voluntary initiatives rather than to be subjected to stringent legislation. Indeed, by 1985 the Canadian Chemical Producer's Association had begun a voluntary environmental management initiative called Responsible Care that was to become the basis for a worldwide program in sector-led environmental self-regulation. By 1989, the British

Standards Institute was beginning to pilot its environmental management system standard. The first company environmental report in Europe was produced in 1989 by Norsk Hydro.

Other environmental and social problems arising from the overall process of development were of such concern that the United Nations commissioned the Brundtland Commission to prepare a report, 'Our Common Future' (1987).

From 1989, some business schools in the UK and USA and parts of Scandinavia began to teach corporate environmental management in their MBA programs. One of the first of these programs was at Manchester Business School in the UK which connected courses on corporate environmental management and corporate social responsibility in the MBA. The first course focused on the management of environmental issues and the concerns of business, from strategy to new product development. The second course focused on community and business relationships, especially partnerships and collaborations, as well as the traditional concerns for corporate responsibility such as corporate giving, diversity policies, responsibilities to consumers and neighbours.

This approach was a clear point of departure in the teaching of corporate responsibility in Europe. However, this approach to management education did not have a long-established tradition unlike the case with business ethics.

This link between business, the environment and society is found in the text of the Brundtland Commission Report (1987) and Agenda 21 (1992), which defined sustainable development as a new approach to economic and social development. The business contribution was set out by the Business Council for Sustainable Development (Schmidheiny, 1992). The intent of sustainable development was not to suppose that companies could be sustainable but rather that companies, operating as economic agents, could contribute to the overall process of sustainable development by working with other actors in the economic and social system. That view of a business responsibility toward sustainable development seems to have eluded most business scholars, with the notable exception of some such as Randers at the Norwegian School of Management. The scholars for whom this perspective made most sense seemed to have been schooled in interdisciplinary or transdisciplinary approaches to management such as systems dynamics, systems thinking and future studies. Teaching on corporate responsibility broadened from its traditional core in business ethics. The fall of the Berlin Wall, the events of Tiananmen Square, combined with the invention of the World Wide Web, all in 1989, enabled the emergence of a more tightly connected and interdependent global economic and financial system that led to the 'internationalization of business and finance'.

The new globally interdependent financial and business system was shaped by technical ideas too – not least by the development of the mathematics on which the valuation of options, futures and other financial derivatives was based (Hull, 1989). Theories arising from the Chicago School of Economics adopted by Margaret Thatcher and Ronald Regan in the mid-1980s began to impact on business and did much to condition the new global financial and economic system.

Neo-liberal economics – trickle-down economics, the free-market based market-efficiency hypothesis, and the notion of agency theory, as a basis for aligning the decisions of senior executives with the interests of shareholders – conditioned the thinking of managers and bankers and also found expression in the PowerPoint presentations and whiteboards of business school professors.

The idea that greater business freedom should be matched by greater managerial responsibility was lost in the heat of globalization and the competitive pressures it provoked.

The consequences that arose from the internationalization of business and finance following 1989 represented possibly the most powerful source of material for teaching and research in corporate responsibility. Internationalization fuelled competition and growth, and the geographic expansion of production to developing economies. Businesses and their managers encountered cultures and societies at different stages of social, institutional and economic development. Mistakes were made by companies: pollution issues as well as concerns around the accelerated use of resources, but also new concerns for international business around child labor as illustrated by Nike (1994), human rights concerns around commodity supply-chains as with the International Cocoa Initiative Foundation (2002), or blood diamonds (1990s). There were also opportunities in this process of internationalization for business to make a positive contribution – closing the digital divide (1995) or providing products and services at the base of the pyramid (1996).

The possible contribution of business was given a focus by the United Nation's Millennium Development goals and the idea that business might play a part in their delivery. The negative aspects seen as human and labor rights issues associated with globalization attracted the attention of policy makers and business leaders through the anti-globalization protests at the World Trade Organization in Seattle in 1999, the G8 meeting in Genoa 2001 and the World Economic Forum in Davos in 2001. Although climate change issues continued to swirl around before and after Kyoto (1997), the face of corporate responsibility in Europe tended to shift toward the social dimensions of international business that dominated this period.

As the challenge of the social and environmental dimensions of global business broadened through the late 1990s, so did the educational and disciplinary backgrounds of those teaching corporate responsibility in the programs of business schools. There were opportunities for inputs from public policy, international relations, public–private partnership as well as more traditional ideas rooted in business ethics, stakeholder theory, institutional theory, environmental thinkers and the systems dynamics, scenario planning and foresight studies. But many of these scholars got little more than some guest classes in the MBA. The audience was still interested in the excitement of the neo-liberal model of business, the emergence of the dot-com revolution and the view of CEO as 'hero'.

UNDERSTANDING THE CHALLENGE

More space for teaching corporate responsibility became possible as the frenetic period of the late 1990s changed course. The dot-com bubble burst in 2000, and as the recovery took hold, we were thrown into further turmoil by terror, first in the skies of America (9/11 – 2001), then in Madrid (2004) and the UK (2005). This caused central bankers to stave off a recession by reducing interest rates. The dialectic between capitalism and communism that had been broken in 1989 was being replaced by a dialectic between capitalism on the one side and other forms of fundamentalism on the other. From this time onwards, international business was not informed by a 'one-world capitalism' perspective but by the emergence of different forms of capitalism as well as those who were opposed to capitalism. Globalization was taking on a new form.

Other issues closer to the heart of business provoked the attention of most of those seeking to embed corporate responsibility in the curriculum – Enron (2001), Worldcom (2002), Parmalat (2004). Despite being evidently larcenous, these events renewed the focus on ethics, codes of practice, accounting and corporate governance practices.

Further interesting territory for teaching corporate responsibility was found in the proliferation of international codes and standards to guide companies and managers, whether the work of the Global Reporting Initiative (1999), ISO 14001 (1996), Social Accountability 8000 (1998) or the Kimberly Process (2001). We can also note the advance of socially responsible investment funds. These issues percolated down from practice to research and then into the management curriculum. The structures, systems and approaches expected of responsible companies became clearer.

In Europe, a final impulse to the development of corporate responsibility was rooted in the European Council's commitment to the Lisbon Agenda (2007) in 2000. That agenda set out the ambition to promote Europe to be 'the most competitive and the most dynamic knowledge-based economy in the world' by 2010. This was to be delivered through innovation as the engine of economic change and competitiveness, and by fostering a learning economy and social and environmental renewal.

This agenda also argued that innovative business provided the link between economic competitiveness and social and environmental renewal. It provided the impetus for the establishment of EABIS, though the reader might note that this agenda from 2001 is remarkably similar to the notion of modernization of business through economic freedoms coupled to greater responsibilities espoused in the UK in the mid-1980s.

For some, the Lisbon Agenda (2007) stood as a new paradigm for the teaching of corporate responsibility in MBA programs and in turn for the orientation of business schools. The foundation of EABIS, and CSR Europe, provided vehicles to advance this through management research and education. In contrast, the response by many academics and business schools was slower and more modest, that is until the credit crisis occurred.

EMBEDDING THE CHALLENGE

EABIS has set about the task of advancing the European agenda for economic change and competitiveness linked to environmental and social renewal. A concerted effort was needed to raise corporate responsibility from the domain of business ethics and corporate codes of practice to a rather more strategic position. With corporate responsibility providing a lever for paradigmatic change, this reflected the emerging position of business in society across the globe, but one found particularly in Europe.

While embedding these ideas in business and in business schools was seen as imperative, not all those in management positions in business schools or even those who teach and research corporate responsibility understood this ambition.

The EC funded the establishment of the Platform for Excellence in Research on CSR, which operated in 2005–7. This established a European network of researchers and educators in business schools in the exchange and the development of ideas on research and education for corporate responsibility and business in society. It sought to find innovative ways to undertake research and education, by bringing businesses and their managers into a much closer connection with researchers and educators, in order to secure both academic rigor and practical relevance in research and teaching.

REFLECTING ON THE CHALLENGE OF THE 'CREDIT CRISIS'

More could be done – for the pace of change is always slower than is wanted by those who lead and always faster than is wanted by those who wish to stay precisely where they are. A telling point here is that in January 2008 *The Economist*, traditionally vehemently opposed to the notion of corporate responsibility, declared in a special issue that corporate social responsibility was a sign (or lagging indicator) of good management.

In contrast to the ideas of *The Economist*, the 'credit crisis' that broke seven months later with the collapse of Lehman Brothers led us to question what 'good management' really involves. Like it or not, most of the bankers who contributed to the crisis were only doing what had been suggested they do – they deployed neo-liberal ideas: compete, perform in the market, create results, succeed, take your bonus, and your own and your company's success means you are building the economy and society. What the credit crisis tells us is that we do not necessarily value the outcomes that follow on from this neo-liberal rhetoric. Moreover, many of the financial institutions that have fallen were equipped with the kind of corporate responsibility programs that had provided the content for many MBA corporate responsibility courses over the previous 10 years or so. The conclusion we might draw from this is that corporate responsibility programs fell far short of the demands of responsible management and governance.

The advent of the 'credit crisis' is not really surprising. While the European Commission was pushing an ambitious program of reform encouraging business schools as platforms for change, the curriculum of business schools was pursuing a different direction. It was pushing for managers to act without responsibility for the impacts of their actions on the systems on which business itself depends.

Rather than expanding the thinking of MBA students to secure economic success, together with social and environmental performance, the educational system was promulgating a more highly individualistic, short-sighted and narrow form of management education. Corporate responsibility was taught on the sidelines, struggling to find its place in a congested curriculum. Many stood by and few dissented. With this background, what then can the deans of EABIS business schools propose to us in their reflections on what has happened?

THE RESPONSE OF THE DEANS OF BUSINESS SCHOOLS TO THE 'CREDIT CRISIS'

The arguments about what went wrong in the business schools in the long leadtime until the credit crisis were prophetically advanced in a posthumous paper by Sumantra Ghoshal (2005). While Ghoshal focused on the contribution of the business schools to the poor management revealed by the rash of scandals in the early 2000s (Enron, Worldcom, Parmalat, etc., identified above), his comments seem to apply equally well to the recent credit crisis: 'Business schools do not need to do a great deal more to help prevent future Enrons: they need only to stop doing a lot they currently do ... we as business school faculty need to own up to our own role in creating Enrons. Our theories and ideas have done much to strengthen the management practices that we are all now so loudly condemning' (p. 75).

More specifically, 'by propagating ideologically inspired amoral theories, business schools have actively freed their students from any sense of moral responsibility' (p. 76).

In the aftermath of the crisis of September 2008, there was a more widely discernible strand of critical discussion in the financial and higher educational press sometimes questioning the role or agency of the business schools in the crisis. We shall not reconstruct this here, but simply indicate the tone of the discourse in headlines such as: 'To what extent are business schools' MBA courses responsible for the global financial crash?' (Walker, 2009); 'What to do?' (Krugman, 2009); 'A greedy giant out of control' (Ford, 2008). Perhaps stimulated into reaction by these publicly critical questions, the deans of business schools were soon engaged in offering a variety of responses. For example, Jordi Canals (2010) from IESE offers an indicative, comprehensive discussion of the problems and challenges in which he constructively reviews the present situation as being full of opportunities for business schools.

The material below derives from three EABIS sources: (1) discussions on the deans' forum of the EABIS website from January to March 2009; (2) a meeting of deans attending the 8th EABIS Colloquium at IESE, Barcelona, in September 2009; and (3) conversations at, and subsequent to, the 2010 EFMD Deans and Directors Forum in Vienna. Consistent with our 'systems approach', we do not claim that these three periods have a specific significance. However, they do reveal something of the contemporary state of thinking in executive education arising through the reflections of some deans of prominent business schools over a period of nearly 12 months. We draw on some illustrative examples of the comments made by deans. Following these comments, we use the final section to make some conclusions.

In the first context, Frank Brown (INSEAD):

Where, I ask, were the bright, well-educated, and especially confident young employees who should have been challenging the logic of this stuff? They were not confident enough, I say. It is uncomfortable to ask for an explanation of an acronym like CDO. What does it mean? What is its real value? Is it sustainable? These are tough questions because they expose the questioner to the smirk of the all-knowing creator of the product. Someone like Fastow, maybe?

… The one thing I do know is that as business schools we need to teach the basics, but we also need to convince our students to be sceptical and to challenge conventional thinking. MBAs need to have the confidence to ask the tough questions and not be satisfied with the answers until they get the facts.

Also, at this time, one of the editors of this book, Alfonse Sauquet (dean of ESADE), said:

Business schools can provide two typical forms of responses to the current turbulence. The first is to resort to the kind of analytical competence for which they have been deservedly praised. They can provide answers to the why and the how this crisis took place. By studying the mistakes, identifying the decision points, analysing institutional dependences and disseminating such interpretations, business schools would be serving their basic academic mission.

… The second type of response is to focus on their role as educational institutions which will not remain the same following the crisis. In that respect, business schools can respond by stressing their developmental role.

... The qualities that will thus be required from such institutions and their programs will encompass the courage to transform; the imagination to create new and better frameworks; a deep sense of commitment and service; and, the ability to learn and partner with different stakeholders. Call this combination a drive towards innovation but, if so, that should be a driven kind of innovation; an innovation that wants to have a positive impact on society. That responsibility has to be accepted as part of the business school's mission.

Dorte Salskov-Iversen (Copenhagen Business School):

CBS curriculum and research programs have a long track record for integrating a business in society perspective. We have a long history of studying and applying insights from e.g. political economy, philosophy, law, anthropology, geography, all of which help students to challenge and push conventional business wisdom.

Also, we are working as hard as ever to insist on extensive work experience for students who wish to pursue an MBA at CBS (9 years for the class of 2009). Once part of our community, MBAs work collaboratively with senior managers taking part in leadership programs (also known as 'grey wolves'). We believe that this interaction reinforces critical learning and a reflection on integrity in management.

And, most recently in 2010, Barbara Igel (Asian Institute of Technology, Bangkok):

Firstly as to the roots of the crisis, there is no blaming here. CSR has always been integral to our business programs for many years and given the entrepreneurial inclinations of Thailand this has resulted in a social approach to entrepreneurship emerging in our courses. We are less interested here in social reporting (seen as reconstructing events around a CSR agenda), and more interested in socialised action. Reporting comes at us nonetheless as a result of regulation of the international supply chains. More critically at a time of resource constraint and industrial recession our economy is in danger of losing market share. We focus on teaching how to change or adapt to changes in the business model. Younger students will bring about change – the experienced executives here are already too entrenched in the profit-only driven practices of the twentieth century. We look to European companies to demand sustainability. Meanwhile until we have got our heads round that ASEAN is still a bit more of a 'business as usual' context. A course itself and alone can make very little difference to practice. A change in the mindset of managers needs to be mainstreamed through all courses.

And Mike Page (Bentley):

Our early response to the crisis was to reconsider the premise of mainstreaming CSR in the curriculum. We found this to be problematic. It seemed to be unconvincing that each of the disciplines would embrace CSR or sustainability in a coherent way – or even agree that such an approach was plausible. We responded alternately by making complex problems and creative solutions a focus of attention. Practice – a practicum – is now an essential part of all courses by which we integrate and systematise learning ... we have tried to drop prescriptivism: it is more important to teach critical thinking than to develop specific course content.

CONCLUSION

What conclusions might we draw from this account of the development of business schools and the orientation and position of corporate responsibility in the management curriculum over the 50 years of MBA provision in Europe leading to the credit crisis of 2008? First, corporate responsibility in Europe has always been more than business ethics and stakeholder theory. But the account of the events in this chapter and the comments of deans arising from the crisis suggest that the management curriculum and the content of corporate responsibility courses did little to contribute to the avoidance of the credit crisis. Indeed, parts of the management curriculum contributed to the crisis while the content of corporate responsibility provided little by way of a counterweight. The credit crisis suggests that management education of the future will need to involve more than a mainstreaming of what is currently understood as corporate responsibility.

A sound understanding of the macro-economic and geo-political context of business is considered very important. Some schools are pondering whether the crisis of the economics discipline, immersed in neo-classical thought and permeating the entire business curriculum, should be met by radical reform on how economics is taught, with a greater diversity from institutional and behavioral economics and re-constituting economics again as a social science. Others are aware that a crisis of modernity is at its heart a crisis of knowledge, and that the way we generate and pass on knowledge is not appropriate for the future, since it consistently fails to question the cognitive limits of the knowledge generated, and does not encourage faculty and students to ask the critical questions you would expect in institutions with a mission of *Universitas litterarum*. They opt, or have opted, for an integrative and interdisciplinary curriculum. Some have even questioned whether knowledge alone, no matter how sophisticated, can suffice to address the complex challenges of a global economy. For them, wisdom needs to complement knowledge.

The 1970s witnessed a consumer revolution, followed by a quality revolution, the 1990s brought us an ICT revolution, and each revolution had deep implications for business and business education. A new revolution calls for an increasing number of informed observers of the sustainability revolution. The realities are there for anyone to see: the planet cannot sustain the externalities of global business models that are increasingly and evidently unstable. Macro trends like climate change, resource depletion, demographic change and geo-political shifts will affect the business environment deeply.

REFERENCES

Agenda 21 (1992) *The Rio Declaration on Environment and Development,* New York. Available at: http://habitat.igc.org/agenda21/rio-dec.htm

Ansoff, H.I. (1979) 'The changing shape of the strategic problem', in D. Schendel and C. Hofer (eds) *Strategic Management: A New View of Business Policy and Planning.* Boston, MA: Little, Brown and Co.

Brundtland Commission Report (1987) *Our Common Future: Report of the United Nations Commission on Environment and Development.* Oxford: Oxford University Press.

Carroll, A. (1979) 'A three-dimensional conceptual model of corporate social performance', *Academy of Management Review*, 4(4): 497–505.

Canals, J. (2010) 'Can they fix it?' *EFMD Global Focus Magazine*, 4(1): 14–18.

Carley, M. and Christie, I. (2001) *Managing Sustainable Development*. London: Earthscan Books. *The Economist* (2008) Special Issue on Corporate Social Responsibility, London, 17 January.

Ford, J. (2008) 'A greedy giant out of control', *Prospect* 152.

Freeman, R.E. (1984) *Strategic Management: A Stakeholder Approach*. London: Pitman.

Friedman, M. (1970) 'The social responsibility of business is to increase its profits', *The New York Times Magazine*, 33: 122–6.

Ghoshal, S. (2005) 'Bad management theories are destroying good management practices', *Academy of Management Learning and Education*, 4(1): 75–91.

Giddens, A. (1986) *The Constitution of Society: Outline of the Theory of Structuration*. Cambridge: Polity Press.

Krugman, P. (2009) 'What to do', *New York Review of Books*, 55(20).

Hull, J. (1989) *Options, Futures and Other Derivative Securities*. London: Prentice-Hall International.

Lisbon Agenda (2007) Available at: http://eur-lex.europa.eu/johtml.do?uri=oj:c:2007:306:som:en:html

Meadows, D.H., Meadows, D.L., Randers, J. and Behrens, W.W. (1972) *1st Report to the Club of Rome – The Limits to Growth*. New York: Universe Books.

Porter, M.E. (1985) *Competitive Advantage*. New York: Free Press.

Porter, M.E. (1987) 'From competitive advantage to corporate strategy', *Harvard Business Review*, May/June: 43–59.

Roome, N. (1988) 'Partnership in practice: retrospect and prospect', *Progress Towards Partnership*, April, 5: 3–4.

Roome, N. (1997) 'Corporate environmental responsibility', in T. Bansal and E. Howard (eds), *Business and the Natural Environment*. Oxford: Butterworth-Heinemann (MBA Series), pp. 40–62.

Schmidheiny, S. (1992) *Changing Course*. Boston, MA: MIT Press.

Walker, P. (2009) Who taught them greed is good?: To what extent are business schools' MBS courses responsible for the global financial crash? *The Observer*, London.

EPILOGUE

Alfons Sauquet Rovira, Mette Morsing and Marc Vilanova

ESADE and Copenhagen Business School

In this final chapter of the book, we want to recap some of the ideas and suggestions that have been advanced in the preceding pages. To do that, we will make two points visible and illustrate them with references to the previous contributions. Furthermore, in this epilogue we will recall the rationale of the book, advance a few reflections on the content and make a last point on the challenges and questions remaining.

THE ORIGIN: PROVIDING A PLATFORM FOR DEBATE

This book, as was explained in the Prologue, is the result of a spark that ignited a small community of academic administrators who felt that for some time business education had been brought to a sort of congressional hearing in which questions about their doings and wrongdoings were implicitly pointing towards their legitimacy.

Yet legitimacy is not a new issue. The relationship between legitimacy and business school education is a long and complex one. It resembles, for better or worse, that of a relationship that grows, matures and probably endures a crisis every now and then.

Indeed, there have been various attempts to make management education a distinctive, regulated professional realm in the USA, with the aim of allowing it to be as comparable and legitimate as other professions are. The founding of AACSB in the early decades of the twentieth century and the Gordon–Howell and other reports in the 1950s are distinct testimonies to this interest in making management education a legitimate activity linked to a profession. More recently, we have witnessed initiatives that pointed in a similar direction. Under the auspices of the UN, the Principles for Responsible Management Education (PRME) were produced to promote a collective commitment to academic institutions using basic assumptions. Also, at the other end of the spectrum, we have seen the proliferation of public discretionary oaths such as the MBA oath promoted by some Harvard Business School students. Both are testimony to the quest for a more legitimate realm.

In addition to that evolution, during the last decade, two phenomena have added pressure to the issue and brought business education more into the public limelight.

First, the financial crisis was eventually tied to real state bubbles in some countries such as Ireland, Spain and to a lesser extent the USA and the UK. Indeed, this unexpected crisis caught the public and the majority of experts by surprise, and its consequences have been significant, nearly knocking down some developed economies. As attribution theory would have rightly foreseen, the magnitude of the blow prompted a public search for those responsible for such effects and for sorting out the causes. In that public search, the immediate attention turned towards the talent providers (e.g. business schools), management incentives (e.g. bonuses) and institutional behavior (e.g. Fed and credit providers). But regardless of the combination of responsibilities assigned to actors and systems, the crisis also brought in a pervasive feeling that there might have been values that had been framing the individual behaviors, so that in the search for individual satisfaction, excessive risk taking and a lack of common sense had been dominant. If this was the case, the question became: what had been the role of the institutions in charge of educating those actors? In other words, the debate turned to analyzing to what extent business schools were to be held accountable, and whether careerism had been overstressed among graduates.

The second phenomenon was a movement that, while it was incubated during the 1990s, was to see its blossoming during the first decade of the twenty-first century as it rode the waves of various corporate scandals of historical magnitude such as Enron, Arthur Anderson or Vivendi. This movement, mostly from the academic community, called for more business accountability, specifically to increase the number of stakeholders that should be taken into account in the private sector. In other words, the movement was proposing that in addition to a monetary payback to the share tenants, generating stakeholder value needed to be included in the measure of success of business. The movement was developed and shaped under different names such as corporate social responsibility; business ethics; sustainability; or corporate citizenship among others, but all these terms shared one common goal: attention was being drawn to how to instil in companies, in management education and in business practices, different modes that would foster a reflection of the long-term consequences of any business decision. As a result, the founding of institutions such as EABIS, the Aspen Institute, APABIS, the UN Global Compact or the above-mentioned UN PRME tried to construct relevant voices and promote debate on the issue of business accountability and stakeholder value. The underlying assumption apparently was that a call for action should be sustained and made consistent to influence both management education and corporate behavior.

All in all, as we have seen in different chapters in Part I of the book, that the question of the role of business schools and their contribution to society filled the tabloids, and the media immediately seized on the opportunity to make quick implicit judgments and express underpinning opinions about how much business schools had contributed with their knowledge – or the lack thereof – to encouraging risk-taking behaviors beyond any sensible assessments (or irresponsible behaviors), to the extent that unrestrained financial misbehaving took place. And in addition to what extent the kind of education provided by business schools was so technocratic and void of value that graduates could not resist the contextual pressure and, once they were placed at a crossroads, made decisions that were against common sense.

This book, as we explained in the Prologue, was born out of the hope of providing a platform from which to voice the standpoint of some business schools. Thus, the purpose of the book was not to provide the best possible answer to the financial crisis from an academic point of view. That is, it was never meant to be a collection of sound assessments about what went wrong, or what should have been done differently. It was not supposed to be a problem-solving toolkit either. Nor was it meant to be a vindication of business schools, taken from a systematic and aggregated perspective. Rather, it has been developed as an opportunity to voice different individual perspectives on the broad question of what business schools contribute to society at large. In this regard, the goal was not to reply directly to any of these questions, but to provide a platform for debate and, more importantly, to show that there is also a significant degree of reflection and debate coming from within the business school community, proposing in many cases drastic changes and foreseeing significant challenges.

The distinctiveness of this book project departs from the assumption that, whatever answers the different authors have provided, it was going to be a response that was both academic and practical as business school leaders face both challenges. At the outset, it was clear that it was not going to represent a narrow academic disciplinary focus such as the sociology of education of philosophical pedagogy. Rather, the mandate of each of the contributing authors was to voice some of the most intimate reflections and debates that were taking part at each of their institutions. After all, most of the authors that have contributed to this book hold a position of responsibility in organizations that are important players in the business education debate. Thus, one could argue whether the contributing authors have been well chosen, whether the organizations they represent have shown leadership or the lack thereof, or even if they did with broad or narrow interests. One could also ask whether they have the discretionary power to effect change or not, or if they have the expertise to discuss some of the issues contained in each chapter. Regardless of all this, one cannot argue that every contributing author has been at the forefront of academic institutions or influential organizations, or that they have made an effort to reflect on the role of their individual institutions in regard to the general mandate of the editors.

Thus, as editors, we have preferred to give ample room to authors to frame their answers in light of their priorities and context. True, we provided some indications of what we understood could be most relevant in each particular case but we were also quite open in considering the validity of individual approaches. Our understanding as editors is that it was important to allow different authors to construct their own voice as they saw fit, and that the manner in which the voice was presented could be just as important as the voice itself. In this regard, we don't see the difference in approaches, languages and structure of the different chapters as a weakness, but rather as a strength. Finally, we would hope that the reader goes through it as if he or she were watching a great and lively debate among leaders and scholars of business education.

SEIZING THE OPPORTUNITY: THE CONTENT

We understand the content of the book as having three potential outcomes. First, each contribution has given authors a unique opportunity to reflect on their institutional task and, very succinctly put, to ask themselves some central questions, such as a simple *What for*? These questions revolve not only around the institution each of them represents, but also indirectly focus on their own leadership. Second, we understand that their work may have an effect beyond their own business schools. Dialogue and debate are sources of transformation, and we expect that some of the suggestions advanced here may generate a sort of ripple effect, spurring on new ideas in other business schools. In this regard, we expect this book to become a bank of ideas where ideas and experiences are accumulated and may serve to stimulate further debate, thinking and action. Also, the book may have a similar effect – for the lack of a better metaphor – that support groups have in that different schools will see their own internal debates and policies reflected in some of its proposals, and will therefore feel that they are going in the right direction, or at the very least that they are not alone in the initiatives undertaken. Third, the book is making a contribution to the development of a collective understanding of the role of business schools by way of making more transparent the thoughts of some central institutions and their leaders.

Regarding its specific content we feel this clearly speaks for itself. Yet when looking at the different proposals presented throughout the book, two central ideas come to mind that are worth underscoring. First, business school education and research is not flat. Second, when business schools are asked about a way to solve knowledge production dilemmas or education challenges, they provide distinctive narratives and ideas.

BUSINESS SCHOOL EDUCATION AND RESEARCH IS NOT FLAT

One of the first conclusions of the book is that the world of business education is far from flat. Despite the growing institutionalization of the field, for instance expressed by way of the task and impact that global accrediting institutions have (such as the AACSB, the EFMD, etc.), or the appearance of more global service providers (GMAC, etc.), the role of business schools strongly differs as their activities develop in different contexts.

Khurana (Chapter 1) warns against an excess of homogenization that does not take into consideration the specifics of the US context. Indeed, the history of business education in the USA is specific and can be written as a long quest for a stable and legitimate base that has resulted in a much institutionalized landscape in which actors have a stable role. Not in vain, the above-mentioned GMAC and AACSB, one in the provision of services and the other in the processes of accreditation, have become something of a reference point and both are originally American organizations that have made an effort to globalize and, in doing so, have contributed to giving a specific shape to the field of business education.

We see this difference clearly when we see look at some of the chapters as is the case, for instance, in Turkey (Tan, Chapter 5) and in Brazil (Fleury and Wood, Chapter 2). In these different chapters, their contributions bring us a vivid and different picture. Unlike the case of US business schools, business education is seen as a factor associated with country development, thus, rather than seeking legitimacy, business schools in such emerging – rather than emerged – economies seem to be clearly enjoying the privileges attached to institutions that provide capacity development; therefore these institutions do not need to seek any further justification. On the contrary, it is widely acknowledged that country elites are trained in such business schools and will be called on to set future strategic frameworks. In that context, the priority is assuring the local audience or stakeholders that the school enjoys an internally solid reputation base which is a proxy of a country gaining international stature. Thus, their priorities are more about becoming a member of a community and to do this there are issues that have to be addressed, such as participating in international discussions, becoming accredited, and the like. In this context, it is less of a surprise that although echoes of the financial crisis can be felt, these are in any case subordinate to the central goal of gaining international reputation externally and capacity building, the latter being a central issue for those economies facing the challenges of modernization and rapid growth. Therefore, it is hardly necessary to justify the public service that business schools provide.

The case of the NUS Business School in Singapore underscores this issue, whereby Yeung and Singh (Chapter 3) leave us in no doubt as to the critical role that business schools have played in recent years and make an even clearer point about their role in the near future. Interestingly, in their view, past, present and future are addressed with a clear understanding of the kind of challenges that derive both from an external context (collaboration being just a newborn concept among Asian business schools) and from an internal context in its reference to governance dilemmas.

The testimonies of St Petersburg University (Katkalo, Chapter 4) and the Warsaw School of Economics (Budnikowski, Chapter 15) also stress contextual factors in the overall meaning of the task of the business school. And, in addition to the other cases, they point to a special facet of the role of business schools. In both cases, business schools seem to have a double role. First, it is clear that they are agents that promote development via capacity development, but also that they play a second role as they themselves become a symbol of a different landscape. They promote and symbolize a transition from one period to another. Their role is more than brute capacity development; what is being asked of them is that they become institutions that can navigate the waters of institutional transformation in periods in which both change and continuity have to be addressed in countries undergoing transition. It thus seems that in addition to upgrading capabilities and training new leaders, providing guidance and symbolizing change are some of the challenges they are facing.

Whereas the above-mentioned cases can avoid excessive justification because of their contexts, Tabellini (Chapter 14) argues that their task can be decoupled from specific contexts and proposes that there is little need for justification of the work of business schools once the appropriate level of analysis has been undertaken. His argument is specifically linked to macro-level institutional development, knowledge production and education to conclude that inasmuch as it is a feature of the scientific method to adequately address the quest for valid inferences and conclusions, there is an inherent value in training students in it. And, as long as this is properly done by educators, students will acquire the values that support the best possible decision-making practices: values that are also the cornerstone of modern valid institutions.

That degree of visibility, being more or less of a lighthouse, is a factor also worth considering and clearly perceived in the case of University College Dublin (UCD) Business School in Ireland (Chapter 10). The Irish case brings in yet another variable, that of country size, and it quickly becomes clear that a business school impact can be very large in a small community. In a small context, the financial crisis has names and surnames, affiliations and board servicing. All in all, this chapter clearly shows that the smaller the country, the larger the visibility of the business school, and, therefore, the lesser the distribution of responsibility.

All these contributions link the role of business school to specific contexts, clearly giving a sense that the institution adapts to serve a specific community by way of linking development and education.

Yet one case approach claims legitimacy can be decoupled from any particular context. Indeed, Tabellini (Chapter 14) links the contribution of business schools to societal development at large. More specifically, he argues that scholarly advances in the social sciences, particularly in economics, have been a cornerstone of institutional development. In this regard, the argument seems to be that as much as advanced societies have progressed, when provided with political systems that frame their interaction, some of the central institutions that form the central system have strengthened and developed thanks to the activities of business schools. For instance, the scientific method has embedded values such as rigor or criticality, which when appropriately followed transmit these values into institutions, organizations and individuals. This value-embedding process is arguably one of the corner-stones in the institutional development of advanced societies. This cycle, which could be seen as a virtuous process, is linked to that of knowledge creation, and more specifically to research. This is the crucial part of the process and one of the central ways in which business school education and research seems to contribute to institutional development.

All in all, using these cases, we learn that business schools are much less context-free than we tend to think. As long as it is true that there is a clear push for comparability in business education via rankings, and as long as accreditation processes indirectly level some of the differences, it also seems clear that there is ample room for interpreting the social role of a business school in different national contexts. In each case, we learn how business school development is tied to the country's future, how business schools are aware of such a demand and, in a sense, how they share and bear a responsibility in many respects.

It could be argued that, in each of the above-mentioned cases, rectors and deans could have minimized their contexts and their relationship to them and in turn engage in a more commoditized discussion about whether business schools are conducting the right research or whether they are training people in the right competencies; yet the stories that these deans, rectors and leaders provide echo all too vividly those of other economies in similar phases of transition.

A quick look at the USA at the end of the 1950s, the aftermath of World War II in the UK or the end of the closed Spanish economy in 1958, shows that these events had a significant effect on how business education was perceived. In all these cases, business schools were regarded as a strategic source of human capital that had a significant impact on the economy. The paradox is that inasmuch as management science remains quite obstinately a-historical, in the sense that it tends to overlook phases and stages in its own development, business schools seem to be much more context-bound and conscious of their different roles and ambitions in their respective contexts.

DISTINCTIVE NARRATIVES

And yet the second point is that business schools cannot measure their contribution merely in light of how much they support their geographical environment. They are professionally bound and they have to respond to basic challenges. Two areas stand out here: knowledge production and knowledge dissemination by way of education. In both cases, there are testimonies of business schools 'looking inward' to find a distinct way to address both issues. In the case of knowledge production, it is a matter of acknowledging the fact that research does not just serve academic interests in the case of education, rather it is a complex process that goes well beyond knowledge transmission and values are embedded in the process as well.

There are two different routes to address research. Whereas Kaptein and Yip (Chapter 12) would bet on syncretism, where they look for a balanced combination of research method-ologies, namely quantitative and qualitative, and offer the Rotterdam School of Management experience to support the case, Barzelay and Estrin (London School of Economics, Chapter 9) advance an original piece that clarifies the process by which, in their proposal, knowledge sticks and makes a difference. Implicit to their argument is that relevant research is the result of consistent effort that requires a number of processes to have an impact. In this regard, none of the different chapters aspire to solve the challenges that are currently under discussion concerning research and management; yet they provide credible approaches as to how the issue of relevance can be tackled. Just recalling the immense workload that served as the basis of Michael Porter's work leaves us with an implicit argument: relevant research is, more often than not, the result of both solid and consistent scholarship combined with those competencies that turn academic results into persuasive arguments. It no doubt remains to be answered whether scholars and institutions are paying appropriate attention to such issues.

In turn, education is a more worrisome and clear-cut case. Whereas conducting good or bad research can have a more relative and filtered effect on society, business education seems to include a more clear and direct narrative, often raising some concern given that there seem to be similarities between some of the education narratives and some of the problems at the heart of the legitimacy debate. Perhaps that is why management education has been placed at the center of the legitimacy debate around business schools. The argument seems to be that business education fosters values and practices that are not primarily addressing the need to build a better society. Therefore, the logical conclusion seems to be that management education needs to introduce responsibility as a central issue. Here we have a group of contributors that address that focus. The cases of ESADE (Losada, Lozano and Martell, Chapter 17), CBS (Irwin, Salskov-Iversen and Morsing, Chapter 8), St Gallen (Bieger, Chapter 11) and Louvain (Swaen, de Woot and Callatay, Chapter 18) share this common inspiring thread: developing responsible leaders is the central concern of the educational endeavor.

Differences are relative and more a matter of focus and degree than of substance. For instance, the case of ESADE mainstreams responsibility so much so as to claim that it should become the focal point of the institution, and therefore activities in principle considered autonomous such as research should be subordinate to that end. In turn, St Gallen's contribution takes a systemic approach that links several internal processes to produce a more valid integrated perspective that links curricula development, scholarly activity and student development in an integrated manner. At Louvain, we are witnessing a combination of initiatives designed to permeate a set of specific values throughout the institution. Central activities to business schools such as research, teaching programs, awards, activities and debates all speak for the desire to give visibility to an understanding of business education that goes beyond the provision of technical competence for professional advancement. In other words, the idea seems to be to train managers who are concerned with contributing to a better and more sustainable society.

With a different emphasis, this set of contributions shares a clear, specific view of business that goes beyond the shareholder approach – one seemingly close to the kind of discourse advanced by institutions such as EABIS and the Aspen Institute, whose open raison d'être is precisely that of streamlining a vision of business education that leapfrogs technocracy.

The chapter from CBS takes an organizational perspective to stimulate the impact of research on society's challenges. CBS introduces business in society platforms on key strategic issues of societal concern, and professors engaging in these platforms will systematically be asked to reflect their research in outreach and educational programs in reply to global concerns such as social and environmental development. Interestingly, some context permeates the approach as rather than privileging the standalone professor, the idea of platforms where researchers work in interdisciplinary teams to advance knowledge seems to echo the Scandinavian tradition for collaborative learning and methods of cooperation.

A different approach, explicitly called for, is patent in the case of the Vienna University of Economics and Business (Badelt and Sporn, Chapter 13), as the university seems to focus on a very specific competence, that of entrepreneurship. In this regard, entrepreneurship is approached under the assumption that, as long as competencies are developed in practice and thus to train in entrepreneurship, there is a need to develop an entrepreneurial context. Schumpeter being a prominent Austrian, the reader is left to wonder whether the chapter may still be a supporting addition to the argument of context dependency.

One major question that remains unanswered is whether these different contributions underestimate the embeddedness of the values in which universities and business schools live and the extent to which these collide or coalesce with their project. Yet it is a remarkable feat that such discourses are present in academic settings as they constitute a considerable degree of complexity.

Lastly, some chapters have taken on board the hard challenge of addressing finance and education at business schools. As expected, there are no simple solutions here; yet a candid discussion of what can be done better is provided. The underlying argument is that disciplines are path-dependent and that the systemic nature of pressures and solutions is too easily overlooked. It seems apparent that there are problems that, regardless of how much we chew on them, remain more intractable than desired. In this regard, the argument seems to be that particularly difficult and complex systemic problems cannot be solved, but rather need to be managed. Therefore, the issue is not so much about solving structural or systemic problems, as about development of individual judgment, where the capacity to face unexpected moral dilemmas is central. Thus, transmitting and embedding values is central. Education can be perceived in a systemic manner, where individual professional behaviors are also subject to the kind of pressures that seem not just to contain but even to dissolve the sense of individual responsibility of business school graduates, and thus the argument underlines the idea that individual development and individual responsibility are a central part of institutional development and responsibility.

LIMITATIONS, CHALLENGES AHEAD AND FURTHER CONSIDERATIONS

Undertaking this reflection around business school legitimacy, the different authors in this book have committed themselves to at least three tasks: first, they have considered the content piece of what they wanted to advance; second, they have decided on the means they wanted to use to persuade their audience; and third, they have developed what we could call a righteousness argument. Consciously or not, they have entered the realm of rhetoric in trying to answer the question and in leaning on various sources for legitimacy.

In any play, some actors are misrepresented; likewise, in any good research there are flaws, and we have to assume that fact. In our case, it is the stories of companies that are underrepresented. No doubt it was worth listening to some of them, but at the same time this would have meant having fewer views from business schools. Thus, there were some necessary tradeoffs, and we opted for a better representation of business schools and selected organizations. Our goal was to focus on those managing business schools and not so much on the different and strategic stakeholders.

The second issue worth mentioning is that criticality in a Kantian sense is relatively absent. Noticeably, a piece by Pugés Chapter 6 makes a point about the limits and dangers of being forgetful of values that are idiosyncratic to European institutions, yet the general trend is towards the sort of optimistic narrative where challenges can be overcome by good design and better management.

Third, it is interesting to think about how business schools see themselves. On the one hand, some of the institutions claiming that they can provide a framework for business education, such as accreditation agencies like EFMD or AACSB – which, let's be honest, one would think of as being naturally relevant for matters concerning legitimacy – are conspicuously absent from the minds of those managing business schools. There is not much better cognitive awareness of Aspen or EABIS, two institutions that have actively set up procedures and standards to influence business education in several ways. Neither are there references to UN PRME, an initiative to which most business schools have given their full support. It would be adventurous to provide a single reason for this forgetful assessment. Yet when there is also no discussion of the role of media, and particularly of business school rankings, it becomes quite interesting to reflect on the role and influence these different tools and initiatives have on business schools as opposed to what they expect. But, more importantly, this lack of influence of these different initiatives begs the question: if not these, then which tools and frameworks influence business school development?

It is also interesting to realize that there is a partial sense of self-consciousness of business schools as part of complex systems of interactions. Interestingly, it appears that whenever it comes to the point of recalling the positive impact of its task, the business school seems to have a better sense of the systemic forces surrounding it and can provide a better account of the social milieu, the drives and roles relevant to its task. However, when the focus turns towards its own practice (education and research), the descriptions tend to pay much less attention to institutional constraints. And, thus, initiatives are advanced more or less as if the authors were change initiators with the purpose of persuading an audience to start committing to a specific course of action. Because there is no doubt it requires some gigantic effort to turn a university into an entrepreneurial institution or to align all academic activities around a basic idea, or to propose a research approach that discards the razor blade of peer review systems and promotions, authors more likely have been discarding constraints to emphasize directions so they may have been writing more as managers than academics.

Equally noticeable is that, in the final analysis, graduates are implicitly assumed to be individual rational decision makers and very often judge situations that turn grave as they escalate, but that are difficult to assess at different moments in time. The reader may be surprised, on the one hand, by how little mention is given to well-known management theories (e.g. path dependency, escalating commitment, problem solving) to explain behaviors and how fast the focus is turned to individual values.

Contributors were selected on the basis of their position rather than on their content knowledge and we are well aware of that fact. They were occupying relevant positions at each of their institutions and that probably created a constraint for each and every one of them. Inasmuch as they were individual authors, they were institutional representatives and they, intentionally or otherwise, could not escape that institutional iron cage. We acknowledge that limitation. In the book, this has sometimes resulted in some degree of over-focusing or overemphasizing their respective institutional realities, and sometimes on perhaps not being as self-critical as they would have hoped. Yet, the very initiative is a clear step and signal on the road towards more accountable leaders and institutions.

Finally, we would like to give due respect to those who have contributed to the book on a different basis. If puns among rectors and deans are commonplace when discussing faculty, no wonder one would think of rectors and deans as not being a more educated species when it comes to editing their work. And, yet, despite one of the editors appertaining to that special category, ours has been a job more engaging and pleasurable than anyone could have foreseen.

INDEX

Tables and Figures are indicated by page numbers in bold.